Corsica

Oda O'Carroll
David Atkinson

Contents

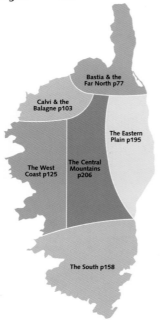

Bastia & the Far North p77

Calvi & the Balagne p103

The Eastern Plain p195

The West Coast p125

The Central Mountains p206

The South p158

Destination: Corsica

What makes Corsica so attractive? Well, its warm Mediterranean climate and breathtakingly beautiful mountain scenery for starters. Those in search of spectacular nature reserves, wonderfully wild forests, fabulous rocky gorges and rivers, and scenic hikes will find Corsica, literally, a breath of fresh air. But that's not the half of it.

With nearly 1000km of clear aquamarine coastline, you'll find some of Europe's best beaches and magnificent child-friendly shallow coves on the island. An equally dramatic underwater landscape shelters a whole slew of exotic flora and fauna – a scuba diver's dream.

The island's buzzing port towns are well removed from the snobbery and pretension of the Riviera. It's mysterious prehistoric sites, its Genoese watchtowers and its striking walled towns are a physical reminder of the island's colourful history. Corsica isn't cheap. But, unlike other island resorts, it doesn't attract package holidaymakers to a string of kiss-me-quick bars and tacky discos.

Corsica's rich cultural heritage, distinct from the rest of France, is still surprisingly intact. Its language, rustic cookery and polyphonic singing are not the stuff of museums but the vibrant currency of everyday life. While this won't suit everyone, those wanting to escape the rigours of the 21st century will have come to the right place.

Don't try to see the island all at once – the death-defying switchback roads will test your vertigo as well as your driving skills and ensure you can't. Take your time. You'll be glad of the excuse to come back and savour this incredible place again and again.

JEAN-BERNARD CARILLET

Corsica's biggest drawcard is its natural beauty. Unesco World Heritage-listed sites and dozens of diverse nature reserves blanket the island. This island of extremes means you can swim in natural pools in the **Réserve Naturelle des Bouches de Bonifacio** (p177), cross spectacular wilderness scenery on the **GR20** (p51), walk through the heart of the Parc Naturelle Régionale de la Corse, or savour the cool, shady trails and splendid rockery of the **Gorges de Spelunca** (p133). The vast lagoon at the **Étang et Réserve Naturelle de Biguglia** (p88) is a hotspot for migrating birds and the largest body of water on the island.

Take a swim in the pristine waters of one of the lakes in the **Vallée de la Restonica** (p214)

SALLY DILLON

SALLY DILLON

Marvel at the natural beauty of Golfe de Porto, protected within **Réserve Naturelle de Scandola** (p132)

Trek through the middle of Corsica's most famous natural feature, **Les Calanques** (p136)
SALLY DILL

TONY WHEELER

Enjoy the scenery on one of the 25 walking trails around **Vizzavona** (p219)

JEAN-BERNARD CARILLET

Admire the island's
wildflowers around **Cargèse**
(p139)

Sail the coastal reserve of **Réserve Naturelle de
Scandola** (p132)

EMILY RIDDELL

Corsica's rugged mountainous interior makes for a dramatic backdrop to a necklace of almost continuous rocky coves, sheltered inlets and sweeping picture-postcard beaches. Near the holiday hub of **Porto Vecchio** (p183) you'll find the famous beaches of **St Giulia** (p182) and **Rondinara** (p182), two of Corsica's best. The **Golfe de Valinco** (p166) with its bustling fishing villages, **Campomoro** (p167) and **Porto Pollo** (p166) at either end of the bay, lead up to the region's capital **Ajaccio** (p143), a haven for water sports. The Golfe de Sagone boasts fine sandy beaches, among them **Le Liamone** (p142) and **Sagone** (p141).

Discover the Genoese towers dotted along the west coast of **Cap Corse** (p89)

OLIVIER CIRENDINI

OLIVIER CIRENDINI

Stay at the seaside resort and fishing town of **Porto** (p128)

Relax on one of the island's most famous beaches, **Palombaggia** (p181)

JEAN-BERNARD CAR

JEAN-BERNARD CARILLET

From Palombaggia, view the beautiful **Réserve Naturelle des Îles Cerbicale** (p181)

JEAN-BERNARD CARILLET

Learn to dive in the beautiful waters of **Archipel des Lavezzi** (p181)

Explore the rock formations on **Île Lavezzi** (p181)

OLIVIER CIRENDINI

For stunning views, visit the high points around **Cap Corse** (p89)

Cycle or walk through the beautiful
Porte de Genes in **Bonifacio** (p173)

Savour the scenery near **Piana** (p138)

Getting Started

WHEN TO GO

During the French *vacances scolaires* in July and August, Corsica is chock-a-block with vistors, mostly French families. The water temperature from July to September is most favourable for water sports. Forget about finding the hotel of your choice without a booking during this period. Prices soar and some of the island's most idyllic sights may be pushed beyond capacity.

Walkers on the GR20 and other routes, the elderly and those travelling with children will surely prefer the less sweltering months of May, June and September, when roads and amenities are also less congested. Or better still, try early spring, late autumn or winter, when the island is at its emptiest.

Bear in mind that if you travel in low season (November to March), a significant number of hotels, camp sites, restaurants, transport and sports facilities will either have shut down completely or be operating at only half steam (see Business Hours, p223).

See climate charts (p223) for more information.

COSTS & MONEY

Corsica is an expensive destination. However, you can economise by travelling in low season and/or by doing at least some self-catering. The interior of the island is also significantly cheaper than the coast.

As a general rule, you can expect to pay at least €90 to €200 for a decent double room in high season (often more in August). You will have to pay the same minimum rates if you are on your own, as there are very few single rooms.

Cut costs by renting lodgings on a weekly or monthly basis rather than by the night, or camping. Sites charge an average of €6/3/3 per person/tent/car.

Most restaurants offer tourist menus for about €15. However, it is often better to choose a good restaurant and have one good course rather than a mediocre complete meal.

Bus and train travel (often seasonal as well) is generally quite expensive if you consider the actual distances travelled. Hiring a car will cost you about €200 per week with unlimited mileage and comprehensive insurance. Perhaps the cheapest and most rewarding way to experience Corsica is to spend a couple of weeks on the GR20 or one of the other celebrated island hikes. Then you are bound to sleep in *gîtes* or in refuges (€9 per night along the GR20) or to camp, and transport is of course free!

HOW MUCH?

An hour's parking in Ajaccio €1.50

A 3½-hour bus journey from Ajaccio to Calvi €23

A five-hour train journey from Ajaccio to Calvi €27.30

LONELY PLANET INDEX

Pint of beer €2.20

1L bottled water €0.40

1L petrol €1.10

Souvenir T-shirt €18

Street snack (savoury crêpe) €5

DON'T LEAVE HOME WITHOUT...

- Your E111 health insurance certificate, if you're an EU citizen
- Your mosquito repellent, especially if camping or hiking (don't believe those hardy locals who tell you mozzies don't exist on the island – they do!)
- Your camera, for the extremely photogenic Corsican landscape
- Some crackers, to go with all that *brocciu* cheese you can't escape

TOP FIVES
FAVOURITE FESTIVALS & EVENTS

Corsicans love to celebrate and there's nearly always something going on around the island. The following is our top five but for a more comprehensive listing of festivals and events throughout the year, see Festivals & Events in the destination chapters.

- **Procession du Catenacciu** (p170) March/April On the eve of Good Friday, in one of the oldest religious (and most bizarre) festivals in the country, a local masked penitent parades in chains through Sartène to purge himself/herself of sin.

- **Les Nuits de la Guitare** (p100) July This family-friendly event attracts a good mix of local and international names and, with its outdoor setting in an amphitheatre complete with menhir statues, is one of the true highlights of the Corsican summer.

- **Fêtes Napoléoniennes** (p150) August 15 & 16 Celebrate Napoleon's birthday with fireworks, live music and a street carnival in Ajaccio.

- **Rencontres les Chants Polyphoniques** (p110) September Feast your ears on Corsica's traditional polyphonic singing in this week-long festival at the cathedral in Calvi.

- **La Tour de Corse** (p150) Mid-October Smell the burning rubber at the French rallying championships, founded in 1956, and running over three days, starting and finishing in Ajaccio.

MUST-SEE COASTAL STRETCHES

From colourful fishing villages to empty coves, Corsica offers a wealth of dreamy seaside escapes. The following list comprises our favourites, but other scenic coastal routes are listed throughout the regional chapters and a rundown of our favourite beaches is listed on p6.

- **Piana to Porto** This stretch of the D81 has got to be one of the contenders for Corsica's most spectacular coastal route. Drive, walk or cycle it but don't miss it. This windy path through the beautiful rock formations, Les Calanques, is best viewed, in full technicolour effect, at sundown.

- **Piana to Plage d'Arone** This elevated cliffside road on the hairpin D824 allows you fantastic views of Les Calanques, Capo Rosso and the whole of the Golfe de Porto.

- **Portigliolo to Campomoro** This equally beautiful, remote, coastal route on the D121 takes you from the splendid 4km-long beach of Portigliolo, through the maquis and high over the Golfe de Valinco.

- **Capo di Fena to Capo Pertusato** This stretch of coast is best seen from the deck of a boat (with a margerita in hand) and there are plenty of companies in Bonifacio who'll oblige. You'll take in the stunning breadth of the chalky cliffs on which Bonifacio is perched, sailing through aquamarine waters to hidden grottos and coves.

TRAVEL LITERATURE

The Corsican visitor's bible, Dorothy Carrington's revered 1971 *Granite Island: a Portrait of Corsica*, also known as *Corsica: Portrait of a Granite Island*, is a travel book only in the sense that it is structured around the author's comings and goings around the island. Its learning and passion for Corsica is immense. Now out of print you may find it in a library, second-hand bookshop or on the Internet.

How exotic Corsica must have seemed to continental writers when they began to discover it in the 19th century, perfect for the purposes of swashbuckler fiction. If you search hard, you may be able to find an old edition of Alexandre Dumas' *The Corsican Brothers*, Guy de Maupassant's Corsica stories or Honoré de Balzac's story 'La Vendetta'. Unsurprisingly, they all deal with honour, murder, implacable hatreds and revenge.

■ **Patrimonio to Pino** At the opposite end of the island, the rugged wilderness of the Cap Corse is best experienced on the twisty D80, passing Genoese towers and windswept fishing villages.

MUST-SEE TOWNS

There's a remarkable variety in the character and atmosphere of Corsica's towns. Our pick of the bunch is as follows.

■ **Bonifacio** (p173) Can't be beaten for its breathtaking coastal scenery and for the buzzing, unpretentious atmosphere in its port and old town.

■ **Sartène** (p168) Perched in the mountains above Propriano, this formidable walled town, with its tall granite houses and narrow streets, retains a charming authenticity, away from the hub-bub of the coast.

■ **Calvi** (p106) With its ritzy, Riviera-like atmosphere, sandy beach, glamorous port and mountainous backdrop, this is a typical picture-postcard town worth a visit.

■ **Corte** (p209) Home of Corsican nationalism and the island's sole university, this historical town attracts plenty of visitors to its renowned museum and bustling old town.

■ **St-Florent** (p96) Visitors to this picturesque little town will enjoy relaxing in its quayside cafés, walking around its citadel or choosing from the wide variety of water sports on its sandy beach.

TOP WALKS

Corsica's stunning and varied scenery, warm climate and abundance of well-marked trails make it a haven for walkers from around the globe.

■ **GR20** (p51) This is undoubtedly Corsica's most famous walk and links Calenzana, in the Balagne, with Conca, just north of Porto Vecchio, 200km away.

■ **Girolata** (p132) This pretty seaside village north of the Scandola Nature Reserve is only accessible by boat or cross-country walk from Col de la Croix. Reward yourself with a swim and cold drink when you get there.

■ **Mare a Mare Centre** (p47) Thirty-six hours coast to coast, this hike, between Ghisonaccia and Porticcio, runs through the hinterland of Ajaccio and the little-known districts of Fiumorbu and Taravo, with charming villages and spectacular landscape.

■ **Ponte Vecchju to Ponte Zaglia** (p134) An easy walk (40 minutes each way) through lush mountain and forest terrain near Ota, with plenty of swimming opportunities in rock pools.

■ **Piscia di Gallo waterfall** (p190) This beautiful, 90-minute inland walk (for all capabilities) takes you through the cool pine forest of L'Ospedale.

For details on Corsican authors, see p33.

Travellers with a good reading knowledge of French will have access to much richer resources. Nicolas Giudici's *Le Crépuscule des Corses* is a brilliant and pessimistic analysis of Corsica's prospects in the world (*crépuscule* means 'twilight').

L'Art du Graffiti en Corse by Pierre Bertoncini is a fully illustrated coffee-table book presenting the history of this illicit art and subculture on the island.

There's something for travellers of all ages to enjoy in *Asterix in Corsica* by R Goscinny, translated into several languages. The subtle historical puns and references may be lost on younger readers, but they'll enjoy this classic romp through the *maquis* as Asterix and chums fend off the Romans.

INTERNET RESOURCES

Though Corsica is hardly the world leader in electronic information, it's coming up from nowhere fairly fast; see p227 for more information on Internet access. Useful sites on Corsica are as follows:

Aller en Corse (www.allerencorse.com) Accommodation listings and other practical information for visitors (French and English).

Clique Corse (www.cliquecorse.com) Practical and cultural information site.

Corse Matin (www.corsematin.com) Corsica's leading daily newspaper (French only).

Corsica Isula (www.corsica-isula.com) The most exhaustive English-language website about Corsica, with links to other useful sites.

L'Agence du Tourisme de la Corse (www.visit-corsica.com) The island's official tourist board site.

Lonely Planet (www.lonelyplanet.com) For succinct summaries on travelling to most places on earth, postcards from other travellers and the Thorn Tree bulletin board.

Itineraries

CLASSIC ROUTES

BETWEEN PORTS
Five days / Porto Vecchio to Porto

Starting in **Porto Vecchio** (p183), ascend the boulder- and pine-fringed D368 to **L'Ospedale** (p189). Continue winding north through the cooler plains of the **Fôret de L'Ospedale** (p189), past the **Barrage de L'Ospedale** (p190), on to the village of **Zonza** (p190) where you could bed for the night. Continue to **Quenza** (p191) and to Aullène, before crossing via the twisty, scenic D420 to Petreto-Bicchisano. Continue up to Ajaccio on the N196, bypassing the town, and head to the coast and Golfe de Liscia on the D81. Stop in either **Tiuccia** (p142) or **Sagone** (p141), the gastronomic hub of the area. Spend a day relaxing on the Golfe de Liscia's sandy beaches before taking the D70 to the bustling inland village of **Vico** (p142). After lunch continue north to **Évisa** (p134), famed for its chestnut festival and the beautiful fôret d'Aitone, on a spectacular road through the **Gorges de Spelunca** (p133). Follow the road to the tiny mountain-top village of **Ota** (p133) and on down to **Porto** (p128) for the night. Finish the journey with a boat trip around the Unesco world heritage site of the **Réserve Naturelle de Scandola** (p132).

This 300km route has everything from lush forests and mountain gorges to fabulous beaches and bustling towns.

STEERING SOUTH

Six days / Ajaccio to Bonifacio

Start your trip with at least a day's walk around **Ajaccio** (p143) and its sights, before hitting the coast road south via Porticcio to **Plage d'Agosta** (p155) for a swim. Continue on the D155 south through the village of Acqua Doria where you should stop to take a walk to the **Capo di Muro** (p157) with its stunning views of the Golfe d'Ajaccio. It's a twisty road south to the busy seaside village of **Porto Pollo** (p166) where you could stay for the night. Detour slightly on the D757 to the magical prehistoric site of **Filitosa** (p164), taking in a fabulous lunch at the riverside **Pont di Calzola** (p165). Double back and get onto the D157 south, via **Propriano** (p160) and on to one of Corsica's best beaches at **Plage de Portigliolo** (p167), where you could stop for a dip before continuing south, taking in the breathtaking coastal views, to the quaint village of **Campomoro** (p167) for a stopover. Heading inland again, the historic walled town of **Sartène** (p168) is only a short distance away but also worthy of a few hours if not an overnight stay. Continuing south, stop at the lion's shape carved out of the rock at **Roccapina** (p172), and head on to the little village of **Pianattoli-Caldarello** (p172) for lunch. All roads from here lead to the wonderful town of **Bonifacio** (p173). After a night on the town, wind up your journey with a boat trip around the **Bouches de Bonifacio** (p181), with views of the spectacular cliffs on which the town rests.

Aquaphiles will enjoy this coast-hugging, 170km route that passes some of the islands most beautiful seaside scenery.

ON THE EDGE
Three days / Cap Corse to the Balagne

Starting from **Bastia** (p79), stop at the **Maison du Cap Corse** (p89) north of town for brochures and information. From here, join the D80 heading north. The entire route essentially now hugs the D80 as it winds up the east coast.

Visit the marina in the lovely little village of **Erbalunga** (p90); it's a great spot for lunch. From here, pass through the rural hamlets of Sisco and Pietracorbara to **Macinaggio** (p91), an ideal place to overnight.

The next day, continue over the top of the cape to **Centuri** (p93), where you can break the journey for lunch or coffee. From here the scenery gets progressively more dramatic as you meander your way down the rugged and far less touristed west coast of Cap Corse. An ideal place to spend the night is **Le Relais du Cap** (p95), a great *chambre d'hôte* just outside Nonza.

From Nonza, the D81 connects the cape with the resort town of **St-Florent** (p96). Then skirt the Désert des Agriates and continue to the Balagne region for the last leg and your destination: the sun-kissed resort town of **Île Rousse** (p115).

A gentle 165km drive on good roads (primarily following the well-maintained D80), taking in the rugged coastal vistas of Cap Corse en route.

TAILORED TRIPS

TOT'S TOUR

With practically a whole coastline of beaches to choose from, a tour of Corsica with young ones can be great fun, without burning a hole in your pocket. Starting in **Ajaccio** (p143), sea-loving kids could try their hand at sailing lessons around the beautiful **Îles Sanguinaires** (p150), tennis or spend a night stargazing at the **Centre Scientifique de Vignola** (p150). A little further south, pet lovers will enjoy watching the 3000 species of turtles at the **A Cupulatta Centre** (p155). In **Porto Pollo** (p166), kids can indulge in a

whole range of water sports from kiteboarding to scuba diving (for over eights). With its shallow beach and clear water it's also the perfect spot for snorkelling or for taking a horse ride on the beach. Down in **Bonifacio** (p173), kids of all ages will enjoy a boat trip around the caves hidden in the town's cliffs, catching the little train up to the Old Town, watching exotic fish at the town's aquarium or, for older kids, quad biking, abseiling or bungy jumping. Junior Tarzans can practice their rope swinging at the **Xtrem Parc** adventure centre (p190) near L'Ospedale.

SUR LA PLAGE

Corsica's beaches are some of the best in Europe. Starting in the far north, the beautiful **Plage de Tamarone** (p92) on Cap Corse is set in the island's wildest and most rugged countryside. Nestling in the Désert des Agriates, the **Plage de Saleccia** (p101) was used as a location in the 1970s film *The Longest Day*, while close by are the smaller but equally stunning **Plage du Loto** (p101) and **Plage de L'Ostriconi** (p101), the latter reputedly having the finest sand in Europe. The west and south coast boasts the island's

best beaches. From Cargèse down to the Golfe de Liscia there are five sandy, white, picture-postcard beaches to choose from. One of our favourites, **Plage de Portigliolo** (p167), has 4km of fine white sand and, by dint of its size, never gets overcrowded. The pebbly **Plage de Santa Manza** (p182) is windy and gloriously empty except for windsurfers and wild goats, while **Plage de Giulia** (p182) has sublime turquoise water and plenty of water sports. Horseshoe **Plage de Rondinara** (p182) is like a lagoon, flanked by pines, and Corsica's most famous **Plage de Palombaggia** (p181) is like a tropical (albeit crowded) paradise.

THE BALAGNE CRAFT TRAIL

Heading out of Calvi, the **Balagne Craft Trail** (p119) not only makes for a very pleasant day's driving around the rustic villages of the Balagne interior, it's also a great way to explore the rich artisan heritage of Corsica's village tradition.

The route hugs the N197 and the coast as far as the charming little village of **Algajola** (p114), from where the D151 drops down through the rural heartland of the Balagne to the village of **Pigna** (p123). This is the most famous spot for browsing the artisan workshops along the route and the location of the famous **Casa Musicale** (p123), a great spot for lunch.

From here, the route winds through tiny villages with signposts pointing the way. Make sure you stop at **Sant'Antonino** (p124), one of the highest Balagne villages and home to the excellent **Cave Antonini** (p124), an artisan winery that uses lemons in its produce. Also worth a visit on your way back to the N197 to return, via Île Rousse, to Calvi, are the splendid villages of **Speloncato** (p120) and **Belgodère** (p119).

Before you set out, pick up a copy of the leaflet *Strada di l'Artigiani*, available from the tourist office in Calvi (p106).

The Authors

ODA O'CARROLL
Getting Started, Itineraries, Corsica Outdoors, Snapshot, History, Culture, Food & Drink, The West Coast, The South, Directory

Having hitched around Corsica with a friend one college summer, played an extra in a film, bummed on beaches and sampled the local *eau de vie*, Oda was quite happy to revisit the haunts of her (not too distant) youth.

This time, with a willing sister in tow, she travelled the switchbacks of the west and south coasts from Girolata to Porto Vecchio and, in between, hiked the hills in search of far-flung places to visit, infiltrating coach tours and dodging stray pigs on the road. Oda has previously worked on Lonely Planet's *France* guide.

MY CORSICA

What struck me on this visit to Corsica is, besides its incredible natural beauty, the sense that when you step onto the island you're leaving the busy 21st century behind. Corsica's rich rural traditions and cultural heritage have remained surprisingly intact. I have so many great memories from this trip, sailing in the **Bouches de Bonifacio** (p181) and swimming in the aquamarine waters of its fantastic beaches, hiking the cool terrain of the **Gorges de Spelunca** (p133) or chatting with locals in **Sartène** (p168). But the highlight has got to be sitting out under the stars on the terrace of the wonderful **Hôtel des Roches Rouges** (p137), overlooking the spectacular Les Calanques, the quiet hills and the sea, and feeling like I'm really at the end of the earth.

DAVID ATKINSON
Itineraries, Bastia & the Far North, Calvi & the Balagne, The Eastern Plain, The Central Mountains, Directory

David Atkinson has has previously written about France for Lonely Planet guides and his travel stories have been published in the *Guardian*, *the Times* and the *Weekend Financial Times*. Bastia was his adopted home in Corsica, and for this book he tried everything from hitching to homestays. He also ate his way through more *fiadone* than he now cares to remember.

CONTRIBUTING AUTHORS

Nicola Williams compiled the Environment and Transport chapters. Nicola lives in Lyon on mainland France. She travelled down, around and up the mountainous spine of Corsica for previous editions of Lonely Planet's *France* guide. *Provence & the Côte d'Azur* and *The Loire* are other French Lonely Planet titles she has authored.

Snapshot

Corsica's political history over the last decade reads like a passage from a hard-boiled gangster novel, with all the spicy crime-novel-by-numbers elements there in full detail – gun running, family feuding, corruption and sexual intrigue. For Corsicans, however, this has been a reality for over quarter of a century.

A landmark 6 July referendum in 2003, which would have given the island's regional assembly greater autonomy on issues such as the environment, tourism and tax, was hotly contested on both sides of the fence. Nationalists called for a yes vote. So, bizarrely, did conservative French President Chirac, saying it would strengthen the island's ties with Paris. Confused? So was the Corsican electorate which, in an embarrassing blow to the 14-month-old Raffarin government already feeling the heat of its unpopular pension reforms, responded with a defiant no. With less than one percentage point, a mere 1500 votes, the institutional reform question was overruled. Many Corsicans believed it would take more than a tokenistic administrative change to end nearly thirty years of struggle.

In a damning twist, Yvan Colonna, son of a former socialist MP and France's most wanted man for the cold-blooded murder of French prefect, Claude Érignac, was found hiding out in a goat shed in the hills near Porto Pollo on the south of the island, just days before the referendum. The 1998 murder had shaken Corsica and Republican France to its core and was the catalyst for the revolutionary Matignon Accords, set up by the then socialist Prime Minister Lionel Jospin (p27). These daring measures were hampered, however, by opposition from both his own party and from Gaullist camps, and by Jospin's need to appease a mostly conservative electorate in the run-up to the presidential election. Consequently for four years the Accord floundered until tough, new, populist interior minister Nicolas Sarkozy seized the baton again and, in an almost personal crusade, staked what many would see as his political career on the passing of the referendum package. Colonna's capture (timed to coincide with the main evening news bulletin) was perceived by many Corsicans as no more than a PR stunt by Sarkozy aimed at placating anti-separatists in the run-up to the crucial referendum. Seen as something of a local hero, Colonna's transfer to a Paris prison in late July sparked renewed violence with bombing on the island and in Nice, and riots on the streets of Ajaccio.

While about 70% of Corsicans would like to wrest more control of regional affairs from Paris, less than 10% want full independence from France.

Fires dominate the headlines of *Corse Matin* every year during the hottest months – the paper-dry maquis-covered hills burn quickly, and fires spread dangerously in an instant. But the majority of the thousands of fires reported each year are set off by arsonists settling old scores, property developers, hunters in search of porcine scrub-eaters and careless picnickers. During the summer of 2003, as temperatures soared and a relentless drought ravaged Mediterranean regions, the worst fires in decades raged across Corsica, seeing tourists airlifted from beaches, water supplies rationed and firefighting costs peak at a whopping €11 million.

FAST FACTS

Population: 262,000

People living in a rural area: 110,000

Unemployment rate: 9.7%

Territory size: 8682 sq km

Visitors entering and exiting Corsica's ports in 2002: 6,000,000

Proportion of women in the workplace: 40%

Percentage of population aged over 60: 25%

Average age of maternity: 30

History

World history is generally told without reference to Corsica at all, except, in passing, as the place that gave birth to world-bestriding Napoleon Bonaparte. Nevertheless, Corsica's history is a fascinating and turbulent one. Its strategic position long attracted the attentions of the major Mediterranean and European powers. Armies from Pisa, Genoa, France, Spain and Britain, not to mention the Moors and the armies of the Roman and Holy Roman Empires, have all fought on Corsican soil. This long history of conflict reflects another battle – the islanders' struggle to assert their identity while dominated by a succession of foreign rulers. Indeed, Corsicans have battled for their independence since the Greeks first enslaved them in 565 BC.

Corsica: The Concise History comes from the Welsh Academic Press' Histories of Europe series. It provide a succinct, thorough account of the island's history.

NEOLITHIC CORSICA

It is likely that the island was inhabited in the Palaeolithic era, but the earliest skeletal remains of Bonifacio Woman, dating from 6570 BC, are from the early Neolithic era.

The first inhabitants of the island probably came from what we now call Tuscany, in Italy, and survived by hunting, gathering and fishing. Rock caves of the kind in which they lived can still be seen at Filitosa (p164) in the south.

Around 4000 BC the inhabitants of the island succumbed to the romance of big stones. At various sites, particularly in the southwestern corner of the island, they erected great standing slabs of stone (menhirs), and shelter-like constructions (dolmens), in which two or more standing stones support a huge, horizontal slab of a stone as a 'roof'. At some point, the menhirs began to resemble statues with carved warrior faces.

Examples of these menhirs can still be seen at various places across the island, including Patrimonio (p100) at the site where the annual Nuits de la Guitare festival is held.

THE TORRÉENS

In about 1100 BC a new race, possibly originating from the eastern Mediterranean, came to the island. These new islanders have come to be known as Torréens, named after their seemingly indestructible signature edifices, the *torri*, or towers, that stand alongside or on the ruins of menhirs and dolmens. Some of the best examples of these towers can still be found dotted along the coastline of Cap Corse (p91).

Evidence suggests that the Torréens routed their predecessors, the menhir and dolmen builders. Those artier folk, with less sophisticated weapons, appear to have migrated or fled to the north. Many of the Torréens, it seems, then headed south to Sardinia, where they built some of the first conical stone edifices, now called *nuraghi*.

The island's architectural development continued, and *castelli* (castles) are the outstanding vestiges of the settled, organised way of life that arose. The remains of two of these can be visited in the mountains between Porto Vecchio and Propriano (p190).

TIMELINE 60,000 BC	4000–1800 BC
First indications of human presence on Corsica	Monoliths and megalithic tombs constructed by the island's inhabitants

GREEKS & ROMANS

In the 6th century BC the Phocaean Greeks founded Alalia at what is now today the conurbation of Aléria (p197) on Corsica's flat eastern plain. Alalia thrived on trade and Corsica soon rose to fame.

For the cosmopolitan, seafaring peoples of the Mediterranean, however, the island was primarily a place for brief port calls. Nobody before Rome actually undertook to invest in and dominate the island, and when Rome did step in it was above all for strategic reasons: to prevent Corsica falling into the hands of its enemies, the Carthaginians.

Rome conquered Alalia, renaming it Aléria, and set about imposing its manners on the islanders, exacting tributes, and even selling some of them into slavery. Rome, though, never went to any great pains to improve the island. In what was to become a recurrent pattern in Corsica, those islanders least willing to bend to invaders sought the protection of the unconquerable mountains.

GOTHS, VANDALS & SARACENS

After the collapse of the Western Roman Empire in AD 476, the distant Byzantine Empire (the Eastern Roman Empire, based in Constantinople) began to take an interest in former Roman territories such as Corsica. The collapse of Rome had initially left Corsica vulnerable to Rome's own despoilers – the Goths under Totila and the Vandals under Genseric. It's likely that the latter sacked Aléria after laying waste to Gaul. Byzantium's equally bloody conquest of the island in the first half of the 6th century ended the brief dominion of the Germanic tribes.

Dorothy Carrington's *Granite Island: a Portrait of Corsica* is possibly the finest book about Corsica in any language.

During the 8th century, Corsica was also increasingly subject to attack by the Moors (Saracens, or Muslims) from North Africa. Whether as organised states or as free-booting pirates, the Moors raided for slaves, and from time to time they took possession of a coastal village or a whole coastal region, or even ventured inland. Between the 8th and 18th centuries, the islanders lived in perpetual fear of invasion.

PISAN SPELL

The 10th century saw the rise to power of the nobility. Important seignorial families, often of Tuscan or Ligurian origin, created fiefdoms on the island and ruled them with a rod of iron. Some historians date the predominance of so-called clans in Corsica from this time. In 1077, at the request of certain Tuscan feudal lords, the Pope appointed the bishop of Pisa to oversee his Corsican interests.

The then-powerful Italian city of Pisa, continually at odds with its rival, Genoa, put commerce ahead of all other values, and its bishop served as a front man for its merchants. Corsica nevertheless also benefited from Pisan overlordship, and this period was one of peace, prosperity and development. Handsome Pisan-style churches were erected in the Balagne, the Nebbio and on and around the northeastern coast. Examples of these, such as Église de San Michele de Murato (p101), can still be visited today.

Pisa's good fortune in Corsica aroused Genoa's jealousy, and Genoese ambitions took a turn for the better when Pope Innocent II, in 1133, divided the island between the two Italian republics. From then on it was simply a matter of gaining ground for Genoa.

565 BC	259 BC
Alalia (Aléria) founded by the Phocaean Greeks	Rome seizes Corsica and holds on to it for more than five centuries

First, Genoa undermined its rival's supremacy by fortifying the town of Bonifacio (p173) in the south. Genoese forces then ventured north, where they turned Calvi (p107) into a stronghold. By the 13th century, despite opposition from some island lords who remained loyal to Pisa, Genoa unmistakably enjoyed the upper hand. Pisa's defeat in 1284 in the sea battle of Meloria, a small island near Livorno, marked the end of Pisan rule in Corsica.

GENOESE OCCUPATION

In *Histoire du Peuple Corse*, Roger Caratini takes the position that the centuries of Genoese rule were Corsica's golden age, while the French long pursued a policy of cryptocolonialism.

Before Italian unification in the second half of the 19th century, Genoa was one of the great early modern merchant states. Indeed, if it had been more ambitious, Genoa rather than Spain might very well have been the first to discover and exploit the Americas; Columbus, after all, was Genoese, whether he was born in Genoa proper or, as some Corsicans would have it, in Genoese Calvi (see the boxed text, p109).

Genoa occupied and dominated Corsica for five centuries, during which time the island was turned into a fortress. The Genoese, however, had little sentiment for the Corsicans, who were often evicted or excluded from towns and put to work on the land to serve Genoa's commercial and economic interests, and to pay taxes. Those who disobeyed were punished severely.

The Genoese administration created towns and set the population to work cultivating olive and chestnut trees, with a view towards turning Corsica into Genoa's breadbasket (see the boxed text, p201). By the mid-16th century, the Genoese believed they at last had Corsica under control. However, the island's strategic importance in Europe would soon prove a catalyst once again.

SAMPIERO CORSO

In 1552 Henri II, king of France, saw an opportunity to gain ground in Italy when the Sienese rose against the Spanish garrison in their city and called on France for protection. Corsica, because of its location, got caught up in the middle of the struggle. In 1553 an expeditionary corps reached Bastia under the command of the Maréchal de Termes and his second in command, the Turkish privateer Dragut, a French ally. The town was captured, shortly followed by others, and within a few days Corsica was declared French territory.

During this campaign, Sampiero Corso, a Corsican colonel in the French army, came to symbolise the fight against the Genoese. Yet his

---

SAMPIERO CORSO 'THE FIERY'

Born in 1498 near Bastelica, Sampiero Corso became known as 'the most Corsican of Corsicans'. He rose to fame on the mainland as a soldier in the French army. Vehemently anti-Genoese, Sampiero fought with great courage alongside the French army in 1553, in a bid to reconquer his native island. Although this first attempt was unsuccessful, he refused to give up hope. He returned to the island with a band of partisans in 1564, having failed to obtain European backing, and managed to destabilise the Genoese but could not vanquish them. Three years later, Sampiero was assassinated.

AD 774	1077
The Moors (Saracens) begin to raid Corsica	The pope appoints the bishop of Pisa to oversee Corsican affairs

THEODOR I, KING OF CORSICA

Born in Cologne in 1694, Theodor de Neuhof sought a land where he could make a name for himself. His interest in Corsica had been awakened when he met some Corsicans in mainland Europe and was touched by their plight. He then raised the money for his expedition from Greek and Jewish merchants in Tunis. Had he had more time and ampler resources, he may even have done the Corsicans some good, but his military strategy was based on the interminable siege warfare that was still the main pillar of military doctrine in Europe. Theodor's Corsican troops were good for lightning strikes and guerrilla warfare, or nothing. Disenchantment was inevitable. When he left Corsica, he did actually crisscross Europe in an effort to rally support – but to no avail. He died in London, penniless, in 1756. A range of artefacts relating to his ill-fated rule are now displayed at the Musée de L'Adecec in Cervione (p203).

popularity and determination were not enough to safeguard the French victory. The Genoese appealed to Charles V, the king of Spain and holy Roman emperor, for support, and Henri, after suffering a series of agonising defeats, signed the Treaty of Cateau-Cambrésis, which recognised Genoese supremacy on the island.

After the breather under the French, the Corsicans found themselves again at the mercy of their familiar enemy and despite a favourable start, Sampiero Corso's independent effort to free the island from the Genoese in 1564 was short-lived.

WARS OF INDEPENDENCE

Corsica's Forty Years' War began in 1729, when an old peasant in a mountain village near Corte balked at paying tax to a Genoese tax collector. The effects of his action snowballed, with more and more Corsicans refusing to pay their taxes each day.

The rebels grew bolder and organised themselves into a group, stealing weapons and gradually weakening Genoese rule. With a revolt on their hands, the Genoese successfully appealed to the emperor of Austria for assistance, and St-Florent and Bastia were subsequently recovered. The Genoese forces were defeated at the Battle of Calenzana (1732) but then regained control of the situation. It was a transient success, however. The revolt recovered momentum and at a meeting in Corte in 1735 the Corsicans drew up a constitution for an independent sovereign state.

A somewhat comical episode followed. In 1736 an eloquent, opportunistic German aristocrat named Theodor von Neuhof disembarked in Aléria. Seeing him as the leader for whom they had been looking, the rebels allowed this peculiar man to declare himself king of Corsica – though, to be sure, under a constitution. His reign, however, lasted only nine months, after which he escaped to London disguised as a priest, where he died, impoverished, 20 years later. Today Baron Theodor von Neuhof is buried in St Anne's churchyard in London's Wardour Street.

The battle continued in Theodor's absence, and the Genoese grew so uneasy that in 1738 they accepted France's offer of assistance. Delighted to be involved in the island's affairs again, this time with Genoa's blessing, the French king, Louis XV, sent an expeditionary corps to Corsica,

'Sampiero Corso's independent effort to free the island from the Genoese in 1564 was short-lived'

1284	1553
Pisa defeated by Genoa in the naval Battle of Melonia, ending Pisan rule	French troops land and capture Bastia, declaring Corsica French territory

paid for by the Genoese, under the command of General de Boissieux. By the time the French left Corsica in 1741, 1000 Corsicans had gone into exile abroad. The rebellion appeared to be over.

In 1753, when the last French regiments pulled out, Corsica was still under Genoese rule.

PASCAL PAOLI & THE REVOLT

In 1755 the troubles resurfaced with an insurrection led by Pascal Paoli. Educated in Naples, Paoli succeeded where everyone else before him had failed: he united the struggle against Genoa. Furthermore, he cobbled together a constitutional state – unique in that still dynastic and absolutist age – which, given time, might have ensured Corsica a happy independence. It was not to be.

In the aftermath of disastrous attempts by the Genoese to regain control of Corsica, France seized the opportunity it had been waiting for. In 1764 France accepted Genoa's offer to occupy the strongholds of Bastia, Ajaccio, Calvi and St-Florent. The Treaty of Compiègne, which sealed the agreement was, however, only the first stage: the Treaty of Versailles, four years later, formalised the Genoese cession of Corsica to France. Now France itself began acting less like a mediator and more like a ruler.

The mobilisation of Paoli's supporters failed to reverse the situation. Their defeat at the Battle of Ponte Novo on the River Golo, northeast of Ponte Leccia, on 8 May 1769 marked the beginning of French rule of Corsica in earnest, and Paoli fled to London.

Published in Glasgow in 1768, James Boswell's *Journal of a Tour to Corsica and Memoirs of Pascal Paoli* was largely responsible for the Paoli and Corsica craze in England.

PASCAL PAOLI – PIONEER

Paoli was born in 1725 in Morosaglia, in the Castagniccia region, and since 1889 his ashes have been buried in the small chapel beneath his childhood family home (p200). He spent his youth in Italy with his father, who had gone into exile during the French occupation. In Naples, where he was educated, he read Montesquieu's *The Spirit of Laws*, Plutarch and Machiavelli. He was barely 30 when he returned to the island, and three months later he was named General of the Nation. The naming ceremony was held near La Porta at the Couvent St-Antoine de Casabianca (p201).

He proceeded to displace the Genoese from everywhere throughout the island except their six fortress towns. His military successes, never decisive, were not his greatest claim to fame. That title is assigned to his relentless constitutionalism. 'Wishing to give durable and constant form to its government', 'the felicity of the nation' – these are phrases from the first of his efforts at writing a framework for governance, and he penned them three decades and more before the Americans convened to try something along similar lines in Philadelphia.

His efforts to root out criminality and in particular Corsica's trademark murderous vendettas were heroic, as also were his efforts to promote public education. The English religious reformer John Wesley called him 'as great a lover of his country as Epaminondas and as great a general as Hannibal'. In America, patriots on the outskirts of Philadelphia met in the General Paoli Tavern, in what was later to become the town of Paoli. (There are in fact now four towns in the US named Paoli.)

But his battle was not winnable, and he spent much of his life in exile in London, where he died.

1559	1729–69
The Treaty of Cateau-Cambrésis recognises Genoese supremacy once more	Corsica's War of Independence ends with the Battle of Ponte Novo and marks the beginning of French rule proper

THE MOOR'S HEAD

It was Pascal Paoli who made the Moor's head Corsica's official emblem. Yet no one really knows why. You see it everywhere – on beer-bottle labels, on the Corsican coat of arms that adorns public buildings and on Corsica's traditional flag. The Moors, or Saracens, in their incarnation as pirates from the Mediterranean's southern shores, were one of Corsica's traditional enemies. During the Crusades, any crusader who had a victory over the 'infidels' could add the Moor's head to his personal coat of arms, suggesting that the Moor's head was a symbol of Corsica's victory over its enemies.

Why, though, does the Corsican Moor wear his bandanna around his forehead, whereas the four Moors on the Sardinian coat of arms wear theirs as blindfolds (as did the Moors so plentifully represented in Corsica before Paoli's time)? Corsican General Ghjuvan Petru Gaffori, when he attacked the Genoese citadel in Bastia in 1745, was perhaps the first to reposition the cloth. 'Corsica at last has its eyes open', Gaffori said. And Paoli commented, 'Corsicans want to see clearly. Freedom must walk by the torch of philosophy. Could we say that we seem to fear the light?' Both of these remarks suggest that Corsica had come to identify with the Moors.

FRENCH RULE

Once again Corsica had a military government of outsiders. In reestablishing law and order and taking control of the administration, the French followed the example of the Genoese, but without their brutality. They proclaimed a new set of laws, known as the Code Corse, particular to the island, and made some efforts to develop agriculture. The period was characterised by Corsica's increasing adaptation to a style of French governance that revolution was about to blow to smithereens.

The French Revolution was initially applauded by many Corsicans. For the impoverished islanders, it gave new voice to popular dissatisfaction. In 1789 a decree proclaimed: 'Corsica belongs to the French Empire and its inhabitants shall be governed by the same constitution as the rest of France'. An amnesty was granted, and Paoli returned to Corsica. But reconciliation between Corsica and France was not complete. In 1793 Paoli was blamed for the failure of the French revolutionary government's Sardinian expedition; he had committed fewer troops than the government had expected. The stern and irreconcilable Revolutionary Convention that had judged and executed Louis XIV and his queen, Marie-Antoinette, ordered Paoli's arrest for counter-revolutionary behaviour. He declared Corsica's secession, and requested help from Britain.

For Britain this was an opportunity of the same kind that Genoa's mismanagement had been for France. On its arrival in Corsica in 1794, the British fleet captured St-Florent, Bastia and Calvi (it was during a battle for the latter that Admiral Horatio Nelson lost the sight in his right eye; see p109). George III, king of England, was proclaimed sovereign in Corsica. Yet the British soon proved a disappointment to Paoli. He had believed Britain to be liberal and enlightened. But Britain did as little to benefit Corsicans as other rulers had. Paoli was passed over for the viceroyalty and again went into exile in London, where he died in 1807.

The Anglo-Corsican kingdom lasted just over two years. Following the English departure in 1796, the island's affairs came once again under the jurisdiction of the French and specifically of Napoleon Bonaparte,

Desmond Gregory's *The Ungovernable Rock* looks into British involvement in Corsica during the revolutionary wars.

a Corsican by birth. His single ambition for the place was to make it French once and for all. Immediately, Napoleon's enforcers bumped up against the clergy, and the conflict resulted in an anti-French insurrection in 1798. Mistrustful of Corsica's own political class, Napoleon excluded Corsicans from island administrative posts, and broke the island up into two departments.

He still managed to make friends in Corsica, and paradoxically – as the island's most famous progeny – did more to Gallicise the island than any other individual.

WWWI & WWII

In the 19th and 20th centuries, Corsica continued to reject some central government decisions from France. The clan structure endured and there was a propensity towards organised crime. During this period levels of rural poverty endured, and attempts to develop infrastructure and agriculture remained frustrated.

Under Napoleon III's (son of Napoleon I's brother Louis) prosperous second French empire, real investment was made in Corsica's infrastructure (such as the Corsican rail network that continues to trundle along today). Corsicans took advantage of the greater employment opportunities available in France in enormous numbers, and they filled many posts in the French empire. The sword, though, has cut both ways: 30,000 Corsicans died for France on the battlefields of WWI.

Corsica fought bravely in WWII as well. In 1940 the island was occupied by more than 90,000 Axis troops, and it was in Corsica that the term 'maquis' was coined for the whole of the French Resistance. Corsica was the first region of France to be liberated and, like its neighbouring islands in the Mediterranean, served as a forward base for the liberation of mainland Europe.

THE CORSICAN MALAISE

Corsica's latter-day difficulties date from the 1960s, when a Corsican autonomy movement was formed to combat what was perceived as

---

NAPOLEON BONAPARTE

Despite his early expressions of Corsican patriotic feeling, Napoleon grew to be extremely ambivalent about his native island, if not hostile to it. In his final exile on the island of St-Helena in the southern Atlantic, he was asked why he had never done more to help develop Corsica's economy. His answer: 'Je n'en ai pas eu le temps' (I didn't have time for it). His mature policy towards Corsica was in fact altogether cold-blooded. Let the Corsicans keep their religion and their priests, he said, but let them love France and let them serve in her armies. A mere two roads, one between Ajaccio and Bastia, one between Bastia and St-Florent, should suffice, he said, for a people whose principal highway should be the sea. Native Corsicans, he decreed, were to be excluded from the administration of the island as they weren't trustworthy.

In 1814, the year of Napoleon's first definitive defeat, the people of Ajaccio threw a bust of Napoleon into the sea as the people of Bastia welcomed British troops. Resentment, however, seems to have passed with time. Ultimately Napoleon was lionised as the homeboy who'd made good in the wider world and brought the island fame. He certainly helps the tourist trade now.

1939–45	1976
Corsica is the first region of France to be liberated by the Allied forces in WWII	Front de Libération Nationale de la Corse (FLNC) formed

France's colonialist policy in Corsica. One particular source of friction was France's use of Corsica's eastern plain for the resettlement of refugees from the French defeat in Algeria. Today this fertile region is also a major centre for tourism.

In 1975 tensions exploded when Corsican separatists, led by the Simeoni brothers, unearthed a scandal involving fraudulent wine-making practices in the eastern coastal town of Aléria whereby immigrant workers benefited. The protesters occupied a building used to store wine, and an attempt by the police to resolve the situation ended in two deaths.

The Front de Libération Nationale de la Corse (FLNC) formed in 1976, and talk of autonomy increasingly turned to talk of independence. In the early 1980s two measures were designed to soothe the nationalists. First, a university was opened in Corte (p212); for many years, after the French had closed down Pascal Paoli's university, higher education was available only on the mainland. Second, the Assemblée de Corse was created; previously, the island had belonged to the Provence-Alpes-Côte d'Azur region. The detente arising from these measures was short-lived, however, and in 1983 the government tried unsuccessfully to shut down the FLNC.

By the 1990s the FLNC had broken into any number of splinter groups, and many other independent groups had come into existence. From 1993 to 1996 these groups warred against each other every bit as furiously as they had previously against the perceived coloniser.

The quarrel continues in various arenas, from economic development policy to environment to language, with tourism a particularly sore point. It should be noted, however, that the separatists have maintained a strict hands-off policy with regard to tourists themselves.

CORSICA TODAY

The assassination of the regional prefect, Claude Érignac, on 6 February 1998 upped the separatists' ante considerably. Érignac was the highest representative of the French state on the island, and his death sparked strong expressions of disgust among Corsicans themselves – as many as 40,000 of them took to the streets to demonstrate.

The new French President Lionel Jospin's government launched a 'Clean Hands' operation, with a view towards re-establishing law and order on the island as part of the ongoing Matignon Accord. This operation did not win the hearts and souls of Corsicans, who felt they had been demonised as terrorists.

In July 2003, after 30 years of nationalist violence and 200 years of French rule, Corsicans were invited to vote on their future status in a referendum linked to plans for decentralisation across France. The vote was split virtually 50:50 right up to polling day, although ultimately the anti-independence movement won out. The result was seen as a snub to Prime Minister Jean Pierre Raffarin's plans to decentralise power but keep Corsica under French rule. As such, Corsica's legacy of terrorism, violence and insularity to the outside world only looks set to continue.

Travellers with a good reading knowledge of French will have access to much richer resources. Robert Colonna d'Istria's *L'Histoire de la Corse*, informed throughout by the premise that Corsica is French and that's the end of it, is one good introduction.

Nicolas Giudici's *Le Crépuscule des Corses* is a brilliant and pessimistic analysis of Corsica's prospects in the world (*crépuscule* means 'twilight').

1998	2003
France's top official on the island, Claude Érignac, is assassinated by nationalist extremists	The anti-independence lobby narrowly wins a referendum on autonomous rule for Corsica

The Culture

REGIONAL IDENTITY

Years of colonisation and invasion have created, one could say, a kind of siege mentality on the island of Corsica. While few could accuse Corsicans of being xenophobic, a deep-seated desire to protect their cultural identity, founded understandably by historical circumstances, has led to an attitude of self-preservation and an acceptance of outsiders that sometimes borders on mere tolerance. The message behind bullet-ridden road signs, with the French placename crossed out and replaced by the spray-painted Corsican version, will be lost on few. In fact, the region's reliance on the tourist industry is something of a pandora's box. According to some nationalists the steady stream of tourists (whose euros are a welcome and provide a significant boost to the greasy till) only serves to exploit the environment and denude the region's cultural fabric. Add to this a love-hate relationship with mainland France and what are seen as its self-interested policies for the region, and you may begin to understand the Corsican psyche. Corsicans are conservative, stoical, tradition-loving people with an integrity that doesn't suffer fools gladly. While Corsicans' reputation for being hostile and unwelcoming is unjustified, there's a grain of truth in the stereotype. Don't expect to find arms wide open to greet you (and your camera-toting coach party) particularly in some of the more remote mountain villages. That said, once you've earned the trust and respect of a Corsican, you won't find a more hospitable, generous host.

LIFESTYLE

Family ties are strong in Corsica. Children often live in the family home until well into their 30s or until marriage, when they may then move out but remain within shuffling distance of the family roof. Outside the main hubs life can be desperately quiet, especially in the mountain villages, in winter when there's a mass exodus of Corsica's young to Marseille, Nice and Paris until the season comes around again.

In early modern times privileged Corsicans pursued education at all levels in Italy. Pascal Paoli (p24) opened the first university in Corsica in 1765, but when the French took over they closed Paoli's university, and for the next two centuries Corsicans seeking a higher education were obliged once again to leave the island for Italy or, as was increasingly the case, for the French mainland. The result was an epidemic brain drain. Corsica's best and brightest left the island to study and often did not return. The situation was only remedied in 1981 when the University of Corsica Pascal Paoli in Corte (p212) opened for business in response to nationalist demand.

Certain rules of inheritance have served to preserve Corsican family unity and continuity. The affiliation to a clan automatically provided an extended family, which also included members of a village community in a structure that was protective of its influence and authority.

However, Corsica isn't one big happy family; ties within families, clans and villages are matched by antipathy for those on the outside – other families, clans and villages.

Corsica's traditions, marked by a code of obligatory hospitality and often wildly disproportionate rough justice, have never been universal on the island or without dissenters. However the response to the violent traditions has often itself been violent. Pascal Paoli, during the brief

DID YOU KNOW?

Corsican families have roughly 1.6 children, lower than the national average of 1.9.

DOS & DON'TS

The Corsica of vendettas and overheated ideas of honour has passed into history.

Corsicans are accustomed to foreigners and are friendly and easy-going. You may want to punctuate conversation with more than the usual number of 'monsieurs' and 'madames'. Instead of just a curt 'Merci', be generous. Say 'Merci, monsieur' or 'Merci, madame'. You'll gain points for showing patience and more points still for taking your time at things rather than rushing. When driving in towns, you may find the road obstructed by a truck whose driver is taking a break, or by two motorists having a chat. Restrain yourself and remember you're on holidays (unless you're racing to catch a flight). It is considered rude to beep or show impatience. The same goes for drivers practising fifteen-point turns on the road – a friendly wave rather than a 30-second honk will do.

You'll also do well to introduce yourself in any conversation that goes beyond a mere exchange of niceties or simple commerce; Corsicans like to know who they are dealing with. In a similar vein, if you enter a bar with a local, it is considered rude if the stranger is not first introduced and their connection to the local person or place established. Remember, it is also more customary to buy rounds than to attempt to divide up a bill. Corsicans will head straight for a bar stool rather than the lounge, which is typically the preserve of women, romantic couples, card players and tourists.

Should you happen to be invited into a Corsican home, there is no need to take your hosts a present. In Corsica, a bottle of wine extended as you cross the threshold may be thought to imply your uncertainty as to whether the house is able to provide.

Corsicans are as *au fait* with the stereotypical Mediterranean *manana* philosophy as their mainland counterparts. Don't expect opening hours to be adhered to, schedules to be kept or plans to move at a northern European pace. Rather than get annoyed, get with the programme and enjoy the easy-going pace.

lifespan of independent republican Corsica in the mid-18th century, perhaps meant to help his countrymen rethink their antique and chilling concept of honour, when he razed the homes of vendetta murderers and put up signposts to publicise the occupants' crimes.

Napoleon went further in trying to bring his countrymen into the modern world: if a murderer could not be apprehended, he had four of the offender's close kinsmen arrested and executed instantly. A sense of honour is a particularly important legacy of the island's turbulent past. Injured pride has been the cause of many a bloody vendetta. The island has spawned a number of 'bandits of honour', outlawed and seeking refuge in the maquis, sometimes for years, after having avenged an offence by violent means. Weapons have always been an important part of Corsican culture – and not only for hunting. Today, though, visitors to the island need not fear getting caught in the crossfire of feuding families or protectionist mafia rackets; apart from the odd burnt-out shell of a building, you might never be aware of the internal machinations of the island's fighting factions.

Corsica's attitude to gays could be seen as less progressive than that of mainland France. Though gay relationships are tolerated, Corsica's traditional mores and society mean that open expressions of affection by same-sex couples might send conservative sensitivities into a spin, especially in the outer regions. And for all the island's tradition of arson, bra-burning didn't make it to the agenda in Corsica. While mothers are held in almost reverential esteem by Corsican men, women's rights and gender equality issues are lagging well behind the rest of Europe. Only four out of ten of the workforce is female and there are no female MPs on the island, an inequality that was due to be addressed had the referendum of July 2003 been passed.

DID YOU KNOW?

Corsican men live to an average age of 72, while Corsican women outlive them by another 10 years.

POPULATION

France's last census of 1999 gave Corsica a population of 260,000, of whom roughly 100,000 live in Ajaccio and Bastia. The record high was 276,000 inhabitants, measured in 1884, and the record low was 170,000 inhabitants in 1955.

A 1990 study by the French National Institute of Economic and Statistical Information suggested that more than 60% of the population at that time was born on the island. Throughout ancient, medieval and early modern times, Corsica assimilated untold numbers of Mediterranean peoples. Corsica opened its arms wide to immigrants in the 20th century as well. Italians settled, as did many of the French who had abandoned their homes in Algeria at the end of the Algerian war of independence in 1962. The arrival of refugees from Algeria, most of them settling in Corsica's eastern lowlands, caused problems, however, and served as an important stimulus for the nationalist movements.

Corsica's birth rate is so low, meanwhile, that approximately 75 of its towns record more deaths than births. The exodus from the inland villages is also worrying. Between the 1960s and 1990s, the mountain communities lost around 15,000 inhabitants, and some regions have a population density approaching that of the Sahara. A quarter of the island's population and one in every three of the inhabitants of the island's mountain villages is now over 60 years old and, as an indication, in the Ajaccio region alone, almost 10% of the female population is aged between 75 and 94. However the island does much to keep its mountain culture alive and the PNRC (p46) encourages tourists to explore its mountainous regions. In 2002 there was a slight increase in the number of births on the island and the level of deaths remained consistent with the previous year, though this was probably helped by the mild winter of 2001. You'll seldom hear English spoken on the island, a rarity in this era of cheap airfares.

To approach the Corsican people from a different angle, it's worth noticing that they tend to have Italianate surnames and French given names.

DID YOU KNOW?

Corsican men, on average, tie the knot at 36, and women at 31.

L'Île sans Rivage by Marie Susini, an author with a love-hate relationship with her native island, looks sceptically at Corsican family structure and island insularity.

SPORT
Adventure Sports

For information on rock climbing, canyoning, diving, walking and horse riding, see the chapter Corsica Outdoors (p42) as well as the activities sections in the regional chapters.

Cycling is popular in Corsica, and you can hire out mountain bikes (called *vélos tout terrain* or VTTs in French) throughout the island. **Objectif Nature** (☎ 04 95 32 54 34 or 06 03 58 66 09; www.Obj-Nature.ifrance.com) in Bastia is an adventure tour company that specialises in VTT. Lonely Planet's *Cycling in France* will also help steer you along the best routes. Bear in mind, though, that the combination of hills and heat can make cycling in Corsica a trying experience.

Skiing facilities on the island are still limited, although there are resorts in Èse and at the Col de Verghio. The best known area, strictly for confident skiers, is the *haute route à ski* which winds through the highest peaks, following the precarious trail of the GR20. Cross-country skiing and snowshoe hikes are also possible with the aid of a professional guide.

Water sports are extremely popular, unsurprisingly, on the island. In the summer you can find companies hiring out windsurfers, dinghies and sports catamarans on some of the island's beaches, including Porticcio (p156), around Porto Vecchio (p185) and St-Florent (p98).

For adrenaline junkies there are plenty of adventure activities such as quad biking (p176) bungy jumping (p176) and 4WD exploring (p155) to fire your energy. See the destination chapters for details.

Spectator Sports

In Corsica, soccer doesn't seem to have the profile that it enjoys on mainland France. Try the first division Bastia SC website: www.sc-bastia.fr.

Several large sporting events are held in Corsica during summer.

Fita Star Kallisté (☎ 04 95 32 25 70) The best archers from around the world compete in Biguglia in April.

Ripcurl (☎ 04 95 73 11 59) Held in Bonifacio in May this competition counts as the French national windsurfing championship.

Corsica Raid Adventure (☎ 04 95 23 83 00) This gruelling competition, taking place over eight days in mid-May, combines various activities, including mountain races, mountain biking and canyoning. It has been held since 1998, and is open to amateurs.

Inter-Lac (☎ 04 95 46 12 48) Held in July this two-stage walking competition covers 28km around the mountain lakes near Corte.

Mediterranean Trophy (☎ 04 95 23 89 00) This international sailing competition, in July, is open to vessels greater than 9m in length.

Tour de Corse (☎ 04 95 23 62 60) This three-day competition is regarded as the rally world championship. The Tour de Corse takes place on the roads (but you should see the roads!) at the end of September each year.

Also worth mentioning:

Route de Sud (☎ 04 95 25 08 13) A cycling event held in May.

La Paolina (☎ 04 95 25 05 99/98 89) A 72km foot race starting at Île Rousse in September.

Six Jours Cyclotouristes de l'Île de Beauté (☎ 04 95 21 96 94) A six-day, 600km cycling event in September.

The theme of Alexandra Jaffe's *Ideologies in Action: Language Politics on Corsica* is self-explanatory. This book will be of interest not just to people on their way to Corsica but anyone with an interest in the survival of 'small' languages.

MULTICULTURALISM

Since 1975 the flow of immigrants from outside France has diminished. The number of mainland French settling in Corsica – *pinzuti*, as the Corsicans call them – has increased. One in six people living on the island is a foreigner. Moroccans account for over a half of these, ahead of Portuguese, Italians and Tunisians. The largest concentration of Moroccans is in Bastia, while Tunisians tend to settle in Ajaccio. In a demographic blip, Calvi has a relatively high proportion of immigrants, many of them Eastern European, thanks to the presence of a French Foreign Legion colony on the outskirts of town (p108). Non-natives are mostly concentrated on the east and south coasts, with outsiders accounting for 40% of the population in the Balagne. In fact, outside l'Île de France (the Paris region), Corsica is the region most occupied by foreigners in France. Of those who come to Corsica, most are, unsurprisingly, young men who find work in the agricultural, building and to a lesser degree tourism sectors. They are easily absorbed during 'the season' but with significant unemployment in the more spartan months and the annual brain drain of Corsica's youth to mainland France, resentments can run rife. It must be noted that some Corsicans are racist, especially against North Africans, who represent a relatively large community on the island.

RELIGION

France is notoriously lax about church attendance, and some observers have taken the position that the country is Roman Catholic in name only. Corsica, however, might be expected to be more conservative in this respect, although one source (a Corsican language-use survey) suggests that 8% attend church regularly, 21% sometimes, 11% rarely, 44% only for social ceremonies and 16% never.

To be sure, religious enthusiasm manifests itself in Corsica in the lavish Holy Week processions in towns such as Bonifacio, Sartène and Calvi; Corsica, for many centuries, belonged to the pope's own diocese. Catholicism in Corsica coexists with vestiges of mystical and superstitious behaviours and beliefs, among them, for example, belief in the *spiritu* (the dead who return from beyond to revisit their terrestrial homes) and the belief that magic spells can cure illness.

ARTS
Music

Corsica's haunting ancient music is undergoing a revival. The most frequently encountered of the traditional secular polyphonic forms is the *paghjella*, which combines three or four male voices in chants for purposes from satire to seduction. The men are usually dressed in black and each stands with a hand over one ear so as not to be distracted by the voice of the person next to him. This is critical, since each voice contributes a different harmonic element: the first provides the melody, the second provides the bass, while the third, more high-pitched, improvises on the theme.

Sound out www.corsemusique.com for the largest who's who of Corsican music on the Net.

The *voceru*, a women's art, is sung, mournfully, at wakes. The women sob and rock to and fro as if in a trance, and their singing is at once halting, monotonous and riveting. In the old days, during vendettas, the *voceri* were typically accompanied by cries for vengeance. In the *lamentu*, a gentler expression of the same general tendency, a woman bemoans the absence of a loved one never to return.

The *chjam'e rispondi* have a call and response form that is similar to that of spiritual or blues music. As *chjam'e rispondi* are improvisational, they lend themselves to competitions.

Corsican vocal music is not of course necessarily performed a cappella. Accompaniment might be by way of wooden or horn flutes, stringed instruments or percussion.

Groups that have recorded the traditional Corsican forms include the hugely popular Canta U Populu Corsu, the Celtic-inspired I Muvrini, A Filetta and I Chjami Aghjalesi. Petru Guelfucci, who performs with the group Voce di Corsica, has become something of a household name throughout France as a soloist; he has even developed a following beyond France.

Older recordings include a set of three LPs, dating from the period 1961 to 1963, under the title 'Musique Corse de Tradition Orale'. This treasure, if you can find it, gives you an idea of how Corsican music must have sounded when it was still more expression than performance. (Some cuts feature the father of Jean-François Bernardini, the leader of I Muvrini.) Another curiosity is the Canzone di i Prigiuneri Corsi in Alimania 1916-1917 (Songs of the Corsican Prisoners in Germany), distributed by the Corsican publisher La Marge; the recordings were made on wax rolls by German ethnomusicologists in WWI prisoner-of-war camps.

Tino Rossi, a pop crooner and balladeer, simply *was* Corsica to mainland France and to much of the world beyond. In the course of his career, from his first recordings in the 1930s through to his death in 1983, he recorded 1014 songs and sold 300 million records.

A new breed of musicians has evolved a hybrid sound that stems from both traditional Corsican and contemporary music. Cinqui So, from Ajaccio, mixed polyphonic music with earthy world music beats in their

2002 album 'Essenza and Isula', and is probably the first Corsican band to produce a trip-hoppy, ambient music that mixes traditional spiritual songs with electronica.

Literature

Native storytelling was for many centuries exclusively oral, and Corsican has only been a written language for just a century or so. Like much oral literature, it wavered between fantastic folk imaginings (*fola*) – talking animals, human-to-animal metamorphoses ('Once upon a time there was a father and a mother who had as a child a little red pig', begins one typical story) – and the more or less artful rendering of incidents from daily life. The stories were told around firesides on cold winter evenings; they were communicated by shepherds on their journeys from summer to winter pasture. Like much oral literature, they were often rendered in poetry or in song – from lovers' serenades to bandits' ballads – in part because it made them easier to remember.

Much of this oral literary heritage has been adopted by modern Corsican polyphonic groups (p32). But there was never a great national epic, though collections have been assembled (for example, the 1979 French-language *Contes Populaires et Légendes de Corse* in the Richesse du Folklore de France series). These narratives resemble traditions elsewhere: the Corsican Gendrillon is the French Cendrillon and the equivalent tale in English, Cinderella.

For some centuries literate Corsicans expressed themselves on paper in Italian. At the end of the 18th century they began to use French instead, and French is of course the language of literary expression today.

Corsica's two most prominent novelists of the 20th century, Angelo Rinaldi and Marie Susini, may be of interest to travellers competent in French; only Susini's *Les Yeux Fermés* (With Eyes Closed) appears to have been translated into English. Rinaldi, Bastia-born in 1940, meticulously describes postwar Corsican society in *Les Dames de France*, *La Dernière Fête de l'Empire*, *Les Jardins du Consulat* and *Les Roses de Pline*. Two contemporary crime writers have made something of a splash. Elisabeth Milleliri, a journalist with the Paris newspaper *Libération*, has published *Caveau de Famille* (1993) and *Comme un Chien* (1995), while Archange Morelli has written *La Maison Ardente* (1997), a detective story set in Corsica at the beginning of the 16th century.

Architecture

Corsica's greatest architectural treasure is ecclesiastical. Hundreds of small churches and rural chapels were built in the early Romanesque period (from the 9th to 11th centuries), but only about 10 survive, and most of these are in ruins. There are more examples of the so-called Pisan Romanesque, a legacy of the end of the 11th century, when Pisa sent architects to Corsica with orders to build small cathedrals. Among the most impressive still standing are the Cathédrale de la Canonica south of Bastia (p89) and San Michele de Murato (p101) in the mountains south of St-Florent, both famous for their polychrome walls. Others can be found in the Nebbio, Castagniccia and Balagne regions.

The Baroque style of church architecture, with its sumptuously decorated interiors and façades featuring triangular or curvilinear pediments, was introduced to Corsica in the 17th and 18th centuries during the period of Genoese domination. Many churches in the Balagne and Castagniccia were built in this style, which was very fashionable in northern Italy. Good examples are the churches and oratories of Bastia (p82)

Journal of a Landscape Painter by Edward Lear is the illustrated memoirs of the poet's visit to the island in the 1860s.

and the cathedrals of Ajaccio (p148) and Calvi (p108), out of a total inventory of about 150.

The island's rich military and defence architecture is outstanding and hard to miss. Of the Genoese watchtowers that girdled the coast, around 60 remain standing today. Some were extended by the French, such as the one in Corte. Citadels dominate numerous coastal towns from Bastia and Calvi all the way down to Bonifacio.

Largely without ornament and fortress-like, traditional Corsican houses bear a resemblance to those found in provincial villages in France or Italy. They are usually constructed from granite (although shale was preferred in the chalky areas of Bonifacio and St-Florent) and four- and five-storey houses are common. Smaller apertures in the façades keep the houses warmer in winter and cooler in summer. The large narrow slates on the roofs vary in colour according to where they are from: grey-blue in Corte, green in Bastia and silver-grey in Castagniccia.

'Ajaccio's Musée Fesch houses the second-largest collection of Italian paintings in France after the Louvre'

Corsica has some impressive 20th-century modernist architecture; the prefecture (town hall) building and the Notre Dame des Victoires church in Bastia, the Lycée Laetitia in Ajaccio, the HLM (a low-cost public housing development) in Olmeto and numerous private villas at Pointe de Spérone are all in their own ways fascinating. A superb 38-page booklet, *Architectures Modernes en Corse*, will point enthusiasts in the right direction. It's available from some larger tourist offices, or contact **Le Service du Patrimoine, Collectivité Territoriale de Corse** (☎ 04 95 51 64 73; 22 cours Grandval, BP 215, 20187 Ajaccio).

Painting

As with architecture, Corsica has tended to import, or imitate, Pisan and Genoese painting rather than develop a school of its own. Ajaccio's Musée Fesch (p145), the biggest museum in Corsica, houses the second-largest collection of Italian paintings in France after the Louvre. Assembled by Napoleon's uncle, Cardinal Joseph Fesch (the Italian commissioner for war and later an astute businessman), it contains dozens of early Italian works. These, by and large, are works that were looted from Italy during the Napoleonic wars.

In the 19th century a handful of Corsican artists such as Charles Fortuné Guasco and Louis Pelligriniles, now all but forgotten, gained a small measure of recognition by studying and working in mainland Europe.

Corsica made a much more important contribution to the graphic arts as one of the many places that continental innovators visited in the late 19th century and early 20th century in search of Mediterranean light. Matisse confided: 'it was in Ajaccio that I had my first vision of the South'. Fernand Léger, early in his career, made repeated visits to Corsica, as did Maurice Utrillo and his mother, the painter Suzanne Valadon. Paul Signac and the American James McNeill Whistler also visited.

Contemporary island painters such as Lucien Peri, François Corbellini, Pierre Dionisi and Jean-Baptiste Pekle are synonymous with Corsica's postwar artistic reawakening. More often than not they have taken their inspiration from the island's stunning landscapes and seascapes.

Environment

THE LAND

Around 30 million years ago a lump of land broke away from mainland Europe, slowly spun around an axis somewhere in the middle of the Gulf of Genoa, and eventually came to a standstill 170km southeast of Nice (mainland France). Corsica was born.

The 8722-sq-km island forms the Corso-Sardinian micro-continent with the neighbouring Italian island of Sardinia, 12km south. Spanning 183km from top to bottom and 85km at its widest point, Corsica is crowned at its northern end by the 40km-long peninsula of Cap Corse.

Mountains run riot. No sooner does the land rise above sea level than it soars into the clouds, climaxing with Monte Cinto (2706m). Plenty of peaks – Monte Ritondu (2622m), Paglia Orba (2525m), Monte Pedru (2393m) and Monte d'Oro (2389m) – give the island's highest peak a run for its money.

Along the western coast, four gulfs – Golfe de Porto, Golfe de Sagone, Golfe d'Ajaccio and Golfe de Valinco – allow for human habitation at sea level. Mountains lunge out of the sea and centuries of erosion have sculpted the ancient magmatic rock base found here into *tafoni* (cavities), dramatic red-rock inlets and the wildlife-rich Scandola nature reserve.

The less-exciting eastern coast is hugged by the long lowland agricultural plain of Aléria. Complex sedimentary and metamorphic rocks, such as schist, make up the island's northeastern fringe, including Cap Corse. This contrasting alpine (schistose) scenery was created, first, from a sedimentary platform formed on the sea floor from deposits produced by the disintegration of existing rocks, and chemical or biological activity (eg shell particles) and, second, from the metamorphosis of these rocks as a result of heat and pressure during the formation of the Alps in the Tertiary era. White chalk rocks characterise the southern foot of the coastline around Bonifacio.

The island's herringbone mountain range and numerous east-west valleys arise from a rift zone that divides the island in half at Corte. Inland, the River Tavignano flows through Corte to Aléria; the 80km River Golo links the Valdu Niellu forest with the Étang de Biguglia and is the island's fastest moving river; and the Liamone, Rizzanese and Taravu Rivers flow out on the western side. Corsica has 43 glacial lakes.

With its stunning variety of ornamental rocks and rare orbicular diorite, the island is a geologist's dream. Diorite, an igneous rock, recognisable by its grey honeycomb structure, is found in Ste-Lucie de Tallano in the Alta Rocca; and you can also see green ophite rocks (a complex magmatic rock created during the major folding periods). Red rocks, the crystalline platform, are in evidence around Pianna and Scandola, and white rocks (chalk) are found near Bonifacio.

WILDLIFE

Corsica shelters a rich variety of flora and fauna, much of which is protected. Travellers who set so much as a little toe into the island's interior will have no trouble meeting up with a menagerie of wild pigs, cows, goats, sheep, mules and other domesticated land animals. Delve deeper into the mountainous terrain (pack patience and a pair of binoculars in your rucksack) and you will be well rewarded.

DID YOU KNOW?

Col (French) and *bocca* (Corsican) mean the same thing – a mountain pass. The Col de Verghio (1467m), midway between Porto and Corte, is the island's highest road pass.

Animals

Corsica's mountain king, the mouflon, reigns in the Bavella and Asco areas. This hardy herbivore, a type of short-fleeced sheep that roamed in the thousands at the beginning of the 20th century but now numbers no more than 500, hangs out in lower valleys between December and February. It retreats to higher altitudes in summer. If the one you meet (look for distinctive white facial markings) has huge 80cm-long coiled horns, it is male.

Bird-watchers have to keep their eyes well-peeled to spot a bearded vulture which, with its soaring wingspan of 2.7m, can resemble a falcon in flight. To distinguish it, look for a black 'beard' under its beak and white or yellowish plumage covering the lower part of its body. The rarest of Europe's four vulture species, the bearded vulture inhabits high-altitude areas (of around 1500m) but descends to lower altitudes in winter. The solitary bird nests in rocky niches, follows the herds and feeds on dead-animal bones. It is most likely to be seen in the Monte Cintu massif. Birds of prey such as the golden eagle and red kite soar overhead in the Vallée de la Restonica near Corte.

The Vallée de la Restonica flutters with the Corsican nuthatch, one of the few species endemic to the island. Discovered at the end of the 19th century, this ground-dwelling bird is recognisable by the white 'brow' across its head. Rarely exceeding 12cm in length, it flits around conifer forests and eats insects and pine seeds. The Corsican finch, sparrowhawk, wren and spotted flycatcher are equally common in this neck of the woods.

In the maquis (p38) the animal kingdom buzzes with activity. The silky-coated wild boar snouts out acorns, chestnuts, roots and fruit; the fist-sized Eurasian scops-owl fills the night with its shrill whistles; and weasels and foxes also skulk around. There are dark green snakes underfoot (not poisonous, but effective nippers) and also shiny back *malmignatte* spiders (look for red stripes on the abdomen), which are rare and venomous. Between mid-November and February Hermann's tortoise – relatively common in Corsica despite its diminishing numbers elsewhere – hibernates in the maquis under piles of leaves. The land tortoise, about 19cm long with orange and black stripes, lives up to 80 years and can be closely observed at the Village des Tortues in the Parc Naturel Régional de Corse. For more information, see the website www .parc-naturel_corse.fr/education/VillageTor.html.

The Corsican red deer, a maquis native since antiquity, disappeared from the island in the 1960s, but was reintroduced in 1985 from Sardinian specimens. Initially confined to protective enclosures in Quenza, Casabianda and Ania di Fiumorbu, the first deer were released into the wild in the late 1990s. The gentle creatures live on brambles, strawberry trees, acorns and chestnuts, and number around 100. Wild boars, foxes, stray dogs and poachers continue to threaten their existence.

The Corsican coastline holds a magnetic lure for wildlife enthusiasts. The audouin's gull, no longer found on mainland Europe, nests among rocks on the Îles Finocchiarola (p39) and is recognised by its dark-red, black-striped, yellow-tipped beak. The shag, a web-footed bird with black-green plumage, is another nesting species on the islands and in the nearby Réserve Naturelle de Scandola. The edge-of-the-world hamlet of Barcaggio (p93) on Cap Corse is prime bird-watching territory. Spring sees storks, herons, spotted crakes and dozens of other migratory birds pass by. The osprey, a formidable fisherman thanks to sharp eyesight and talons, can also be spotted around Cap Corse and on the rocky coasts and headlands of the Réserve Naturelle de Scandola where it nests. The peregrine falcon is another known nester here.

Birds of Corsica by Jean-Claude Thibault and Gilles Bonaccorsi makes an invaluable reference guide for any half-serious, Corsica-bound spotter.

UNDERWATER ANIMALS

Corsica's fish life will leave you goggle-eyed.

- Bogue – this vegetarian species lives in shoals above Poseidonion beds and feeds on the leaves. It is silver in colour with horizontal golden markings. Born male, it grows into a female.

- Brown meagre – this predator (40cm to 80cm long) swims in shoals near the rocky sea floor or above Poseidonion beds. Look for silvery-grey markings and an arched back.

- Cardinalfish – this red 'king of the mullet', about 15cm long, lives near cave entrances or beneath overhangs.

- Damselfish – these fish congregate in compact, slow-moving schools near the water's surface and close to shallows. Look for grey and black markings and scissor-shaped tails.

- Forkbeard – two forked barbels under the chin distinguish this shade-loving brown fish.

- Grouper – the thickset darling of scuba divers, sometimes growing to 1.5m in length, is distinguished by its enormous thick-lipped mouth and by the whitish flecks on its brownish scales. It spends most of its time in holes. Born female, specimens change sex when they get older.

- John Dory – this fish with superb stripes on its dorsal fin owes its French name, St-Pierre to the tale that the black spot on its flank was left by St Peter after Jesus instructed him to catch the fish and remove the gold coin from its mouth.

- Labridae – this family's colourful representatives include the inescapable rainbow wrasse, the most 'tropical' fish in the Mediterranean. A maximum of 20cm long, it is found near the surface and has remarkable turquoise and red mottled markings.

- Moray eel – this fierce predator waits in crevices, from which only its mouth is visible. Growing to 1.5m, it is distinguished by its speed, its sharp teeth and its dark, sometimes yellow-flecked markings.

- Red scorpion fish – known locally as *capon*, the red scorpion fish lies in wait for its prey on the sea floor, using its camouflage skills to blend in with its surroundings. Its body is covered in poisonous spines and outgrowths.

- Sargo – extremely common, sargo swim alongside divers who go near the rocky sea floor. The most widespread variety is the silvery white bream (around 40cm long), which has two characteristic black marks on its gills and tail.

- Swallow-tail sea perch – usually found at the entrances to caves or wrecks and away from the light, this is a small, graceful, orange-red fish.

Endangered Species

Of France's seven endangered and eight critically endangered mammals on the Red List (www.redlist.org), one is endemic to Corsica. Generally tucked inside a black and brown striped shell, the green-bodied Corsican snail (*helix ceratina*) faces extinction. Having not been seen since 1902, the molluscs were discovered around Ajaccio, on Corsica's southwestern coast, in 1995. The six hectares of coastal land they inhabit is now protected, and a captive breeding programme has been implemented.

With fewer than 250 breeding pairs in Europe, the bearded vulture is also endangered. Food shortage poses one of the biggest threats to the carrion-eating bird. Since 1998 an EU-funded LIFE project in the Parc Naturel Régional de Corse has allowed park authorities to monitor its 10 pairs of vultures and supply them with additional food (goat and sheep carcasses) at sites in Ascu and the Forêt de Tartagine.

The **Mediterranean monk seal**, another European creature facing extinction, has not been seen in the Réserve Naturelle de Scandola – once home to a small colony - since 1995.

Divers keen to know exactly what's what through that mask should get hold of Kurt Amsler's *Corsica Diving Guide*, a detailed look at 26 of the island's most thrilling dive sites and the 130-odd marine species divers could see.

Plants

Corsican flora (which counts 2000-plus species) splits neatly into three zones: the legendary maquis, oak, olive and chestnut trees that grow in the so-called Mediterranean zone (up to altitudes of 1000m); the pine and beech forests in the mountain zone (1000m to 1800m); and the low and sparse grasses and small mountain plants of the higher alpine zone (above 1800m). Just 15% of Corsican land is cultivated; forest and maquis carpet more than half of the island.

Corsica's heavily scented maquis, covering around 200,000 hectares, positively bursts with sweet-smelling species, most of which flower in spring and early summer. Typically scrubby and short, the maquis is tough enough to survive summer's intense heat, burns quickly, but grows quickly. It provides a safe-haven for most of Corsica's 40 orchid species. Rock rose, a shrub with either white flowers with yellow centres or pinkish-mauve flowers, is the most common maquis species, closely followed by the white-flowering myrtle that blossoms in June and is treasured for its blue-black berries (used to make some excellent liqueurs), and the tiny blue-violet flowering Corsican mint with its heady summertime aroma. Tree heather grows 2m tall and its white flowers exude a honey-like scent. Fruit trees include the mastic, the red fruits of which turn black to exude a resin-like fragrance, the white-flowering Asphodel and the more common strawberry tree.

Holm oak, cork oak (the bark of which is peeled off every 10 years or so to fashion stoppers for wine bottles) and olive trees all grow below 600m and are other maquis inhabitants. Otherwise, the cork oak is most common in the south, around Porto Vecchio, while the olive (pressed to make oil) thrives on sunny coastal slopes, particularly in the Balagne on the northwest coast.

Citron, kiwi and avocado trees grow in the eastern lowlands, as does the chestnut tree. Introduced to the island in the 16th century, the chestnut quickly lent its name – La Castagniccia – to the eastern plains on which it was cultivated. Its husks open in October to expose a flavourful brown fruit, which is used in local cuisine or ground into flour. See p201 for more chestnut details.

The main constituent of the forests in the higher mountain zone is the Corsican or laricio pine. As it ages, the tree spreads its foliage horizontally like a parasol and lives for an age. Some island specimens – including in the Forêt de Vizzavona - are reckoned to be 800 years old. Another mountain-zone inhabitant, found anywhere between 800m and 1800m, is the prickly pear, a member of the *Cactaceae* family brought back from Central America by Christopher Columbus. Resembling a cactus, with prickly, oval-shaped 'arms' and yellow flowers, its sweet, thick-pulpy fruits are known as prickly pears or barby figs.

UNDERWATER PLANTS

Don a snorkel and mask, and get ready to be dazzled by the Corsican coastline's extravaganza of flora – as rich and as brilliant underwater as on dry land.

- Poseidonion – endemic to the Mediterranean, this green plant (from Poseidon, the god of the sea), forms vast grassy meadows on the sand creating a choice biotope, home to numerous species of fish seeking shelter or spawning in the foliage.

- Seaweed – there are several forms: brown, green or red, hard or soft. Calcified varieties can have superb mineral formations. Certain species of red algae are recorded nowhere else in France.

NATURAL PARKS

The single most decisive step in the preservation of Corsica's unique wildlife was the creation of the Parc Naturel Régional de Corse (PNRC) in 1972. Protecting more than two-thirds (350,510 hectares) of the island, the reserve is the island's biggest promoter of environmental consciousness. Unlike national parks in France, which can only protect uninhabited areas, the populated PNRC (pop 26,700) 'protects and stimulates the survival of natural, cultural and human heritage' – hence the creation of some 2000km of marked footpaths, not to mention costly measures taken to preserve endangered species and to educate through guided nature walks, information centres and other ways.

On the island's western coast lies the astonishing Réserve Naturelle de Scandola, a 919-hectare pocket of land and 1000 hectares of sea that swims with 125 fish species and 450 types of seaweed. So rich in marine life is this reserve that it is inscribed on the Unesco World Heritage list. Neighbouring Cape Porto, Cape Girolata and the red cliffs staggering south along the coastline to Piana are also listed; while the coastline immediately north of the reserve around Galéria forms the Réserve de Biosphere de la Vallée du Fangu, 23,400 hectares dedicated to scientific research.

A good chunk of the remaining one-third of Corsican land falling outside the PNRC and UNESCO orbit is protected by three other small reserves. Off the northernmost tip of Cap Corse lie the Îles Finocchiarola, three pin-prick islands (four hectares in all), off limits to visitors between 1 March and 31 October to allow several rare birds to breed in peace.

South of Bastia, the Réserve Naturelle de Biguglia provides a safe haven for more than 100 bird species and serves as a vital stopover between Europe and Africa for migrating birds. Up to 20,000 birds winter around the shallow, 1450-hectare lagoon that forms Corsica's largest and most important wetland.

In the far south, more islands are protected by the Réserve Naturelle des Bouches de Bonifacio. Of the six islets in the Lavezzi archipelago, two – Île de Cavallo (nicknamed Millionaires' Island) and Îlot de San Baïnsu – have strangely escaped the 80,000-hectare protected zone. Marine life is particularly rich here, accounting for the 12,000 hectares of water off limits to divers with oxygen cylinders. The nature reserve is best known for its revived brown grouper population – protected since 1993 after decades of unregulated fishing practically wiped them out from the western shores of the Mediterranean.

Heading north along the eastern coast, the Réserve Naturelle des Îles Cerbicale – a cluster of five islets northeast of Porto Vecchio – protect marine bird life and some unique flora.

www.parc-naturel
-corse.fr
It might be in French only but the website of Corsica's largest protected area is crammed with useful, practical and fascinating facts about the island and its fauna and flora.

WATCH YOUR STEP

Rooting pigs and careless hikers threaten Corsica's 40-odd highland lakes. The PNRC has therefore implemented a programme whereby seasonal workers collect the rubbish that summer visitors leave behind at the most popular lakes – Melu, Nino and Creno – and at the same time enforce the camping bans. As a further precaution, the GR20 has been diverted from the grassy areas around Lac de Nino. Walkers should respect the rules: no fires, no rubbish and no heedless tramping.

Intensive pasturage threatens *pozzines* (from the Corsican *pozzi*, meaning 'pits') – little water holes linked together by small rivulets over an impermeable substratum (like peat bogs). Underfoot they feel like a carpet of cool moss. Watch your step around Lac de Nino and on the Plateau de Coscione, between the GR20 and the Refuge de la Bergerie de Bassetta.

Park	Features	Activities	Best Time to Visit
Réserve Naturelle de Biguglia	reed-bed wetland with all types of warblers, migratory herons, osprey, red-footed falcon, black- and white-winged terns	bird watching, walking	spring, winter (migratory birds)
Réserve Naturelle des Bouches de Bonifacio	archipelago reserve with rich marine life including 68 fish species, including the grouper	scuba diving (restricted)	summer
Réserve Naturelle des Îles Cerbicale	five-islet reserve with 136 flora species packed into 36 hectares	botany, bird watching, walking	spring
Parc Naturelle Régional de Corse	Corsica in a nutshell: maquis, forest, mountains, stunning coastline	walking, climbing, horse riding, wildlife watching, thematic nature expeditions	spring, summer, autumn (rutting season)
Réserve Naturelle des Îles Finocchiarola	protected nesting islets for audouin's gulls, cory's shearwater, scopoli's shearwater, comorants	bird watching	Nov to Feb (closed rest of year)
Réserve Naturelle de Scandola	natural treasures of world renown including osprey, peregrine falcon, brown grouper	diving, snorkelling, walking, bird watching, botany	spring (walking & botany), summer (diving)

ENVIRONMENTAL ISSUES

Corsicans are devoted to the ecological well-being of their island. Exhibit number one is the popular uprising in 1973 against offshore toxic-waste disposal by an Italian multinational during the so-called *boues rouges* (literally 'red slicks') affair. Corsican eco-nationalism, as it is called (which, in 1973, consisted of Corsican terrorists bombing the waste-dumping Italian ships), still persists. And while bomb threats can hardly be defended as civilised, they do make property developers think twice about lining Corsica's coastline with mega-hotels and fast-food outlets.

Fires pose the biggest threat to the island's sun-sizzled environment. As sweet-smelling as the Corsican maquis is, the scrubland burns in a flash. Of the thousands of fires reported each year, some 90% are started by arsonists or irresponsible visitors on picnics, campers, cigarette smokers and so on. Other culprits include hunters setting fire to forests to drive out wild boar, property developers, shepherds who burn expanses of land to make meadows for grazing, and farmers who burn stubble to produce potash, which is used to improve soil quality.

Between 1973 and 2001 no fewer than 283,000 hectares of land burnt. As many as 20 fires are reported on a single summer's day – an alarming trend that Mediterranean Europe's increasingly drier and hotter climate is only exacerbating. In the summer of 2003 unrelenting temperatures cost Corsica almost €11 million in fire-fighting expenses as fire swept across 27,000 hectares of land – the worst fires for 30-odd years. Severe drought, moreover, saw island-wide water restrictions.

Preventative measures taken by local government include a summertime ban (until 30 September) on camp fires, barbecues and other outdoor fires island-wide, and a ban on smoking in forests and the maquis. Lighting up (anything) warrants a €750 fine. To protect fauna already ravaged by fires, the Corse-du-Sud prefect banned hunting game (wild boar, pheasant, woodcock, hare, etc) in fire-scarred areas in southern Corsica for the 2003/4 season.

Measures taken by the **Office National des Forêts** (ONF; www.onf.fr, French only), which manages the island's national forests, include making more fire breaks, educating the public through forest visits (the ONF provides seasonal guided visits to the national forests of Bavella, Bonifatu, Marmaro, Chiavari, Valdu Niellu, Aïtone, Pineta, Fangu, Vizzavona and l'Ospedale); and planting more fire-tolerant foliage such as subterranean clover (*trifolium subterraneum*).

Pigs also threaten forests, as Corsican farmers continue, as they always have, to allow their livestock to range freely. Pigs contribute to deforestation by disturbing the soil in their search for food.

On the coast, environment protection is tackled head-on by the **Conservatoire du Littoral** (www.conservatoire-du-littoral.fr). The public body has built protective barriers around the Roccapina and Barcaggio dunes to prevent further erosion by tourists and over-grazing livestock who trample across the fragile sands and so destroy the stabilising plants. More significantly, it has bought (hence protects) 9084 hectares of threatened coastal sites – 21% of the 1000km of Corsican coastline – including the 5495-hectare Désert des Agriates (considered as a nuclear-testing site until the Conservatoire intervened in 1989); southern Corsica's dune-rich Sartenais coastline (2001 hectares); the Bouches de Bonifacio; and the tip of Cap Corse.

'Protection measures include planting more fire-tolerant foliage'

CORSICA OUTDOORS

For such a small island, less than 200km long and less than 90km wide, Corsica is a great destination for an activity-based holiday. Almost 1000km of coastline with clear warm waters and top scuba diving and water-sports facilities makes it a water-lover's oasis. The lush mountainous scenery and multitude of well-marked forest trails will appeal to hikers, climbers and horse riders alike.

DIVING

If you're a diver, Corsica will show you about as good a time as you'll find anywhere in the Mediterranean. The inlets and beaches are numerous. The dramatically rugged landscape on the dry side of the shoreline continues underwater in the form of yet more mountains and canyons, needles, sharp peaks, rocky masses and scree. The onshore maquis scrub, meanwhile, transforms underwater into a handsome carpet of yellow-flowering anemone, red coral and gorgonian. The underwater inhabitants include grouper, brown meagre and dentex. There are a number of easily accessible wrecks. In summer, the clarity and temperature of the water are such that, despite the latitude, the feel of this underwater world borders on the tropical.

'If you're a diver, Corsica will show you about as good a time as you'll find anywhere in the Mediterranean'

A further plus is that Corsica's superb underwater kingdom has been remarkably well preserved, thanks to the careful management of two internationally renowned marine nature reserves (the Réserve Naturelle de Scandola and the Réserve Naturelle des Bouches de Bonifacio), the absence of an intensive commercial fishing industry and an almost total lack of polluters and pollution.

Finally, Corsica's 30-odd diving centres have first-rate personnel and excellent facilities, and the opportunities for *après*-dive are abundant.

Diving Conditions

In winter the water temperature in Corsica hovers around a rather chilly 13°C to 14°C. In May it rises to around 17°C and in June from 20°C to 21°C. It peaks in August at around 25°C. In September it remains pleasant at around 23°C and a bearable 20°C in October. These temperatures, though, are as measured at the surface. Further down they will be lower. In order to stay warm, you will do well to wear a wet or dry suit with a hood.

The clarity of Corsican waters is legendary. In summer average visibility runs to 25m, although in August, in good weather, visibility sometimes runs as high as 40m. The wind, particularly the southwesterly *libecciu* can, on the other hand, produce a heavy sea swell that will roil the waters in some of the less protected gulfs and inlets.

Prime Diving Spots
AROUND PORTO VECCHIO

A dozen or so dives can be taken in this area, mainly in the vicinity of the Îles Cerbicale. The small island of Le Toro (The Bull), at the southeastern end of this archipelago, is ideal for all abilities because it has a number of protected little coves and shallows with a maximum depth of around 40m.

Of the two wrecks to be visited in the area, the more famous is the *Pecorella*, a 45m-long cement carrier that sank in a storm in 1967. The state of preservation of this wreck is remarkable, and its bridge and helm, gangways, engine room, cement holds and chain lockers can all be explored safely. Though there are few fish in the area apart from a handful of brown meagre and some red scorpion fish, organisms such as red coral and sea anemones decorate the vessel's hull. The site is regularly used for introductory dives, night dives and underwater photography.

BONIFACIO
The waters around Bonifacio are the most dived in Corsica, and there's a reason: the Réserve Naturelle des Bouches de Bonifacio (p177), a 20-minute boat trip southeast of the coast, offers a stunning stage set and exceptional conditions for divers of all abilities. The turquoise-green water and chiselled granite rocks are reminiscent of more tropical climes. The small inlets seem to have been designed for novice divers, and the more renowned sites – some of them quite famous – provide thrills for more experienced divers.

GOLFE DE VALINCO
The Golfe de Valinco (p166) is treasured by divers for its underwater relief – even more dramatic than that of other parts of the western coast – with depths of up to 800m. It's home to an abundance of sessile organisms such as gorgonian, parazoa and the jewel of the Mediterranean, red coral. The density of the fauna increases as you approach the wilderness around the mouth of the gulf, and the most appealing dives are over rocky mounts close by the shore at the northern and southern entrances to the gulf. For beginners there are sheltered inlets closer to Propriano.

'The Golfe de Valinco is home to the jewel of the Mediterranean, red coral'

GOLFE D'AJACCIO
Dozens of sites can be found along the scalloped border of the Golfe d'Ajaccio, from the surprisingly little-visited Îles Sanguinaires in the north to Capu di Muru in the south. Le Tabernacle, at the northwestern end of the gulf, is the main site on this part of the coast. It's ideal for beginners, with a plateau descending from 3m to 22m as if along paving stones. Forkbeard, rock lobster, brown meagre, sargo and even grouper are the sea life here.

The most spectacular dives in this area are found mainly in the southern section, between the Tour de l'Isolella (also known as the Punta di Sette Nave) and Capu di Muru.

GOLFE DE LAVA
Because of its relative inaccessibility north of the Îles Sanguinaires, the Golfe de Lava tends not to be visited much, yet it boasts one of Corsica's most stunning dive sites, the Banc Provençal which is out in open sea towards the Golfe de Liscia. This is a memorable dive, only in calm seas and only for the initiated.

GOLFE DE SAGONE
This huge gulf boasts several exceptional dives. On the southern shore, towards the Golfe de Liscia (a kind of suburb of the Golfe de Sagone), experienced divers can have fun with the series of drops at Castellaci. Nearby the plateau extends out from the coast in a series of wide steps (15m to 30m, 30m to 50m) honeycombed with caves.

GOLFE DE PORTO
The Golfe de Porto, with its granite walls plunging fast to abysses 800m beneath the surface and its teeming marine life, is Corsica's jewel. Yet the

dozen sites between Punta Muchillina in the north and Capu Rossu in
the south are exploited by only three diving centres. Although the area
is glorious, diving here is complicated by two problems. Boat trips to
the best sites, close to the northern and southern edges of the gulf, are
sometimes made difficult if not impossible by the westerly wind; and
diving is prohibited within the fauna-rich Réserve Naturelle de Scandola
just above the gulf.

AROUND CALVI
The many contrasts in the area around Calvi make it attractive to divers.
The southern part of the bay is admittedly nothing to write home about,
but the wilderness around the Pointe de la Revellata, to the west, is extraordinary, and the Baie de Calvi contains one of the most highly rated
sites in all Corsica in the wreck of a B-17 bomber. The bomber is for
experienced divers only, because of the depth at which it lies, though
centres in Calvi are currently taking level 1 divers to where they can at
least see it from a distance.

'Baie de
Calvi
contains
one of
the most
highly rated
sites in all
Corsica in
the wreck
of a B-17
bomber'

BAIE DE ÎLE ROUSSE
There are few sites in the Baie de l'Île Rousse, but the handful that do
exist – rocks rising from a sandy floor and cloaked with magnificent
gorgonian – might well be pronounced the most beautiful anywhere in
Corsican waters.
Le Naso, the most famous of the Île Rousse sites, is a huge rock descending from 13m to 32m, and distinguished by the concentration of
conger and moray eel in the crevices around its base. The site is appropriate for divers at all levels of proficiency.

GOLFE DE ST-FLORENT
The Golfe de St-Florent boasts about a dozen regularly visited sites
between the Désert des Agriates to the west and the low chalky cliffs to
the east, which beneath the waves turn as holey as a Swiss cheese.
Two wrecks can be found near the citadel in St-Florent: *L'Aventure*, at
10m, and the *Ça Ira*, at 18m. The latter, a hospital ship dating from the
Napoleonic era, has been closely studied by an archaeological group.

BASTIA
Diving enthusiasts have tended to disdain Corsica's eastern coast. True,
this side of the island lacks peaks and canyons and dramatic drops
plunging into abysses, and gorgonian and red coral are also rare. On
the other hand, the gently sloping sand-and-silt sea bed is strewn with
rocky outcrops that provide refuge for a whole range of creatures. And
those divers who particularly like to explore disaster sites will be in their
element here. Wrecks can be found up and down the coast from Bastia
harbour to the Tour de l'Osse on Cap Corse to the north.

Diving Centres
There are diving centres in nearly all the gulfs. Virtually all are affiliated with the Fédération Française d'Études et de Sports Sous-Marins
(FFESSM; French Federation of Submarine Studies and Sports) and
welcome all divers, regardless of their training.
Like most leisure activities and tourist facilities in Corsica, diving is
highly seasonal. Of some 30 centres on the island, only a handful are
open year-round, and some open only on demand. Most open at the end
of April and close at the end of October, but in April, May and October

---

SAFETY GUIDELINES FOR DIVING

Before embarking on a scuba diving, skin diving or snorkelling trip, carefully consider the following points to ensure a safe and enjoyable experience:

- Possess a current diving certification card from a recognised scuba-diving instructional agency (if scuba diving).
- Be sure you are healthy and feel comfortable diving.
- Obtain reliable information about physical and environmental conditions at the dive site (eg from a reputable local dive operation).
- Be aware of local laws, regulations and etiquette about marine life and the environment.
- Dive only at sites within your realm of experience; if available, engage the services of a competent, professionally trained dive instructor or dive master.
- Be aware that underwater conditions vary significantly from one region, or even site, to another. Seasonal changes can significantly alter any site and dive conditions. These differences influence the way divers dress for a dive and what diving techniques they use.
- Ask about the environmental characteristics that can affect your diving and how local, trained divers deal with these considerations.

---

they really just tick over. The season proper starts in June and reaches its peak in July and August.

Whatever time of year you go, always book at least a day in advance.

COSTS & FACILITIES
Corsica's diving centres offer a wide range of services, such as introductory dives (for children over eight, and adults), night dives, exploratory dives and training for diving qualifications. The price of an introductory dive includes equipment hire, while the price of an exploratory dive varies according to how much equipment you need to borrow.

Generally clubs have a price for 'equipped divers' and an 'unequipped price' (anything from €18–40 for either). Packages of three, five or 10 dives are invariably cheaper than single dives.

CHOOSING A CENTRE
Like a hotel or restaurant, each diving centre has its own personality and style. Some people may be more comfortable with the intimacy and slightly seat-of-the-pants feel of a smaller establishment, while others will prefer the well-oiled machinery, the logistics and the no-nonsense professionalism of a larger, American-style centre.

If you are unsure about a centre, go somewhere else, and be wary of word of mouth. Each centre has its admirers and critics, especially when there are several centres in one area.

All of the centres listed in the regional chapters are authorised diving centres. They employ qualified instructors, have modern, well-maintained equipment and observe strict safety regulations. The lists in each chapter, however, are not exhaustive.

'Corsica's diving centres offer introductory dives, night dives and exploratory dives'

WALKING
Arguably the best way to explore Corsica is on foot. It will slow you down and make it impossible not to savour the extraordinary landscapes and the fresh mountain air, and this is even before you calculate what it will do for your calves and your overall well-being.

The island, moreover, is crisscrossed with paths leading coast to coast and into otherwise inaccessible mountain redoubts. Walking options range from the most challenging two- or three-week hike, such as the 200km-long GR20 (see the special section, p51) to the easy afternoon stroll along the coast; there is something for all tastes, all levels of ambition and all abilities. Well-known and much enjoyed walks across the island include the Mare e Monti and Mare a Mare trails, outlined briefly here (below). Although less publicised than the GR20, these routes take in some spectacular mountain and coastal scenery, with the added bonus of ending each day comfortably in a village. They also offer a shorter and less daunting physical challenge, for those who doubt their ability to cope with the GR20.

'The Mare e Monti and Mare a Mare trails take in some spectacular mountain and coastal scenery'

The Parc Naturel Régional de Corse (PNRC) is an excellent source of information for walkers. If you can access the French Minitel system, there's a Minitel service: 3615 Rando.

The PNRC, created in 1972, is a protected area totalling 350,510 hectares, and includes many of its most beautiful areas and more than 1500km of hiking and walking paths. The Golfe de Porto, the Réserve Naturelle de Scandola (a Unesco World Heritage area) and the island's highest peaks, including the Aiguilles de Bavella, are all part of the PNRC.

The **Maison d'Information Randonnée du PNRC** (PNRC walking information office; ☎ 04 95 51 79 10; www.parc-naturel-corse.com; 2 rue Sergent Casalonga, Ajaccio; ☉ 8am-7pm Mon-Fri, 8am-noon & 2-7pm Sat) publishes a wealth of information about the park in English, Spanish and French, along with a number of walking guides (mostly in French).

The Mare e Monti Routes

As the name suggests, these are paths between the sea *(mare)* and the mountains *(monti)*.

MARE E MONTI NORD

The Mare e Monti Nord (literally 'Sea to the Northern Mountains') is a superb (and not very demanding) walk linking Calenzana (p121) in the

---

SAFETY GUIDELINES FOR WALKING

Before embarking on a walking trip, consider the following points to ensure a safe and enjoyable experience:

- Pay any fees and obtain any permits required by local authorities.
- Be sure you are healthy and feel comfortable about walking for a sustained period.
- Obtain reliable information about physical and environmental conditions along your intended route (eg from park authorities).
- Be aware of local laws, regulations and etiquette in relation to wildlife and the environment.
- Walk only in regions, and on trails, within your realm of experience.
- Be aware that weather conditions and terrain can vary significantly between regions, or between trails in the same region.
- Seasonal changes can significantly alter a trail and these differences influence the way walkers dress and the equipment they carry.
- Ask before you set out about the environmental characteristics that can affect your walk and how local, experienced walkers deal with these considerations.

Haute-Balagne region to Cargèse (p139), south of the Golfe de Porto. It is divided into 10 days of four to seven hours each, and its highest point is 1153m. It passes through several exceptional natural sites, such as the Forêt de Bonifatu, the Réserve Naturelle de Scandola and the Gorges de Spelunca, and stops in some charming villages, notably Galeria, Ota and Évisa.

The route is passable year-round, but the periods before and after the main season (May to June and September to October) are preferable to avoid the worst of the heat. The path crosses the Mare a Mare Nord (below) in two places: Évisa and nearby Marignana.

MARE E MONTI SUD

This path runs between the bays of two well-known seaside resorts in the southwest of Corsica – Porticcio (p155) and Propriano (p160). It's divided into five days of five to six hours and ascends to a maximum height of 870m. There are stops in Bisinao, Coti-Chiavari (which towers above the two bays), Porto Pollo and Olmeto. The walk ends in Burgo (7km north of Propriano).

There are only two *gîtes d'étape* on the route, one in **Bisinao** (☎ 04 95 24 21 66) and one in **Burgo** (☎ 04 95 76 15 05). In the other villages you can stay in a hotel or at a camping ground, or in Propriano at the Ferme Équestre de Baracci (p162).

The highlights are the views over the bays, the historic Genoese towers and the beaches (the Baie de Cupabia and Porto Pollo). Like its northern counterpart, this path is passable year-round and is not particularly difficult. Spring and autumn are the best times. The path meets the Mare a Mare Sud (p49) in Burgo.

The Mare a Mare Routes

Three Mare a Mare (Sea to Sea) paths link the west and east coasts via the mountains in the centre of the island.

MARE A MARE CENTRE

The Mare a Mare Centre provides an excellent opportunity to explore the more traditional, inland areas of Corsica. The route can be completed in seven days, each with three to seven hours' walking. Starting in Ghisonaccia on the east coast, and finishing in Porticcio (p155) on the west coast, it passes through the little-known districts of Fiumorbu and Taravu before crossing the hinterland of Ajaccio.

Unlike the GR20, which stays high in the mountains away from settlements, the Mare a Mare Centre passes through some of the prettiest villages on the island. The route is generally less taxing and less crowded than the GR20. It offers considerable comfort with *gîtes* (restaurants) and hotels every night.

The maximum altitude is 1525m at Bocca di Laparu, so the best time to do the walk is between April and November. Take a detailed map (as the markings are not very regular). Didier Richard's 1:50,000 (*Corse du Sud* and *Corse du Nord*) and the 1:25,000 IGN blue series available from PNRC offices, bookshops and some tourist offices, are best. There are no ATMs on the trail and the *gîtes* don't take credit cards.

MARE A MARE NORD

From Moriani on the east coast to Cargèse (p139) in the west, this path passes through vastly contrasting areas and is split into 10 days, each lasting from four to six hours and reaching altitudes of up to 1600m. For the final section of the walk, between Evisa and Cargèse, the route

'The highlights of the Mare e Monti Sud are the views over the bays, the historic Genoese towers and the beaches'

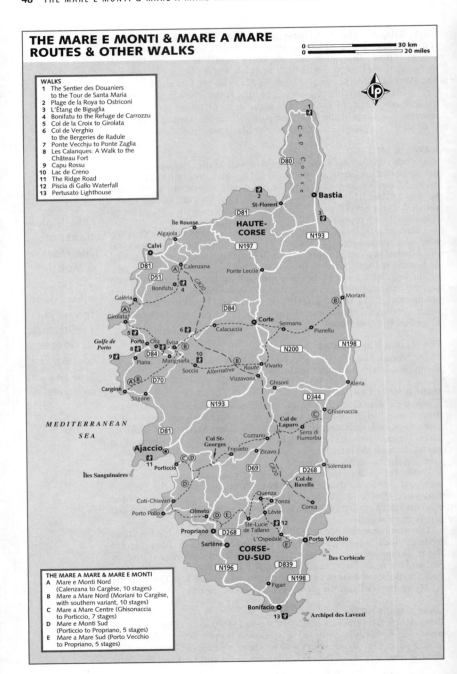

THE MARE E MONTI & MARE A MARE ROUTES & OTHER WALKS

0 — 30 km
0 — 20 miles

WALKS
1 The Sentier des Douaniers to the Tour de Santa Maria
2 Plage de la Roya to Ostriconi
3 L'Étang de Biguglia
4 Bonifatu to the Refuge de Carrozzu
5 Col de la Croix to Girolata
6 Col de Verghio to the Bergeries de Radule
7 Ponte Vecchju to Ponte Zaglia
8 Les Calanques: A Walk to the Château Fort
9 Capu Rossu
10 Lac de Creno
11 The Ridge Road
12 Piscia di Gallo Waterfall
13 Pertusato Lighthouse

THE MARE A MARE & MARE E MONTI
A Mare e Monti Nord (Calenzana to Cargèse, 10 stages)
B Mare a Mare Nord (Moriani to Cargèse, with southern variant, 10 stages)
C Mare a Mare Centre (Ghisonaccia to Porticcio, 7 stages)
D Mare e Monti Sud (Porticcio to Propriano, 5 stages)
E Mare a Mare Sud (Porto Vecchio to Propriano, 5 stages)

merges with that of the Mare e Monti Nord (p46). It is better to avoid the period between November and April, when parts of the route may be under snow.

MARE A MARE SUD
This route is passable year-round. It is a famous, easy walk that links Porto Vecchio (p183) in the southeast to Propriano (p160) in the southwest. The walk is divided into five days, each of which lasts an average of five hours, and reaches a maximum altitude of 1171m. With fine views to the Aiguilles de Bavella and Monte Incudine, it crosses through the magnificent region of Alta Rocca and many of the island's most beautiful villages. The third day of the trail offers three options: a short version that skips the Plateau de Jallicu, a detour through the village of Aullène or a long version via Zonza, which adds a day to the itinerary.

Strolls & Country Walks
Walking in Corsica is by no means limited to the GR20 (p51) and the Mare a Mare and Mare e Monti walks (above). There's every bit as much, and perhaps more, for those who prefer an easy walk of a single day, half a day or less. Details of some of the best short walks are in the regional chapters of this guide.

The PNRC can provide brochures on easy 'country walks' it has designed around the villages of Alta Rocca, Bozio, Fiumorbu, Niolu, Taravo, Venachese and Giussani – all in interior parts of the island that visitors don't often see. These walks, all three to seven hours in length for the round trip, are perfectly suited to casual walkers and even to families.

'Horse-riding treks take you to places that are inaccessible to vehicles'

HORSE RIDING
The variety of landscapes in Corsica, from rocky mountain trails and inland forest paths to sweeping beaches, makes it an ideal place to see on horseback. Whether you choose an hour's trek or a themed tour of one or two weeks (which includes accommodation in *chambres d'hôtes* or camping), there are a whole host of reputable riding schools to cater to most needs and abilities. The best thing about riding is you'll often find that treks take you to places that are inaccessible to vehicles, allowing you to discover relatively uncharted terrain. In all, there are 1900km of bridle tracks open to riders on the island.

Expect to pay between €18-28 an hour for a lesson or ride. There are riding centres all over the island; some also offer accommodation and most are open year-round. The best time to trek is in spring or autumn, when it's a bit cooler and the roads are less crowded, though summer excursions usually explore the cooler mountain areas.

On organised tours, a day's riding (roughly four to six hours) may be split into two half-days – either the early morning or the late afternoon –

- **Association Régionale pour le Tourisme Equestre** (☎ 04 95 46 31 74; 7 rue Colonnel Ferracci, Corte) The national body can provide information on equestrian holidays.
- **Comité Régional d'Équitation Corse** (☎ 04 95 22 28 35; cre.corse@wanadoo.fr; 19 ave Noel Franchini, Ajaccio) Has a list of its 53 CRE-affiliated riding centre members.
- **Ride in France** (www.rideinfrance.com) This specialist travel agency organises riding holidays, some coupled with castle accommodation, spa therapies or wine trails, all over France.

to avoid the midday heat. Riding centres will provide you with a hard hat and sometimes boots. It's advisable though to wear suitable trousers and good strong footwear (runners or shoes with a flat sole aren't suitable). See the destination chapters for more details of individual riding centres.

ROCK CLIMBING & CANYONING

The most mountainous of the Mediterranean islands, Corsica is something of a holy grail for rock climbers. Its highest peak, Monte Cinto, is at 2710m, but 50 other peaks on the island exceed 2000m. The most popular climbing spot is around the granite needles of Aiguilles de Bavella and Popolasca in the south.

'Corsica is something of a holy grail for rock climbers'

Canyoning is hiking through water, down falls and over rocks and natural obstacles with the use of mountaineering equipment. You must know how to swim to take part. A relatively good degree of physical fitness is needed for both sports. Adventure centres that offer canyoning and climbing (see the destination chapters) provide neoprene suits, helmets and harnesses. A day's canyoning will set you back around €50 to €80 and usually includes a light picnic lunch. Bring your own water and snacks such as dried fruit and energy bars.

Via Ferrata is an equipped peak near the Aiguilles de Bavella (p192) that is especially useful for beginners; there are metal gangways, steps and safety harnesses.

Canyoning is somewhat weather-dependent and therefore seasonal. It is recommended that you do not go out in storms or heavy rain, as rocks become treacherously slippery in wet weather and visibility is hampered.

■ **Comité Régionale Corse Montagne et Escalade** (☎ 04 95 48 05 22; compagnieamm@club -internet.fr; Syndicat Intercommunal de Niolu, rte de Cuccia, Calacuccia) Organises guided individual or group mountain treks for all levels of fitness with a mixture of climbing and canyoning on a daily or weekly basis. Daily treks cost between €80 and €160 per person, and weekly treks cost roughly €500.

■ **Corsica Forest** (☎ 06 16 18 00 58; www.corsica-forest.com) This adventure company organises canyoning in the wilderness and climbing on the Via Ferrata.

■ **Objectif Nature** (☎ 04 95 32 54 34; http://obj-nature.ifrance.com/obj-nature/) Based in Bastia, they organise canyoning in valée de la Gravons and the Aiguilles de Bavella.

The GR20

GR20 FACTS

Duration	15 days
Distance	168km
Difficulty	demanding
Start	Calenzana
Finish	Conca
Nearest Towns	Calenzana (p121), Porto Vecchio (p183)

Summary A legendary, if demanding, walk through the granite ranges of inland Corsica. Experience the isolation and grandeur of the mountains well away from the coastal crowds.

HIGHLIGHTS

- Navigating the treacherous climb out of the glorious **Cirque de la Solitude** (p57)

- Walking along the carpet-like pozzines around **Lac de Ninu** (p60), and at the foot of Mount Incudine

- Crossing the **Aiguilles de Bavella** (p65) along the Alpine Route

- Passing through heavily scented maquis on the way to **Conca** (p66) on the last day

The GR20 is the most famous of the *grandes randonnées* (long-distance, waymarked walking routes), attracting 10,000 brave souls to take on its heights from all over Europe every year. It was created in 1972, linking Calenzana, in the Balagne, with Conca, north of Porto Vecchio, and has since become something of an institution.

This renowned high-level walk stretches diagonally from northwest to southeast, following the island's continental divide (hence its Corsican name, Fra Li Monti, which means 'Between the Mountains'). The diversity of landscapes makes this an exceptional walk, with forests, granite moonscapes, windswept craters, glacial lakes, torrents, peat bogs, maquis, snow-capped peaks, plains and *névés* (stretches of ice formed from snow).

Consider using the resources available close to the route. You can stop off and stock up at villages linked to the GR20. The paths connecting the GR20 to the villages below are marked with yellow painted lines (these can sometimes be confusing or inadequate on some of the less frequently used paths). For a description of villages where you can join or leave the GR20, see the boxed text on p55.

PLANNING
When to Go

The GR20 can be comfortably walked any time between May and October, although some parts of the route remain snow-covered until June, making them tricky to negotiate. The peak-season months of July and August are best avoided if you have an aversion to crowds. From mid-August to the end of September, there are frequent storms, especially in the afternoon.

What to Bring

The GR20 is a long and challenging walk, and requires some preparation. You will need to carry food with you for at least part of the trail as some of the *refuges* (refuges or mountain huts) only provide light snacks. Depending on the amount of time at your disposal, plan on making detours to local villages for further supplies. Don't forget to carry a good supply of cash, as there are no ATMs on the GR20 and credit cards are only accepted in a few places. As a general rule, you'll need between €10 and €25 per day.

Lack of water can also be a real problem on the GR20. You will be able to find water

WARNING

Take note of and observe PNRC rules and regulations; in particular, lighting fires at any point along a route in the park is strictly forbidden, as is camping outside the designated areas near *refuges*.

As far as drinking water from streams is concerned, safety is not guaranteed: do not use it unless strictly necessary, and then purify it.

at every *refuge*, but between stops there are very few sources of drinking water. These have been detailed in the walk description.

Camping gear is also essential, as there is only a limited number of places available in *refuges* along the way. Note that reservations cannot be made at the PNRC-run *refuges*. When camping you do not have access to

equipment inside the huts, and fires are prohibited, so bring your own stove and fuel.

Weather in the mountains can fluctuate quickly between extremes, so come prepared for all conditions. You can call ☎ 08 92 68 02 20 for the latest weather reports in French. A length of rope is a handy addition, as it will allow you to lower

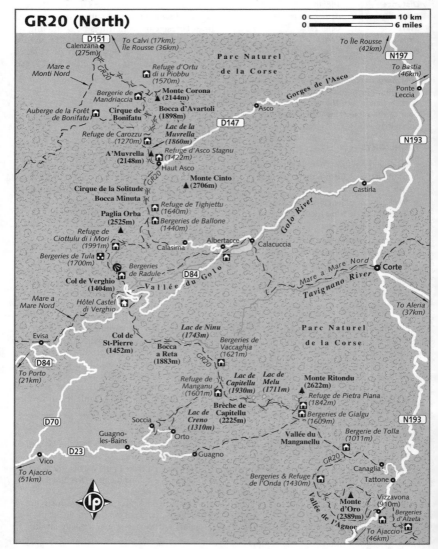

your backpack down particularly steep sections of the trail, leaving you free to descend without extra bulk.

Books

The excellent Fédération Française de la Randonnée Pédestre (FFRP) Topo-Guide À Travers la Montagne Corse (No 67) details the GR20 route. Cicerone's *Corsican High Level Route: GR20* is a handy English-language companion for the trail.

Maps

For the GR20 route, choose IGN 1:25,000 maps or Didier Richard's 1:50,000 No 20 *Corse du Nord* and No 23 *Corse du Sud*.

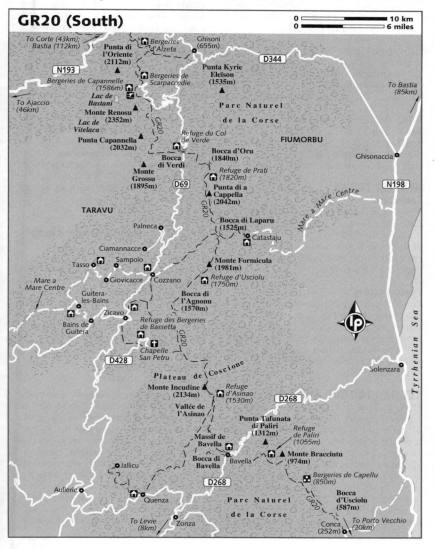

GR20 (South)

0 — 10 km
0 — 6 miles

To Corte (43km); Bastia (112km)
Ghisoni (655m)
Punta di l'Oriente (2112m)
Bergeries d'Alzeta
D344
N193
Bergeries de Capannelle (1586m)
Bergeries de Scarpaccedie
Punta Kyrie Eleison (1535m)
To Bastia (85km)
To Ajaccio (46km)
Lac de Bastani
Monte Renosu (2352m)
Lac de Vitelaca
Parc Naturel de la Corse
FIUMORBU
Punta Capannella (2032m)
Refuge du Col de Verde
Bocca d'Oru (1840m)
Ghisonaccia
Bocca di Verdi
Refuge de Prati (1820m)
Monte Grossu (1895m)
D69
Punta di a Cappella (2042m)
N198
TARAVU
GR20
Bocca di Laparu (1525m)
Palneca
Catastaju
Mare a Mare Centre
Ciamannacce
Monte Formicula (1981m)
Tasso
Sampolo
Refuge d'Usciolu (1750m)
Giovicacce
Cozzano
Mare a Mare Centre
Guitera-les-Bains
Bocca di l'Agnonu (1570m)
Zicavo
Refuge des Bergeries de Bassetta
Bains de Guitera
GR20
Chapelle San Petru
D428
Plateau de Coscione
Solenzara
Monte Incudine (2134m)
Refuge d'Asinao (1530m)
D268
Vallée de l'Asinao
Punta Tafunata di Paliri (1312m)
Refuge de Paliri (1055m)
Massif de Bavella
Jallicu
Bocca di Bavella
Bavella
Monte Bracciutu (974m)
Bergeries de Capellu (850m)
Aullerie
Quenza
D268
Bocca d'Usciolu (587m)
Parc Naturel de la Corse
To Levie (8km)
Zonza
Conca (252m)
To Porto Vecchio (20km)
Tyrrhenian Sea

While the 1:25,000 maps are more detailed, you'll need six (Nos 4149OT, 4250OT, 4251OT 4252OT, 4253OT, 4253ET) of them to cover the GR20, whereas you'll only need two of the 1:50,000 maps.

NEAREST TOWNS
Calenzana
Thirteen kilometres from Calvi (p106), Calenzana (p121) is the northern starting point for the GR20 and is also on the route of the Mare e Monti Nord (Sea to Northern Mountains) walk (p46), making it very popular with walkers.

Porto Vecchio
Porto Vecchio (p183) is the nearest town of a reasonable size to Conca (p192), at the end of the walk. It makes a good base for exploring the surrounding areas, especially the Alta Rocca region, Bocca di Bavella and the spectacular coast north and south of the town.

GETTING TO/FROM THE WALK
Start walking at Calenzana. There is no public transport from Conca, at the end of the walk, to Porto Vecchio. However, staff at La Tonnelle (p192) in Conca can arrange a shuttle service on request to Porto Vecchio (€6). However, you will have to wait until there is a minimum number of people ready to leave – no problem in the high season.

Some of the alternative access points to the GR20 are served by public transport.

Haut Asco (Day 3; p56) is accessible on the D147, which meets the N197 2km north of Ponte Leccia.
Castel di Verghio (Day 5; p135) is served by a daily bus between Corte and Porto via the D84.
Tattone (reached via a side trip on Day 8) is on the Bastia–Vizzavona–Ajaccio train line. It takes just seven minutes and €2.40 to get from Tattone to Vizzavona by train or by phoning for a taxi (p60).
Vizzavona (Day 9; p219) is on the train route between Ajaccio (€8.40) and Bastia (€23.50). Trains stop four times a day in each direction. Two of the services continue beyond Bastia to Île Rousse (€14.90) and Calvi (€17.60).
Cozzano (reached on a side trip on Day 12) is linked to Ajaccio daily except Sunday by buses operated by **Autocars Santoni** (☎ 04 95 22 64 44).
Zicavo (a detour on Day 13) is also served by buses run by **Autocars Santoni** (☎ 04 95 22 64 44) between Ajaccio and Zicavo daily except Sunday (€13).
Bavella (Day 14; p192) can be reached daily except Sunday in the peak season by an **Autocars Balesi** (☎ 04 95 70 15 55) on the Ajaccio–Porto Vecchio line (only Monday and Friday in the low season).
Quenza (Day 14; p191) can be a departure point from the GR20. **Autocars Balesi** (☎ 04 95 70 15 55) buses stop daily except Sunday (only Monday and Friday in the low season) on the Ajaccio–Porto Vecchio service.

THE WALK
Day 1: Calenzana to Refuge d'Ortu di u Piobbu
7 hours, 10km
You are confronted with the tough conditions of the GR20 from the very outset. This day is one long ascent, crossing a series of ridges, with hardly a downhill break and long stretches without shade. There's no guaranteed source of water, so bring at least the recommended 2L per person.

NORTH TO SOUTH OR SOUTH TO NORTH?

From which direction should you tackle the GR20? Nearly two-thirds of walkers opt for the north–south route, as does this guide. There are various reasons for this – access to Calenzana is easier, the main guide to the route is in this direction, habit – but logic would dictate going from south to north. The southern section between Conca and Vizzavona is easier, giving your body a chance to get used to the effort. Going in this direction also means that you don't have to walk with the sun in your eyes.

ALTERNATIVE ACCESS POINTS ALONG THE ROUTE

Completing the GR20 will give you a sense of pride and achievement, and rightly so. It is a demanding course that requires commitment. But while the goal of many is to walk it end to end, there is no shame in biting off just a small section. Even a couple of days on the traverse will allow you to experience the beauty of Corsica's mountain wilderness and sample the physical challenges of the trail.

The obvious way to divide the GR20 is into two sections: from Calenzana to Vizzavona (over nine days), and south from Vizzavona to Conca (in six days). Vizzavona is the most convenient midway point, with train and road links to Ajaccio and Bastia.

Between Calenzana and Vizzavona, it's possible to join the trail at several villages along the way: Haut Asco (at the end of Day 3), Castel di Verghio (at the end of Day 5) and Tattone, a short side trip from the main trail (on Day 8). For just a small taste of the GR20, Days 4 and 5 take in some of the most spectacular scenery of the whole walk, across the Cirque de la Solitude.

In the southern section of the GR20, Cozzano (Day 12), Zicavo (Day 13), and Quenza and Bavella (Day 14) are all popular access points for walkers. Reaching Cozzano, Zicavo and Quenza involves a detour from the GR20, but these traditional villages, tucked away in remote valleys, are the very soul of Corsica and well worth exploring in their own right.

For details of transport links to places along the GR20, see p54.

The walk starts in Calenzana by winding up to the top of the village, then the path starts to climb steadily through ferns, with good views back to Calenzana and Moncale, another hillside village. At the well-signposted 'Carrefour de Sentiers' (550m), less than an hour from Calenzana, the Mare e Monti Nord route (p46) splits from the GR20. Soon after, the trail reaches the rocky Bocca di Ravalente at 616m.

From the pass, the trail skirts a wide terraced valley, staying fairly level and passing a few small streams that usually dry up later in the season, before climbing relatively gently to 820m. After this easy stretch the trail becomes steeper, zigzagging uphill to another pass, Bocca a u Saltu (1250m). About 3½ hours from the start, this is a perfect spot for lunch. Over the other side of the ridge, on the northeastern face of Capu Ghiovu, the trail starts to climb even more steeply; you may have to use your hands to hoist yourself up some of the rocks. About halfway up this stretch is a stream that is a good source of drinking water if it hasn't dried up.

The wide grassy expanse at **Bocca a u Bassiguellu** (1486m), 5½ hours into the walk, is dotted with shady pine trees and makes another good place for a rest stop. From here the trail crosses a rather rocky and unsheltered stretch but stays fairly level. The *refuge* comes into view across the valley, into which you descend before a final short climb brings the day to an end.

Refuge d'Ortu di u Piobbu (camping €3.50, dm €9; meals €7), at 1570m, has 30 beds and plenty of camping space. However, it has just one rather primitive toilet and shower; there is a water source about 200m beyond the *refuge* along the GR20. There are a few meals and drinks on offer as well as snacks.

Side Trip: Monte Corona
2½–3 hours
Walkers who still feel strong may want to climb nearby Monte Corona (2144m). A trail, marked by cairns and flashes of paint, goes up the slope directly behind the *refuge* to Bocca di Tartagine (1852m). From there head south and climb the rocky ridge until you see the rounded summit, which is covered in loose stones and marked by a cairn. The spectacular view stretches from the *refuge* below to the north coast.

Day 2: Refuge d'Ortu di u Piobbu to Refuge de Carozzu
6½ hours, 8km
Two routes exist for this day. The one fully described in this section is graded demanding. It cuts across a range of mountains, with rocky and often spectacular scenery. The alternative low-level route skirts the mountain range crossed by the main route. It leads off to the west from the Refuge d'Ortu di u Piobbu, meeting a road after a couple of kilometres, which it follows for about 5km down the valley to the Auberge

de la Forêt de Bonifatu (540m). From the auberge retrace your steps up the road for 1.5km before climbing to rejoin the GR20, just beyond the Refuge de Carozzu.

The day's walk starts with a gentle ascent through pine forest to a ridge (1630m). In front of you is a sharp drop to the valley bottom and then a long, steep ascent (500m) to an even higher ridge on the other side.

The trail descends quickly to the valley floor, passing the ruined **Bergerie de Mandriaccia** (1500m) shepherd's hut and the Mandriaccia stream, then starts the long climb up the other side. About halfway up this unrelenting ascent there's a good source of drinking water, probably the only one you'll come across all day.

Eventually, about three hours from the start, you'll come to Bocca Piccaia (1950m). There's very little shade.

The trail does not cross the ridge immediately but stays on the northern side, remaining at a fairly high altitude until it crosses to the other side and gently descends to Bocca d'Avartoli (1898m). Traversing the southern and western faces of the next ridge, the trail drops steeply before climbing sharply to cross the next pass. It then goes to the eastern side of the ridge, crossing back again to the western side at **Bocca Carozzu** (Inuminata; 1865m), about five hours into the walk.

From here the route begins the long and somewhat tedious descent to the *refuge*. At the start of the descent it's worth looking back at the wonderful views enjoyed in the last couple of hours of the walk. It's only towards the end of this descent that you'll find some shady trees. A short distance before the *refuge* the trail crosses a stream.

Refuge de Carozzu (camping €3.50, dm €9; meals €4-7), at 1270m, is in a magnificent setting, hedged in by sheer rock faces on three sides, but with an open terrace looking down the valley. It sleeps 26 and there are plenty of camp sites in the surrounding woods. Corsican cheese omelettes, soup and other food are on offer. Beer, wine, soft drinks, sausage, cheese and other supplies are also sold.

If you follow the path from the *refuge* towards Lac de la Muvrella for 10 minutes, past a passage of rocks with cables, you'll come to a stream with a series of delightful (albeit chilly) swimming pools. You might also spot some *mouflon* here.

Day 3: Refuge de Carozzu to Haut Asco
6 hours, 6km

This part is graded moderate. Note that there is little water once you've left the Spasimata River behind.

The day starts with a short, rocky zigzagging path up through the forest to a ridge, then a slightly longer drop to the Spasimata River at 1220m. This is crossed on a rickety suspension bridge that is not for the faint-hearted. At first the trail edges along above the river, crossing long sloping slabs of rock. At some points plastic-coated cables offer handholds, which are reassuring, but note that these rocks can be dangerously slippery when it rains.

Leaving the river with its tempting rock pools, the trail then starts a long, rocky ascent to **Lac de la Muvrella** (1860m), which is reached after three to 3½ hours. The lake water is not safe to drink. If you look back during the final stages of the ascent, you'll see Calvi on the north coast. From the lake it's only a short scramble to the knife-edged ridge. After a short drop on the other side, the trail soon starts to climb again, skirting around the side of A'Muvrella to Bocca a i Stagni (2010m). The total time of ascent from the river is roughly four hours. You can make a one-hour detour from Bocca a i Stagni to the summit of A'Muvrella (2148m).

The day is less taxing than the previous two, ending with a long, 600m descent to **Haut Asco**, visible far below. Haut Asco looks like any ski resort in the off season – bare, dusty and forlorn – but it's a haven for walkers after the spartan conditions of the last couple of days. Changes are in store, however, as there are plans to demolish some of the buildings in coming years.

Refuge d'Asco Stagnu (camping €3.50, dm €9; menus €13), at 1422m, has 30 beds in rooms for two, four or six people. It also has hot showers, a huge kitchen and a dining area as well as a terrace. There's plenty of camping space on the grassy ski slopes and campers can use the showers at the *refuge*. The welcoming wardens offer a choice of Corsican soup, spaghetti bolognaise, Corsican cheese and desserts.

You can also stay at the **chalet** (☎ 04 95 47 81 08; d with shower & toilet €39-46; gîte with/without half board €26/6.50; menu €15, meals €7-11; open 15 May–end Sep) at Haut Asco.

A **small shop** (open 11am-8pm) sells trekking essentials, including freeze-dried food, sausage, cheese, bread, energy bars, chocolate, cereals, fresh fruit and even hiking shoes!

Day 4: Refuge d'Asco Stagnu to Bergeries de Ballone

7 hours, 8km

This is generally held to be the most spectacular day on the GR20, crossing the Cirque de la Solitude, which requires some technical climbing. There is water at the Refuge d'Altore, and from there to the Bergeries de Ballone the trail follows a mountain stream.

From Haut Asco the trail starts on the left (south) side of the ski run. It's easy to lose the trail at the start when it heads away from the ski slope into the trees. If you do wander off the trail, it's not a problem: you can rejoin the route when it climbs above the valley and the ski slopes to cross the glacial moraines. The views over the valley and Haut Asco are stunning.

Allow about two hours to reach the site of the old Refuge d'Altore at 2000m. From the small lake at the site, a steep 45-minute climb leads to Bocca Tumasginesca, or Col Perdu (Lost Pass), at 2183m. From the pass the **Cirque de la Solitude** falls dramatically away beneath your feet. For most walkers this is the highlight of the entire GR20, and one's first reaction is probably sheer amazement that its navigation is possible.

The descent and ascent of the Cirque de la Solitude is more of a rock climb than a walk. However, there are chains bolted into the rock face to make the climb easier. Since other walkers are often almost vertically below you, it's important to take great care not to dislodge rocks or stones as you climb. Typically it takes about 2½ hours to cross the cirque (a steep-sided basin formed by the erosive action of ice).

From Bocca Tumasginesca it's 200m down to the scree-covered valley floor, where many walkers stop for lunch. On the other side the route crosses rock slabs, often guided by fixed cables, and makes a series of steep, rocky, chain-assisted ascents before emerging into an equally steep gully (or *couloir*) filled with loose rocks and stones. Towards the top the climb becomes a little more gentle, before emerging 240m above the valley floor at **Bocca Minuta** (2218m), the second-highest point on the GR20.

Past the ridge the scenery is dramatically different: much wider and more open. The trail makes a long and at times steep descent down the Ravin de Stranciacone before reaching the Refuge de Tighjettu about 1¼ hours after leaving Bocca Minuta.

Refuge de Tighjettu (camping €3.50, dm €9), at 1640m, has limited camping space, so many campers prefer to pitch their tents lower down, by the river. Note that the river rises rapidly when there are storms. The warden sells food, such as Corsican cheese and sausage, but doesn't prepare meals.

It's only another 30 minutes' walk down the valley to the **Bergeries de Ballone** (camping €3.50; menu €14; 🕑 Jun-Oct), at 1440m. There are lots of good spots at which to pitch your tent around the *bergeries* and camping or bivouacking is free. Beds are also available in a large tent for €5.

The *bergeries* has a popular **restaurant** and **bar**, with beer, wine, snacks and breakfast, and three-course Corsican meals.

Day 5: Bergeries de Ballone to Castel di Verghio

7 hours, 13km

Day 5 contains a half-day option, with the possibility of breaking the journey at the Refuge de Ciottulu di i Mori, with access to the villages of Calasima and Albertacce – from Bergeries de Ballone (see the Side Trip, p58). It has been graded moderate.

The day begins with a gently undulating ascent through pine forests where streams tumble down from the hills to the west to join the Viru River at the valley floor. Across the valley to the east you can see the road leading up from Albertacce to Calasima, at 1100m the highest village in Corsica. The trail turns west round the eastern slope of Paglia Orba and then emerges from the forest for the steep and rocky slog up to Bocca di Foghieghiallu (Col de Fogghiale; 1962m) after about three hours.

On the other side of the pass a wide valley opens out to the south, but the route continues west, crossing the slopes of Paglia Orba and climbing slightly to reach the *refuge*.

Refuge de Ciottulu di i Mori (camping €3.50, dm €9; meals €5-7), at 1991m, is the highest *refuge* in the entire GR20; it has 26 beds. Along one side of the building there's a terrace looking out over the valley below. Directly behind the *refuge* is Paglia Orba (2525m), the third-highest peak in Corsica. Climbers may want to make the three-hour round trip to the summit of the mountain via the Col des Maures, but the final stretch includes some reasonably challenging rock climbing. This is not an ascent for beginners.

The route continues round to the western side of the Vallée du Golo, descending slightly to 1907m before dropping steeply down to the river at 1700m, just below the ruins of the Bergeries de Tula. For the next couple of hours the walk follows the impressively rocky ravine of the **Golo River**, passing a series of appealing rock pools. The **path** tracing the lower part of the valley was, for many centuries, a traditional route along which farmers took their livestock when migrating to summer pastures.

The valley narrows before the trail reaches the Cascade de Radule (1370m) and the **Bergeries de Radule**, after five to six hours. Cheese is sometimes sold at the *bergeries*. For the final hour you walk through the beech forests of the Valdu Niellu, passing the signposted turn-off to the Fer à Cheval bend (many walkers choose to join the GR20 at this point) and crossing the Mare a Mare Nord trail (p47) before finally emerging on the D84 just 100m west of Castel di Verghio (1404m). The ski slopes are on the other side of the road.

Side Trip: Calasima & Albertacce
3 or 5 hours return
You can get to Calasima (1100m) in 1½ hours from the Bergeries de Ballone. The only facility in Calasima is the **Bar du Centre**, but it's only another 6km downhill to Albertacce, which is on the D84.

Albertacce has a range of shops, cafés and restaurants; see p216.

Day 6: Castel di Verghio to Refuge de Manganu
5½ hours, 14km
This day of the GR20 follows a particularly shady route and is of moderate difficulty. Water is available at a spring in a shrine just above Lac de Ninu and at a stream

flowing from the lake close to the night's stop.

The GR20 runs gently through pine and beech forests, dropping gently to 1330m before making a sharp turn to the right (west) and climbing to the small shrine at Bocca San Pedru (Col de Saint Pierre; 1452m), reached after about 1½ hours.

From the pass the route continues to climb, following the carefully laid stones of an ancient mule path and offering superb views to the east. The trail climbs to a ridge, drops off it, climbs back on to it and eventually reaches Bocca a Reta (1883m). It then descends to Lac de Ninu (1760m), about 3½ hours from the start. Surrounded by grassy meadows and *pozzines* (interlinked waterholes – see the boxed text on p60), the lake makes a wonderfully tranquil stop for lunch.

The trail continues east, following the course of the Tavignano stream, which drains the lake, across meadows and then through patches of beech forest past the remains of an abandoned *refuge* to the **Bergeries de Vaccaghja** (1621m), one to 1½ hours from the lake. The *bergeries* usually sells wine, cheese and bread. From here you can see the Refuge de Manganu, less than an hour's walk across the valley. The trail drops gently from the *bergeries* to Bocca d'Acqua Ciarnente (1568m) and finally makes a short, sharp ascent, crossing a bridge over the Manganu stream to the Refuge de Manganu.

The pleasant **Refuge de Manganu** (camping €3.05, dm €8.40), at 1601m, has 26 beds and plenty of grassy camping space around the building, good showers and toilets and a selection of tempting swimming spots in the Manganu stream. Cheese, cooked meats and drinks should be available.

Day 7: Refuge de Manganu to Refuge de Pietra Piana
6 hours, 10km
This is a hard day, as the route climbs to the highest point on the GR20 before teetering round a spectacular mountain face that drops down to glacial lakes. Water is available from streams during the first ascent and from another stream on the final descent to the Refuge de Pietra Piana.

After crossing the bridge from the Refuge de Manganu, the GR20 immediately begins to climb, emerging onto a small meadow after 30 minutes, climbing again to another brief, horizontal break at around 1970m and then ascending even more steeply up a rocky gully. This finally becomes a scramble to the **Brèche de Capitellu** (2225m), a spectacular small slot through the spiky ridge line of peaks. Around 2½ hours from the *refuge*, this crossing is the highest point on the GR20 and the view to the east is breathtaking.

The trail bends to the southeast and edges around the eastern face of the ridge, high above the lake. There's often snow on the path well into the walking season, so take great care; it's a long way down. Just before another small pass at 2000m, where the trail crosses to the southern side of the ridge, another trail diverges off to the east and drops down to Lac de Capitellu. It's possible to continue down from there to Lac de Melu (1711m) and then climb back up to the GR20 at Bocca a Soglia.

The main route climbs slightly to reach Bocca a Soglia (2050m), about an hour's walk from the Brèche de Capitellu. Lots of day-trippers drive into the valley from Corte to walk up to the lakes.

The trail then bends to the northeast, high above Lac de Melu, climbing to the soft-edged little Bocca Rinosa (2150m) and passing Lac de Rinosa before reaching Bocca Muzzella (Col de la Haute Route; 2206m), about five hours from the start of the day. From here it's less than an hour, downhill all the way, to the Refuge de Pietra Piana.

The small, 28-bed **Refuge de Pietra Piana** (camping €3.50, dm €9; meals €5-7), at 1842m, is nicely situated right on the edge of the ridge, looking south down the Vallée du Manganellu. There's plenty of grassy camping space and good facilities. There are two toilets and two solar-heated showers that sometimes have hot water. Various hot dishes, home-made cakes, snacks and bread are also sold.

Side Trip: Monte Ritondu
3 hours return
Keen walkers may consider climbing Monte Ritondu (2622m), the second-highest mountain in Corsica. This is not a technically demanding climb, although the 800m ascent may be a little tiring at the end of the day.

Cairns mark the route to a meadow and dried-up lake just above the *refuge*. The trail then zigzags uphill before crossing the ridge

at 2260m, south of the peak. Don't descend from the ridge towards the small lakes below – continue north along the eastern side of the ridge, crossing patches of snow until the large Lavu Bellebone lake comes into view. The trail drops down to the lake's southern end and edges round the southeastern side before starting the steep climb up the slope of the rocky gully that leads to the spiky rock marking the Col du Fer de Lance. From here the trail turns west and climbs to a small metal-roofed shelter, huddled just below the summit. There are superb views in all directions from the summit.

Day 8: Refuge de Pietra Piana to Refuge de l'Onda
5 hours, 10km
An easy, mostly shady day's walk, the trail follows streams almost all day so water is no problem.

After the dramatic ascents and descents of the previous day, this section of the walk is gentle and predominantly downhill. As soon as the trail leaves the *refuge* there's a choice between following the main GR20 through the Vallée du Manganellu or taking an alternative high-altitude route (with double-yellow markings), which follows ridges to the Refuge de l'Onda. The high-altitude route is quicker but less interesting. It takes four hours, includes some technical and exposed stretches and has superb views over Ajaccio.

The main GR20 starts to drop almost immediately and soon reaches the Bergeries de Gialgu (1609m). The trail continues to drop, following an ancient mule track of neatly laid stones that winds down the hill to the Manganellu stream at 1440m. It then plunges through often dense forest to the **Bergerie de Tolla** (1011m), about three hours from the start. This pleasant little haven sells the usual supplies, and also serves snacks and meals.

Just below the *bergerie* a bridge crosses the Manganellu stream (940m). From here you can detour off the GR20 to the villages of Canaglia and Tattone (p60).

The GR20 turns upstream from the bridge and almost immediately passes over the Goltaccia, which flows into the Manganellu. Do not cross over this bridge but continue upstream and uphill beside the Goltaccia. Eventually the trail crosses the river and climbs away to the north side, soon reaching the **Bergeries de l'Onda** (camping €3.50; meals €5-7), a summer hive of activity next to the Refuge de l'Onda's grassy camping site. The *bergeries* sells wine, bread, cheese, sausages and prepared meals. It is surrounded by fences to keep the many pigs and sheep from poking around the site.

Refuge de l'Onda (dm €9) itself is higher up the hill, overlooking the *bergeries* and camp site from 1430m. It has 16 beds, one shower and one toilet, but is not as appealing as the *bergeries*.

Side Trip: Canaglia & Tattone
2 or 4 hours return

The walk is between a half and one hour from the Manganellu bridge on the GR20 to the pretty village of Canaglia. The wide track running alongside the river and the string of little pools make this a popular route with walkers. At Canaglia's small restaurant, the **Osteria u Capitan Moru**, trout and Corsican dishes are a speciality. There's a phone in the restaurant.

From Canaglia it's 4km by road to Tattone. For a taxi call Alain (☎ 04 95 47 20 06, 06 07 89 16 10) in Vivario.

In Tattone, the **Bar Camping du Soleil** (☎ 04 95 47 21 16; camping €6; pizzas €5-8), near the train station, has a **pizzeria** and a **bar** that also sells snacks.

Refuge Chez Pierrot (☎ 04 95 47 20 65, 06 14 66 42 20, gîte with/without half board €26/11) has 18 beds in three dorms and two bathrooms with hot showers. Pierrot is a real character and offers local specialities as well as snacks. Bookings are essential.

From Tattone, Pierrot (of the eponymous *refuge* on the N193) will come and pick you up in Canaglia or Vizzavona and will take you to your preferred departure point the following day. This is a good way to short-circuit the GR20 route between Pietra Piana and Vizzavona.

Day 9: Refuge de l'Onda to Vizzavona
5½ hours, 10km

This is traditionally the mid-stage of the GR20, and ends in Vizzavona, the best-equipped stop along the GR20. Water is plentiful along this part of the trail.

This moderately graded route sets off northwards, following the high-altitude alternative route to the Refuge de Pietra Piana, but soon doubles back to head south up the long climb to the **Crête du Muratellu** (2020m), reached after 2½ hours. From this windswept height the rest of the day's walk is a long descent.

An alternative route, marked only by stone cairns, continues up the Crête du Muratellu and turns slightly northeast to Bocca di u Porcu (2159m), from where it turns southeast to climb to the summit of Monte d'Oro (2389m), the fifth-highest mountain in Corsica. There are stretches of difficult rock climbing on this route, which should not be attempted by inexperienced climbers. It rejoins the main GR20 route just before Vizzavona and adds about three hours to the day's walk.

The main GR20 makes a steep and rocky descent (which can be slippery in the rain) from the Muratellu ridge into the

---

HIGH-ALTITUDE LAKES & POZZINES

Corsica's 40-odd high-altitude lakes, formed from the glaciers that used to cover the mountains, were unknown to scientists until the 1980s but are now actively monitored by PNRC personnel. A number of different analyses have shown that some are endangered by the digging of pigs and the pollution caused by tourist overpopulation in the summer. The PNRC has implemented a protection programme for the most popular lakes – Melu, Ninu and Creno – in the summer. Seasonal workers collect the rubbish left by walkers and ensure that the camping bans are upheld. The GR20 has even been diverted so that it does not contribute to the destruction of the grassy areas around Lac de Ninu. Respect the rules: no fires, no rubbish and no walking at inappropriate places.

The *pozzines* (from the Corsican *pozzi*, meaning pits) are also a fragile environment, threatened by intensive farming. *Pozzines* are little water holes that are linked together by small streams and are on an impermeable substratum – they're like peat bogs. They feel like a carpet of cool moss to walkers. They are found near Lac de Ninu and on the Plateau de Coscione, between the GR20 and the Refuge des Bergeries de Bassetta.

upper heights of the Vallée de l'Agnone. The descent becomes less steep and the surroundings greener as the route drops below 1600m and passes the remains of an abandoned *refuge* at 1500m. The trail passes a high waterfall, the **Cascades des Anglais** (1150m), roughly four hours from the start, and continues through pine forests, sometimes high above the tumbling stream. Monte d'Oro broods over this scene from the northeast.

A **snack bar** and a bridge over the Agnone hint at the proximity of civilisation, and from here into Vizzavona (p219) the route makes the transition from walking path to a track quite suitable for cars. There are several turns, several bridges and what seems like an interminable trudge before the trail finally emerges onto the road right in the middle of the village of Vizzavona, only a short distance from the train station.

Day 10: Vizzavona to Bergeries de Capannelle
5½ hours, 13.5km

This section of the walk, graded moderate, is punctuated by magnificent views as you approach Monte Renosu against a background of laricio pine and beech trees.

From the station in Vizzavona, follow the marked route for the GR20 Sud, which passes in front of Hôtel I Laricci. It first crosses the access path to the GR20 Nord on the right and then crosses a little bridge before climbing to rejoin the N193 and the ONF (Office National des Forêts; National Forestry Office) house, which you'll reach after 15 minutes. The trail then joins a wide path leading to a sign that tells you that Bergeries de Capannelle is five hours away. Shortly after, the GR20 leaves this path and ascends to the left. You'll then come to a fork (the right fork leads to a spring 450m away).

The route quickly leaves the dirt track behind and makes a twisting ascent to a high-voltage power cable (about an hour from the start) that marks the start of a long, flat trek through the undergrowth. A steep little path leads straight ahead until it intersects with a path with yellow markings. Here the GR20 goes off to your left, but make a detour 100m down the right fork for a wonderful **view** of Monte d'Oro and Vizzavona below.

Back on the GR20, the path emerges from the undergrowth into a bare, almost lunar landscape from where you can see Bocca Palmente (1647m) ahead. Pay attention to the markings and the junction where the GR20 turns right to the pass, just over 15 minutes' climb away.

The path goes back down towards the Bergeries d'Alzeta before continuing level. After about 30 minutes a hairpin bend marks the left turn-off that leads to Ghisoni. This **turn-off**, with a stunning view over the Monte Renosu massif, is an ideal spot for a picnic.

The GR20 continues along the hillside and goes through a forest of laricio pines, some of which are an impressive size. About 1¼ hours later it reaches the charming Bergeries de Scarpaccedie.

A short distance on, the route bears to the right before a steep uphill stretch (a good 20 minutes of solid effort) to a wonderful view of Monte Renosu (2352m). You'll then see a sign extolling the virtues of the beer on tap at the Gîte U Fugone at Capannelle. It's a 20-minute walk from the sign to the Bergeries de Capannelle, which is at the foot of the ski lifts in the resort area of Ghisoni (not the village). Although there is only one remaining shepherd, all the *bergeries* kept by local families now serve as cottages for holidaymakers and hunters.

Straight ahead from the Bergeries, the **Gîte U Fugone** (☎ 04 95 57 01 81, 04 95 56 39 34; dm with half board €28; menus €9.20-18.50; ☾ May-Sep) offers good value for money. The dorms have four or five beds, and showers and toilets are in a big building that resembles a high-altitude restaurant. There are 70 beds all up and half board is preferred. A little grocery sells basic foodstuffs; the restaurant has *menus* based on Corsican specialities and generous meals for those who opt for half board.

The **Gîte U Renosu**, 300m away, is only open in winter.

Just before the Gîte U Fugone is the **PNRC refuge** (dm €4.50). Although in a charming house made entirely of stone, the *refuge* is somewhat dubious in terms of comfort. The fee is collected by the warden of the Gîte U Fugone, where you can have a hot shower (€2.50). Information about the rest of the GR20 is sometimes displayed here.

You can also **camp** for free near the Gîte U Fugone. Cold showers are available and also free but you can have a hot shower at the *gîte*.

Day 11: Bergeries de Capannelle to Bocca di Verdi
5 hours, 11.5km
This day is relatively short and easy, keeping largely to a plain at around 1500m. If you wish to extend the day, a two-hour detour to the *pozzi* plain is an attractive option. The route begins at the foot of the ski lifts (follow the white-and-red markings to Bocca di Verdi and not the path leading to Lac Bastani) and rapidly leads into a forest of beech trees that hint at the once idyllic setting of the Bergeries de Capannelle before the construction of the ski resort.

It will take less than 30 minutes to reach the Bergeries de Traggette (1520m). You then follow a fast-flowing stream down to the D169, which you should reach within an hour. Fifty metres further on, the route heads uphill again. There are views over the Fiumorbu region and the Kyrie Eleïson range before the path enters a thick forest of pine and beech.

After 45 minutes, the GR20 rounds a hairpin bend to the right. When the snow is melting you will have to cross a string of streams here, some of which may require acrobatic skills. Another 45 minutes later there's a second hairpin bend, this time in the open.

You are now halfway through the day's walk and right next to Punta Capannella (2032m); above you, the Lischetto stream, which flows from the little Lacs de Rina (1882m), cascades down in a profusion of small waterfalls.

Once you have crossed the Lischetto, it will not take more than 30 minutes to get to the **Plateau de Gialgone** (1591m), with an invigorating view over Bocca di Verdi. In front of you is **Monte Grossu** (1895m) and, at the edge of the plain, a wooden sign directs you to the *pozzi*, a magnificent grassy plain that may be worth the detour (allow two hours to get there and back).

The GR20 itself carries straight on towards Bocca di Verdi and begins an impressive zigzagging descent that culminates some 30 minutes later in a little wooden bridge straddling the Marmanu stream.

A few metres on you'll see the remains of a giant fir tree that once rose to the amazing height of 53.2m. The path then continues

level until it reaches a big group of rocks. Here the trail widens out and after about 15 minutes reaches a large picnic area.

To the right is a path through the forest that goes to the village of Palneca, while a path to the left leads to Bocca di Verdi (Col de Verde) after about 300m.

Relais San Pedru di Verde (☎ 04 95 24 46 82; camping per person/tent €4/5; dm with/without half board €27/10; daily special €12; ☽ May-15 Oct), better known as the Refuge du Col de Verde, is in a lush green setting on the edge of the D69. The main, wooden cottage has a dorm for 20 people and is equipped with a stove. The sanitation facilities are in good order and the two showers (included in the price) are hot.

One of the best things about this *refuge* is its lovely terrace, where you can enjoy salads and grilled and cooked meats. The place is sometimes overrun by walkers wanting to lunch there.

Day 12: Bocca di Verdi to Refuge d'Usciolu
7–7½ hours, 14km
This is one of the longer and more difficult days of the GR20, including some very steep sections and occasional high winds on the exposed ridges.

After crossing a minor road, the trail ascends gently through a pine forest to a turn-off (10 minutes). Once it turns left, the real climbing begins. It takes 20 minutes of sustained effort to reach an intermediate plateau – the end of the first section.

A stream marks the start of the second steep section (which is at least shaded by beech trees). After another hour of tough, unshaded climbing, you'll reach **Bocca d'Oru** (1840m), with excellent views over the eastern plain.

A very pleasant walk then leads, after about 15 minutes, to **Refuge de Prati** (camping €3.50, dm €9; meals €8) at 1820m. It has been totally rebuilt after being destroyed by lightning. This PNRC *refuge*, which has 28 beds and one (cold) shower, attracts many walkers who prefer to add two hours to Day 11 in order to make Day 12 easier. The *refuge* also has other attractions: it's in a beautiful setting with a lawn that's ideal for camping and has a friendly warden who has good hot and cold food on offer.

You should fill your flask at the *refuge*'s water fountain, as there are no other water sources for the rest of the day. The GR20 follows the path to the right (a path to the left marked in yellow goes down to the village of Isolacciu di Fiumorbu) and leads straight on to the ridge.

This very steep stretch only lasts about 20 minutes, but the rest of the path remains steep and rocky. Make the most of the view (over the villages of Palneca, Ciamannacce and Cozzano) because you will need all your strength to negotiate the next 30-minute section up through large rocks (this can be dangerous in bad weather conditions – so take great care). For the next 1¼ hours the path along the ridge is rocky and difficult, coming very close to some frightening precipices at times. However, you do get some spectacular views.

Once past Punta di a Cappella (2042m), the trail skirts round the Rocher de la Penta before moving off the ridge and into a little forest that is an ideal spot for a picnic. From here it's less than 30 minutes to **Bocca di Laparu** (1525m), where the route crosses the Mare a Mare Centre walk (p47). There's a sign to a spring here. Count on three hours to go from the Refuge de Prati to Bocca di Laparu. The trail to Cozzano leaves the GR20 from here (see below).

After the pass, the trail continues along the ridge, climbing steadily up to **Monte Formicula** (1981m), the highest point of the day and a little less than 500m above Laparu. Allow between 1¾ and two hours for the climb. You'll walk along the east side of the ridge before shifting to the windier western side.

Once past Monte Formicula, it is not much further to the Refuge d'Usciolu (roughly 30 to 45 minutes) and, rather like a Sunday afternoon walk, it's downhill all the way.

Leaning against the mountain, **Refuge d'Usciolu** (camping €3.50; dm €9; meals €7) has a bird's-eye view over the whole valley. The *refuge* (the only accommodation on this day) has 32 beds and is clean and well kept. The **camp site** is just below the *refuge*. The warden will prepare pasta and meat dishes on request and has a range of supplies fit for a grocery: cooked meats, cheese, bread, chocolate, sweets and drinks.

Side Trip: Bocca di Laparu to Cozzano
5 hours return

The route to Cozzano forms part of the Mare a Mare Centre walk (p47). It descends

from Bocca di Laparu for about 25 minutes before crossing two streams and entering a splendid forest of laricio pine. It then leads to a forest track. Turn left and before long you'll pass a fast-flowing stream. There's a natural spring next to the path 200m farther on. Follow the path for half an hour until you see a sign for Cozzano pointing towards a little path heading down into the forest.

Forty minutes later the trail joins a recently made forest road that continues down. After 10 minutes you'll come to a small stream on the left; at a bend a few hundred metres farther on, the path goes back into the forest. Be careful as it's easy to miss the orange markings (don't follow the red markers). The path is lined with oak trees and majestic *châtaigniers* (chestnut trees) and crosses the forest road, before following a dry river bed, which starts at a pigsty on the left.

After three hours of downhill walking, you'll hear a **large stream**, where you can bathe, and finally to a sealed road. Turn left and the road will take you into the centre of Cozzano; turn right and you'll reach the *gîte rural*.

On the other side of the village, towards Palneca (to the north), a large building houses the **Gîte Rural Bella Vista** (☎ 04 95 24 41 59; camping per person €5, dm/d €10/28, half board per person €28; breakfast €5), which has six dormitories for six people each. You can camp in the garden and there is a self-catering kitchen. For those who don't feel like cooking, an evening meal is offered.

There are two snack bars in Cozzano, one at either end of the village: **U Mezzanu** (☎ 04 95 24 40 82; meals €5.35-9.20, sandwiches €3.80; ☼ May-Sep) and **Snack Bar Terminus**.

Cozzano is the only village in the area with a **pharmacy** (☎ 04 95 24 40 40; ☼ 9am-12.30pm & 3-7.30pm Mon-Sat); it's in the main square. The main square also contains a well-stocked **grocery** (☼ 9am-noon & 3-7pm Mon-Sat & Sun morning). For information on public transport links to Cozzano, see p54.

Day 13: Refuge d'Usciolu to Refuge d'Asinao
7½–8 hours, 14.5km

It's possible to do this section over two days, with a detour to the village of Zicavo (not described here) or a stop-off at the Bergeries de Bassetta, climbing Monte Incudine on the second day.

From the Refuge d'Usciolu, a short, steep path leads back up to the ridge. There's a sign to Cozzano, where it is possible, but not very practical, to stop off. From here it's a tightrope walk along the **ridge**, which is particularly steep at this stage, for a good two hours.

The altitude is an almost constant 1800m, but the trail goes up and down in a continual series of tiny ascents and descents, making the going very hard, particularly across large slabs of rock. There's no shade and the signs are not always easy to find, but the views are sublime.

Two hours from the start the trail passes a distinctive U-shaped gap, then drops down towards a grove of beeches on the western side of the ridge.

After about three hours you'll reach a wonderful, shady clearing – an ideal place for lunch. The pastoral setting, with streams and majestic beech trees, is in stark contrast to the barren austerity of the route along the top of the ridge. There's also a spring, which is signposted. About 10 minutes from here the trail reaches the crossroads at Bocca di l'Agnonu, about 3¼ hours from the start of the day.

The route continues among the beech trees for about 20 minutes, leading to an overhang with wonderful views. The trail then moves out of the beeches and onto the hilly plain. The route is easy until it reaches the foot of Monte Incudine, which you summit later in the day. After about an hour the trail reaches the southern junction with the alternative route via Zicavo and the Refuge des Bergeries de Bassetta to the west.

Another option, if you would rather complete this section over two days, is the impeccably run **Refuge des Bergeries de Bassetta** (☎ 04 95 25 74 20, 06 87 44 04 08; dm €11, half board in chalet per person €30.50; menu €17, daily special €8), roughly 1½ hours' walk off the GR20 (with only a slight change in altitude). This private *refuge* is a converted old *bergerie* and is well worth the detour as this is a very picturesque area. It is 1.5km from the Chapelle San Petru and is also accessible by road from Zicavo, about 14km away along the D428 and D69. The refuge has 17 beds, some in the former *bergerie*, others in small, recently built chalets. Excellent Corsican meals are served in a big communal room with a fireplace.

Shortly after the junction for the Bergeries de Bassetta, the trail crosses a rickety wooden footbridge over the Casamintellu and the ascent of Monte Incudine begins. After about 30 minutes, you reach **Aire de Bivouac i Pedinieddi**. This little plateau used to be home to the Refuge de Pedinieddi, until it was destroyed by lightning. It's possible to **bivouac** here and there is a water supply.

About one hour's walk from the footbridge, you reach **Bocca di Luana** (1800m), which is on a ridge. The route turns to the right and begins the difficult climb to the ridge leading to the summit. A strenuous 1¼ hours from Bocca di Luana, you'll reach the cross on the summit of **Monte Incudine** (2134m). It is not uncommon for there to be snow here until June.

All that's left now is the descent to the *refuge*. The first 15 minutes is an easy walk along the ridge. The trail reaches a junction and you can see what lies ahead: the path plummets down to the *refuge* 500m below. The slope really is impressive, and your joints will certainly feel it. Allow 1¼ to 1½ hours to descend from the summit to the Refuge d'Asinao.

Refuge d'Asinao (camping €3.50, dm €9), at 1530m, only has room for 20 people. Basic refreshments (cooked meats, honey, cheese, beer and wine) are sold and the warden sometimes prepares soup (€3 to €4). From the *refuge* you can see the Bergeries d'Asinao below.

Day 14: Refuge d'Asinao to Refuge de Paliri via the Alpine Route
6¼ hours, 13km

This day offers a spectacular alpine alternative to the main trail not long after starting out. From the Refuge d'Asinao, the GR20 path heads west before gradually turning south to reach the valley, where you ford the Asinao River after about 30 minutes' walk. On the way you will pass a sign indicating a turn-off to Quenza, a jewel among villages on the Mare a Mare Sud trail (p49). It is three to four hours from the GR20 and boasts a *gîte d'étape*, several hotels, as well as two grocery stores, a post office and telephone boxes.

On the other side of the Asinao River the path climbs gently and then evens out along the side of the mountain at an average altitude of 1300m. The route is easy and pleasant, following a ledge above the Asinao for about one hour. In places you can just about see through the foliage to the towering foothills of the Massif de Bavella.

After about 1½ hours of walking you reach a crossroads. Straight ahead is the main GR20 route, which skirts the Bavella mountainside to the southwest of the massif. Taking off at 90° to the left of the normal path, the **Alpine Route** takes you to the heart of the massif and is marked out in yellow – it is, without doubt, one of the highlights of the GR20. The two paths converge shortly before Bocca di Bavella.

Deviating from the official GR20 trail, the Alpine Route is one of the most beautiful. However, it is also technically demanding, passing through fallen rocks and stones and requiring you to use your hands across a chained slab of rock in one section. If you get vertigo or feel uneasy, it is advisable to take the main route. It is also worth avoiding this option in the wet, as there is a real risk of slipping.

The climb up the mountainside is very steep. There is a short respite for about 10 minutes, then the path leaves the wooded section and continues to climb towards **Bocca di u Pargulu** (1662m), reaching it after an hour. Towards the end, the rock faces, with their knife-edge points, can feel overwhelming. When you get to the top and see the panoramic views, however, it will all seem unimportant. In the jagged landscape you can make out peaks that look like huge sharp teeth – these are the **Aiguilles de Bavella** (Bavella Needles).

From here the path descends steeply through a stony gully for about 30 minutes until it reaches the famous chain across a smooth, steep slab, about 10m in width. This should pose no problems in dry weather. After another 30 minutes of tricky progress along rocky slopes you reach a pass, where you have a wonderful view of the peaks and the village of Bavella, close by to the east. The path to Bavella plunges through a deep gully of pink granite. The markings are sometimes less than adequate during this difficult descent.

Roughly four hours after you set out, the path rejoins the normal route of the GR20.

It is then only a short stroll through a pine forest to Bocca di Bavella car park.

Go past the *Madone des Neiges* (a statue of the Virgin Mary) and take the sealed road (one of the few concessions to civilisation on the GR20) to the left for about 300m. This leads into the village of **Bavella** (p192).

It may be worth stopping off in Bavella, as the Refuge de Paliri, at the end of the day, does not provide refreshments. Some walkers choose to leave the GR20 here, although this is a shame as the last stage of the traverse is quite picturesque.

If you wish to continue to the Refuge de Paliri, allow another 2¼ hours. The only difficult section is around Bocca di Foce Finosa. When you reach the Auberge du Col de Bavella on the road into Bavella, take the turn-off to the right, which changes into a forest track 50m farther on.

The walk is pleasant and easy, and follows a level route through a forest of pine trees and ferns for 15 minutes. The path then narrows before forking to the left and descending to a small stream. About 10 minutes later you come to a forest track – follow it to the right for 50m. Turn left at the fork and cross the Volpajola stream on the small concrete bridge.

Opposite, to the east, is a long range of mountains, which you will cross via Bocca di Foce Finosa. Five minutes from the stream, the path forks to the right to begin the ascent. It takes a strenuous 45 minutes to climb 200m in altitude to Bocca di Foce Finosa (1214m).

The last section of the route is the hour's walk to the Refuge de Paliri (1055m), down the east face of the range. The descent starts sharply, then turns northeast and levels out. A small peak just before you reach the *refuge* marks the end of this long section.

Built on the site, and with the stones, of a former *bergerie*, the little **Refuge de Paliri** (dorm camping €3.50, dm €9) has 20 beds and is not lacking in style. It is also in a magnificent setting. On a clear day you can see as far as Sardinia to the south. The warden has looked after the *refuge* since 1981, and it is clean and well maintained. There are toilets and a kitchenette area with equipment but the *refuge* does not sell any food. The only source of drinking water is a stream 200m below the *refuge*.

Day 15: Refuge de Paliri to Conca
5 hours, 12km

From the *refuge* the path descends briefly before coming to the heart of a superb forest of maritime pines and ferns. On the left is the imposing spectre of the Anima Danata (Damned Soul) at 1091m, with its distinctive sugar-loaf shape. After a short walk along a ledge, you can easily make out the Monte Bracciutu massif to the east and Monte Sordu to the southeast (25 minutes away). The path then follows a ridge that curves northeast round a cirque, in the middle of which are the peaks of the Massif du Bracciutu.

Looking back you can see the hole in the Punta Tafunata di i Paliri, which almost looks like a bull's-eye in the line of mountains extending from northeast to southwest. Follow this ledge for about 30 minutes (there's no shade), until you reach Foce di u Bracciu (917m). At this point the trail turns to head due south.

The trail follows the contour line for about 10 minutes before tackling the ascent of **Bocca di Sordu** (1065m). It takes 30 minutes of difficult climbing to reach the pass, with its distinctive masses of fallen rock. The view from here stretches as far as the sea.

Just after the pass you climb 50m down across a relatively steep granite slab (it could easily become a natural slide in the wet). This leads to a sandy path that slices through a pine forest (about two hours from the start). Five to 10 minutes later the trail emerges at a little plateau dotted with granite domes and strangely shaped piles of rocks. In the background is maquis and a few maritime pines. After about 15 minutes in this setting the path starts to descend. About 2½ hours after setting out you will reach the ruins of **Bergeries de Capellu** (850m). A signpost leads to a spring about 300m to the left of the main path, a good spot for a picnic.

The path leads steadily down to the Punta Pinzuta stream, which you can hear running through the valley.

After three to 3½ hours from the start, the trail fords the stream, then follows its course for a while before crossing back at a large bend. There are big **rock pools** here where you can cool off. A good 20-minute climb takes you out of this steep-sided valley and up to a pass. The path continues along the mountainside, almost level, for 45 minutes until it reaches **Bocca d'Usciolu** (587m), a narrow U-shaped passage through a wall of granite.

The descent into **Conca** (p192) in the valley below (20 to 30 minutes) passes through thick undergrowth, emerging at a sealed road (about five hours from the Refuge de Paliri). Turn left, follow the road to a crossroads and then take the road leading down. You will soon be able to see the main road.

Food & Drink

You might be at a loss, understandably, if asked to distinguish Corsican cuisine from French. You'd be forgiven for thinking that, as a region of France, its cuisine might be simply derivative of its mainland mentor's. But the cuisine of Corsica is far more complex than that. Of course there are elements of French gastronomy evident in its cooking methods, such as the stewing of meat *en daube*, in red wine and garlic, but Corsican cuisine owes its distinct characteristics to a whole host of factors. Firstly, its location in the Mediterranean provides a wealth of raw materials: fragrant olive oils, sun-loving fruits and vegetables, and cured meats, easily and economically preserved in the Mediterranean heat. Some staples from the Italian kitchen have crossed the short passage of water to the island and, especially on the east coast, it's common to see a regional variation of polenta, cannelloni and lasagna on the menu. But most importantly, Corsican food has evolved, historically, from the agrarian peasant diet of the mountains. In the 18th century most Corsicans, under threat from would-be colonisers, retreated to the safety of the mountains, a terrain that lent itself well to pig, sheep and goat rearing. Inland streams provided trout and eels, and the carpet of maquis covering the peaks yielded an abundance of aromatic herbs – wild mint, fennel, nepita, rosemary and laurel – and natural produce such as honey and the versatile chestnut.

Remarkably, little has changed in the intervening years. It wasn't until the 20th century when people began reclaiming the coast that the wealth of fish and seafood around the island began to find its way to the table.

However, despite the influence of Italian and French cuisine on its menus, Corsican cuisine has been preserved for centuries and remains relatively untouched by exterior trends, so while you gladly won't see a chipper or McDonald's on its streets, neither are you likely to see a juice bar or sushi restaurant. The endurance of this wonderful earthy style of cooking that takes full advantage of the fruits of the land is all the more refreshing in an increasingly globalised world.

> Lonely Planet's *World Food: France* takes an in-depth look at the whole country's food history and culture.

DID YOU KNOW?

Corsicans began relying on the chestnut tree to produce flour as early as the 16th century when the Genoese began taking the island's grain crop back home

STAPLES & SPECIALITIES

The ingredients that make Corsican cuisine distinctive are above all the regional charcuterie (cooked, cold pork meats), the chestnut, the local seafood and *brocciu* (fresh sheep or goat cheese, also spelled *bruccio* and *brucciu*).

Charcuterie & Other Meats

Carnivores will have found their spiritual home in Corsica. Meat of every species, shape and genesis dominates the local diet. Of the various charcuterie, *figatellu*, a thin liver sausage, is Corsica's pride, but also watch out for *lonzu, coppa, salamu, salciccia* and *prizuttu*. If among these you think you recognise cognates of more familiar salami and prosciutto, you will not be mistaken. But Corsican charcuterie has a distinctive flavour, because the meat generally comes from *cochons coureurs* (free-ranging pigs), which feed primarily on chestnuts and acorns. The *assiette de charcuterie* you will see as a starter on many a *menu Corse* will consist of a sampling of thin slices of four or five of these meats. If you want to know which is which, ask your server. Most of the pork-based charcuterie are made during winter. Unlike some of the other meats which may cure over anything from six months to a couple of years, *figatelli* (plural) is

---

VEAL WITH OLIVES

To make this typical Corsican dish, cut the veal into small pieces and brown it in a little olive oil until it is golden. Then sauté some white or red onions in a casserole dish with one clove of chopped garlic. Add a little tomato juice, a glass of white or rosé' wine, a pinch of salt, some pepper and a few bay leaves.

Allow to simmer for half an hour, then add some stoned green olives. Continue to cook on a medium heat for half an hour and serve with fresh tagliatelle.

---

generally eaten soon after production. If you're offered it in summer, it's probably the frozen variety, which may have less flavour.

Main courses, generally speaking, will answer to your idea of French cookery, but look out for the local speciality of veal with olives (rarely made using Corsican veal), and *sanglier* (wild boar), particularly in long-simmering stews called *civets* in French or *tiani* (*tianu* in the singular) in *menu Corse*. *Sanglier* is best eaten during the hunting seasons of autumn and winter. *Stufatu* and *ghialadicciu* are slow-braised mutton and pig's stomach stews respectively (popular in winter), *premonata* is beef stewed with juniper berries and *cabri* (kid) is roasted with rosemary and garlic. Most of these dishes will be served with *pulenta*, a Corsican variation of Italian polenta, made with chestnut flour.

Seafood

The warm waters of the Mediterranean provide an ample and varied net of produce: sea bream, squid, sardines, scorpion fish, crayfish and red mullet. Oysters and mussels are a speciality around the east coast, and *langoustes* (Dublin Bay prawns) appear on menus all around the coast both in *ziminu* (or *aziminu*), the Corsican version of the soup bouillabaisse (normally only served for two people) and served with pasta, simply cooked in a little olive oil and garlic. Sardines stuffed with *brocciu* are generally delicious, and inland you'll come across plenty of farmed trout, stuffed with either almonds or a selection of herbs from the maquis. *Rogets a la bonifacienne* is a southern speciality featuring mullet cooked with anchovies, tomatoes and garlic.

For everything you ever wanted to know about Corsican cheese but were afraid to ask, see www.fromages-corse.org.

Cheese

It's impossible to visit Corsica without coming across *brocciu*, which can be found on practically every single menu, in a variety of guises. This mild, crumbly, white cheese, not a million miles from ricotta, is made from the *petit-lait* (whey) of either goat's or ewe's milk, and is the only cheese accredited with an AOC (Appellation d'Origine Contrôlée). True *brocciu*, as opposed to the inferior-tasting *brousse* (made from imported or powdered milk), should be available only from about November to June, when the lactating goats or sheep provide their characteristic milk. Corsicans take this distinction seriously; a restaurant caught passing off *brousse* as *broccio* can be closed down. *Brocciu* can be eaten fresh, as a creamy *fromage frais*, baked with the zest of oranges or *cédrat* (a sweeter type of lemon) in a *fiadone* cheesecake, or drained, salted and aged for use in savoury dishes. Be sure to try an omelette of *brocciu*. The cheese combines particularly harmoniously with mint, with which it will almost always be paired in an omelette. You can also enjoy *brocciu* in pasta dishes, such as cannelloni and lasagne, or stuffed into vegetables. *Brébis* and chèvre are the overall names given to a range of sheep's and goat's cheese. *Bastelicaccia* is a soft creamy sheep's cheese with a natural crust, and *sartinesi* is a raw, hard-pressed, sharper tasting sheep's cheese. *Tomme Corse* is a semi-hard, granular, raw, ewe's milk cheese. *Niolincu* from the south and *Vénacu* from the Alta-Rocca are both popular soft cheeses. Hard cheeses are often served as a starter or instead of a dessert (or even as a bar snack), with a basket of crusty bread and a dollop of sweet fig jam, which acts as a delicious relish against the sharp flavour of the cheese. Pregnant women should check whether certain cheeses have been pasteurised, and should avoid raw varieties altogether.

Snacks

The 'sandwich Corse' seen on many café menus, is a *panino* (grilled sandwich, an Italian term) of charcuterie and cheeses. Varieties include the Libecciu, the Stellu (according to the menu, 'the most Corsican of panini'), the Velacu and the Astu. Merenda, the company that assembles and distributes these little masterpieces throughout the island, tells us that in earlier times these are what shepherds ate for a midday meal in their pastures.

The official Corsican wine site has good links to other gastronomy-related sites: www .vinsdecorse.com.

Traditional Corsican soups are served in winter and are a meal in themselves. Vegetarians beware. The vegetable soup, made with butter beans and garden vegetables, will often be made with meat stock, or even contain *lardons* of pork or sausage. Check before you order.

Dessert

For dessert, try the wonderful *fiadone* (a light flan made with *brocciu*, lemon and eggs), *brocciu* fritters or *canistrelli* (biscuits made with almonds, walnuts, lemon or aniseed). Corsican jams (made with oranges, figs, chestnuts and so on) are also delicious.

Crepes can be made either of *froment* (wheat) or *sarrasin* (buckwheat) flour. Purists distinguish a crepe (made with wheat flour) from a *galette* (made with buckwheat flour). Two distinctively Corsican crepe fillings are *brocciu* cheese with mint, and chestnut.

You'll see a variety of cakes, tarts, biscuits and *beignets* (a type of doughnut), especially inland, made from the subtle-tasting chestnut flour.

There are six official varieties of Corsican honey produced at different times of the year, mostly scented with chestnut, aromatic herbs from the maquis or fruits.

DRINKS
Alcoholic Drinks

Two breweries on the island produce eight different beers. La Pietra is an amber beer whose ingredients include chestnut flour from La Castagniccia. Enthusiasts contend that, even though the beer doesn't taste of chestnuts, its flour is nevertheless largely responsible for the beer's unique characteristics. Serena is a lighter product of the same brewery; the label bears a Corsican Moor's head. The pale Colomba beer, launched in 1999, is flavoured with maquis herbs, principally myrtle. The Tribbiera brewery

---

RECIPE FOR FIADONE

If you liked it in Corsica, you can make it at home. Finely grate the zest of one lemon and mix with 500g of *brocciu* (or ricotta, if you can't find *brocciu*), six beaten eggs and 350g of superfine sugar in a bowl. Beat until you have a smooth paste. Then turn this mixture into a buttered flan dish and cook at a medium heat until the surface of the *fiadone* is golden in colour (between 45 minutes and one hour).

CORSICAN WINE IN NUMBERS

About 48% of Corsican wines are reds, 29% are rosés and 23% are whites. Approximately 413 different producers on the island bottle some 347,000 hectolitres (hl) annually. Of the total, over 91,000hl are of *Appellations Contrôleès* standard – of sufficient quality to justify a kind of trademark protection. More than 181,000hl are *vin de pays*, or high-quality table wines. About 76,000hl are simple table wines. *À votre santé!*

---

uses mountain spring water to make Dea, Prima, Apa (with Corsican honey), Ambria and Mora (Mora is a dark beer).

Corsica has nine AOC-labelled wines produced mainly from the original rootstocks of the country, using varieties of grape such as Vermentinu, Sciacarellu and Niellucciu. There are now roughly 10,000 hectares of vineyards on the island, notably in the Nebbio and on the eastern coast, and these vineyards can be visited (see the relevant chapters for details). Corsican wines (red, white and rosé) can be bought in stores for as little as €4 a bottle (or even less), and the mark-up in restaurants is not scandalous. These are not necessarily the most distinguished of wines but, unless you're celebrating a golden wedding anniversary, they'll be better than good enough.

'The *eaux de vie* at 45% alcohol by volume are like rocket fuel'

Cap Corse Mattei, invented by Louis Napoléon Mattei in 1872, is a local wine-based aperitif, comparable to red Martini, made from Muscat wine. Casanis is a *pastis*, and although not strictly from Corsica (it's from Marseille), it was developed by a Corsican with the good Corsican name of Casabianca, and the label still has the Corsican Moor's head on it. You won't be shot for asking for a Ricard or a 51, but ask for a Casa anyway and pronounce it ca-*zah*.

The *eaux de vie* (brandies or *acqua vita* in Corsican) for consumption after dinner are particularly good when based on a citrus fruit the Corsicans call *cédrat* (for all practical purposes, a lemon) or on myrtle or other maquis plants. These are generally home-made and at 45% alcohol by volume are like rocket fuel. If at the end of dinner your server puts down a little plate with a couple of sugar cubes on it and an unlabelled bottle, you are to pour a little of the contents of the bottle over the sugar cubes and suck them. This is a very old custom and a very good one.

CELEBRATIONS

Corsicans take their food seriously and the revered fruits of the earth are celebrated in a whole host of festivals throughout the island.

February

A Tumbera: Foire du Porc Coureur (☎ 04 95 26 65 35) Festival and competition featuring a characteristically Corsican variety of mountain pig; held in Renno on the first weekend of the month.

March

Fête de l'Olive (☎ 04 95 78 80 13) The olive festival takes place in mid-March in Ste-Lucie de Tallano.

April

A Merendella (☎ 04 95 35 81 26) This fair features local farm products and takes place in Piedicroce (Castagniccia) at Easter weekend.

Journée du Brocciu (☎ 04 95 27 82 05) Everything you wanted to know about Corsica's world-famous cheese; held at the end of the month in Piana.

May
A Fera di u Casgiu (☎ 04 95 47 00 15) This cheese fair takes place in Vénaco.
Festimare d'Île Rousse (☎ 04 95 60 04 35) Dating from 1998, this now annual celebration of the pleasures of the sea and its produce is aimed at young people.

June
St-Érasme Fishing boats are blessed in Ajaccio, Bastia, Girolata and Calvi on 2 June.
La Foire de la Mer (☎ 04 95 57 48 94) This fair celebrates the people who earn their living from the sea, the sea's pleasures and sea ecology; it's held in the middle of the month in Solenzara.

July
Foire de Vin de Luri (☎ 04 95 35 06 44/04 17) The island's leading annual wine event, held on Cap Corse.
Santa Severa (☎ 04 95 35 06 44) A festival of the sea and night-time carnival at Luri harbour.

September
Fêtes de Notre Dame à Bonifacio A religious festival held on 8 September; a chance to try stuffed aubergines made the Bonifacio way.
Mele in Festa (☎ 04 95 22 67 39) A honey festival in Murzo at the end of the month.

November
Fête du Marron d'Évisa (☎ 04 95 26 20 09) Honouring chestnuts and mushrooms.
Journèes de la Pomme et des Produits Naturels (☎ 04 95 28 71 83) In honour of the apple and other fruits of nature's bounty; held in Bastelica.

December
Foire à la Chataigne (☎ 04 95 27 41 76) The oldest and most important fair in Corsica honours the chestnut. It takes place mid-month in Bocognano.

WHERE TO EAT & DRINK

As in mainland France you can take your pick of where to eat, anywhere from a bar to a restaurant, café or *ferme auberge*. Corsicans take their meals seriously. You could set your watch by the exodus from offices and businesses at midday for lunch, so to avoid queues you might be better to wait till at least after 1pm. For Corsicans, dinner at home is normally eaten between 8pm and 9pm (many people don't knock off work until 7pm or after), but in restaurants it can be later.

You can pick up a snack such as a sandwich, *panini* or salad in a bar theoretically at any time of the day. Bars normally open around 7am and many serve until 2am or 3am, though the kitchen will probably close at about 10pm, and you may not get a salad or hot dish before midday. Restaurants usually open from midday (almost never before) to 3pm, and any time after 6.30pm until 11pm or midnight. Cafés will normally open for breakfast and close just before dinner. Their menus (somewhere between those of a bar and restaurant) usually provide a choice of hot meals and a good selection of desserts and pastries. They often offer better value than restaurants, especially if you feel like taking your main meal of the day at lunchtime. *Fermes auberges* are restaurants based on farms, which primarily use home- and farm-produce on the menu. Some places double up as accommodation, but the restaurant is usually open to non-guests and will offer good-value meals of an excellent standard.

Around the coast and in busier towns, you'll find that most restaurants close outside the tourist season (November to April), and during the season they open for both lunch and dinner, seven days a week. Prices

'Cafés often offer better value than restaurants, especially if you feel like taking your main meal of the day at lunchtime'

must be indicated outside the restaurant, but you may need to ask if restrictions apply to *menus* (they might, for example, serve between certain hours or on certain days).

Since Corsicans are well used to catering to visitors' needs during the season, nothing is too much trouble – children are accepted at any hour, and solo or female travellers are made to feel comfortable. In some of the mountain villages, however, solo women might feel like a local curiosity in the small, male-dominated bars.

Tipping

French law requires that restaurant, café and hotel bills include the service charge (usually 10% to 15%), so a *pourboire* (tip) is neither necessary nor expected. If you want to leave something extra, that's up to you. A cover charge (for bread and tap water) is also included in the price of the meal.

Quick Eats

Except for stalls selling caramelised nuts and fish stalls on the beach, you won't come across many street vendors. Many of the bigger villages and most towns will have at least one day of the week when they hold a market, which will include food stalls. Check with the local tourist office, as this is where you'll find a wealth of fresh local produce for picnics (fruit and cheeses, olive oils, wine and charcuterie). The quality is invariably good and the price is often a fraction of that in a supermarket.

VEGETARIANS & VEGANS

Corsica is a nation of meat lovers, and though vegetarians won't go hungry, it has to be said that they will inevitably find menus limited and repetitive. There are only so many omelettes and *lasagnas au brocciu* a person can eat in one holiday.

Staples will be salads, soups, crepes, omelettes, cheeses, bread products and, if you are not averse, fish. On the east coast, especially, you're more likely to find restaurants serving pizza and pasta. There are no vegetarian restaurants in Corsica per se, so you'll have to shop around to get away from the charcuterie and meat stew on practically every menu. Dishes such as stuffed aubergines and tomatoes *(farcies)* are common, and though a vegetable platter might strike some Corsican restaurateurs as a novelty, they do serve vegetables as side dishes and might be willing to assemble a plate of several vegetable side dishes for you. You'll have to rely on those eggs and *brocciu*, though, for your protein. Certainly don't be afraid to ask.

Beware of dishes that ostensibly look like vegetarian options, only to reveal a 'healthy hint' of meat beneath the surface. Many Corsicans innocently consider it no harm to add a piece of meat to a mainly vegetable dish, so if in doubt, ask. Corsican vegetable soup often contains meat stock, if not meat pieces, and *aubergine a la bonifacienne* is stuffed with minced meat and breadcrumbs.

L'Ortu (p204), outside Vescovato, is Corsica's only organic and vegetarian eatery. In the bigger towns you may find an Indian or Chinese restaurant, which will add some spice to your otherwise homogenous diet.

DINING WITH KIDS

With Corsica's increasingly low birth rate and proportionally elderly population, suffice to say that Corsicans welcome children with open arms. Most restaurants have high chairs and all, with few exceptions, will allow accompanied juniors to dine at any hour. Children's menus though, if they exist at all, may not appeal to more sensitive tastes. Where restaurants offer a special children's menu, it will usually consist of a simplified, mostly meat-based version of the adult's, sometimes with chips. Depending on how cultivated your little ones' palates are, you may find yourself resorting to savoury crepes, pizza, pasta or omelettes. A picnic might give you the opportunity to make up a few healthy and nourishing favourites for at least one meal of the day.

If travelling with a baby, you should consider bringing enough formula (especially if it's soy-based) for the whole journey. Brands differ and though many of the more common types are available in supermarkets and pharmacies, you may not find your particular brand. You don't want to discover on holiday that your bundle of joy has a taste for only one type of milk. There is a limited selection of baby food in jars, so either carry a few for emergencies or mix up a small portion from your own meal in a restaurant; servers will generally oblige you by mincing meat or fish if necessary). Be careful if adding soup, which may have salt already added. See also p223.

The 1970s food bible *Guide gourmand de la France* demystifies local specialities from all the regions.

HABITS & CUSTOMS

Corsican food is not eaten on the run, and is generally eaten at certain specified hours of the day. Between noon and 2 or 3pm, many businesses shut their doors so that employees can eat a proper lunch. Portions are smaller than in many other countries, but courses are more numerous. Lunch and dinner are usually accompanied by wine.

But start with breakfast. Corsican *petit déjeuner* consists of croissants, *pain au chocolat* (bread with chocolate filling) or *tartines* (pieces of French bread smothered with butter). Coffee is generally *café créme* or *café au lait* (coffee with lots of hot milk).

At *déjeuner* (lunch) and *dîner* (dinner), you generally begin with an *entrée* or *hors d'oeuvre* (starter or appetiser), followed by a main dish, and finish with a dessert or cheese and finally coffee. You can, to be sure, short-circuit this ritual by ordering just a main dish à la carte or by eating at a café.

EAT YOUR WORDS

To discover the difference between a *ghialadicciu* and a *fiadone* (and we suggest you do), here are some handy phrases for you to digest.

Useful Phrases

I'd like the set menu.	*Je prends le menu.*
I'm a vegetarian.	*Je suis végétarien/végétarienne.*
I don't eat meat.	*Je ne mange pas de viande.*
Could you recommend something?	*Est-ce que vous pouvez recommender quelque chose?*

I'd like to reserve a table.	*J'aimerais resérver une table.*
Do you have a menu in English?	*Est-ce que vous avez un menu en anglais?*
I'd like a local speciality.	*J'aimerais une spécialité régionale.*
Please bring the bill.	*Je voudrais l'addition s'il vous plaît.*
Is service included in the bill?	*Est-ce que le service est inclu?*
Where is the bathroom?	*Où sont les toilettes?*

Menu Decoder
STARTERS & SOUP
bouillabaisse – Mediterranean-style fish soup, originally from Marseille, made with several kinds of fish, including rascasse (spiny scorpion fish); often eaten as a main course
croûtons – fried or roasted bread cubes, often added to soups
potage – thick soup made with puréed vegetables
soupe de poisson – fish soup
soupe du jour – soup of the day

COMMON MEAT & POULTRY DISHES
blanquette de veau or d'agneau – veal or lamb stew with white sauce
bœuf bourguignon – beef and vegetable stew cooked in red wine (usually burgundy)
cassoulet – Languedoc stew made with goose, duck, pork or lamb fillets and haricot beans
chou farci – stuffed cabbage
choucroute – sauerkraut with sausage and other prepared meats
confit de canard or d'oie – duck or goose preserved and cooked in its own fat
coq au vin – chicken cooked in wine
civet – game stew
fricassée – stew with meat that has first been fried
grillade – grilled meats
marcassin – young wild boar
quenelles – dumplings made of a finely sieved mixture of cooked fish or (rarely) meat
steak tartare – raw ground meat mixed with onion, raw egg yolk and herbs

DESSERTS & SWEETS
beignet – doughnut
canistrelli – dry biscuits
crêpes suzettes – orange-flavoured crêpes flambéed in liqueur
figatone – chestnut flan
flan – egg-custard dessert
frangipane – pastry filled with cream flavoured with almonds or a cake mixture containing ground almonds
galette – wholemeal or buckwheat pancake; also a type of biscuit
gâteau – cake
gaufre – waffle

English-French Glossary
BASICS

air-conditioning	*la climatisation*	(non) smoking	*(non) fumeur*
bakery	*la boulangerie*	salt	*du sel*
beer	*de la bière*	tea	*du thé*
bill	*l'addition*		
breakfast	*le petit déjeuner*		
coffee	*du café*		
dinner	*le dîner*		
grocery store	*l'épicerie*		
lunch	*le déjeuner*		
milk	*du lait*		

MEAT, CHICKEN & POULTRY

bacon	lard	horse meat	cheval
beef	bœuf	kidneys	rognons
blood sausage (black pudding)	boudin noir	lamb	agneau
brains	cervelle	large sausage	saucisson
braised pig's stomach	ghialadicciu	liver sausage	figatellu
chicken	poulet	liver	foie
chop of pork, lamb or mutton	côte	meat	viande
		minced beef	bœuf haché
		mutton	mouton
cooked or prepared meats (usually pork)	charcuterie	pigs' trotters	pieds de porc
		pork fillet	lonzu
cured ham	prizuttu	pork	porc
cutlet	côtelette	poultry	volaille
duck liver pâté	foie gras de canard	rabbit	lapin
duck	canard	smoked sausage	saucisson fumé
goat (and can also refer to goat's cheese)	chèvre	snail	escargot
		spare pig's rib	coppa
		steak	bifteck
goose	oie	steak	steak
ham	jambon	tripe	tripes
		turkey	dinde
		wild boar	sanglier

FISH & SEAFOOD

anchovy	anchois	salmon	saumon
clam	palourde	sardine	sardine
crab	crabe	scallop	coquille St-Jacques
crayfish	langouste	seafood	fruits de mer
fish stew	chaudrée	shrimp	crevette grise
fish	poisson	small saltwater crustacean	langoustine
king prawns	gambas		
lobster	homard	squid	calmar
mussels	moules	trout	truite
oyster	huître	tuna	thon
prawn	crevette rose		

VEGETABLES, HERBS & SPICES

aniseed	anis	cucumber	concombre
artichoke	artichaut	French (string) beans	haricots verts
asparagus	asperge	garlic	ail
aubergine (eggplant)	aubergine	garlic mayonnaise	aïoli or ailloli
avocado	avocat	green pepper	poivron
beans	haricots	herb	herbe
beetroot	betterave	kidney beans	haricots rouge
button mushroom	champignon de Paris	leek	poireau
cabbage	chou	lentils	lentilles
carrot	carotte	lettuce	laitue
celery	céleri	mushroom	champignon
cep (boletus mushroom)	cèpe	olive	olive
		onion	oignon
chopped raw vegetables	crudités	parsley	persil
		parsnip	panais
courgette (zucchini)	courgette	peas	petits pois

VEGETABLES, HERBS & SPICES *CONTINUED*

potato	*pomme de terre*
rice	*riz*
salad or lettuce	*salade*
spice	*épice*
spinach	*épinards*
sweet corn	*maïs*
tomato	*tomate*
truffle	*truffe*
vegetables	*légumes*
white beans	*haricots blancs*

Bastia & the Far North

CONTENTS

Bastia was for many centuries the number one urban centre in Corsica. Indeed the balance of regional power only began to shift in favour of the southern city of Ajaccio during the time of Napoleon I. Today the principal hub of Haute Corse, Bastia remains a place for doing business and making serious money. The south, meanwhile, is regarded as the domain of pen-pushers and bureaucrats. Indeed, while some parts of the north may lack the tourist developments of the far south, the northern region has a grittier, edgier feel overall. While people in the south are often accused of putting off anything today that can be done at some unspecified date in the future, the north retains a certain businesslike dynamism.

This merchant's mentality is also evident in other areas of the far north – from the bustling harbour-side villages of rugged Cap Corse to the wine-makers of Patrimonio. The Nebbio region, meanwhile, stands apart from the rest of the island in both geography and character with its huge natural attraction, the Désert des Agriates.

HIGHLIGHTS

- **Dining**
  Sample staple Corsican favourites at **Osteria U Tianu** (p86) in Bastia's Vieux Port

- **Wining**
  Taste **Patrimonio**'s (p99) famous AOC wines on a vineyard visit

- **Chill-Out Spot**
  Spend a night serenaded by the ocean at **Le Relais du Cap** (p95), near Nonza

- **Funky Festival**
  Listen to everything from folk to jazz to salsa at the international **Nuits de la Guitare** (p100) in Patrimonio

- **Kids' Stuff**
  Enjoy the programme of free summer events and entertainment in Bastia's **place St-Nicolas** (p82)

- **Beach Bum**
  Feel the fine white sand of superb **Plage de Saleccia** (p101) in the Désert des Agriates

- **Meet the Family**
  Spend a night at **Chez Madame Vignon** (p85) in Bastia

- **The Open Road**
  Drive down the less explored **western cape** (p95) of rugged Cap Corse

Western Cape ★

Le Relais du Cap ★

Bastia's Osteria U Tianu & Chez Madame Vignon

Plage de Saleccia ★

★ Désert des Agriates

★ Patrimonio's Vineyards & The Nuits de la Guitare Festival

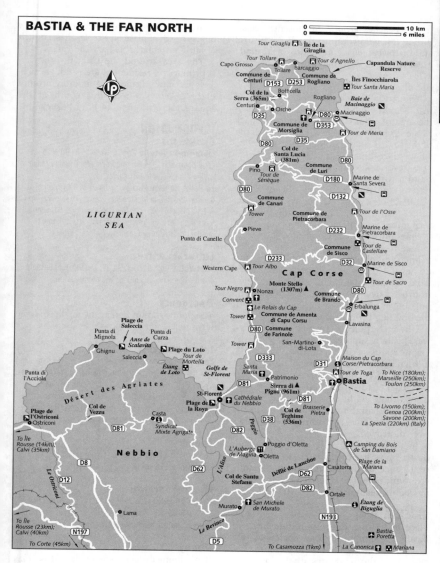

BASTIA

postcode 20200 / pop 38,000

Economically the most dynamic Corsican city, Bastia has a certain rough-round-the-edges charm and a much more cosmopolitan feel than Corsican village life.

In terms of passenger traffic through its port, it ranks second in France only to the English Channel port of Calais, with thousands of passengers flooding the city in high season. The problem in the past has been encouraging them to stay. Traditionally many people have departed Bastia straight for Cap Corse or headed to the beaches around St-Florent. Recent initiatives to promote Bastia's cultural and historical legacy have, however, made great strides in keeping visitors in town for at least a few days. Those who do linger are not disappointed.

The city of Bastia was officially founded in 1372, although there were settlements in the area of what is now Bastia as far back as the Roman times. The Genoese governor of the time, residing in the poorly defended Château de Biguglia in a malaria-infested area several kilometres away, decided to build a fortress (or *bastiglia* – hence Bastia) on the only really significant rocky headland on a coastline that was otherwise rather featureless. The site thus became recognised as strategically important.

Freedom-minded Corsicans, however, tended to see the fortress, or citadel, as the prime symbol of Genoese oppression, and on several occasions villagers came down from the mountains and sacked the town in protest over Genoese taxes. Despite the ongoing instability, Bastia continued with the building programme.

Under Napoleon, revolts in the town were brutally suppressed and in 1811 Bastia lost its status as capital to Ajaccio. In 1943, in what has to have been one of the cruellest mistakes of WWII, US Air Force bombers savaged the town even after the last Axis troops had withdrawn. Several people, joyously celebrating their liberation in the streets, were killed and numerous buildings were destroyed.

In the post-war period the strength of Bastia's port has contributed, to the town's resurgence as the island's most dynamic economic pole. The Haute-Corse prefecture moved its headquarters to Bastia in 1975.

ORIENTATION

Place St-Nicolas is the pumping heart of Bastia and home to its café society as well as a slew of shops, banks and facilities. The city's main thoroughfares are the east–west ave Maréchal Sébastiani, linking the southern ferry terminal with the train station, and the north–south blvd Paoli, the domain of serious shoppers.

Quieter and less touristy is the place de Hôtel de Ville, a few blocks south of place St-Nicolas, which is home to a good produce market every morning (be sure to get there

early). The Togo Marina, meanwhile, a few blocks north of place St-Nicolas, has a bunch of fairly unremarkable bars and cafés.

The area around the Citadel, however, is primarily a residential area and, as such, feels far more authentic – notably around place d'Armes where, just south of the square, there's a great 24-hour bakery.

INFORMATION
Bookshops

Librairie-Papeterie Papi (☎ 04 95 31 00 96; 5 rue César Campinchi; ☼ 8am-noon & 2-7pm) Sells a range of walking maps and tourist guides.

Le Point de Rencontre (☎ 04 95 31 23 10; cnr blvd Général Giraud & la Montée Ste-Claire; ☼ 9am-12.30pm & 1.30-7.30pm Mon-Sat) This bookshop cum arts centre has a range of local-interest texts plus acts as home to regular exhibitions and readings by local authors.

Cultural Centre

'Una Volta' (☎ 04 95 32 12 81; ☼ Sep-Jun) Bastia's cultural home has exhibitions and literary events.

Emergency

The police station is near the northern ferry terminal.

Internet Access

Café Taz (cours Henri Pierangeli; €3 per hr; ☼ 9am-2am) A lo-fi but effective place with computers across two floors.

Cyber Oxy (☎ 04 95 34 22 31; 1 rue Salvatore Viale; €3.10 per hr; ☼ 10am-2am) This is a smart and comfortable cyber-café but, bizarrely, has no access to yahoo email due to server problems. A good spot for an hour's idle Net-surfing, though.

Laundry

Le Lavoir du Port (25 rue du Commandant Luce de Casa-bianca; €5.5 per wash; ☼ 7am-9pm)

Medical Services

Bastia hospital (☎ 04 95 59 11 11; ☼ 24 hrs) Bus No 1, which leaves from opposite the bus station on blvd Général Graziani, terminates at the hospital (€1.50).

Money

Banks lining the perimeter of place St-Nicolas include Banque Nationale de Paris, Société Générale and Crédit Agricole; all have ATMs and offer to exchange money.

Post

Bastia post office (ave Maréchal Sébastiani; ☼ 8am-7pm Mon-Fri, 8am-noon Sat) Has a photocopier, poste restante and an ATM facility.

BASTIA

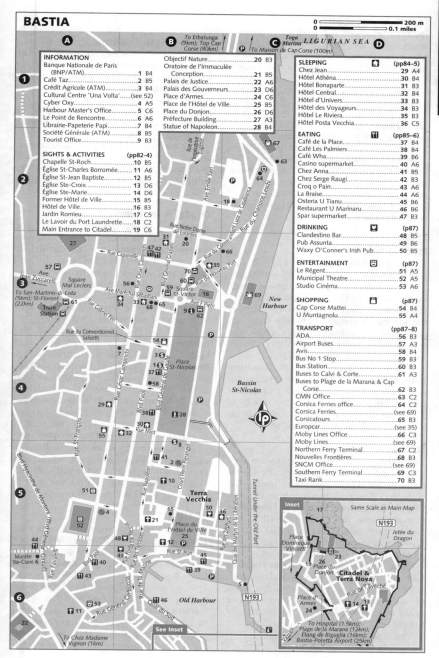

0 — 200 m
0 — 0.1 miles

INFORMATION
Banque Nationale de Paris
  (BNP/ATM)..............................1 B4
Café Taz..2 B5
Crédit Agricole (ATM).....................3 B4
Cultural Centre 'Una Volta'......(see 52)
Cyber Oxy..4 A5
Harbour Master's Office..................5 C6
Le Point de Rencontre......................6 A6
Librairie-Papeterie Papi..................7 B4
Société Générale (ATM)...................8 B5
Tourist Office.....................................9 B3

SIGHTS & ACTIVITIES   (pp82–4)
Chapelle St-Roch..............................10 B5
Église St-Charles Borromée..........11 A6
Église St-Jean Baptiste...................12 B5
Église Ste-Croix................................13 D6
Église Ste-Marie...............................14 D6
Former Hôtel de Ville......................15 B5
Hôtel de Ville....................................16 B3
Jardin Romieu...................................17 C5
Le Lavoir du Port Laundrette.......18 C2
Main Entrance to Citadel...............19 C6

Objectif Nature...............................20 B3
Oratoire de l'Immaculée
  Conception.....................................21 B5
Palais de Justice..............................22 A6
Palais des Gouverneurs..................23 D6
Place d'Armes...................................24 C6
Place de l'Hôtel de Ville.................25 B5
Place du Donjon...............................26 D6
Préfecture Building..........................27 A3
Statue of Napoleon.........................28 B4

SLEEPING   (pp84–5)
Chez Jean..29 A4
Hôtel Athéna....................................30 B4
Hôtel Bonaparte..............................31 B3
Hôtel Central.....................................32 B4
Hôtel d'Univers................................33 B3
Hôtel des Voyageurs.......................34 B3
Hôtel Le Riviera...............................35 B3
Hôtel Posta Vecchia........................36 C5

EATING   (pp85–6)
Café de la Place................................37 B5
Café Les Palmiers............................38 B4
Café Wha...39 B6
Casino supermarket........................40 A6
Chez Anna...41 B5
Chez Serge Raugi.............................42 B3
Croq o Pain..43 A6
La Braise...44 A6
Osteria U Tianu................................45 B6
Restaurant U Marinaru...................46 B6
Spar supermarket............................47 B5

DRINKING   (p87)
Clandestino Bar.................................48 B5
Pub Assunta.......................................49 B6
Waxy O'Conner's Irish Pub............50 B5

ENTERTAINMENT   (p87)
Le Régent...51 A5
Municipal Theatre............................52 A5
Studio Cinéma...................................53 A5

SHOPPING   (p87)
Cap Corse Mattei..............................54 B4
U Muntagnolu....................................55 A4

TRANSPORT   (pp87–8)
ADA...56 B3
Airport Buses....................................57 A3
Avis..58 B4
Bus No 1 Stop...................................59 B3
Bus Station...60 B3
Buses to Calvi & Corte.....................61 A3
Buses to Plage de la Marana & Cap
  Corse...62 B3
CMN Office...63 C2
Corsica Ferries office.......................64 C2
Corsica Ferries...........................(see 69)
Corsicatours......................................65 B3
Europcar......................................(see 35)
Moby Lines Office.............................66 C3
Moby Lines.................................(see 69)
Northern Ferry Terminal.................67 C2
Nouvelles Frontières.......................68 B3
SNCM Office...............................(see 69)
Southern Ferry Terminal.................69 C3
Taxi Rank..70 B3

LIGURIAN SEA

To Erbalunga
(9km); Top Cap
Corse (40km)

Toga
Marina

To Maison de Cap Corse (100m)

New
Harbour

Bassin
St-Nicolas

Terra
Vecchia

Old Harbour

Train
Station

To San-Martino-di-Lota
(5km); St-Florent
(22km)

Square
Mal Leclerc

Place
St-Nicolas

Place du
l'Hôtel de Ville

Tunnel Under the Old Port

To Chez Madame
Vignon (1km)

See Inset

Inset   Same Scale as Main Map

Citadel &
Terra Nova

Place
Dominique
Vincetti

Place du
Donjon

Place d'
Armes

Jetée du
Dragon

To Hospital (1.5km);
Plage de la Marana (12km);
Étang de Biguglia (16km);
Bastia-Poretta Airport (25km)

Tourist Information

Tourist office (☎ 04 95 54 20 40; www.bastia-tourisme
.com; place St-Nicolas; ☒ 8am-8pm) This is one of the
better organised offices on the island and staff are more
highly trained than in many other places. It offers a range
of brochures, including a town plan and a walking guide
to Cap Corse, plus advice on how to find accommodation
in town.

Travel Agencies

Corsicatours (☎ 04 95 31 03 79; rue Maréchal
Sébastiani; ☒ 8.45am-noon & 2-6.30pm Mon-Fri) This
company acts as the agent for ferry and bus tickets.
Nouvelles Frontières (☎ 04 95 32 01 62; rue Maréchal
Sébastiani; ☒ 9am-noon & 2.30-6pm Mon-Fri, 9.30am-
noon Sat) Across from the post office, this is the best
agent for deals on international flights, flights to mainland
France and package deals.

SIGHTS
Place St-Nicolas

The beating pulse of Bastia's city life, this
nearly 300m-long, 19th-century square has
a string of cafés lining its western edge, snack
kiosks within its perimeter and a lively flea
market on Sunday mornings. Throughout
the summer it comes to life with free concerts held on makeshift stages within the
square and is home to a huge July 14 fireworks display to mark Bastille Day.

The square also boasts an imposing
statue of Napoleon (p83); his powerful torso
is draped in a Roman emperor's tunic and
his eyes are peering out to sea towards Elba.
The latter, the place of his first exile, is located 40km to the east of the city.

Terra Vecchia

This oldest part of the town has always been
considered the most authentically Corsican quarter. From place St-Nicolas, rue
Napoléon files past two Baroque chapels,
Chapelle St-Roch and **Oratoire de l'Immaculée
Conception**; the latter once served as the
seat of the Anglo-Corsican parliament. Its
throne was meant for King George III and
its organ played *God Save The King*.

Opposite the chapel is **place de l'Hôtel de
Ville**, also known as place du Marché, with
some handsome four-storey buildings and
the old town hall complex. The blue colour
of the roofs is said to be due to the use of a
unique local stone, *lauze*.

The **Église St-Jean Baptiste**, located in
the southwestern corner of the square, is
recognisable by its twin bell-towers. The
church was completed in 1666 and in the
18th century was redecorated in the Baroque
style. From the square, narrow sidestreets
wind their way between tall houses down
to the Vieux Port (old harbour) and **quai des
Martyrs de la Libération**. The buildings nearest
the harbour took a battering during WWII
bombing missions designed to drive out
Axis occupiers. Today it is given over to al-
fresco eateries (p85).

The area behind the square is better preserved, particularly as you climb towards
the **Église St-Charles Borromée**. It is hidden
behind tall, narrow buildings, some of
which have been recently restored.

Citadel & Terra Nova

From the southern quay of the Vieux Port
(p83), the **Jardin Romieu** (☒ 8am-8pm, winter
8am-5pm) leads through to the citadel via
the steps of the **rampe St-Charles**. In 1452
this citadel fortress, built by the Genoese
ruler of the time, became the provincial
capital of Corsica and, as such, the seat of
the governors. The Terra Nova quarter grew
up around the fortress.

Unlike the buildings in Terra Vecchia,
however, the buildings in Terra Nova have
been refurbished, and the ochre, red, yellow and green façades of the narrow streets
gleam in the sunlight. Approaching from
Jardin Romieu, you enter the citadel via
place du Donjon with the **Palais des Gouverneurs**
(Governors' Palace) immediately on your
right. The latter has been earmarked to
house the new **Musée d'Ethnographie Corse**,
which aims to showcase Bastia's Baroque
art history. It's a good plan but, several
years down the line from the initial discus-
sions, everyone's still waiting for it to be
built. Don't go holding your breath.

ACTIVITIES

A long-standing pioneer of Corsica's adventure sports scene, **Objectif Nature** (☎ 04 95
32 54 34 or 06 03 58 66 09; http://Obj-Nature.ifrance.com;
3 rue Notre-Dame de Lourdes; ☒ 8am-7pm Mon-Sat,
8.30am-noon Sun) is a friendly little company.
It offers good advice on, and helps to organise, a slew of adventure trips throughout
Corsica. Activities range from canyoning
in the Golo valley (€46) through to sea-
kayaking along the Désert des Agriates
(€43). Closer to home they rent mountain

bikes (€16 per day) and run night-fishing trips out of Bastia harbour with dinner on board (€55). The owners speak English and Italian.

From April to October, the tourist office helps to run two-hour **walking tours** (☎ 06 81 89 80 80; adult/child €7/free) under the themes of Baroque Bastia, Genoese Bastia and Bastia under Napoleon III. Groups meet at the tourist office each morning at 9am. The guide speaks Italian; no English is spoken.

WALKING TOUR

The following walking tour of Bastia looks at the city's rich historical heritage and the influence of various invading forces on its architecture and spirit.

Starting outside the **tourist office (1)** at the north end of place St-Nicolas, walk south past the **statue of Napoleon (2)**, gazing up en route to the buildings that encircle the square on its southern and western flanks. These high apartment blocks, reminiscent of those in any number of smaller Italian cities, with their steep interior stairs, visible from the street, date from the 17th and 18th centuries.

From the main square, cours Henri Pierangeli weaves through into the Terra Vecchia, the oldest part of the town, where **place de l'Hôtel de Ville (3)** is home to the former town hall building (now used primarily for weddings) and the Église St-Jean Baptiste.

- Distance: 4km round-trip
- Duration: 2 hours

From the church, cross rue St-Jean, a quaint little backstreet that is home to some of the restaurants in Bastia (p85), and go down via the stairs to the **Vieux Port (4)**. Today this area is mainly a tourist attraction, although the harbour master's office still rents berths for yacht owners. As Bastia grew as a major port, a new commercial port was built to the northeast, leaving this sunny strip to the restaurateurs and café owners.

Hugging the curve of the port, the quai du Sud leads, via the rampe St-Charles, to the shady **Jardin Romieu (5)**. Beyond this lies the entrance to the citadel proper with steep

stone stairs leading up into **place du Donjon (6)** with the Palais des Gouverneurs immediately on the western flank.

From here cut through the narrow streets, heading southeast via rue Notre Dame and west along rue de l'Évêché, to reach the imposing yellow and white façade of the **Église Ste-Marie (7)**. A plaque on a house to

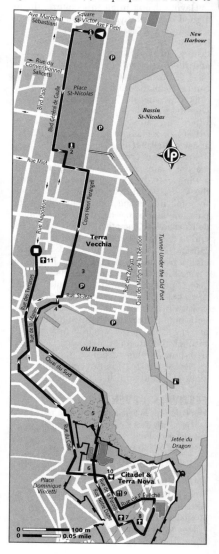

BASTIA & THE FAR NORTH

its right tells you that Victor Hugo lived there as an infant and toddler (from 1803 to 1805) when his father was a general in the town's garrison. Skirting the side of the church, you will come to the **Église Ste-Croix (8)** where the black crucifix is regarded as a magical item; it was supposedly pulled from the sea by fishermen in 1428.

Having drunk in all this culture, this is a good opportunity to stop for some light refreshment. **A Cava (9;** ☎ 04 95 31 65 17; 3 rue de la Paroisse) is an old-style shop offering free tastings of traditional Corsican products, and the owner will be happy to proffer a taste of his favourite house liqueur: a 40% *eau de vie* made from local maquis.

Follow rue de la Paroisse northeast, winding back through to place du Donjon where you can stop for a fortifying coffee (€1.50) or a glass of house sangria (€3.80) at **Bar la Citadelle (10).**

From here cross the square and exit via the main entrance to the citadel, following rue du Colle north and skirting the Vieux Port to rue des Terrasses, home to some interesting local craft shops, and past the imposing façade of the **Oratoire de l'Immaculée Conception (11)**. Towards the end of the 18th century the British Admiral Horatio Nelson had conquered the town after a two-month siege, and the British remained in the driver's seat for the next two years. During this time the new rulers would often hold planning sessions in the church's lavishly ornate interior. The Brits have long gone but the interior remains suitably lavish, and the statue of the Virgin is now paraded through the streets of town each December in a show of religious pomp.

Place St-Nicolas (1) is now clearly back in sight just to the north.

FESTIVALS & EVENTS

Processions de la Semaine Sainte (late March to early April) Holy Week is celebrated fervently with colourful processions.
Festival of St Érasme (2 June) Nautically themed festivities, food stalls, boat rides and amusements in the harbour celebrating the patron saint of fishermen.
Relève des Gouverneurs (☎ 04 95 54 20 40; 2nd Sat July) A historical re-enactment of the changing of the governors ceremony amid much pomp and ceremony.
Musicales de Bastia (☎ 04 95 32 75 91; starts October) Five days of Baroque music, polyphonic singing (p32), blues and popular song.

Festival du Film et des Cultures Méditerranéennes (☎ 04 95 32 08 86; starts November) A celebration of Latin-based language cinema.

Check with the tourist office (p82) and the daily newspaper *Corse Matin* (www.corsematin.com) for the latest details.

If you understand French, you'll find the latest information on cultural events in Bastia on Radio Corse Frequenza Mora on 101.7MHz FM.

SLEEPING

Bastia, like much of Corsica, needs more good-quality accommodation so don't expect great value for your money overall. Thankfully there are some simple but decent hotels in the centre of town that make for a suitable base.

Given the huge amount of traffic passing through town from the port during high season, however, you will need to book ahead. Off season, expect rates to fall and some properties to close up all together.

Budget

Hôtel d'Univers (☎ 04 95 31 03 38; 3 ave Maréchal Sébastiani; s/d/tr/qd €50/60/75/90; 🕮) Across from the post office and handy for both train and bus stations, this good budget option has clean, bright rooms with a touch of comfort. The bathrooms are spotless and there's a phone and television in every room. Don't expect much of a welcome from the rather surly owners but, given that it's reliable, centrally located and open year-round, it remains the pick of the bunch.

Hôtel Central (☎ 04 95 31 71 12; www.centralhotel.fr; 3 rue Miot; s/d €55/70) This hotel has rather dark, battle-scarred rooms and a welcome at times worse than a wet weekend, but at least it's clean. Ask for one of the garden-view rooms, which are quieter than those on the street. A few larger rooms have a useful kitchenette for self-caterers (€78).

Other recommendations:
Camping du Bois de San Damiano (☎ 04 95 33 68 02; €12.60) The pick of the local camp sites is 5km south of Bastia at the Plage de la Marana. There are good facilities, bungalows for hire on a weekly basis and bus connections from Bastia twice daily (once Sundays; see boxed text Bastia's intercity bus connections p88).
Chez Jean (☎ 04 95 31 50 13; 19 rue César Campinchi; d/qd €35/65) Still going strong after many long years of service, the cheapest option in town definitely has the

least frills in town but, in the absence of a youth hostel, is the true budget option.

Mid-range
Hôtel Posta Vecchia (☎ 04 95 32 32 38; www.hotel -postavecchia.com; quai des Martyrs de la Libération; d without/with sea view €48/70; ✖) This is a nice little property with homely rooms and some tasteful flourishes in its use of decoration – larger rooms even come with sea views. Previously the larger rooms also boasted refrigerators – great for keeping drinks cool in summer – but, sadly, the owners are in the process of taking these refrigerators out of the rooms. If this property is full, the hotel management also run a sister hotel, **Hôtel Athéna** (☎ 04 95 34 88 40; 2 rue Miot; s/d €50/60), which has spick-and-span modern rooms in a quiet location. Even the smaller rooms have air-conditioning and a television.

Hôtel Bonaparte (☎ 04 95 34 07 10; www.hotel -bonaparte-bastia.com; 45 blvd Général-Graziani; s/d from €58/67; P ✖) A smart, upmarket property with well-appointed rooms and a central location. This is a handy spot for those needing to be close to the ferry port for an early departure.

Hôtel des Voyageurs (☎ 04 95 34 90 80; www .hotl-lesvoyagers.com; 9 ave Maréchal Sébastiani; s/d €60/ 80; ✖) The only three-star place in town is, by default, the most expensive. And from the outside it looks like a good option worth splashing out a little extra for. Once inside, however, the rooms are rather small and dark, while the po-faced receptionist will try to palm you off with a room overlooking the back yard. Overpriced for what you get.

If all of these are full, **Hôtel Le Riviera** (☎ 04 95 31 07 16; 1 bis rue Adolphe Landry; s/d €50/60) makes a good port-in-a-storm.

Top End
There are no top-end hotels in Bastia so, for better quality, you will need to drive 20 minutes out of town (direction Cap Corse) to the rural hamlet of San-Martino-di-Lota, about halfway between Bastia and Erbalunga. There are two excellent options here.

La Corniche (☎ 04 95 31 40 98; www.hotel-lacorniche .com; r/with half-board from €62/73; P ✖ ✖) A rural village location and great views out to sea make this an ideal spot for some R 'n' R away from the big city. Rooms are tastefully decorated with some artistic flourishes

while the restaurant serves a range of Corsican favourites (*menus* €20/23).

Château Cagninacci (☎ 04 95 31 69 30; r with breakfast €78; P ✖) A converted 17th-century Capuchin convent perched high on a hillside with spectacular views out to Elba from the terrace. The four spacious rooms, each with antique furnishings, are a cut above anything available in Bastia. There is no restaurant here.

EATING
The best of the action for eating out is to be found around place St-Nicolas and the Vieux Port area, the latter being ideal for summer al fresco dining. Bastia, being more of a year-round city, is also a good place to sample local dishes without suffering the mass-produced, touristy *menus Corse* that most restaurants tend to passively serve up in high season.

Cafés
Instead of a pricey hotel breakfast, a far better option is to head for the nearest *boulangerie*, pick up a *pain au chocolate* and install yourself at one of the cafés on place St-Nicolas for your morning coffee. **Café de**

la Place, with its wicker chairs and baskets of fresh croissants, and **Café Les Palmiers** are both worth a try for a *grand créme* (€2.50) and a spot of people watching. **Chez Serge Raugi** (☎ 04 95 31 22 31; 2bis rue Capanelle) is a well-regarded ice-cream maker; its terrace is consistently packed on summer nights.

Restaurants

By far the best place for dinner is also the best-value eatery in town. **Osteria U Tianu** (☎ 04 95 31 36 67; 4 rue Rigo; ☻ 7pm-1am Mon-Sat) is an atmospheric, family-run place tucked away down sidestreets behind the Vieux Port. What sets this place apart is that locals eat here, but visitors are also made welcome so everyone mixes in together. The five-course *menu* of traditional Corsican favourites, accompanied by as much wine as you can drink, has hardly changed in over 20 years – which is probably why people come back again and again. At €19 it represents not only unbeatable value but it is also a great introduction to the traditional flavours of Corsica.

Chez Anna (☎ 04 95 31 83 84; 3 rue Jean Casale; mains €10-12, menu Corse €17.50) is a nice little spot with a flower-covered façade and meals served on a streetside terrace. The portions are really generous, so mains or giant salads are quite filling enough by themselves if you don't feel like working your way through a full set *menu*.

If you can't face another *fiadone*, **Café Wha** (☎ 04 95 34 25 79; Vieux Port; snacks €9–12; ☻ 11am-2am) is a fun place for cocktails and cheap and cheerful Mexican snacks. This is not only quite a hip hang-out for Bastia's student crowd but makes for a good escape from the charcuterie and cheese treadmill of the *menu Corse*.

For something a bit more classy, try **Restaurant U Marinaru** (☎ 04 95 32 45 99; quai du Sud; daily specials/menu €14/15.50), which is known for its fish dishes. The daily special, often a seafood *pot-au-feu*, is worth a try, while there's a children's *menu* (€8) and a gastronomic *menu* (€27) for those actively seeking to spend and eat large.

Quick Eats

Croq 'o' Pain (☎ 04 95 58 80 95; 2 blvd Paoli; ☻ 10am-10pm) A friendly snack joint with two good-value *menus*: sandwich and drink (€4.70) and sandwich, drink and dessert (€6.40).

Self-Catering

There are several **Spar supermarkets** around town, notably a large branch next to Chez Serge Raugi (above) on rue Capanelle (☻ 8am-12.30pm & 3-8pm) with another branch just off blvd Paoli (☻ 8.30am-12.30pm & 3.30-7.30pm). There's also a large **Casino supermarket** next to Croq 'o' Pain (☻ 8.15am-12.15pm & 2-7pm Mon-Sat) on blvd Paoli.

THE AUTHORS' CHOICE

La Braise (☎ 04 95 31 36 97; 7 blvd Hyacinthe de Montera; ☻ noon-2pm & 7pm-late Mon-Sat) Chez La Blaise is a long-established favourite for artists and actors visiting town – hence the photos adorning the walls from the legendary French actor Jean-Paul Belmondo to the singer Dario Moreno.

The septuagenarian owner, Jo, is a former musician who saw plenty of action playing gigs with a young Johnny Halliday in Nice jazz clubs during the 1950s. After marrying a Corsican woman, he moved to Bastia over 30 years ago and set up this traditional pizzeria, a stone's throw from the Palais de Justice and the theatre. Today it remains a great place to savour the traditional flavours of Corsica.

'The essence of Corsican village food is all about hearty fare and simple, fresh ingredients,' says Jo, stoking the fire of his wood-burning oven for the lunchtime rush. 'So we leave all the fresh produce in my wife's village in La Castagniccia (p199) at an altitude of 800m and simply bring down the fresh supplies each week.'

Jo's signature dishes change with the seasons: summer brings *torte au fromage frais* and *torte aux herbes* (both €5), while the winter season is all about charcuterie (cold meats), notably *figatellu*, a pork sausage that has been hung and dried for six months before serving. Pizzas remain the year-round staple while the house speciality desserts – a *fiadone* (cheesecake; €5.50) served with a splash of *eau de vie* (a local spirit) or a banana wood-fired in its own skin (€5.50) – are perennial favourites.

DRINKING & ENTERTAINMENT

Bastia has more of a nightlife scene than most Corsican cities but everything still closes up by 2am. In summer many places close all together while locals head back to the family village. Off season the city can actually feel more lively with bars and cafés bolstered by the student population.

There are a few discos, notably **L'Apocalypse** (☎ 04 95 33 36 83) at Plage de la Marana south of Bastia but, unless teenagers shimmying to bad French rock like a high-school disco is your thing, don't bother.

The two bars on rue Fontaine Neuve are more worthwhile. **Pub Assunta** (☎ 04 95 34 11 40) has a pool table and local bands playing on Thursday evenings and most weekends. The **Clandestino Bar** (☎ 04 95 30 88 81) is more of a tapas-style bar but it serves good cocktails and has Latin-influenced music. Both open 10pm-2am and don't get going much before midnight.

Waxy O'Connor's Irish Pub (☎ 04 95 32 04 97; 6pm-2am), working in collaboration with **Café Wha** (☎ 04 95 34 25 79; Vieux Port; 11am-2am), has drinks promotions and occasional live bands. There's Murphy's, not Guinness, on tap; it's deserted before 11pm.

There are also two cinemas in town: **Le Régent** (☎ 04 95 31 30 31; rue César Campinchi; www.leregent.fr), a multi-screen cinema with the latest releases; and **Studio Cinéma** (☎ 04 95 31 12 94; rue Miséricorde; www.studio-cinema.com) near the Palais de Justice, with both French and international releases.

SHOPPING

Bastia's most famous shop is **Cap Corse Mattei** (☎ 04 95 32 44 38; 15 blvd Général de Gaulle; 9.30am-noon & 2.30-7.30pm Mon-Sat). The interior of this gloriously retro shop has hardly changed since the day Louis-Napoléon Mattei first opened the business in 1872. During its 100-plus years of service it has continued to sell not only its celebrated brand-name Cap Corse apéritif, but various spin-off products that make ideal souvenirs. Look out for local specialities such as fig jam, olive oil and fruit liqueurs.

Of all the various shops around town selling supposedly traditional products, **U Muntagnolu** (☎ 04 95 32 78 04; 15 rue César Campinchi; 9am-12.30pm & 2-8pm Mon-Sat) is the best for charcuterie, cheese, wine and honey; they'll post purchases anywhere.

GETTING THERE & AWAY

Air

Bastia-Poretta airport (☎ 04 95 54 54 54), 20km south of downtown Bastia, has charter connections to the UK (p233) and connections to mainland France with Air France (☎ 0820 820 820) and Air Littoral (☎ 08 25 834 834).

Boat

There are two ferry terminals in Bastia: the northern terminal has showers, toilets and a welcome kiosk (7am-9pm) for timetables and information; the southern terminal has a ticket office for same-day and advance travel for SNCM, Corsica Ferries and Moby Lines. Note: the ticket office for CMN is located opposite the northern terminal in a separate building. The main operators and routes are as follows. Fares change with the seasons and bookings are recommended at peak times. For more information on ferry services see p235.

CMN (☎ 04 95 55 25 55; www.cmn.fr; 8am-noon & 2-6pm Mon-Fri, 8am-noon Sat) Overnight services to Marseilles.

Corsica Ferries (☎ 04 95 32 95 95; www.corsicaferries .com; 8am-noon & 2-6pm Mon-Fri, 8am-noon Sat) Services to Nice and Toulon in France, and to Savone and Livorno in Italy.

Moby Lines (☎ 04 95 34 84 94; www.mobylines.de; 8am-noon & 2-6pm Mon-Fri, 8am-noon Sat) Services to Genoa and Livorno.

SNCM (☎ 04 95 54 66 90; www.sncm.fr; 7.30am-7pm Mon-Fri, 8am-noon Sat) Services to Marseilles, Nice and Toulon.

Bus

The main bus station (a grand term for a little parking area with no ticket sales counters) is at the bottom of rue du Nouveau Port to the north of place St-Nicolas. Confusingly, certain bus companies leave from other stops around town. It's a complex system so for details of destinations and operators see the boxed text (p88).

And check with the Bastia tourist office (p82) for seasonal schedule changes. For details of buses to Cap Corse see p90.

Bus operators are:
Autocars Antoniotti (☎ 04 95 36 08 21)
Autocars Cortenais (☎ 04 95 46 02 12)
Eurocorse (☎ 04 95 21 06 30)
Les Beaux Voyages (☎ 04 95 65 15 02)
Les Rapides Bleus (☎ 04 95 31 03 79)
Transports Santini (☎ 04 95 37 04 01)

BASTIA'S INTERCITY BUS CONNECTIONS

Destination	Operator	Frequency	Departure Time	Price	Duration	Stop
Ajaccio	Eurocorse	2 daily Mon-Sat	7.15am & 3pm	€18	3 hr	Route du Nouveau Port
Calvi	Les Beaux Voyages	1 daily Mon-Sat	4.30pm	€12.50, €1 (bags)	1½ hr	Outside train station
Corte	Autocars Cortenais	Mon, Wed, Fri	12.10pm	€10	1 hr	Outside train station
Porto Vecchio	Les Rapides Bleus	2 daily Mon-Sat	8.30am & 4pm	€18.50	2½ hr	Opposite post office (ave Maréchal Sébastiani)
St-Florent	Transports Santini	2 daily Mon-Sat	11am & 6pm	€5	45 mins	Bus station
La Plage de Marana	Autocars Antoniotti	2 daily Mon-Sat	11.30am & 6pm	€2.50	20 mins	Camping San Damiano
Route du Nouveau Port	Autocars Antoniotti	Sun	8.30am	€3.50	30 mins	Beach

Car

Most of the car-hire firms have branches both in Bastia and at the airport. Advance booking is recommended in high season.

In town, try:

ADA (☎ 04 95 31 48 95; 35 César Campinchi; ✆ 8am-noon & 2-7pm Mon-Fri, 9am-noon Sat)

Avis (☎ 04 95 31 95 64; 40 blvd Paoli; ✆ 8.30am-noon & 2-6pm Mon-Sat)

Europcar (☎ 04 95 31 59 29; rue Adolphe Landry; ✆ 7am-8.30pm Mon-Sat, 7-9am & 11am-2pm & 6-10.30pm Sun)

At the airport, try:

ADA (☎ 04 95 54 55 44)
Avis (☎ 04 95 54 55 46)
Budget (☎ 04 95 30 05 04)
Europcar (☎ 04 95 30 09 50)
Hertz (☎ 04 95 30 05 00)
Sixt (☎ 04 95 54 54 70)

Train

The **train station** (☎ 04 95 32 80 61; ✆ 6am-9pm) is at the western end of ave Maréchal Sébastiani. There are daily connections to Ajaccio (€23.50, four hours, four daily), Corte (€11, two hours, five daily), Casamozza (€3.30, 30 minutes) and Calvi (€17.80, three hours, four daily); the latter requires a change at Ponte-Leccia (€7, 1½ hours).

GETTING AROUND
To/From the Airport

The **airport bus** (€8, 30 minutes) leaves from in front of the **Préfecture building**, which is on the roundabout opposite the train station. Times change by season and are posted at the bus stop.

Airport taxis (☎ 04 95 36 04 05) cost day/night or Sundays €30/35.

Taxi

Taxis Radio Bastiais (☎ 04 95 34 07 00) and **Taxis Blues** (☎ 04 95 32 70 70) operate 24 hours per day. Rates, for up to four passengers, are €10 to Erbalunga, €15 to Macinaggio and €40 to St-Florent.

AROUND BASTIA

ÉTANG ET RÉSERVE NATURELLE DE BIGUGLIA

This stretch of coast running south from Bastia is home to a vast 11km lagoon enclosed by a long sandy beach, la Marana. With a total surface area of 1450 hectares, it is the largest closed body of water in Corsica.

Declared a nature reserve in 1994, it is an important area for Corsican flora and migrating fauna (p36). More than 100 species of bird can be observed here, while eel and mullet are farmed in the waters. Though sailing and bathing are prohibited, a **footpath** follows the northern and eastern shore for walkers, and a small **information kiosk** (☎ 04 95 33 55 73; ✆ 9am-noon & 2-5pm summer only) opens on the eastern side of the lagoon.

Driving south from Bastia towards la Marana is the **Brasserie Pietra** (☎ 04 95 30 14 70; ☺ 9am-noon & 2-5pm summer only; free visit), the brewery that produces Corsica's favourite dark beer, as well as the lighter malt beer Serena and the maquis-scented blond beer Colomba. Visitors are welcome; out of season, appointments are mandatory.

The sandy **Plage de la Marana** itself, 16km along the N193 from Bastia, is devoted to tourism with shops, holiday homes and a few tacky discos. A narrow stretch of sand more than 10km long between the Étang de Biguglia and the sea, the beach is nothing special, but at last you can stretch out your beach towel. Best park up at the car park and make your way to the beach on foot. If you're feeling more active, in summer a track bordering the eastern fringe of the lake is frequented by rollerbladers and cyclists, and there is windsurfing on the lake.

At the southern end of the Étang de Biguglia, 25km south of Bastia, is the archaeological site of **Mariana**, with its remains of Roman baths, and the Pisan **Cathédrale de la Canonica**, consecrated at the beginning of the 12th century. The strange little menagerie of animals on the decorative arched moulding over the western entrance of the cathedral is definitely worth a look.

GETTING THERE & AWAY

In summer, **Autocars Antoniotti** (☎ 04 95 36 08 21) buses leave Bastia's bus station twice daily at 11.30am and 6pm (Sundays once daily at 8.30am) for Camping San Damiano (p84); €2.50, 15 minutes). They run onto Plage de la Marana and Étang de Biguglia (€3.50, 30 minutes).

CAP CORSE

The maquis-covered Cap Corse peninsula, 40km long and around 10km wide, stands out from the rest of Corsica, giving a giant geographical finger to the French Riviera. This wild and rugged region is often called an 'island within an island'.

For many long years, the Cap Corse peninsula was ruled by important noble families from the city and republic of Genoa and surrounding Liguria, the coastal region of Italy closest to the border with France. As these families prospered on trade in wine and oil, the Genoese and Ligurians became accustomed to considering Cap Corse an ally. History rarely proved them wrong.

This part of Corsica was an important centre for merchants and trading. It also has a long maritime tradition and is, apart from Bonifacio, the only area within Corsica where the inhabitants have made a living from fishing. Indeed, the inhabitants of Cap Corse were the first islanders to broaden their horizons overseas – many of them went on to find fame in the French colonies in North Africa and the Americas. Then, once they had made their fortune, many returned to Corsica, where some had colonial-style houses built; some of these so-called 'American houses' can still be seen in the region, particularly around Sisco (p90).

Today, girdled by numerous old watchtowers built under the Genoese to protect the vulnerable peninsula from Saracen raiders, the cape is dotted with charming coastal fishing villages and small communities perched precariously in the hills.

Cap Corse doesn't, however, offer particularly good value – especially in high season when the population of these tiny hamlets increases tenfold, and proprietors hike prices to squeeze the tourist Euro before another long winter when most places close up and the place is deserted.

To find the places going against this grain you will need a car and a decent grasp of French.

The west coast offers a less touristy glimpse of life, not to mention some of the best scenery and death-defying switchback roads. But stock up in hubs such as Erbalunga and Macinaggio, as facilities can be sparse en route; these places also have the only two ATMs on the entire cape.

If you drive fast, you can 'do' the cape in a day by following the D80. Ideally, though, you'll take your time to stop, admire the view and get off the main drag into some inland hamlets.

When asking directions be aware that Cap Corse comprises, and is known by, its 22 *communes*; places therefore are – confusingly – sometimes identified by both their *commune* and village name.

Information

The **Maison du Cap Corse** (☎ 04 95 31 02 32; www .destination-cap-corse.com; ☺ 9am-noon & 2-6pm Mon-Fri), next to Toga Marina and 800m north of place St-Nicolas in the *commune* of Pietrabugno, is not an actual tourist office per se but it can handle email and phone enquires.

It also offers a practical guide (in English) and a map of walking routes (in French). Buses to Cap Corse stop outside the office but the stop is not marked. Virtually opposite the office is a large **Geant shopping centre** (8.30am-8pm Mon-Sat) and a **post office** (8.30am-5.30pm Mon-Fri, 8.30am-noon Sat).

Getting There & Away
Bus operators dominate Cap Corse and have a bad habit of changing timetables at will. The Bastia tourist office (p82) and Maison du Cap Corse (p89) should have the latest schedules.

ERBALUNGA
postcode 20222 / pop 1500
Erbalunga, within easy striking distance of Bastia by bus or car, is a popular stop on the Cap Corse to the Balagne classic route (p15) with good facilities for travellers, including food shops, a large free car park and a **post office/ATM** (9am-noon & 2-3pm Mon & Thu, 9.30am-noon & 2-4.30pm Wed & Fri, 9am-noon Sat). The beach is pebbly but the charming harbour makes a good spot for a lunch stop. The **Dolphin Dive School** (06 07 08 95 92), opposite A Piazetta (see below), has diving trips and kayak hire, both from €35 per day.

Lavasina, 2km south of Erbalunga, has little to offer aside from a look around the village church, a pilgrimage destination in early September.

Pozzo, 3km from Erbalunga, is the trailhead for climbing Monte Stello (1307m) with a sign 'Monte Stello 3 hours' indicating the path through the maquis from the main square.

Sleeping & Eating
Castel Brando (04 95 30 10 30; www.castel brando.com; d/ste €134/160; Mar-Oct; P X) The only hotel in town is a venerable and stylish three-star affair with spacious, airy rooms and top-notch facilities. Indeed, the place has an opulent feel suitable for any French film stars who just happen to drop by. Ask, if possible, for a room on one of the upper floors as these rooms offer by far the best views. There's a decent buffet breakfast (€10) served each morning on the terrace

CAP CORSE BY BUS
Buses out of Bastia for Cap Corse are operated by **Société des Transports Interurbains Bastiais** (STIB; 04 95 31 06 65) and stop opposite the Bastia tourist office on route du Nouveau Port.

- To **Erbalunga** (€2, 20 minutes, 20+ buses weekdays 6.30am–6pm, 12 buses Sat 6.30am–7.10pm, 11 buses Sun 8am–7pm)
- To **Macinaggio** (€6.40, one hour, three buses daily Mon–Sat 7am–7pm)
- To **Sisco** (€2.30, 25 minutes, 10–12 buses daily 7.30am–7pm) and onto **Pietracorbara** (€2.60, 30 minutes, 6–8 buses daily 7.30am–7pm)

by the swimming pool. Private villas are also available for a minimum of five nights during high season.

A Piazetta (04 95 33 28 69; pizzas €7) The local pizzeria is the pick of Erbalunga's eateries, with meals served on a tranquil outdoor terrace in a shady square. The food is simple but satisfying; what really gives this particular place top marks is the delightful harbour-side setting.

Just east of this, **Le Corona** (04 95 33 42 50; giant salads €7-9) is a good refuelling spot with more of a snack-style *menu* and a good range of main courses for a leisurely lunch.

For something more special – at a price – **Le Pirate** (04 95 33 24 20; menu €64; dinner & lunch Wed-Sun) has the best views across the harbour, attentive service and haute cuisine fare. It's a set, all-inclusive menu.

SISCO
postcode 20233 / pop 750
The *commune* of Sisco comprises a scattering of rural mountain hamlets, which trace a trail down through the maquis to a small marina and none-too-sandy beach. The latter forms the *commune* hub on the D80 Cap Corse to the Balagne classic route (p15).

It's a quiet place but there is a **post office** (8.50am-noon & 2-4.30pm Mon-Fri, 8.50-11.30am Sat) – buses to Bastia stop right outside – and a **Cocci Market shop** (7am-1pm & 2.30-8pm Mon-Sat, 7am-1pm Sun) next door to a *tabac* heading west (inland) from the post office.

Sleeping

Hôtel-Restaurant U Pozzu (☎ 04 95 35 21 17; www
.u-pozzu.com; d/qd €62/104; ❄) With the Hôtel
de la Marine now converted into apartments on a strictly weekly-let basis only,
this is now the only proper hotel in town.
It's a friendly enough place if slightly lacking in atmosphere with modern rooms;
evening meals (€16) are served on the
restaurant terrace.

The most recent addition to the area is
the **Gîte Le Relais** (☎ 04 95 35 28 85; r €45), located 1.5km west of the post office, which
has basic but adequate rooms with private
bathrooms in a rural setting.

Eating

A Casaíola (☎ 04 95 35 21 50; pizzas €9) This popular restaurant is a mainstay of the Sisco
scene given its pleasant beachside location.
Meals are served on a shady terrace opposite a small chapel, or you can choose to eat
on a wooden deck directly overlooking the
waves. The owners also hire canoes (€9 per
hour) and run a nearby **camp site** (☎ 04 95 35
20 10; sites for 2 people €15).

Osteria A Stella Sischese (☎ 04 95 35 26 34; menu
€18.50) is a well-regarded local favourite for
hearty Corsican specialities served amid an
earthy ambience. There's a children's *menu*
(€12.50) and a gourmet *menu* with seven –
count 'em – gut-busting dishes (€23) to
showcase traditional flavours. Reservations
highly recommended.

PIETRACORBARA
postcode 20247 / pop 430

The *commune* of Pietracorbara is best
known for its sandy beach with tourists
congregating at the **Marine d'Ampuglia** on the
coast, 4km downhill from the isolated inland hamlet. This place is so quiet it makes
Sisco look positively animated, but it does
have some decent sleeping options.

Hôtel-Restaurant Macchia e Mare (☎ 04 95 35
21 36; www.macchia-e-mare.com; r without/with sea views
€42/47; meals €18.50, obligatory half-board in August €53/
59) This two-star property at the southern
entrance to the marina has a quiet restaurant terrace and modern rooms – it's worth
paying the extra for the sea view.

Hôtel-Restaurant Les Chasseurs (☎ 04 95 32 21
54; d without/with half-board €45/80; menus €12 to €20;
P) has rather dated but adequate rooms
and an outdoor restaurant.

GENOESE TOWERS

Around 60 of the 85 Genoese towers that
the Banco di San Giorgio built in Corsica
in the 16th century remain standing today.
Mostly round but occasionally square, these
fortified structures are about 15m high and
are particularly common in Cap Corse.

The towers were supposedly intended
to protect the island from Saracen raiders, but you can't help thinking that in
building them Genoa also sought to protect its strategic and commercial interests
in Corsica from European challengers.
Placed around the coastline so that each
was visible from the next, the towers formed
a vast surveillance network. A system of
signals enabled a message to circle the
island in one hour.

On Cap Corse, Pino (p94), Erbalunga
(p90) and the Sentier des Douaniers
(p93) all have fine examples of Genoese
towers.

MACINAGGIO (MACINAGHJU)
postcode 20248 / pop 460

The hub of the eastern cape, Macinaggio
(*commune* of Rogliano) is *the* place to stay
overnight and stock up on supplies before
going 'over the top'. It has the best facilities for travellers and marks the terminus
for buses from Bastia. Its little harbour –
crammed with luxury yachts and swarthy
Mediterranean types in designer shades –
is reputed to be one of the island's best
moorings.

Information

The Macinaggio **post office** (✆ 8.30am-noon &
2.30-4.15pm Mon-Fri, 8.30-11.30am Sat) has one of
two ATMs on the whole of the cape (see
also p90) and is clustered in a little square
150m west of the marina along with a **laundrette** (€7 per 5kg wash; ✆ 9am-1pm & 3.30-8pm)
and a **Spar supermarket** (✆ 8.30am-12.30pm &
4-8pm Mon-Fri, 8.30am-noon Sun).

The small but friendly **tourist office** (☎ 04 95
35 40 34; www.ot-rogliano-macinaggio.com; ✆ 9am-noon
& 3-7.30pm) is above the **harbour master's office**
(capitainerie; ☎ 04 95 35 42 57) at the southern
end of the marina at the entrance to town.
The former has the entire cape's only facility for public Internet access (20 centimes
per minute) and offers a range of maps,

CORSICA'S TWISTED FIRESTARTERS

Napoleon Bonaparte, Corsica's most famous son, famously once remarked that he could smell the island of his birth from his exile on Elba. He was probably referring to the maquis, a dense shrub composed of sage, juniper and myrtle, that covers thousands of square hectares of the renegade Mediterranean island. Indeed, each spring when the maquis explodes into a carpet of pink and yellow flowers, its uniquely pervasive fragrance provides most visitors to the island with an olfactory souvenir they never forget.

But every year, as Mediterranean temperatures nudge the mid-30s, thousands of hectares of the spiny shrub across Corsica turn into death-trap towering infernos. Indeed, tales of fire-fighters risking everything to tackle huge bush blazes dominate the summer news bulletins, and reports of walkers caught unawares amid burning scrubland are the high season mainstay of *Corse Matin*'s front-page splash.

Corsicans suspect that a large number of the fires are started quite deliberately. Some locals blame the shepherds, accusing them of burning the ground to force new shoots to sprout through the parched ground; others cite dastardly real-estate agents seeking to commandeer grazing land for another shipping magnate to build his holiday home. Other possible culprits include careless tourists and deliberate troublemakers. Everyone is alleged to have a vested interest in Corsica's pyromania problem.

But not everyone is prepared to sit back while the island goes up in flames. 'The truth is that fires generate a lot of money and keep a lot of people in work. The fires benefit everyone except the island itself and its people,' says Roger Filippe, president of **L'Amichi di u Rughjone** (☎ 04 95 35 05 04; www.amichidiurughjone.org), a community action group set up out of frustration with the local administration's inability to resolve the fire issue.

The 300-odd members, all volunteers, work to repair damage to the local environment, maintain safe hiking trails and lobby to raise awareness of the way bureaucracy keeps the fires burning.

In recent years Cap Corse has been particularly badly affected with the *commune* of Sisco bearing the brunt of the most recent infernos. Having witnessed the worst blazes for 20 years has only served to strengthen L'Amichi di u Rughjone's resolve. 'It's no use waiting for the politicians – the action must come from us, the people,' says Filippe, sipping his morning coffee on the veranda of his home in the Cap Corse *commune* of Luri. 'Besides, as Corsicans, we are born fighters.'

including one for the ever-popular **Sentier des Douaniers** walking trail (p93).

For the more active traveller, **Cap Corse Location** (☎ 06 21 26 28 30; ⏲ 8.30am-12.30pm & 5-8pm) shares premises with Europcar next door to the post office and rents mountain bikes for €15 per day.

Families may prefer boat trips along the protected coastline with the **San Paulu** (☎ 04 95 35 07 09; www.lebateau.fr.st; adult/child €15/10), which is moored directly opposite the tourist office. The two-hour round-trip includes a stop for swimming en route, but there is no time allocated to spend time actually exploring around Barcaggio.

Otherwise, the **Plage de Tamarone**, one of the region's most stunning beaches, is the main draw in the region for beach bunnies. It's 2km north of the marina, just past Camping U Stazzu (p93) and has a kiosk for snacks but no showers or toilets.

Sleeping & Eating

Hôtel Les Îles (☎ 04 95 35 41 51; r without/with sea views €48/53) This waterfront hotel is the cheapest in town. The rooms are small and fairly unspectacular but they have bathrooms and breakfast is included in the price. It offers the best central location in the marina. As such, it remains the most popular spot in town – be prepared to book ahead. You're better off saving on the extra money for sea views and instead opting for one of the quieter rooms at the back of the hotel for a better night's sleep.

Auberge U libecciu (☎ 04 95 35 43 22; www.u-libecciu.com; d without/with half-board €95/130; **P**) This auberge has chalet-style accommodation in a quiet location away from the marina's social hub. The rooms are spacious, albeit rather sparse, but at least you won't be disturbed by late-night revellers. The food served as part of the half-board deal

LE SENTIER DES DOUANIERS (CUSTOMS OFFICERS' ROUTE)

Hikers and walkers will love this rugged coastal path that leads away from the beach at Macinaggio and, winding its way through the fragrant maquis of the Capandula Nature Reserve, hugs the protected shoreline. As you stroll, the view is spectacular with various sections grazing the coastline looking out to the **Îles Finocchiarola** and passing the Genoese **Tour de Santa Maria** and **Tour d'Agnello** en route.

The trail leads on to complete the first stage at Barcaggio – allow up to three hours for this section.

From here, and if you're not already flagging in the sun, the path continues for another 45 minutes on to Tollare. From Tollare it's a hefty but spectacular four-hour trek to the harbour at **Centuri** (right). It's not a particularly hard walk but make sure to take a hat and plenty of water, and avoid the midday sun – it can be especially ruthless along the strip of coast.

If the walk is proving too much, then **Loc'Ago** (☎ 06 19 47 77 13) has guided excursions on quad bikes from €25 per person. Otherwise, the company that runs the San Paulu boat (p92) also runs a water shuttle (€7) to rescue overly ambitious souls who can't face the hike all the way back to Macinaggio; it leaves Barcaggio daily at noon.

does seem rather mass produced, which makes sense given the preponderance of coach parties that stay here.

U Ricordu (☎ 04 95 35 40 20; www.hotel-uricordu.com; s/d €140/160; P X R) Just north of the post office, this is the smartest option in the area. The rooms and facilities are unrivalled but, during the high season, the pricey half-board deal is obligatory, as is a minimum seven-night stay. This place is one for the high rollers only. They'll transfer you to Bastia-Poretta airport for €30.

If you've escaped the half-board thrust on people by most hotels around here, then **Maison Bellini** (☎ 04 95 35 40 37; menus €14/22) has reliable seafood dishes served on a terrace at the northern end of the marina. In summer it also runs a small snack kiosk

on the water's edge for sandwiches and crepes (€5).

Other recommendations:

Résidence Stella Marina (☎ 04 95 35 07 04; www.stella-marina.com; 2-/4-person villa per week €457/542; P R) Modern villas in a family-friendly resort complex open year-round.

Camping U Stazzu (☎ 04 95 35 43 76; €12.50 camping for two people) Signposted 800m west of the marina, this shady spot is handy for Tamarone beach.

AROUND MACINAGGIO

The eastern cape can feel pretty crowded – especially during high season – so the answer is to jump in the car and escape the hordes. Following the D80 inland from Macinaggio, the *commune* of **Rogliano (Rugliano)** makes for a short but dramatic drive.

After a particularly sharp intersection, the D53 drops down to **Bettolacce**, the main hamlet and home to **Hôtel-Restaurant U Sant'Agnellu** (☎ 04 95 35 40 59; www.hotel-usantagnellu.com; s/d €80/72), a smart and cheery three-star with 14 nicely decorated rooms and fantastic panoramic views from the terrace over dinner.

Backtracking to the highway, the D80 snakes across to Botticella from where the narrow D253 winds its way through the maquis for 10km before reaching Corsica's northernmost village, **Barcaggio (Barcaghju)**. This remote spot has an end-of-the-world feel – even in summer – and its only hotel, **Hôtel La Giraglia** (☎ 04 95 35 60 54; r €75), exploits this fact mercilessly, charging top whack for mediocre rooms. They don't do evening meals but breakfast is included in the price.

Capo Grosso, to the west of Barcaggio and the hamlet of Tollare, has the best views on the cape – if you can handle following the unmarked and heavily rutted road off the D153 for 2.5km. Having then drunk in the scenery, you can rejoin the D153, which winds back to Botticella. From here the road connects back to the D80 and pushes onwards towards the similarly unexplored western cape.

CENTURI

postcode 20238 / pop 230

Despite the swelling population in summer, Centuri still has a hidden treasure feel about the place. Its focal point is the small stone harbour (a traditional home of rock-lobster fishing) that feels a lot more earthy than the flash yachts and Gucci shades that dominate the landscape in Macinaggio.

From the D80 the road makes a steep switchback turn onto the D35 that drops down to the *commune* of Centuri, passing several outlying hamlets en route – notably Orche, 4km from Centuri harbour and home to the only **post office** (☼ 9am-noon & 1.30-3.30pm Mon-Fri, 9-11.30am Sat) in the area. From here the road goes down to a large free car park, beyond which lies the marina with severely restricted access to vehicles.

There's not much of a beach here – just a strip of pebbly shoreline heading along the D35 route via the *commune* of Morsiglia. Centuri is a particularly welcome sight for walkers as the harbour marks the terminus of **Le Sentier des Douaniers** (p93).

Within the marina there's a **boulangerie** (☼ 7.30am-8pm) for fresh *patisserie* and two shops, the best stocked being **Mini Market Agostini** (☼ 8am-7.30pm), just west of the hotel, Le Vieux Moulin (see below).

Sleeping

Hôtel-Restaurant du Pêcheur (☎ 04 95 35 60 14; r €50/60) You can't miss this hotel north of the harbour – it's painted bright pink. The rooms are rather dark and small, but it's a cheerful spot and the cheapest option in town. At least the rooms have private bathrooms and some offer a great vista across the harbour at sunset. However, one big word of warning: if you take a front-facing room, don't expect an early night given the noise from the late-closing Bar Dominci opposite. In summer you're obliged to eat dinner in the restaurant downstairs (€15 menu) – the portions are a bit on the small side, but there's usually some fresh seafood options and a good choice for mains.

Hôtel-Restaurant U Marinaru (☎ 04 95 35 62 95; tolaini@wanadoo.fr; obligatory half-board €90) Tucked away 200m east of the harbour, this hotel has simple but quiet rooms, some with balconies overlooking the harbour and many with proper baths (not just showers). Despite the enforced half-board deal, this is one place where guests actually have a wide choice from the €20 menu rather than being restricted to a few set options.

Hôtel-Restaurant Le Vieux Moulin (☎ 04 95 35 60 15; www.le-vieux-moulin.net; s/d with obligatory half-board in high season €94/140, bungalow s/d/tr/qd €123/ 166/230/290 P ⏶) Centuri's most prestigious lodging knows its place and sticks rigidly to the formula. It caters exclusively to a very moneyed clientele – hence the stylish décor and haute cuisine restaurant. Accommodation is also available in comfortable bungalows with terrace (also on a half-board basis). On-site there's a tiny cave-like **disco** (☼ 10pm-late Fri & Sat), supposedly the oldest on the island, which opens only in summer. Expect free entry, pricey drinks and lots of French, soft-rock ballads.

Heading 4km along the D35 from Centuri harbour, **Camping L' Isolottu** (☎ 04 95 35 62 81; €14) is a well-respected year-round camp site with good facilities.

Eating

Cavallu di Mare (☎ 06 16 20 14 19; omelettes €4, giant salads €8) Opposite Mini Market Agostini on the south side of the harbour, this simple but friendly eatery is the best budget option – indeed the best option for any budget – given its generous portions and friendly service. By way of a welcoming gesture, a free apéritif is offered to every customer and, while you munch, you can look out from the stone terrace across the harbour. It opens during summer only but caters for the whole gamut of needs from morning coffee, through lunch to dinner and snacks.

A Macciotta (☎ 04 95 35 64 12; menus €15.50/21) Alongside Hôtel-Restaurant du Pêcheur, this is an upmarket option serving seafood on a terrace decorated with fisherman's garb. The gourmet seafood buffet (€41) is only worth considering if you are seriously, *seriously* hungry.

PINO

postcode 20228 / pop 150

The D80 splits just before the tiny hamlet of Pino between the D80 (direction Nonza) and the D180, which leads back, via the *commune* of Luri, across the cape and onto the east coast at Santa Severa marina. From here it rejoins the D80 classic route (p15) back to Bastia. **Luri** is home to a major **wine fair** (p71) that is held each July and attracts viticulture experts and blatant old wine soaks alike from every corner of the island. There's a new wine museum, **A Mimoria di u Vinu** (☎ 04 95 35 06 44; adult/child €3/free; ☼ 10am-1pm & 4-6pm Wed-Sat) that looks at the history of

Corsica's wine industry through a range of implements, documents and testimonials.

Rustic Pino itself is a coffee stop, not an overnight stop. There's no accommodation here – unless the Maison du Cap Corse (p89) can find you a *chambre d'hôte* in the region. Pino does, however, boast a useful **Spar supermarket** cum petrol station (☺ 8.30am-12.30pm & 2.30-7pm Mon-Sat, 8.30am-12.30pm Sun), the **Bar les Platanes** (☎ 04 95 35 07 95) for drinks and snacks and a smart restaurant, **La Tour Génoise** (☎ 04 95 35 12 29; menus €15/20/26). The restaurant is a good spot for a leisurely lunch and a chance to recharge the batteries while watching the yachts from the terrace.

NONZA
postcode 20217 / pop 70

Dating from medieval times, this charming little village, standing 150m above a blackened shingle beach, is the main stopping point for travellers skirting the western coast of the cape. Not only is it the nicest spot on this side of the cape with its highly dramatic ocean backdrop, but it also is blessed with the best facilities for travellers.

Nonza's hub is the village fountain with its bust of the ubiquitous Pascal Paoli (p24) and **Café de la Tour** (p96), the focal point of Nonza's buzzing social life. There's a small **grocery shop** (☺ 8am-8pm) 50m north of the fountain, a **boulangerie** (☺ 7.15am-12.30pm & 5-7.30pm; sandwiches €3) 50m to the south of

the fountain and a **post office** (☺ 9am-noon & 2-4pm Mon-Fri, 9-11.30am Sat) a further 50m south again from the *boulangerie*.

Well worth a look as you stroll around the village is the 16th-century **Église Ste-Julie**, whose ochre façade rises from the roadside. The path opposite the grocery shop descends to the **Fontaine Ste-Julie**, dedicated to Corsica's patron saint, where a memorial plaque recalls that, in AD 303, 'St Julie was martyred and crucified for her Christian beliefs. After her death, her breasts were cut off and hurled against the rock, whence this miraculous spring arose'.

Below the fountain the path drops sharply down to the beach. Beware: it's steep going down, murderous coming back up, and hot – especially in summer. Otherwise, by car, head 2km back towards Centuri where a narrow paved road leads to the shore. If you are beach-bound, there are no showers or toilets and very little shade; bathing is prohibited due to strong currents.

Back opposite the fountain, narrow and rather steep streets lead up to the 16th-century **Genoese tower** (free entry; ☺ 8am-sundown), famed for the incident when, besieged by the French in 1768, a lone villager, Jacques Casella, took on the might of the French army. Incredibly he actually managed to convince his adversaries that there was a whole battalion in defence of the tower. When Casella finally surrendered – and emerged from the tower entirely alone –

THE AUTHORS' CHOICE

Le Relais du Cap (☎ 04 95 37 86 52; www.relaisducap.com; r €55/65; 🖳) Four kilometres south of Nonza at Olmeta du Cap, this family-run lodging is ideal for people looking for something a little more individual. It offers an infinitely superior base to anything on offer accommodation-wise in St-Florent (15km away via the Patrimonio wine route; p99) and is the pick of accommodation available down the western side of Cap Corse.

There are four double rooms and one self-contained apartment for up to four people, which is rented on a weekly basis (€550/650). Overall the rooms are unfussy but well-appointed with a few nice, homely touches that show the owners have genuinely put some thought into making the place stand out from the crowd.

A BBQ and communal cooking facilities are available to guests downstairs, while the all-you-can-eat breakfast buffet (€5) – served on a terrace with a spectacular vista across the crashing ocean – will set you up for the whole day ahead.

The pebble beach is just a few steps away from the lodge's front door, and the owners can advise on places to eat and things to do in the area. It makes a good base for walking and beach-combing trips but you will need your own transport to get around.

This is one place among the rather mediocre selection of Cap Corse lodgings that is truly worth seeking out. Ask the owners about off-season promotions.

the French were, naturally, pretty damn flabbergasted.

Today the tower offers some superb views across the village and the gulf beyond. As such, it's a real shame that some bright spark has come up with the idea that using the ramparts to sell tacky tourist souvenirs and tired old generic photographs of wistful Corsican panoramas would be a suitable use of such a major historical monument. Shame on them.

Sleeping & Eating

Overlooking the fountain the family-run **L'Auberge Patrizi** (☎ 04 95 37 82 16; menu €22, mains €14) is now just a restaurant – albeit a rather good one with the best setting in the village and a small but well-considered *menu*. Previously the owners ran a *chambre d'hôte* but now their daughter has taken over the accommodation side of the business. She now runs **Chambre d'hôte Casa Lisa** (☎ 04 95 37 83 52; d €63), which has quiet and homely rooms overlooking gardens. It is located down a set of winding paths directly opposite the fountain and is signposted en route.

Nonza's other *chambre d'hôte* is the smart and modern **Casa Maria** (☎ 04 95 37 80 95; d/f €80/140; 🞉), which has well-equipped rooms with large bathrooms. Located along the trail ascending to the tower, it's rather on the pricey side for a *chambre d'hôte,* but the rooms are a good size for a family and the whole place has a newly refurbished feel about it.

Next to the grocery shop, **U Franghju** (☎ 04 95 37 82 16; menu €20) has decent food but needs to expand its terrace for more space, while **Le Café de la Tour** remains *the* spot for people-watching and summer drinks in the shade of the chestnut trees. This is the place to take the pulse of the local community.

THE NEBBIO

This region is a bit of a mixed bag with extreme tourist overload and rugged, wild scenic beauty all squashed into a region bridging the gap between the northern hub of Bastia and the Balagne coastline with its beaches and tiny villages.

The busy resort town of St-Florent is the rather disappointing hub town of the region. It's the obvious place to stay and eat, but most people don't realise that beyond the tack and chintz of St-Florent are the vineyards of Patrimonio (p99) and the raw beauty of the Désert des Agriates (p101).

St-Florent is served by buses from Bastia and boats ply the water-bound route to the Désert des Agriates. Outside of these two options a car is pretty much essential to explore further, especially if you are hoping to escape the hubbub of the high-season crowds.

ST-FLORENT (SAN FIURENZU)
postcode 20217 / pop 1500

Locals call this major resort town a 'Petit St-Tropez'. Truth is, however, that St-Florent has all of the attitude and few of the facilities of the jewel of the French Riviera. Indeed, in high season it is absolutely rammed with well-to-do French and Italian holidaymakers – they're the ones parking their flash yachts in the small harbour. Expect a major price hike as soon as the first yacht of the summer drops anchor in the marina.

Given that there's plenty of far nicer places nearby – notably Île Rousse (p115) and Patrimonio (p99) – St-Florent really is one place you can consider leaving off your itinerary.

Orientation

St-Florent is little more than a village and is easily navigable on foot. The main road from Patrimonio skirts the northeasterly side of the town and leads into place des Portes, St-Florent's social hub. The narrow streets of the old town stretch north towards place Doria, the best spot for dinner. Crossing the River Poggio, the D81 continues south towards Oletta with the sandy Plage de la Roya, the beach bunnies' and watersports fiends' mecca, stretching outwards to the west.

Information

The nearest hospital is 23km away in Bastia. For details of a doctor on call, check at the tourist office, where details are posted outside.

Crédit Agricole (🕙 8.10-11.55am & 1.40-4.40pm Mon-Sat) Opposite the Société Générale, it has a similar raft of services.

Post office (🕙 9am-noon & 2-5pm Mon-Fri, 9am-noon Sat) Located in the centre administratif, along with the tourist office and the town hall, it has an ATM.

Presse Centrale (place des Portes; ⏰ 7.30am-8.30pm
Mon-Sat, 7.30am-noon Sun) Sells foreign newspapers,
maps and film.
Société Générale (⏰ 8.25am-noon & 1.45-4.50pm
Mon-Fri) On the road to the post office, this small branch
exchanges travellers cheques and has an ATM.
Tourist office (☎ 04 95 37 82 16; ⏰ 9am-noon &
2-5pm Mon-Fri, 9am-noon Sat) The staff here are big on
dishing out brochures, but sometimes not so big on advice.

Sights
Perched above the harbour, the sandy-
coloured but ruined **citadel**, built under the
Genoese, looks strangely like a Moroccan
kasbah. Sadly there's not enough of it left
standing to divert you for more than a few
minutes.

More interesting is the **Cathédrale du
Nebbio** (Église Santa Maria Assunta), a
fine example of religious architecture
about 1km east of the town centre on the
site of the ancient Roman city. It makes
for a nice little stroll after lunch and you
can still visit the church. Ask at the tourist
office if the church is open – if not, it will
cost €1 and they'll need to hold onto your
passport as security before they will lend
you the keys.

Activities
Altore (☎ 04 95 37 19 30 or 06 83 39 69 06) is a specialist tour operator that can help arrange
adventure-based trips for independent
travellers.

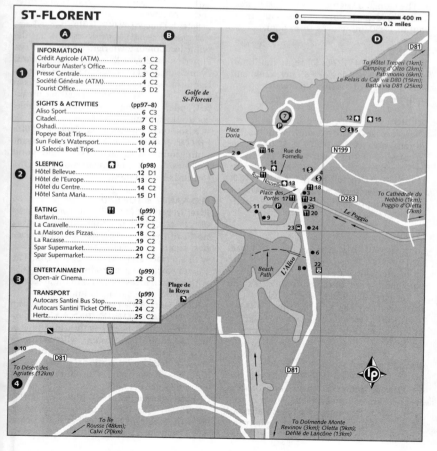

BOAT TRIPS

From June to September two companies organise daily boat trips to the superb **Plage du Loto** on the edge of the Désert des Agriates (p101), in turn an easy 30 minutes' walk from the equally superb **Plage de Saleccia**. Stock up on all necessary provisions before you leave as there are few facilities on arrival. En route the trip passes the ruined Genoese Tour de la Mortella but visits are not possible.

The **Popeye II** (☎ 04 95 37 19 07; adult/child €10/5) is an old fishing boat, recognisable by its painted Rolling Stones mouth, which departs six times daily from 8.45am to 3.15pm. The ride to **Plage du Loto** takes around 30 minutes; last return 7.30pm.

The launch **U Saleccia** (☎ 04 95 36 90 78; adult/child €10/5) departs three times daily from 9am to 11.30am; returns from 4pm.

CYCLING

Aliso Sport (☎ 04 95 37 03 50) rents mountain bikes for €18 per day or €85 per week, and sells a range of fishing and water-sports equipment.

DIVING

There are several dive outfits in the St-Florent area. **CESM** (☎ 04 95 37 00 61; http://cesm.free.fr), in the water-sports facility at La Roya beach, has a five-dive package for €144 (€316 with full board). **Aquado** (☎ 04 95 37 27 43; www.aquado.com/index; quai de l'Aliso) is in town, opposite the bridge which leads to La Roya beach.

QUIRKY

For a taste of an alternative lifestyle, **Oshadi** (☎ 04 95 37 00 21; quai de l'Aliso) is an organic shop/café selling a range of healthy eating supplements and organic produce. It's one of the few such places on the island (see also boxed text The Authors' Choice, p204). It also offer various styles of massage by appointment only; prices range from €38 per hour.

WATER SPORTS

Beach bums make a beeline directly for the **Plage de la Roya**, a long ribbon of sand around 2km southwest of the town centre. From June to September **Sun Folie's Watersport** (☎ 06 13 07 39 83) rents watersports equipment, ranging from pedalos (€18 per hour) to sea scooters (€125 per hour plus extra for petrol and bond) from its beachside base.

Sleeping

St-Florent offers poor value overall and is absurdly busy in summer. The best accommodation is actually out of town (see boxed text, p95) though, if you are planning to stay in town, be sure to book well ahead in high season.

BUDGET

The best budget option is the no-frills but functional and very centrally located **Hôtel du Centre** (☎ 04 95 37 00 68; rue de Fornellu; d/tr €38/54). It's not the most flash place but the more expensive rooms do have a bath and TV, while most rooms also offer harbour views.

Hôtel de l'Europe (☎ 04 95 37 00 03; place des Portes; r with street/sea views €55/58; menus around €15) has the prime location in town right on the place des Portes but, sadly, really rather dreary rooms. Even if you don't overnight here, however, its café terrace and restaurant are useful places to know. They serve a decent €6.60 set breakfast, and the evening set *menus* are a reliable, good-value option.

Also recommended is **Camping d'Olzo** (☎ 04 95 37 03 34; site for 2 €16.50), a three-star campground with shady sites and good facilities. It's 2km northeast along the D81 (towards Patrimonio).

MID-RANGE & TOP END

Hôtel Treperi (☎ 04 95 37 40 20; r with half-board €90; P ⚑) Hidden among the vineyards north of the town, this homely little place has smart and welcoming rooms, each with a terrace and a view over the gulf. The friendly owners have produced a leaflet (€5) with a dozen ideas for walks in the area, and are a good source of local information.

Hôtel Santa Maria (☎ 04 95 37 04 44; www.hotel-santa-maria.com; d/tr €110/130; P ✗) An upmarket three-star property with a nice line in design, comfortable rooms with balconies and a clutch of maritime-theme furnishings. A half-board option is available in the on-site Marinuccia restaurant for an extra €25 per person.

Hôtel Bellevue (☎ 04 95 37 00 06; d/ste €147/155; P ✗ ⚑) is a big family-friendly resort hotel with decent facilities but hefty prices for what you actually get.

Eating

La Maison des Pizzas (☎ 04 95 37 08 52; pizzas €10) Right on place des Portes, this long-standing eatery does a fine line in wood-fired pizzas served on a buzzy terrace. It is the perennial favourite in town as it opens late and is the *only* place in town to stay open year-round. You can eat in or, for a picnic pizza, there's a little serving hatch for take-away orders.

Otherwise, for something lighter, a good option is **Bartavin** (☎ 04 95 37 04 48; place Doria; 🕒 6pm-late), a tapas bar with tables spilling out onto a terrace on place Doria. Try the mezze plate (€13) washed down with a glass of local AOC Patrimonio wine (€4).

La Rascasse (☎ 04 95 37 06 99; quai d'Honneur; menu €20) A smart option for a more classy night out; the seafood comes with a view across the marina and a flourish of stylish presentation. But, if you pay for your seafood by weight, expect a larger than average bill.

For a quick snack, **La Caravelle** (☎ 04 95 37 00 27) is a simple place just south of places des Portes. It has good, giant salads (€8) and panini (€5.50). Self-caterers should head for the twin **Spar supermarkets** (🕒 8.30am-12.30pm & 3.30-7.30pm) on either side of the River Poggio.

Entertainment

The **open-air cinema** (☎ 04 95 31 12 94; €6.50; 🕒 Jul & Aug from 9pm) is 350m south of place des Portes along the Oletta road.

Getting There & Away

BOAT

The **harbour master's office** (capitainerie; ☎ 04 95 37 00 79; 🕒 8am-9pm) has showers, and information about weather forecasts and berths.

BUS

Autocars Santini (☎ 04 95 37 02 98; office opposite bus stop; 🕒 10am-noon & 6-8pm Mon-Sat) Buses run to Bastia twice daily Monday to Saturday at 6.45am & 2pm (€5, 45 minutes). The bus stop is 170m south of place des Portes. In summer only, buses run to Île Rousse twice daily Monday to Saturday at 9am and 4.30pm (€10, one hour).

CAR

Hertz (☎ 04 95 37 16 19; 🕒 9.30am-12.30pm & 3-7.30pm Mon-Fri) is open during summer in the Corse Plaisance building south of the River Poggio.

PATRIMONIO

postcode 20253 / pop 650

This peaceful little village, 6km outside of the resort town of St-Florent, has two principal – and worthy – claims to fame. They are its vineyards (below) and its world-renowned guitar festival (p100).

The wine, primarily muscat and a range of almost indecently fruity rosés, is excellent. Indeed, the area as a whole was the first such region in the whole of Corsica to be granted an *Appellation d'Origine Contrôlée* (AOC) seal of quality for its wine. Today a dedicated *route des vins* is signposted from St-Florent through the vineyards of Patrimonio, and around 600 hectares of land are cultivated for wine by some 30-odd growers.

Many of the wineries in this region welcome passing visitors for tastings without appointment. It is, of course, implicit in this that you will be purchasing some wine – but it's not mandatory.

If you have a car, a tour of the vineyards makes for a great half-day trip and is a far better way to spend the day than loafing around St-Florent. Sadly, as yet, there are no sleeping options in the immediate area, but Le Relais du Cap (see the boxed text, p95) is just a short drive away and a more than suitable base.

Patrimonio is served by buses between Bastia and St-Florent (p88).

Of the 30-odd local winemakers, *caves* that are recommended include:
Domaine Gentile (☎ 04 95 37 01 54) The most exclusive *cru*.
Domaine Lazzarini (☎ 04 95 37 13 17) Liqueurs and fruit wines.
Cave Orenga de Gaffory (☎ 04 95 37 45 00) The pick of the full-bodied reds.
Clos Montemagni (☎ 04 95 37 14 46) Good quality rosés.
Dom Pastricciola (☎ 04 95 37 18 31) Owned by the mayor of Patrimonio. According to local sources he has plans afoot for opening some *chambre d'hôte* accommodation in the village.

Eating

Osteria di San Martinu (☎ 04 95 37 11 93; menus €15 & 20) is a popular spot for visitors to the Nuits de la Guitare festival (p100) as it's just by a car park en route to the festival grounds. It has the standard wood-fired pizzas and local specialities served on a large, open terrace.

NUITS DE LA GUITARE

The **Association Les Nuits de la Guitare** (☎ 04 95 37 12 15; www.festival-guitare-patrimonio.com) is the organising body behind this major cultural event, one of the highlights of the summer calendar in Corsica.

The event has gone on from humble beginnings to become a mainstay of the Corsican summer and has, with the support of the wine-making local mayor, also helped put the tiny Nebbio village of Patrimonio on the map as a cultural powerhouse – for a fortnight a year at least.

During the festival, proceedings get under way at 9.45pm each night as a diverse group of musicians takes the stage – from local jazz heroes to visiting Cuban salsa groups and many internationally known names along the way. The programme each year is deliberately as eclectic as it is geared to please the crowd – a mix of holidaying mainlanders and local culture vultures with a healthy dose of foreign tourists thrown in.

The action all takes place in the Théâtre de Verdure de Patrimonio and features an outdoor stage set in an atmospheric amphitheatre complete with menhir statues.

For those travelling with children, have no fear. The whole thing is a decidedly family-friendly affair with an easy-going atmosphere and plenty of stalls and snack kiosks doing a brisk trade. There's only one hitch: finding a parking space is no joke.

Tickets (€25 to €35) are available from selected music and bookshops across Corsica; contact the organising office for more details.

For something more special, **Les Jardins du Menhir** (☎ 04 95 37 01 11; route de l'église; menu €20) is a refined place set in the grounds of an old amphitheatre, and is owed by the local mayor's son. It's not the cheapest option but well worth splashing out – just for the setting alone. It's also the eatery closest to the festival grounds when the guitar festival is in full swing. Book well, and we mean *well*, ahead.

THE INLAND NEBBIO

A tour of the Nebbio's inland villages makes for an easy half-day's drive from St-Florent, and is a pleasant escape from the crowds of Corsica's least appealing resort town.

High up on the island's raised backbone, the **Col de Teghime** (536m) marks the midway point between Bastia and St-Florent with breathtaking views in both directions, as far as the island of Elba to the east and the Désert des Agriates to the west. The dizzying mountain pass is an essential part of the inland Nebbio trail.

About 10km from Bastia and just before the pass, however, there is a less compelling site: a large open-air rubbish tip covered with a carpet of birds. It's crying out for attention from the local authorities and has been doing so for longer than some care to remember.

More aesthetically pleasing is the summit of the **Sierra di Pigno** (961m), a moderate 4.5km climb from the pass road, with magnificent views over Cap Corse – despite the radio masts that increasingly obliterate the view out to sea.

Best known of the inland villages are the tiny hamlets of **Oletta** and **Poggio d'Oletta**, which cling to the hillside between St-Florent and Bastia, 9km to the south of Col de Teghime via the D38. The former is known for its artisan workshops, while the latter is dominated by the 18th-century Église de San Cervone. If it's not open, ask at the town hall for the key. At the northern entrance to Oletta, just off the D38, **L'Auberge A Magina** (☎ 04 95 39 01 01; d €40; menus €15) has great views across the Nebbio from its panoramic terrace dining room at sunset.

About 4km south of Oletta, the roundabout at the Col de San Stefano marks the edge of the **Défilé de Lancône**, where two roads overhang the narrow gorges: the D82 joins the N193 at Ortale, while the more spectacular D62 follows the contours over to Casatorra. The D62 is narrow, however, and becomes difficult if traffic is heavy, making this an accident black spot. If you're driving, take it slowly. This stretch of road already has too many statistics.

Murato, 5km southwest via the D305, is a larger village and, during Corsica's brief independence in the 18th century (p23), it was the seat of the mint in which the coins of the new state were struck. The village is also the birthplace of Giuseppe Fieschi and the father of Raúl Leoni (below).

The main claim to fame, however, is the Pisan **Église de San Michele de Murato** with its distinctive green and white hues. The white (chalk) came from St-Florent and the green (ophite) was taken from the bed of the nearby River Bevincu. The colours are laid out first in horizontal stripes, then in an irregular patchwork. It dates from around 1140, and local legend has it that the church was built in just one night by angels – they missed a bit.

If you're peckish, **Ferme-Auberge Campo di Monte** (☎ 04 95 39 03 68; menus €15) has a decent restaurant but no accommodation.

DÉSERT DES AGRIATES
Between St-Florent and the mouth of the Ostriconi river lie 30km of arid landscape known as the Désert des Agriates, with its low chalky mountains and a maquis so sun-scorched that even the plants seem rocklike.

It's hard to believe this area was once used to grow food for Genoa. Indeed, right up until the 20th century, life in the area was governed alternately by seasonal livestock-grazing and sowing. In October shepherds from the Nebbio highlands and the Vallée d'Asco would bring their goats and sheep down for the winter. In June farmers arriving by boat from Cap Corse would take over the area. The region was even once as famous for its olive groves as those of the Balagne villages (p118). The widespread use of écobuage (cultivation

on burnt stubble) and fires fanned by the prevailing winds are mainly to blame for transforming the once fertile soil into a stony, barren desert.

The 40km Agriate coast, by contrast to the nearby resort of St-Florent, offers spectacular back-to-nature scenery and a chance to escape the trashy designer-shades set swanking around the marina. The highlight of this Agriates region is undoubtedly the outstanding **Plage de Saleccia** – the setting for the film The Longest Day (1960) – which stretches for nearly 1km and ranks easily alongside the best of what any tropical island has to offer. The smaller but equally stunning **Plage de Loto** and **Plage de l'Ostriconi**, at the eastern and western edges of the Agriates region respectively, are also superb. Some partisans claim that the latter has the finest sand in all of Europe.

When various harebrained schemes were proposed to transform the desert in the 1970s – including building a Club Med–style holiday complex – the Conservatoire du Littoral stepped in to avert the disaster and bought the 5000-odd hectares of land. This, together with the adjoining common land, today makes up the protected natural site of the Désert des Agriates, managed by the **Syndicat Mixte Agriate** (Joint Agriate Association; ☎ 04 95 37 09 86; ☽ 9am-noon & 2-4pm Mon-Fri). Its office is on the D81 towards the hamlet of Casta. Staff here provide good information as they are charged with protecting this area of outstanding interest and beauty. They will advise visitors on walks suitable for their ability and also offer information on

THE PRESIDENT & THE TERRORIST
At the age of 58 Raúl Leoni was voted president of Venezuela in the December 1963 elections. His Murato-born father, Clément Leoni had left Bastia for Caracas at the age of 22 to try his luck in the South American republic about a decade before the future president was born there. Raúl Leoni made his first and only visit to Corsica in 1970, but father and son are both now heralded as symbols of successful Corsican migration. Leoni's opponent in the 1963 election, Arturo Uslar Pietri, a distinguished man of letters, was also of Corsican descent.

Born in Murato in 1790, Giuseppe Fieschi was yet another kind of émigré. A sometime shepherd, sometime solider, he organised an attempt on the life of the Orleanist citizen king of France, Louis-Philippe, and the royal family, during the fifth-anniversary celebration of the July 1830 revolution that overthrew the last Bourbon monarch, held in Paris. The daring assassination attempt failed but 19 people were killed and many more injured. Fieschi and his accomplices were condemned to death and they were executed a year later.

Fieschi is better remembered in Murato than Raúl Leoni is.

the local fauna, including a slew of bird, butterfly and plant species.

Plage de la Roya to Ostriconi Walk

The D81 is the only road that attempts to penetrate the desert, skirting its southern fringe en route to the resort town of Île Rousse. The brave – some would suggest downright foolish – can meander their way through the desert by sticking to the coastal path that starts at St-Florent's **Plage de la Roya**. This, however, is no easy walk and divides into three clear sections: St-Florent to **Saleccia** (five hours 30 minutes), Saleccia to **Ghignu** (two hours 45 minutes) and Ghignu to **Ostriconi** (six hours 30 minutes) in the far west.

The journey requires you to overnight en route, and you will have to avoid the searing midday sun by leaving at around 5am. Take a hat and *plenty* of water. Alternatively **St-Flo Quad** (☎ 06 18 66 10 94) offers half-/full-day quad-bike trips (€90/140), including lunch, drinks and fuel.

Sleeping & Eating

If you're desperate for some quality beach time away from the day-trippers, it is possible to overnight in the desert – but options are severely limited and camping on the beach itself is prohibited.

The pick of a fairly poor bunch is the **Relais de Saleccia** (☎ 04 95 37 14 60; d without/with terrace €45/50), located at Casta 12km west of St-Florent. Rooms are simple but at last the price includes your breakfast. The owners run a small restaurant next door with a good-value Corsican menu (€17.50) and rent mountain bikes.

Camping U Paradiso (☎ 04 95 37 82 51; sites/bungalows with half-board €12/40) is located at the end of the track that leads from Casta to the Plage de Saleccia, 12km from the D81. This track is only accessible by mountain bike or in a 4WD. It's pretty basic with only a handful of facilities, but at least the Plage de Saleccia is just about 100m from the entrance.

Village de l'Ostriconi (☎ 04 95 60 10 05; sites for 2 €18.60), on the western side of the D81 close to Plage de l'Ostriconi, has better camping facilities and rents functional bungalows with kitchenettes for four people (€400 per week). Bookings are essential.

Getting There & Away

BOAT

The most pleasant way of getting to the Plage du Loto jetty is by boat in an easy day-trip from St-Florent (p98).

BUS

Autocars Santini buses to Île Rousse (p118) run along the D81, skirting the fringe of the desert.

CAR

There are limited options for self-drive given the harsh nature of the local terrain. There are two roads that lead off from the D81 into the desert proper. Both about 12km long, one leads to Saleccia while the other terminates at Ghignu. Don't expect an easy ride. Both are suitable only for 4WDs as they're rough and very stony. What's more, these two rudimentary tracks are even worse when the rain has dug deep ruts in the ground that are then baked hard by the sun. Always ask advice on conditions before setting off – either your lodgings or the Syndicat Mixte Agriate (p101) are a good source of advice.

Calvi & the Balagne

CONTENTS

CALVI & THE BALAGNE

The Balagne area of Corsica has one of the island's largest micro-regions – that's why it's sometimes called the 'orchard of Corsica'. The landscape of the countryside has a certain gentleness to it that distinguishes it from the turbulence of so much of the island's other topography. The supremely fertile soil here supports citrus-fruit plantations and olive groves, making the inland Balagne area an important centre for the island's agricultural turnover.

Despite its rural heartland legacy, however, the Balagne was also one of the first regions on the island to open up to tourism and Calvi in particular has attracted large numbers of holiday-makers since between the two world wars. Today the coastline that runs from Calvi to Île Rousse has some of the best – but also sometimes the busiest – beaches in Corsica. These regions are packed with French and Italian tourists during the high season. Expect prices to be hiked, cafés to be crowded and standards of service to suffer during high season.

The small villages of the Balagne's interior area, meanwhile, are rich with artisans, local produce and breathtaking views. Even during the high season these tiny nooks and crannies are thankfully spared the full tourist onslaught. Indeed, if you have a car, this is one of the most rewarding areas of the island to visit.

HIGHLIGHTS

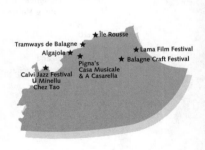

- **Dining**
  Sample some proper, traditional Corsican cooking at **U Minellu** (p112) along Calvi's blvd Wilson

- **Shopping**
  Follow the **Balagne craft trail** (p119) through the villages inland from Calvi

- **Go Glam**
  Dress up and enjoy the atmosphere on a posh night out at **Chez Tao** (p112) in Calvi's citadel

- **Escape the Crowds**
  Enjoy the chilled-out atmosphere in the unspoilt village of **Algajola** (p114)

- **Soak up Some Culture**
  Listen to the best of the best at the renowned jazz festival in **Calvi** (p110) or watch European films at the festival in **Lama** (p119)

- **Catch a Ride**
  Jump aboard the **Tramways de Balagne** (p113) for an unforgettable trip along the coastline

- **Time for a Quick Half**
  Enjoy a sundowner at A Casarella in the village of Pigna before heading for dinner at the nearby **Casa Musicale** (p123)

- **Get Sporty**
  Try a new water sport along the beach at **Île Rousse** (p115)

CALVI & THE BALAGNE

THE BALAGNE

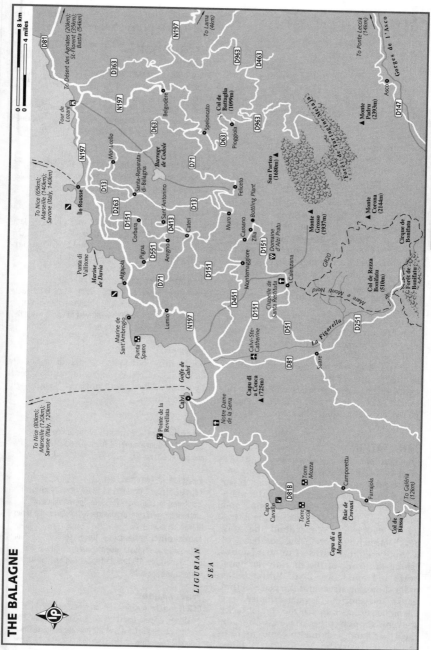

0 8 km
0 4 miles

LIGURIAN
SEA

To Nice (65km);
Marseille (140km);
Savone (Italy, 140km)

To Nice (80km);
Marseille (120km);
Savone (Italy, 120km)

To Désert des Agriates (20km); St-Florent (35km); Bastia (54km)

To Lama
(4km)

To Ponte Leccia
(14km)

Gorges de l'Asco

D81

N197

D363

N197

D963

D463

D147

Asco

Monte Padru
(2393m)

Tour de
Lozani

Monticello

Ile Rousse

Santa-Reparata-
di-Balagna

Belgodère

Spéloncato

Col de
Battaglia
(1099m)

D63

Pioggiola

D963

Forêt de Tartagine Melaja

San Parteo
(1680m)

Monte Grosso
(1937m)

Monte Corona
(2144m)

Punta di
Vallitone

Marine
de Davia

Corbara

Pigna

D551

Aregno

Caterì

Sant'Antonino

D413

Muro

Feliceto

Cassano

Zilia

Bottling Plant

Barrage
de Codole

D13

D71

Domaine
d'Alzi Pratu

Montemaggiore

Calenzana

Mare è Monti Nord

GR20

Col de Rezza
Bonifatu
(510m)

Cirque de
Bonifatu

Forêt de
Bonifatu

Algajola

Marine de
Sant'Ambrogio

Punta
Spano

Lumio

N197

D71

D451

D151

Chapelle de
Santa Restituda

Calvi-Ste-
Catherine

D51

La Figarella

D251

Golfe de Calvi

Pointe de la
Revellata

Calvi

Notre Dame
de la Serra

Capu di
a Conca
(725m)

Suare

D81

Capo Cavallo

Torre
Truccia

Torre
Mozza

D81B

Camporettu

Farrajola

Baie de
Crovani

Capu di a
Marsetta

Col de
Bassa

To Galéria
(12km)

CALVI & THE BALAGNE

CALVI

postcode 20260 / pop 5400

Calvi, the 'capital' of the Balagne region, is a thriving little town that stretches lazily along Calvi bay under the watchful eye of the local twin giants: the citadel and Monte Cinto (2706m). It is the island town closest to the Mediterranean coast of metropolitan France and, in many respects, resembles any number of the smaller towns along the French Riviera with a thriving café culture and a sandy strip of beach.

Calvi, accordingly, attracts more holidaymakers than any Corsican destination other than Porto Vecchio and the Ajaccio area. And, as such, some visitors may well turn up their noses at what they take to be just another tacky resort town. It's certainly not the cheapest place – a simple coffee can set you back an increasingly alarming sum as you move down the marina's strip of cafés stretching towards the citadel end of town – but as a tourist resort it serves its purpose well.

Calvi is a major access point for one of the more attractive parts of the island: the villages of the Balagne Interior (p118). So, if after a few days you are starting to feel Calvi too tacky, simply hire a car, or jump on the Tramways de Balagne (see boxed text p113), and get off the tourist track. Île Rousse (p115) and, in particular, Algajola (p114) are just a short hop away and far less crowded.

ORIENTATION

The citadel – also known as the upper town (*haute ville*) – is built on a promontory to the northeast of the lower town (*basse ville*); the latter provides the main thrust of the town's eating, sleeping and shopping options. The hub of the activity by day is centred around the long beach stretching out to the southeast of town. By night it transfers to quai Landry (along the front of the marina) for bars, beers and brasseries. Blvd Wilson is the main shopping street and the place to find banks and shops. The pedestrianised rue Clemenceau has more in the way of tacky souvenir shops but rue Alsace Lorraine, on the other hand, is home to some interesting artisan workshops and craft studios; the latter street is also now part of the cobblestone pedestrianised area.

INFORMATION

Bookshops

Maison de la Presse (☎ 04 95 65 17 43; ave de la République; ◷ 7am-10pm) A large range of French and foreign newspapers and magazines.

Black 'n' Blue (☎ 04 95 65 25 82; 20 blvd Wilson; ◷ 9am-7pm Mon-Sat, 9am-noon Sun in summer) Foreign-language books, guides, maps and a selection of Corsican CDs.

Internet Access

Café de l'Orient (☎ 04 95 65 00 16; 16 quai Landry; 1€ connection plus 0.10€ per min; ◷ 8am-2am) Water-side café with a set of computer terminals indoors.

Laundry

There are two **laundrettes** in town (◷ 8am-9pm; €5.5 per wash), one on blvd Wilson and the other in the car park of the Casino supermarket on ave Christophe Colomb.

Medical Services

Emergency Medical Centre (☎ 04 95 65 11 22; route du Stade; ◷ 24 hr) Essentially a branch of the hospital in Bastia; the centre is 250m southwest of the Auberge de Jeunesse BVJ Corsotel off route de Santore.

Money

Banks line blvd Wilson, including Société Générale, Crédit Agricole and Crédit Lyonnais. All of them have ATMs and will change money.

Post

Post office (cnr blvd Wilson & ave de la République; ◷ 8.30am-5pm Mon-Fri, 8.30am-noon Sat) Has an ATM and poste restante.

Tourist Information

Tourist office (☎ 04 95 65 16 67; www.tourisme.fr /calvi; port de Plaisance; ◷ 9am-8pm) A range of brochures is available, including a town plan and a series of walking maps (€6).

Tourist office annexe (◷ 10am-1pm & 2.30-5.30pm Mon-Sat Jun-Sep) Just inside the citadel; offers audio-guided tours (€6, 1½ hr). Staff speak English, Italian, German and Spanish.

Travel Agent

CCR (Corse Consignation et Représentation; ☎ 04 95 65 01 38; ◷ 8.50am-6pm Mon-Fri, 8.50am-noon Sat) The agent for ferries in Calvi is at the harbour opposite the Colombo Line office.

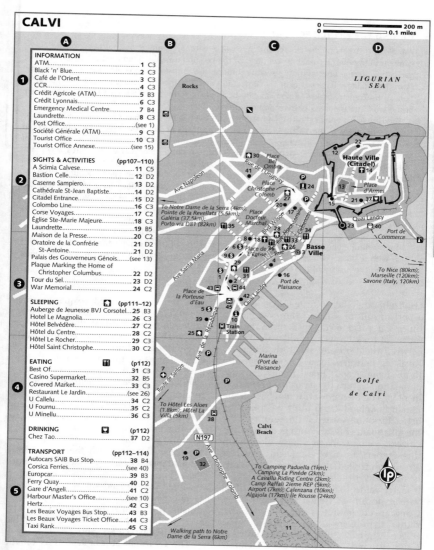

CALVI

| | 0 ————— 200 m |
| | 0 ————— 0.1 miles |

INFORMATION
ATM...**1** C3
Black 'n' Blue.............................**2** C3
Café de l'Orient..........................**3** C3
CCR...**4** C3
Crédit Agricole (ATM)................**5** B3
Crédit Lyonnais..........................**6** C3
Emergency Medical Centre........**7** B4
Laundrette..................................**8** C3
Post Office................................(see 1)
Société Générale (ATM).............**9** C3
Tourist Office...........................**10** C3
Tourist Office Annexe..............(see 15)

SIGHTS & ACTIVITIES   (pp107–110)
A Scimia Calvese.......................**11** C5
Bastion Celle............................**12** D2
Caserne Sampiero.....................**13** D2
Cathédrale St-Jean Baptiste......**14** D2
Citadel Entrance......................**15** D2
Colombo Line............................**16** C3
Corse Voyages..........................**17** C2
Église Ste-Marie Majeure..........**18** C3
Laundrette................................**19** B5
Maison de la Presse..................**20** C2
Oratoire de la Confrérie
   St-Antoine.............................**21** D2
Palais des Gouverneurs Génois.....(see 13)
Plaque Marking the Home of
   Christopher Columbus............**22** D2
Tour du Sel...............................**23** D2
War Memorial............................**24** C2

SLEEPING   [hotel icon] (pp111–12)
Auberge de Jeunesse BVJ Corsotel...**25** B3
Hotel Le Magnolia.....................**26** C3
Hôtel Belvédère.........................**27** C2
Hôtel du Centre.........................**28** C3
Hôtel Le Rocher........................**29** C3
Hôtel Saint Christophe...............**30** C2

EATING   [fork/knife icon] (p112)
Best Of.....................................**31** C3
Casino Supermarket...................**32** B5
Covered Market.........................**33** C3
Restaurant Le Jardin...............(see 26)
U Callelu..................................**34** C3
U Fournu..................................**35** C2
U Minellu.................................**36** C3

DRINKING   [glass icon] (p112)
Chez Tao..................................**37** D2

TRANSPORT   (pp112–114)
Autocars SAIB Bus Stop.............**38** B4
Corsica Ferries.......................(see 40)
Europcar..................................**39** B3
Ferry Quay................................**40** D2
Gare d'Angeli............................**41** C2
Harbour Master's Office...........(see 10)
Hertz..**42** C3
Les Beaux Voyages Bus Stop.......**43** B3
Les Beaux Voyages Ticket Office..**44** C3
Taxi Rank..................................**45** C3

SIGHTS
Citadel

Built at the end of the 15th century by the Genoese, Calvi's citadel still towers over the town from atop its 80m-high granite promontory. A handful of cafés and restaurants set out tables in the shadow of its ochre walls but, unlike its Bonifacio counterpart (p175),

it's not an integral part of the town and the majority of its buildings are closed to the public. Still, the citadel is definitely worth a visit for its peaceful atmosphere, its interesting religious edifices and the spectacular view it offers across the Golfe de Calvi.

It was in the 1st century AD that the Romans laid the foundations of the town of

JOINING THE FRENCH FOREIGN LEGION

Wander the streets of the citadel and you will eventually come across members of the 2ieme Régiment Étranger de Parachutistes (REP) of the Légion Étrangére. Identified by their distinctive garb, they are the ones cutting a swathe through the tourists and enjoying some off-duty time from their military base out near the airport in Calvi. These burly recruits are the latest incarnation of the French Foreign Legion, an elite body of crack troops for whom a tour of duty in one of the world's danger spots is second nature.

The Legion is a career choice that has been shrouded in mystery ever since King Louis Philippe founded the force in the 1830s. Many of the myths of the Legion now look rather outdated but there are two maxims that still hold true: anonymity is guaranteed and, in return for five years of service, soldiers can earn French citizenship – not to mention a decent wage. That's why many of today's recruits who put themselves through the notoriously challenging entrance exam hail from the war-torn Baltic States and disparate fragments of the former Soviet Republic.

The secretive nature of the force also persists although, since troops have recently seen action in Kosovo and Sierra Leone, these days they are trying to be more open with a public still fascinated by the romance of the Legion's legacy. Indeed Calvi's Camp Raffali opens its doors to the public twice yearly – late April and late September. The opening of their base affords a rare glimpse of the daily life of the 1000-odd legionnaires based in Calvi.

The April opening coincides with a major procession of the regiment through the streets of Calvi with recruits dressed in all their finery. Bizarrely, the parade celebrates one of the worst defeats in the history of the French military.

Calvi, although the Golfe de Calvi had been a port of call for sailors from even earlier times. Later laid to ruin by Saracen raiders, Calvi got back on its feet under the Pisans between the 11th and the 13th centuries. Rivalries between local lords, especially those from Cap Corse, finally led the population to turn to Genoa for protection in 1278. The then powerful republic on the Italian mainland could not have asked for better luck and wasted no time in turning the inhabitants of Calvi into good Genoese citizens. Using Calvi as a base, along with the southern town of Bonifacio (which it already controlled), Genoa was able to exert its power over the rest of the island.

Calvi came to be so utterly identified with its loyalty to Genoa that many other Corsican communities considered Calvi, rather than Genoa, the oppressor. The finger is, in fact, still sometimes pointed at Calvi, even today. It was under the Genoese influence, however, that the citadel was built in Calvi and fortified against the outside world. Over the centuries of Genoese overlordship, Calvi would nevertheless be put sorely to the test.

In the mid-16th century Corsica got caught up in the rivalry between Henri II of France and Charles V of Spain (king of Spain and also holy Roman emperor). In 1553 France dispatched a squadron made up of French troops and Turkish forces under the command of the Turkish privateer Dragut. This fleet captured Bastia, St-Florent and Bonifacio but failed to take Calvi. It was on this occasion that Genoa gave the town its motto in recognition: *Civitas Calvi Semper Fidelis* (City of Calvi forever faithful). Today, crossing place Christophe Colomb, you reach the citadel through a porch over which the town motto remains inscribed.

From here little alleyways then lead to the place d'Armes, with the former **Palais des Gouverneurs Génois** (Genoese Governors' Palace) on the left. This imposing building, renamed **Caserne Sampiero**, was built by the Genoese in the 13th century and extended during the 16th; it now houses the barracks and mess hall for the French Foreign Legion (see boxed text above).

The **Cathédrale St-Jean Baptiste** is on the other side of the place d'Armes, halfway up a little alley. Built in the shape of a cross, this 13th-century church narrowly escaped complete destruction when an adjacent powder store exploded in 1567; it was rebuilt and consecrated as a cathedral in 1576. The dome is superb and the interior boasts a high altar of polychrome marble dating from the 17th century, to the right of which is the *Christ des Miracles*. This ebony statue has been venerated since the town was besieged in 1553. According to legend, the ships of the besieging forces simply sailed back out to sea after the population of Calvi carried the statue in a procession through their streets. The *Vierge du Rosaire* (Virgin of the Rosary), a large statue also in this church, has three different robes: a black one for Good Friday, a purple one for the Wednesday after Palm Sunday and a rich brocade one for use in processions. The space is now often used to host polyphony singing (p32) evenings in summer.

If you retrace your steps to the place d'Armes and take a little street to the left, you will come to the **Oratoire de la Confrérie St-Antoine** (Oratory of the St Antoine Brotherhood), a charitable institution that has been active in Corsica since the 14th century. Behind the ornate façade of the building, which features a slate lintel depicting the abbot St Antoine, are walls covered in frescoes from the 15th and 16th centuries (some badly timeworn, unfortunately) and an ivory Christ attributed to the Florentine sculptor Jacopo d'Antonio Tati, known as *Le Sansevino*.

The citadel has five **bastions**, erected one after another and now providing wonderful views. These were formally used as lookouts for invading forces. One of the most famous attacks on the citadel came in 1794 when the town, which Genoa had ceded to France in 1764, came under attack from the British army and separatist forces led by Pascal Paoli. It was heavily bombarded and largely destroyed during the fighting – a battle that also cost Admiral Horatio Nelson the use of his right eye. Following the onslaught, Calvi eventually capitulated and ceded to the combined forces. The Anglo-Corsican kingdom was short-lived, however, and Calvi returned to French control in 1796.

To the north-west is the **Bastion Celle**, flanked by a stone sentry box suspended over the ramparts to keep an eye on the surroundings. Nearby is a marble plaque marking the alleged birthplace of Christopher Columbus (see boxed text below). At the far end of the ferry quay, and standing under the shadow of the citadel, the **Tour de sel** is a medieval lookout tower.

Église Ste-Marie Majeure

Behind the pink exterior of the Baroque Église Ste-Marie Majeure, at the very heart

CALVI & THE BALAGNE

A CALVIAN CALLED COLUMBUS?

Today an ancient house in the Calvi citadel still bears a **plaque** attesting to the birth therein of the obsessed explorer credited with the discovery of the New World. A little 72-page book, *Christophe Colomb, Corse*, written by Joseph Chiara and available from the Calvi tourist office (but only in French, regrettably), makes the case for Columbus' Calvian birth.

Roger Caratini, however, in his masterly *Histoire du Peuple Corse* (1995), mocks the Corsican 'amateur historians' who have made 'dogma' of Columbus' Calvian origins. All serious scholars and documents agree, Caratini asserts, that Columbus was the son of a Genoese weaver; the person first to argue the case for Columbus' birth in Calvi, in the mid-19th century, was a 'credulous churchman'.

But Chiara believes that Columbus' birth in Genoa (distinct from his undisputed Genoese 'citizenship') will itself never be more than a hypothesis. He suggests that when Columbus went looking for underwriting at the Spanish court, he could not very well admit to being of Calvian origin because the Calvians had massacred a Spanish garrison, thus putting an end to Spanish ambitions in Corsica, in 1521. Chiara's arguments, supported by reference to Columbus' name and own recorded use of language, have irresistible romantic appeal.

Moreover, there's actually something at stake for Corsica in the dispute. If Corsica gave the world Napoleon but not Columbus, well, maybe it was just chance. If Corsica gave the world both Napoleon *and* Columbus, then there begins to be a pattern, which could be seen to indicate an inherent Corsican desire to dream more boldly and travel further than other ethnic groups. It remains true that wherever Columbus himself was born, numerous Calvians figured in his crews, and by the mid-16th century Calvians were living in the New World in numbers out of all proportion to the Corsican population.

of the lower town, is an impressive domed ceiling. Built between 1765 and 1838, it stands as testimony to the rapid growth of the lower town during this era. The church houses 16th- and 18th-century paintings and a statue of the Assumption that is carried through the town every year during the Assumption Day procession at the end of August.

ACTIVITIES
Beaches
The beach in Calvi stretches 4km from the marina along the bay to the east. To get to it by foot from the town centre, simply follow ave Christophe Colomb south. After the Casino supermarket, a path branches off to the left, leading directly down to the beach.

The Tramways de Balagne railway (p113) links Calvi to a series of smaller and often more charming beaches that pepper the coast all the way through Algajola and onto Île Rousse.

Boat Trips
Between April and October **Colombo Line** (☎ 04 95 65 32 10; www.colombo-line.com) organises excursions in glass-bottomed boats from its kiosk-style office right on the harbour. The trips are dependent on having good weather so check and reserve your place in advance for departures. Children aged four to 10 pay half-price; children under four go free. There are three tours to choose from:
Tour 1 Departs Calvi daily at 9.15am and sails via the Réserve Naturelle de Scandola and Girolata, returning to Calvi by 3pm (€50).
Tour 2 Departs Calvi daily at 2.30pm and sails via the Réserve Naturelle de Scandola, returning to Calvi by 5.15pm (€40).
Tour 3 Departs Calvi twice-weekly at 9am and sails via the Réserve Naturelle de Scandola and Ajaccio, returning to Calvi by 5.15pm (€65).

CALVI FOR CHILDREN
The adventure sports company **Altore** (☎ 06 83 39 69 06; www.altore.com), to the east of Calvi along the D151 between Montemaggiore and Cateri, offers a range of both summer and winter sporting activities from paragliding to cross-country skiing. Their latest attraction, however, is **A Scimia Calvese** (adult/child €15/12; ☺ 10am to 6pm Wed, Sat & Sun May–Oct), an elevated 700m-long structure of bridges,

ladders, beams, logs, pulleys and cables that you negotiate from end to end. It's located in La Pinède, a pine wood at the southern end of the beach; a harness is provided.

A Cavallu Riding Centre (☎ 04 95 65 22 22; http://acavallu.online.fr) offers trail rides and lessons (€18 per hour) 2km from the centre of town along the N197 in the direction of the airport.

TOURS
Les Beaux Voyages (☎ 04 95 65 11 35; www.lesbeaux voyages.com; résidence le Vieux Chalet; ☺ 9am-noon & 2-7pm Mon-Sat) acts as the ticket agent for bus and ferry tickets and offers coach trips from Calvi. The various trips include:
Fôret de Bonifato (half-day €10; departs Mon 2.30pm)
Cap Corse (full-day €26; departs Tue 7am)
Villages of the Balagne (half-day €13; departs Wed & Fri 2.30pm)
Maquis circuit (full-day €26; departs Thu 7am)
Corse Voyages (☎ 04 95 65 00 47; blvd Wilson; ☺ 9am-noon & 2-7pm Mon-Sat), in conjunction with Autocars Mariani, organises a similar set of excursions with very similar prices; its tours run on different days, however, so if one operator's tour is full for the day, simply try the other one (for another day). Both companies offer reduced fares for children.

FESTIVALS & EVENTS
Calvi hosts a range of festivals with the majority crammed into the sun-drenched and tourist-dominated summer months; check with the tourist office (p106) for the latest details.
La Passion (☎ 04 95 65 23 57; late Mar-early Apr) A major Corsican-language event during Holy Week retracing the Passion of Christ.
Processions de la Semaine Sainte (late Mar-early Apr) Fervent Holy Week celebrations.
St-Érasme (2 Jun) The blessing of the fishing boats.
Rencontres d'Art Contemporain (☎ 04 95 65 16 67; mid-Jun–mid-Sep) Works by contemporary painters and sculptors are exhibited in the citadel throughout the summer months.
Calvi Jazz Festival (☎ 04 95 65 00 50; last wk Jun) Open-air and indoor concerts plus a range of jam sessions featuring big names from the international jazz scene.
Rencontres de Chants Polyphoniques (☎ 04 95 65 16 67; mid-Sep) Festival of polyphonic musical expression (p32) held at various venues in the citadel.
Festival du Vent (☎ 01 53 20 93 00; www.lefestivaldu vent.com; late Oct) An annual festival celebrating the role

of the wind in the arts, science and sport to round off the end of the tourist season.

SLEEPING

Calvi has a comparatively decent range of accommodation options that includes one of Corsica's few actual youth hostels and some of the island's most exclusive hotels. In high season, however, advance booking is recommended. The best of the accommodation is actually to be found outside of the town centre itself.

Budget

Auberge de Jeunesse BVJ Corsotel (☎ 04 95 65 14 15; ave de la République; dm €22) This auberge has clearly seen better days, but for the price, and with breakfast thrown in, it remains the best-value option in town – especially if you're travelling on your own during high season. Indeed, it's one of the few youth hostel-style establishments of its kind on the whole island. The rooms are simple and dormitory-style with bunks for up to eight people per room and slightly mouldy shared bathrooms. You don't have to belong to an affiliated youth hostel network to stay here but it's worth knowing that the reception opens 7.30am–1pm and 5–10pm – if you miss it, there's nowhere to leave your bag securely.

Hôtel du Centre (☎ 04 95 65 02 01; 14 rue Alsace Lorraine; d/tr with shower €42/50) Converted from an old prison, this cheap but cheerful place still has a rather cell-like feel with its stark and gloomy rooms. Thankfully the owner's friendly welcome helps to compensate. It also represents better value than the *auberge de jeunesse*, if you are happy to share larger rooms; two-person studios are also available (€320 per week). The reception opens 8am–9pm.

Other recommendations:

Camping La Pinède (☎ 04 95 65 17 80; €19) A useful site with a good range of facilities about 1.5km south of the town centre and close to the beach; it's also possible to hire caravans (€200-320 per week).

Camping Paduella (☎ 04 95 65 06 16; €17) This is the nearest campground to town but facilities are basic.

Mid-Range

Hôtel Les Aloes (☎ 04 95 65 01 46; www.hotel-les -aloes.com; d with sea/garden view €58/50; P) About 2km west of the train station in a quiet residential area, this is the best mid-range

option. It's far superior to anything in town, however, with nicely furnished rooms, a large breezy terrace for breakfast (€6) and some nice retro kitsch design flourishes. It's also a quiet spot for couples seeking some quality time away. You will really want your own car to get here – it's quite a walk in the sun.

Hôtel Le Magnolia (☎ 04 95 65 19 16; rue Alsace Lorraine; d with half board €150; P) Back in town, this is the best option for those preferring accommodation right in the heart of the action. Converted from a 19th-century mansion and overlooking a vine-shrouded garden, this is charming spot – albeit a little pricey for what you get. Rooms are smart and comfortable, although single travellers face a hefty single supplement. The adjoining restaurant, **Le Jardin** (☎ 04 95 65 08 02; menus €23/35), serves good, wholesome Corsican food with a nod towards *haute cuisine*.

Hôtel Belvédère (☎ 04 95 65 01 25; www.resa -hotels-calvi.com; place Christophe Colomb; d/tr €115/130;) Looking fresh after a refit, this central hotel has small but comfortable rooms. The breakfast is served on an outdoor terrace but isn't really worth the extra €6.50 per person per day. Better to grab a *pain au chocolate* at a nearby patisserie.

Hôtel Le Rocher (☎ 04 95 65 20 04; www.visit corse.com/lerocher; blvd Wilson; d/tr/qd €173.50/209.50/ 245; P) This hotel, opposite the post office, has smart, newly refitted rooms. The staple continental-style breakfast is included in the price but, at those rates, you'd really expect a bit more than a croissant first thing in the morning.

Top End

Hôtel La Villa (☎ 04 95 65 10 10; www.hotel-lavilla.com; 2-person villa/ste from €300/560; P) One of Corsica's few four-star properties, this is a seriously luxurious experience for the seriously loaded visitor. It's 5km west of town in a secluded location and the raft of in-house facilities includes four pools, a beach club with its own water-sports equipment and a Michelin-starred restaurant. If rubbing shoulders with holidaying French film stars and Italian politicians is your thing, then you'll love it.

Hôtel Saint Christophe (☎ 04 95 65 05 74; www .hotel-saint-christophe.com; place Bel'Ombra; d with sea view/half board €155/195, f with sea view/half board €211/ 265; P) The big resort hotel in town is a family-friendly place and blessed with a good range of facilities, including a nice swimming pool with its own terrace's snack bar. However, this place tends to be rather dominated by package tours in summer and it does feel a little soulless overall. As a result, although it's a good spot to catch up on a few home comforts, there is really very little here to remind you that you're actually in Corsica.

EATING

Pizzerias and restaurants offering traditional Corsican *menus* abound but only a few are genuinely worth seeking out as many seem to cater solely to the transient tourist Euro that doesn't know its *fiadone* from its *eau de vie*. This scenario particularly holds true along the strip of eateries lining quai Landry and rue Clemenceau. The area around blvd Wilson, however, has a few hidden gems well worth seeking out.

Budget

For a quick snack on the run, **Best Of** (☎ 04 95 65 06 82; 1 rue Clemenceau; ⊗ 11am-late) has a good range of sandwiches (€3-7).

The **covered market** (⊗ 8am-noon Mon-Sat), situated along rue Alsace Lorraine heading towards the citadel from Église Ste-Marie Majeure, has some excellent fresh produce and local Corsican goods. It's a great place for some mouth-watering browsing and, if your French is up to it, talking your way into a little tasting session. The large and very well-stocked **Casino supermarket** (ave Christophe Colomb; ⊗ 8.30am-8.30pm Mon-Sat), south of the train station, caters for self-caterers' needs comprehensively.

Mid-Range & Top End

U Minellu (☎ 04 95 65 05 52; traverse de l'Église; menu Corse €16) This is the pick of the local eateries for some genuine Corsican fare; it's a traditional place with a good-value menu and a decent range of local AOC Corsican wines. This is one place where you feel you are genuinely eating like a Corsican and the setting is superb with meals served on a covered terrace overlooking Église Ste-Marie Majeure. This place attracts locals and tourists in equal numbers; as you would expect, the food really is top-notch. Unbeatable.

U Fournu (☎ 04 95 65 27 60; menus €16/20) Raised above blvd Wilson on a shady terrace, this little eatery also has a good line in genuine Corsican fare. If you're not peckish enough for the set *menus*, there's a good choice of mains (€16-20). It's also a shady little spot for lunch on a summer's day.

If you're prepared to splash the cash and head for the harbour, **U Callelu** (☎ 04 95 65 22 18; quai Landry; menus €20) is the best bet and well known for its fresh fish dishes.

DRINKING & ENTERTAINMENT

The hottest spot in town – and the place to spot any passing celebrities who just happen to be in the area – is **Chez Tao** (☎ 04 95 65 00 73; rue St-Antoine; ⊗ 11pm-5am May-Oct). Actually located within the citadel walls, this opulent nightspot has become a Corsican institution over its long years of indulging the whims of the glitterati. The lavishly decorated venue was conceived by Tao Kanbey de Kerekoff, who served in a White Cavalry regiment during the Crimea War and then, defeated in battle, headed west to seek fame, fortune and a nice little bolthole for a quiet half.

Having found his way to Corsica, he fell in love with the citadel, acquired what was once the palace of the bishops of Sagone and, in 1935, opened Corsica's first ever cabaret club. The venue has been passed down through the generations onto his children, who continue to run it in the spirit of Monsieur Tao's legacy. These days it is best known as a piano bar (drinks from €12, champagne from €150 for the high rollers), but it also doubles as a restaurant with a wonderful view over the bay – at a price, of course (count on from €40 a head).

There are also a few open-air discos along the N197 heading out of town but they're the usual disappointing school disco fare. Think teenage clientele, overpriced drinks and very, very bad French rock. Don't do it.

GETTING THERE & AWAY
Air

Calvi-Ste-Catherine airport (☎ 04 95 65 88 88) is 7km southwest of town. There are no ATM or *bureau de change* facilities available at the airport. Calvi has earned a reputation as a bit of a problem airport in that, as the runways are so close to the mountains, when winds are high, flights have a habit of being redirected to Bastia – a good few hours away by train or bus.

Boat

La Méridionale (CMN; ☎ 04 95 55 25 55; www.cmn.fr; low/high season €30/41; 3hrs) has daily connections to Nice.

Corsica Ferries (☎ 04 95 32 95 95; www.corsica ferries.com) also has daily services to Nice (low/ high season €20/32; 3hrs) and Savona (day, low/high season €16/31; night €21/31; 3-6hrs). Corsica Ferries sells tickets in Calvi through Les Beaux Voyages (p110) and has a ticket office at the ferry quay. For more information on ferry crossings, see the Transport chapter (p235).

The **harbour master's office** (☎ 04 95 65 10 60; ⏰ 7.30am-9pm) is beneath the tourist office.

Bus

Les Beaux Voyages (☎ 04 95 65 11 35; résidence le Vieux Chalet; www.lesbeauxvoyages.com) runs buses Monday to Friday from Calvi to Bastia (€12.50, 1½ hours), Île Rousse (€3.50, 30 minutes), Ponte Leccia (€8, one hour). In July and August the company also runs buses daily Monday to Saturday to Galéria (€5.30/6.10 without/with baggage, 45 minutes) and twice daily Monday to Saturday to Calenzana (€4.60/5.30 without/with baggage, 20 minutes). Buses leave across the road from their offices on place Porteuse d'Eau.

In summer **Autocars SAIB** (☎ 04 95 22 41 99) runs buses daily from Calvi to Porto via Col de la Croix, where the footpath for Girolata starts (see boxed text p132). Buses leaves from opposite the Casino supermarket at 3.30pm (€16, 2½ hours) during summer only.

Car

At the airport:
Avis (☎ 04 95 65 88 38)
Budget (☎ 04 95 65 36 67)
Europcar (☎ 04 95 65 10 19)
Hertz (☎ 04 95 65 02 96)

In town:
Hertz (☎ 04 95 65 06 64; place de la Porteuse d'Eau; ⏰ 8am-8pm Mon-Sat)
Europcar (☎ 04 95 65 10 19; ave de la République; ⏰ 8am-1pm & 2.30-7.30pm Mon-Sat) Located 50m north of the Auberge de Jeunesse BVJ Corsotel.

Train

From Calvi's **train station** (☎ 04 95 65 00 61; ave de la République) there are four departures daily to Ajaccio (€20.50, five hours), Bastia (€13.40, three hours) and Corte (€11.20, three hours); all journeys require a change at Ponte Leccia.

GETTING AROUND

Calvi itself is easily navigable on foot and the beach can be reached on foot from the town centre.

To/From the Airport

There is no public transport to or from the airport other than taxis (see below). A taxi

---

THE TRAMWAYS DE BALAGNE

Every year the spectacular beaches and hidden coves of the Balagne coastline suddenly come to life with the first tourist's beach towel of the summer season. The lifeline that connects these isolated coves is the Tramways de Balagne, an offshoot of the **Chemins de Fer de la Corse** (www .ter-sncf.com; p241).

This bone-shaking little engine trundles between Calvi and Île Rousse every day in summer, stopping at up to 18 stations en route between 6am and 6.40pm. Even today many of these stops are request-only with bronzed groups of bathers and hikers popping out from behind a rock to hail the iron horse as she chugs slowly by. Someone will come around during the trip to collect the fare and make a note of where you want to get off.

Like much in Corsica, there has been talk of improving the rail system for many years but, so far, little has changed. And while Le Micheline, the main train that plies the route from Bastia to Ajaccio, is most likely to receive the first benefits of any make-over work, the Tramways de Balagne is a low priority on the list for refurbishment. Perversely, however, it's exactly this uniquely lo-fi quality that is the main source of its charm. Indeed, rail enthusiasts from all over the world now converge on Calvi to ride the Tramways de Balagne before she is finally put out to pasture.

The one-way fare from Calvi to Île Rousse is €7.60 (45 minutes); if you're likely to be making multiple journeys, such as return day-trips from Calvi to the Balagne beaches, consider buying a *carnet* of tickets (€8).

---

from the airport to the centre of town costs day/night €12/17.

Bicycle
Gare d'Angeli (☎ 04 95 65 02 13; place Christophe Colomb; 1/2/7 days €17/32/94) rents mountain bikes.

Taxi
There's a **taxi rank** (☎ 04 95 65 30 36) on place de la Porteuse d'Eau. Taxis run excursions for two to four people to the Forêt de Bonifatu (€35), Galéria (€55) and Calenzana (€23).

AROUND CALVI

POINTE DE LA REVELLATA
This outcrop of land, just 3km west across the sea from Calvi's citadel quarter, offers a little foretaste of the still wilder and more beautiful coastline that lies beyond Calvi along the west coast (see boxed text below).

There's a sandy beach here and a slew of tiny coves that are frequently lapped by turquoise waters but, quite frankly, little else. The D81B (towards Galéria and Porto) will get you so far but, after you reach the footpath down to the cape, the choice is

---

DRIVING FROM CALVI TO PORTO

The D81 between Calvi and Porto (known as the D81B as far as Galéria) traverses some spectacular coastal scenery before plunging into the Parc Naturel Régional de Corse (PNRC).

If you're driving and not accustomed to this kind of road you'll probably be too busy avoiding a premature date with your maker to enjoy the view. The switchback bends are unrelenting and rock falls common, while the tarmac has been patched up again and again but is still ridden with unexpected cavities.

Indeed, the narrowness of the road surface makes passing other vehicles – not those in your own lane but those coming *at* you – a nerve-racking game of chicken. This is definitely not a road trip for the faint hearted and not a journey that is easily forgotten.

---

either on foot or by mountain bike only. In dry weather, however, a 4WD could just about make it.

NOTRE DAME DE LA SERRA
Five centuries old, this tiny chapel stands on a wild and windswept hill, situated 1.5km down a trail from the D81B. To get there turn left away from the sea at the point where the track branches off towards Pointe de la Revellata (left).

A statue of a shrouded Virgin Mary can be seen here gazing out over the Golfe de Calvi in silent contemplation. The chapel makes for an easy afternoon hike and a welcome escape from the tourist throng crowding the streets of Calvi.

ALGAJOLA
postcode 20220 / pop 250
This charming and pleasantly sleepy little town, roughly half way between Île Rousse and Calvi along the Balagne coastline, remains one of the few relatively unspoilt places in Haute Corse. It does attract its fair share of tourists in high season with people flocking to its long sandy beach (150m east of the tourist office), but, although Algajola has all the facilities you could ever need, it retains a sense of calm and tranquillity long since lost in most Corsican resorts.

All in all, Algajola makes for a great little base from which to explore the Balagne region and an ideal spot to dodge the crowds of its neighbours, Calvi (p106) and Île Rousse (p115).

Facilities include a **laundry** (7am-11pm; wash/dry €5.30/2) and a **post office** (9am-noon, 2-6pm Mon-Fri, 9am-noon Sat), 50m east of the tourist office. Speaking of which, the small but friendly **tourist office** (☎ 04 95 62 78 32; 10am-noon, 2.30-6.30pm) is 100m east of the train station.

Sleeping
Hôtel-Restaurant Stella Mare (☎ 04 95 60 71 18; www.hotel-stellamare.com; d without/with half-board, compulsory in August, €88/140; P) A very smart and comfortable two-star property with recently renovated, spacious rooms and a tranquil location. There are great sea views from the terrace where a buffet breakfast (€7) and evening sundowners are served. The owners can advise on local activities and walking trails, while there are plans

currently afoot to add an on-site sauna and spa for future seasons.

L'Esquinade (☎ 04 95 60 70 19; s/d €50/68) This simple, clean little place right next to the post office is the best budget option and the best bet for single travellers. Ask for a room overlooking the garden for the best views and you'll wake up to church bells and a superb Mediterranean vista. All rooms have bathrooms while the bar downstairs is a friendly spot for a snack. This is where breakfast (optional, €5) is served.

Hôtel Beau Rivage (☎ 04 95 60 73 99; www.hotel -beau-rivage.com; d without/with half-board, compulsory in summer, €58/69; P) Right on the beach, this large, family-run operation has clean but unremarkable rooms with small balconies. Single travellers pay a hefty €23 single supplement but a third person sharing pays only €21 extra. The owners also let well-equipped, self-contained apartments for up to four people in a nearby annexe on a weekly basis (€650).

Eating

U Fournu (pizzas/salads €7/7) is the local homely little pizzeria. There's a sunny terrace, a range of good-value eat-in or take-away pizzas and a decent wine list featuring some local AOC wines. It opens for lunch and dinner in summer.

La Veille Cave (☎ 04 95 60 70 09; menus €16-22; ✹ closed Mon lunch) is the pick of the mid-range options with pizzas, seafood and the usual gamut of Corsican staples, all served in a picturesque, red-hued square.

Self-caterers should head for the **Super Service shop** (✹ 8am-12.30pm, 4-7.30pm), opposite the post office.

Getting There & Away

In summer the Tramways de Balagne (p113) links Algajola with Île Rousse (€1.60, 15 minutes) and Calvi (€2, 30 minutes). There are up to 12 trains daily in summer.

ÎLE ROUSSE (ISULA ROSSA)

postcode 20220 / pop 2700

Compared to tacky St-Florent or tourist-trap Calvi, Île Rousse feels a lot more like how a typical Corsican beach resort should be: sun-kissed by day, mellow by night. It's more relaxed, easy to navigate and home to more than its fair share of little places to while away the time.

With its long sandy beach and string of beach-side cafés, plus a slew of ferry arrivals in summer maintaining strong links with mainland France, it's more than a little ironic that the omnipresent Pascal Paoli (p24) originally founded the town as a centre of Corsican nationalism. If he knew how his vision for a utopia had become a tourist resort for well-to-do outta-towners, he would probably be spinning in his grave.

Orientation

Paoli's efforts in shaping Île Rousse were rewarded with a large **statue** in – wait for it – place Paoli, now the social hub of town with its café society. It's also the place to hunt for bargains at the Sunday morning flea market.

Immediately north of place Paoli is the covered market and the town's primary dining and shopping area. The ferry quay is on the Pietra peninsula, 500m north of the train station, which marks the western limit of the town, while the beach runs east along the Promenade A Marinella.

Information
BOOKSHOPS
Maison de la Presse (ave Piccioni; ✹ 7am-8.30pm) Books, maps and foreign-language publications.

INTERNET ACCESS
Cyber One Café (15b ave Paul Doumer; €3 per hour; ✹ 10am-2am Mon-Sat, 3pm-2am Sun) 300m west of the post office.
Movie Store Cyber (€3 per hour; ✹ 10am-2am Mon-Sat, 3pm-2am Sun) Inside a video shop at the start of the N197, heading southwest out of town.

LAUNDRY
The local **laundry** (✹ 7am-midnight; wash/dry €5.30/ 2) is just south of L'Ostéria, on the corner of rue Napoléon.

MEDICAL SERVICES
The nearest hospital is 27km away in Calvi; check the tourist office for details of local doctors on call.

MONEY
Société Générale (ave Piccioni; ✹ 9-11am & 2-4pm) Offers ATM and currency exchange facilities.
Crédit Agricole (ave Paul Doumer; ✹ 9-11am & 2-4pm) ATM and currency exchange, next to the Casino supermarket.

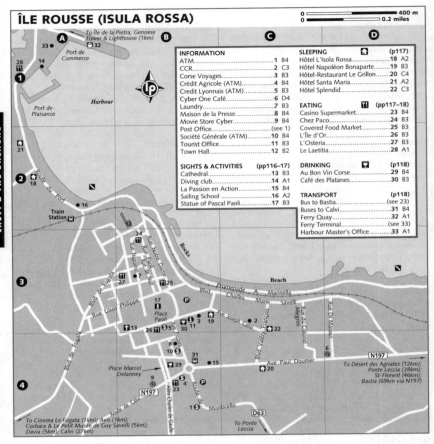

ÎLE ROUSSE (ISULA ROSSA)

INFORMATION		
ATM	1	B4
CCR	2	C3
Corse Voyages	3	B3
Crédit Agricole (ATM)	4	B4
Credit Lyonnais (ATM)	5	B3
Cyber One Café	6	D4
Laundry	7	B3
Maison de la Presse	8	B4
Movie Store Cyber	9	B4
Post Office	(see 1)	
Société Générale (ATM)	10	B4
Tourist Office	11	B3
Town Hall	12	B2

SIGHTS & ACTIVITIES	(pp116–17)	
Cathedral	13	B3
Diving club	14	A1
La Passion en Action	15	B4
Sailing School	16	A2
Statue of Pascal Paoli	17	B3

SLEEPING		(p117)
Hôtel L'Isola Rossa	18	A2
Hôtel Napoléon Bonaparte	19	B3
Hôtel-Restaurant Le Grillon	20	C4
Hôtel Santa Maria	21	A2
Hôtel Splendid	22	C3

EATING		(pp117–18)
Casino Supermarket	23	B4
Chez Paco	24	B3
Covered Food Market	25	B3
L'Île d'Or	26	B3
L'Osteria	27	B3
Le Laetitia	28	A1

DRINKING		(p118)
Au Bon Vin Corse	29	B4
Café des Platanes	30	B3

TRANSPORT		(p118)
Bus to Bastia	(see 23)	
Buses to Calvi	31	B4
Ferry Quay	32	A1
Ferry Terminal	(see 33)	
Harbour Master's Office	33	A1

Crédit Lyonnais (place Paoli; ⊗ 9-11am & 2-4pm) ATM and currency exchange.

POST
Post office (route de Monticello; ⊗ 8.30am-3pm Mon-Fri, 8.30am-noon Sat) ATM but no currency exchange, 50m south of the Calvi bus stop.

TOURIST INFORMATION
Tourist office (☎ 04 95 60 04 35; www.ot-ile-rousse.fr; place Paoli; ⊗ 9am-7pm Mon-Sat, 10am-6pm Sun) Small but helpful with a full range of maps and brochures. The office has plans to move for future seasons to a location right on the seafront – watch this space.

TRAVEL AGENCIES
CCR (Corse Consignation et Représentation; ☎ 04 95 60 09 56; ave Joseph Calizi; ⊗ 9am-noon & 2.30-6pm Mon-Fri, 8.30am-noon Sat) Agent for ferry tickets to and from Corsica.

Corse Voyages (☎ 04 95 60 11 19; place Paoli; ⊗ 9am-12.30pm & 2.30-7pm Mon-Fri) Agents for ferry tickets to and from Corsica.

Festivals & Events
Festivoce (☎ 04 95 61 77 81), held in July, is a festival of music and song in the Balagne, along the stretch from Île Rousse to Calvi.

Sights
The beach is the main draw around these parts and its long strip of sand is very busy during summer.

There are always a few hardy souls walking out to the Île de la Pietra, 1km west of the train station, where there is a **Genoese tower** and a lighthouse.

Five kilometres from Île Rousse in the tiny village of Corbara, **Le Petit Musée de Guy Savelli** (☎ 04 95 60 06 65; place de l'Église; free but donations welcome; ☼ 3-6pm) is a small but impressive little museum of Corsican historical artefacts and is a veritable treasure trove. The art historian owner, Guy Savelli, has devoted 40 years of his life to building up a collection of over 50,000 items, having first become interested in researching and restoring *objets d'art* as they were collected for the family home by his grandfather.

Some of his most prized possessions include a book of Corsican history written in 1594; an original of a book written by Boswell, dating from 1769, that tells the story of his voyage to France and his meeting with Pascal Paoli; and a set of 18th-century postcards. The exhibits sprawl across several rooms and each piece, lovingly collated and researched by Monsieur Savelli, has its own unique story to tell.

Most of all, he treasures a set of fighting knives. 'In the old days, even the women used to carry these knives – it was for protection,' says Savelli ominously.

Activities

For water sports, the western edge of town is home to the local Île Rousse **diving club** (☎ 04 95 60 36 85) and **sailing school** (☎ 04 95 60 36 85). **La Passion en Action** (☎ 04 95 60 15 76; ave Paul Doumer; ☼ 7am-8pm) rents mountain bikes for €16/77 a day/week.

Sleeping

For a small town, Île Rousse has some good options for all budgets, many of them a mere stone's throw away from the beach. But make sure you book well ahead in summer as these places fill up quick.

BUDGET & MID-RANGE

Hôtel-Restaurant Le Grillon (☎ 04 95 60 00 49; ave Paul Doumer; s/d €32.20/41.10, compulsory half-board in August €54.20/79.20; P) With simple but effective rooms and a well-received restaurant at ground level, this place offers by far the best value for single travellers and those looking to economise. The reception is in the bar downstairs.

Hôtel Splendid (☎ 04 95 60 00 24; www.le-splendid-hotel.com; blvd Valéry François; s/d €59.50/88.50; P ☼) A reliable two-star hotel with an aura of faded charm, this place represents the best of the mid-range options. It has a good range of facilities with a particularly nice little swimming pool and pool bar area by the main gates. And don't forget to stock up on the all-you-can-eat breakfast buffet – it's included in the room price.

Hôtel l'Isola Rossa (☎ 04 95 60 01 32; route du Port; d/t €105/121e; ☼) This place has older rooms, some with sea-facing balconies, and is very close to the harbour. The owners are, however, making an effort to update the place and have recently converted the top floor into two apartment-style attic rooms (€105), which would be suitable for a family.

TOP END

Hôtel Santa Maria (☎ 04 95 63 05 05; www.hotel santamaria.com; route du Port; P ☼ ☼) This well-appointed three-star place remains the best address in town with luxurious rooms and direct access to a private beach. The owners have renovated two self-contained apartments in the grounds – these now make for a smart and comfortable base for a family. Of the two, the three-room Roc e Mare (€4250 per week) has less frills. The four-room Cala Rossa (€5300 per week), however, comes with a sauna and a spa. Both properties come with maid service.

Hôtel Napoléon Bonaparte (☎ 04 95 60 06 09; www.langleytravel.com; place Paoli; d without/with half-board €162/188; P ☼ ☼ ☼ ☼) This hotel is the former palace home in exile for Mohammed V, erstwhile King of Morocco. Now, however, it has been taken over by a Scandinavian tour company on a long lease and, given the huge numbers of coach parties from Norway arriving every week in high season, there's little opportunity for passing travellers to find a room. It's rather a shame as the facilities here are excellent and include, notably, a well-run kids' club. It may be worth calling by to see if there is any space but be sure to brush up on your Norwegian before doing so. More information about package deals can be found on the company's website.

Eating

Easy-going snack joints and cafés line the southern edge of place Paoli – try **L'Île d'Or**

(☎ 04 95 60 12 05; menus €12-30) for lunch – while, across the square, the ancient **covered food market** is a great place to sample and buy local produce each morning. Stall holders are generally receptive to handing out a few samples and talking interested travellers through their wares – that is, if you're planning on making a purchase.

There's also a string of restaurants that line the beach front and, although none of them will be winning any Michelin stars, many have tables placed quite deliberately in the sand and offer decent three-course dinner *menus* (€20).

L'Osteria (☎ 04 95 60 08 39; place Santelli; menus €17/19) is an old favourite with its no-nonsense Corsican specialities and rustic setting. This one is more of a dinner spot and the candlelit atmosphere is good for the romantically inclined. **Chez Paco** (☎ 04 95 60 03 76; rue Paoli; menus €22/28) has speciality seafood dishes; try the house-special paella (€18) or bouillabaisse (€28).

By the harbour, 300m north of the Hôtel Santa Maria (p117), **Le Laetitia** (04 95 60 01 90; route du Port) opens for lunch and dinner with seafood specialities; count on paying about €20 per head.

There's a large and very well-stocked **Casino supermarket** (ave Paul Doumer; ☼ 8.30am-8pm Mon-Sat, 8.30am-1pm Sun), which covers all the needs of self-caterers.

Drinking & Entertainment

There's not much going on around here after dark aside from hanging out in the cafés of place Paoli. **Café des Platanes** (☎ 04 95 60 00 36), with its sprawling wicker chairs across the square, has been doing the business for customers since 1928 and is still going strong today. Meanwhile **Au Bon Vin Corse** (☎ 04 95 60 15 14; place Marcel Delanney) is a shopfront for local liqueurs, honeys and olive oil *and* a wine bar for a little pre-dinner pick-me-up. Try the obscenely fruity *vin aux fruits* (€2.2).

The only other option is the open-air **cinema le Fogata** (☎ 04 95 60 00 93; blvd de Fogata; ☼ summer only from 9.30pm), along the N197 heading southeast out of town.

Getting There & Away

AIR

Île Rousse is 25km from Calvi-Ste-Catherine airport (€40 by taxi). There is no public transport connection.

BOAT

From the ferry terminal, **SNCM** runs high-speed boats to Nice (low/high season €30/41; 3hrs) and Marseilles (low/high season €35/53; 11½hrs), and **Corsica Ferries** (www.cmn.fr; low/high season €16/31; 3hrs) links Île Rousse to Savona, Italy. For more details on ferry crossings, see the Transport chapter (p235).

BUS

Les Beaux Voyages (☎ 04 95 65 11 35), in Calvi, runs buses Monday to Saturday from Île Rousse to Calvi (€3.50, 30 minutes), Bastia (€10, two hours) and Ponte Leccia (€7, one hour). The stop for Calvi is unmarked on the corner of ave Paul Doumer and ave Piccioni; for Bastia, it's again unmarked in front of the Casino supermarket.

Autocars Santini (☎ 04 95 37 02 98) runs buses twice daily Monday to Saturday from Île Rousse to St-Florent (€10, one hour) in summer.

CAR

Avis (☎ 04 95 60 21 79) has an office opposite the open-air cinema le Fogata.

TRAIN

The **train station** (☎ 04 95 60 00 50) is at the western edge of town. There are four departures daily from Île Rousse to Bastia (€14.70, 2½ hours), Corte (€11.80, two hours) and Ajaccio (€24.20, four hours); all require a change at Ponte Leccia station.

Tramways de la Balagne (p113) links Île Rousse with Algajola (€3.10, 15 minutes) and Calvi (€4.10, 50 minutes) 12 times daily between June and September.

THE BALAGNE INTERIOR

This verdant inland area offers a vision of the real Corsica away from the tourist cafés of Île Rousse (p117) and the souvenir shops of Calvi (p106). Think dramatic scenery, even more dramatic switchback roads and a real chance to penetrate the living, breathing village life that Corsicans tend to hold so dear. Indeed, during the summer, many city-dwelling Corsicans return to their family village for their annual sojourn. It is seen as a chance to maintain the strong family ties and traditions so often lost on the younger generation.

THE BALAGNE CRAFT TRAIL

Anxious to show how the Balagne region has preserved its traditional range of crafts and artisan skills, the association **A Strada di l'Artigiani** (☎ 04 95 32 83 00; 3 rue Marcel Paul, Bastia) has strived to create a dedicated Route des Artisans de Balagne.

The route essentially hugs the N197 running north from Calvi to Île Rousse with the odd detour inland to snake through some of the Balagne mountain villages. Clearly marked signposts indicate a range of traditional crafts and artisans from stringed-instrument makers to wine-makers and potters. Many of these artisans' workshops are open to the public and visits are free. Of course, they'll be more than happy for you to relieve them of their wares.

The leaflet *Strada di l'Artigiani* is available from the tourist office in Calvi (p106).

If you have a car, you can visit the Balagne villages in an easy day's circuit, stopping regularly en route for coffee, lunch and a chance to wander around some of the artisan workshops that form part of the Balagne Craft Trail (see boxed text above). This driving route from Calvi traces a path through the villages. Be warned, however, there is no public transport in this region.

LAMA

postcode 20218 / pop 140 / elevation 400m

Heading inland along the D8 from Île Rousse, the glorious village of Lama has gone from a soulless cultural wasteland to one of the most dynamic villages in Haute-Corse (see boxed text The Rebirth of a Village, p120). Today, with its film festival, flower festival and over 50 converted *gîtes* for tourists, it's a lively place and has a healthy association with British tour operators who send clients to this region.

The **tourist office** (☎ 04 95 48 23 90; www.ot -lama.com; ☺ 9am-noon & 2-5pm Mon, Tue, Thu, Fri; 9am-noon & 2-6pm Wed & Sat, 11am-noon & 2-7pm Sun) produces a tourist guide leaflet and can offer advice to travellers in the region.

In the upstairs section of the building that houses the **town hall** (☎ 04 95 48 21 05) there is free Internet access available (☺ 10am-3pm Mon-Fri),

next to a small café/bar, **Chez Jules** (☎ 04 95 48 23 92; summer only). In the same building but downstairs there is an exhibition hall, U Stallo, with old, black-and-white photos tracing the history of the village through the ages.

There's also a small **post office** (☺ 9am-noon Mon-Sat), a **grocery store** (☺ 8.30am-noon & 6-8pm) and, in the spirit of the village's communal facilities for all to share, a **swimming pool** for the exclusive use of *gîte*-dwellers (☎ 04 95 48 24 04; ☺ summer noon-7pm).

Sleeping & Eating

All accommodation is based around the converted *gîtes* (see boxed text, p120); bookings are handled via the tourist office.

Campu Latinu (☎ 04 95 48 23 83; www.campu latinu.fr; menu Corse €25; ☺ Tue-Sun lunch & dinner) This is a suitably chic venue given that its owner is also the village's urbane mayor. Expect fantastic panoramic views across the mountains and high standards of cuisine (mains €15, children's *menu* €9). Watch out for passing French film stars snatching some quality time away from the spotlight.

BELGODÈRE (BELGUDÈ)

postcode 20226 / pop 380 / elevation 310m

This tiny village high above the olive groves in the Vallée du Prato, at a distance of 15km from Île Rousse, has a timeless, tranquil feel. The focus of the village is the church with its Baroque altarpiece, while the tranquil village square it looms above has a couple of cafés, a post office and a pharmacy. It is mooted that a dedicated tourist office is due to open for future seasons.

Behind the village square there's also a ramshackle old fort, from where there's a wonderful view over the surrounding valleys. It's tucked away through an archway between the two cafés behind the war memorial.

Sleeping & Eating

A few hundred metres from the square and 50m past the *Mairie* building along the road to Ponte Leccia, **Hôtel-Restaurant Niobel** (☎ 04 95 61 34 00; www.niobel.com; s/d/tr with half-board €66/105/140; P) has 12 unfussy but clean rooms, all with bathrooms and some with balconies overlooking the valley. Rather eerily this panoramic vista includes a clear view across to the cemetery. Guests are required to spend at least one night on a half-board

---

THE REBIRTH OF A VILLAGE

Many of the Balagne villages have sadly seen better days with dwindling populations and the collapse of their traditional village crafts and industry. The village of **Lama** (p119), however, stands out as one place that has managed to bring off a major change in its fortunes. And this spectacular economic U-turn is primarily the result of 25 years of hard work by its charismatic local mayor, Monsieur Simon Bacculli.

During the Genoese era (p22), Lama had blossomed as a thriving rural community and a major centre for olive oil production. This golden period continued for many centuries until a massive fire devastated the region, leaving 35,000 hectares of olive groves burnt to cinders. With its primary industry destroyed and the community spirit torn asunder overnight, the population dwindled from 400 to 60 within just a few short years. These were dark days for the people of Lama.

The turning point came, however, in 1989 when the local authority, under Bacculli's direction, decided to devote the village to tourism. The key point, though, was that they deemed this conversion should be executed in a responsible manner that empowered residents to make a livelihood without destroying the village's community fabric.

Old houses that had fallen into disrepair were rebuilt and converted into holiday homes for tourists. Within a few years the village had become a glowing example of how to set up a responsible tourism project – and get it right.

Such was the success of the project that the Government's ministry of tourism – amazed at how a tiny Corsican village could bring itself back from the brink of economic stagnation – awarded Lama with a major tourism prize, the Grand Prix National de l'Innovation Touristique. It was Lama's finest hour and a chance to finally banish the spectre of the village's dark past.

'For Lama, tourism is all about discovery,' says Bacculli, sipping an after-lunch café at his restaurant, Campu Latinu (p119).

'Our aim has always been not to foster tourism for tourism's sake but to do so with intelligence. It has always been our primary aim to showcase Lama as a place where the visitor can get an insight into the personality of the island,' he adds.

To this end, Lama first played host to the **Festival Européen de Cinéma et du Monde Rural** (European Festival of Rural Film; festival_lama@yahoo.com) in 1993. Today the event attracts about 6000 visitors to the village during the first week of August when films by big name European directors are projected onto the façades of the some of the village's finest Tuscan-style mansions.

'At first we were working hard to survive but now,' smiles Bacculli, finishing his espresso, 'we are working hard not to take things too far. We can't stop the people of Lama converting their homes for tourists but we can encourage them to always do so with a degree of charm.'

---

basis but, thankfully, the terrace restaurant has some decent *menus* (lunch/dinner €15/19). The owners speak some English, Italian and German; the hotel is part of the Logis de France group (p222).

SPELONCATO (SPILUNCATU)

postcode 20226 / pop 222 / elevation 600m

Eleven kilometres southwest of Belgodère via the D71, a road that snakes dramatically up the mountains, Speloncato is generally regarded to be one of the most beautiful villages in the Balagne. Perched at an elevation of 600m, and not far from the site of an ancient Roman encampment, it owes its name to the nearby grottoes (known as *e spelunche* in Corsican) and its charm to its little streets with their densely packed stone houses. Given the altitude, the whole village is often shrouded in an eerie mist and even in high summer it can have a pleasantly cool feel about it.

The **Église St-Michel**, which is Romanesque in style, has a handsome Baroque choir dating from 1755, and it is worth a visit not only for its paintings and sculptures but also for its magnificent Tuscan organ (1810). The bell-tower was added in 1913.

There's also a small **grocery shop** (9am-7pm Tue-Sat, 9am-noon Sun).

Sleeping & Eating

The only public lodging in the village, **Hôtel A Spelunca** (04 95 61 50 38; d with street/mountain view €53/61; Apr-Oct; (P)), has quite a history. The building was constructed in 1850 by Cardinal Savelli, the director-general of the police in Rome under Pope Pius IX and a native son of Speloncato. Its 18 comfortable rooms, built around a central staircase, are lavishly furnished with period furniture that captures the spirit of its opulent past. This is a good place for a taste of history.

Bar **Le Gallieri** (menus €15-20) makes a pleasant bolthole for lunch in the tiny central square.

FORÊT DE TARTAGINE MELAJA & PIOGGIOLA

As the D63 winds south from Speloncato, it traverses its way across the Col de Battaglia (1099m) towards the Forêt de Tartagine Melaja, marking the outer boundary of the Parc Naturel Régional de Corse (p210).

The forest itself, which covers 2700 hectares, is rather inaccessible due to the poor quality of the roads – count on one hour to drive to the edge of the forest. The village of Pioggiola, 3km beyond the Col de Battaglia, is the area's tiny hub.

From here the D963 winds through 16km of stunning landscapes before reaching the forest proper. Initially, the scenery on the drive into the forest seems a little inanimate (except for the livestock you're likely to encounter on the narrow mountainside road) but then the scattered pine trees begin to cluster more densely. The road reaches the forestry lodge about 3.5km after the sign indicating the start of the forest.

After following the trail for a few hundred metres you can swim in the river, have a picnic or go for a walk along one of the marked paths (including a firewall path) that stretch out along the stream in the shade of the pine trees.

Sleeping & Eating

In Pioggiola, **Auberge Aghjola** (☎ 04 95 61 90 48; r with half-board €61; (P)) is a pretty, ivy-covered house with comfortable rooms and one of the highest swimming pools in Corsica.

Hôtel A Tramala (☎ 04 95 61 93 54; d €65; (P)), at the junction of the D63 and the D963, 2km out of Pioggiola in the direction of the forest, is a big stone house with spacious double rooms. The room price includes a hearty breakfast.

FELICETO

postcode 20225 / pop 200 / elevation 350m

Following the D71 southwest from Speloncato, Feliceto has little by way of attractions to discourage you from simply passing on through – aside, that is, from one rather good hotel, the **Mare e Monti** (☎ 04 95 63 02 00; d/tr €94/111; (P)). This is one of the rare hidden gems that nestle up here among the Balagne villages. A converted, blue-shuttered 'American house' it offers comfortable rooms with some nice design touches, such as terracotta floor tiles, and great views across the mountains. The whole place has been refurbished and there's a new, mosaic-lined outdoor swimming pool with an adjoining restaurant. This is a great spot to settle back with a cold drink and admire the view.

Next door, the winery **Domaine Renucci** (10am-noon & 4.30-7.30pm Mon-Sat), run by the son of the Mare e Monti's owner, is a well-respected winery producing a range of good-quality AOC wines.

CALENZANA

postcode 20214 / pop 1500 / elevation 300m

The largest of the villages in the Balagne, Calenzana is also the trailhead for both the GR20 (p51) and the Mare e Monti Nord walking trails (p46) – hence it's always busy with walkers either setting out or looking for some R'n'R on their way back from the hike.

Work on the **Église St-Blaise** in the village square – as ever the complete focal point of the village – began in 1691 and took 16 years to complete. The cornices, decorated with acanthus leaves, were added in 1722 and the high altar in polychrome marble (based on drawings by Florentine architect Pierre Cortesi) in 1750. The splendid Baroque belltower was built between 1862 and 1875.

Calenzana was once a major pocket of opposition to the Genoese occupation (p22) and the village was the site of a major battle during the Corsican uprising against Genoese troops and their German mercenary allies. The field adjacent to the church is now the resting place of 500 Germans killed in a bloody conflict on 14 June 1732.

Given its regular through-traffic of hungry and thirsty hikers, Calenzana is well blessed with services. There's a **post office**

CALVI & THE BALAGNE

(8.30am-noon & 2-4.15pm Mon-Fri, 8.30am-noon Sat) 40m east of the town hall, plus shops, a *tabac* and even a small branch of the Crédit Agricole bank.

Sleeping

Gîte d'Étape Municipal (04 95 62 77 13; dm/tent €14/9.60) A few hundred metres along the D51 in the direction of Calvi, and just past the service station on the right-hand side, this is a favourite spot for hikers. It has clean, comfortable dormitories for up to eight people as well as shady ground for you to pitch a tent nearby and there are good kitchen and washing facilities. The site is also home to a useful **mountain information office** (9am-10pm Mon-Fri, 3.30m-10pm weekends) with details of walks in the area. The shelter opens year-round and the showers are hot. Recommended.

Hôtel Bel Horizon (04 95 62 71 72; s/d/tr €45/55/60), opposite the church, has clean rooms with a shared toilet; the rooms, however, have showers. Book ahead as this is also popular with weary walkers seeking a level of comfort after their trek.

Eating

About 200m north of the church, **L'Olmia** (04 95 47 35 22; menus €14 & 20) is a bright and breezy pizzeria with the standard Corsican favourites on offer. Virtually next door, **Le GR20** (04 95 60 66 30; menu €17) has a nice little back-garden terrace where walkers gather to contemplate their achievements over a cold beer or two.

On the main road, 30m north of the church, **Chez Manu** (04 95 62 81 97; menu €14.50, take-away pizzas €8.50) is a reliable little spot with a shady terrace. Of late it has had a few mixed reviews from readers.

Getting There & Away

Les Beaux Voyages (04 95 65 11 35; www.lesbeaux voyages.com) runs buses to Calenzana from place Porteuse d'Eau in Calvi. In summer buses run twice daily Monday to Friday (€4.60/5.30 with baggage, 20 minutes); off-season they run once daily Monday, Tuesday and Thursday to Saturday.

AROUND CALENZANA
Chapelle de Santa Restituta

About 1.5km east of the village is the Romanesque Chapelle de Santa Restituta,

dedicated to the martyred patron saint of Calenzana who was beheaded on the village square in the early 4th century. The townspeople originally intended the chapel, built in the 11th or 12th century, to be in a different spot but changed their plans when, according to the local legend at least, the building materials were found to have moved mysteriously in the course of each night. The spirit of Restituta herself, they concluded, must have been communicating with them to indicate where she wanted the chapel built. These days nobody seems to have a link with the spirit world to determine what she thinks of her remains being paraded each year through the villages in late May. For a poke around, ask for the key to the chapel at the nearby tobacconist's.

Montemaggiore
elevation 400m

A few kilometres north of Calenzana, on the D151, the village of Montemaggiore is known for its 17th-century Baroque **church of St-Augustin**. The village was formerly a major centre for olive oil production before fires devastated the area in the 1940s (p120). Today its small population (maybe 100 people in winter – if that) celebrate its former halcyon days with an **olive oil fair** each July. There's little else here apart from a friendly little café-*tabac* and Chez Francoise, where you can stop for a coffee or to buy water.

Zilia

Driving southeast from Calenzana along the D151, just before Zilia, a slightly overgrown sign marks the entrance to the cellars of **Domaine d'Alzi Pratu** (04 95 62 75 47; 8am-noon & 2-7pm Mon-Fri). The winery is near the former convent of the same name. This is a silver medal-winning winery and staff here sell wines direct to the public at reduced rates, as well as offering a range of olive oils and liqueurs. This is a good spot for souvenir hunting and a chance to stock up on the pick of local produce at more than attractive prices.

From here it's just a 100m further along the D151 to the turn-off to **Zilia mineral water spring** (04 95 65 90 70), production site for one of Corsica's most popular bottled waters. It accepts visitors by appointment only (closed on weekends).

FORÊT & CIRQUE DE BONIFATU

The word Bonifatu means 'place of good life' and, in the early years of the 20th century, this area was frequented by convalescents who came to take advantage of its pure air. The purity of the local ecosystem has also made it popular with Corsican fauna, including foxes, bearded vultures, Corsican nuthatches and wild boars. Flora-wise, the forest, which covers over 3000 hectares and ranges in elevation from 300m to 2000m, consists of maritime and laricio pines, green oaks and other broad-leafed trees.

Back in the mists of time this forest, and its surrounding area, was traversed by shepherds who were busy taking their flocks between winter and summer grazing grounds. These days the area is mainly frequented by walkers tackling the rigours of the GR20 walking trail (p51).

If you're not an ambitious walker, then you will probably want wheels to get here. From Calvi take the road towards the airport (D251) and continue for about 20km more. There's a sign for the Forêt de Bonifatu 7km after the turn-off for Calenzana. Two kilometres further on is Col de Rezza (510m), which overlooks a barren landscape sometimes called the Chaos de Rezza. The pass is a little before the forestry lodge, an inn and a car park where you are expected to park (cars/camping cars €3/4.5).

A little footpath known as the **Sentier du Mouflon** (Mouflon Path) starts from the car park. It's not a very shady forest track and has some uphill parts but it takes you on a forest circuit in about 2½ hours. About 20 minutes from the car park, the track leads to the paths that take you to the **Refuge de Carrozzu** (two hours further) or the **Refuge d'Ortu di u Piebu** (about three hours further) on the GR20 route (p51). There are plenty of rockpools en route for a spot of bathing if you need to cool off.

Sleeping & Eating

The **Auberge de la Forêt** (☎ 04 95 65 09 98; with half board €40), next to the car park, has reasonable rooms with their own bathrooms but a shared toilet. There are also two basic but clean dormitories with bunk beds for up to 16 people (half board €30). It's a popular spot with GR20 walkers but more by necessity than actual choice. Given that it's not an overly welcoming place then, if you have transport, you will probably want to push on.

PIGNA

postcode 20220 / pop 200 / elevation 450m

Nestled among the twists of the D151 and a short hop from both Algajola and Île Rousse, Pigna is a nice little spot for wandering around the artisan workshops highlighted by the Balagne Craft Trail (p119). It's a deservedly popular place with tourists so aim to go late afternoon to avoid the crowds and to soak up the sunset. Most of the village's artisan workshops open from 10am to noon and 3pm to 7pm daily.

Sadly, while Pigna is big on craft shops, it has few practicalities for the passing traveller.

Sleeping & Eating

One of the most talked-about hotels in Haute-Corse, **Casa Musicale** (☎ 04 95 61 77 31; www.casa-musicale.org; r with mountain/sea views €56/75; starters €8–11, mains €22) is no longer the hidden gem it once was, but it remains a consistently good-value and unusual place. The rooms are highly atmospheric with frescoes on the walls and the restaurant, converted from an old olive press, serves a small but satisfying *menu* of hearty village fare. Most of all, though, it's known for its regular traditional Corsican music nights with visiting bands. It is also the focus of regular traditional music festivals and recitals during the summer months.

A new addition to the village scene is **U Palazzu** (☎ 04 95 47 32 78; www.hotel-palazzu.com; r €140), a bright and modern *chambre d'hôte* with a few nicely decorated rooms. The terrace restaurant has a €20 *menu* of local dishes, focusing on the use of local produce. It's all rather nicely done but not the best value for what you actually get.

A nice little tucked-away spot to rest your legs at the bottom of the village is **A Casarella**, an organic juice bar with a fantastic terrace overlooking the ocean. Try the fresh organic juice (€2.50) or the home-made ice cream (€3), then sit back and soak up the view. It's one of the best views in the whole of the north.

SANT'ANTONINO

postcode 20220 / pop 70 / elevation 550m

One of the highest and certainly one of the prettiest villages in the Balagne, rustic Sant'Antonino also offers one of the best 360-degree panoramic views in Haute-Corse. In summer the village is a mix of deserted cobbled side streets and bustling postcard stalls with a handful of places to eat, just above the car park. It's well worth a detour to soak up the atmosphere of Balagne village life.

The small square, where both the free car park and the Baroque **Église St-Annunziata** are situated, is also the departure point for donkey rides around the village (€8, every 20 minutes from 3.30pm).

At the bottom of the village, and a welcome little spot to rest up a while, is **Cave Antonini** (☎ 04 95 61 76 83), a family-run business that has been producing wines, honey and preserves since 1868 – all using lemons as their base ingredient. The current owner, Olivier, is happy to chat to visitors, sets out free-to-use picnic tables for passing tourists to take a pew, and serves up glasses of refreshing lemon juice over crushed ice (€2) – delicious. The house speciality lemon wine makes for an ideal and unusual souvenir.

Sleeping & Eating

The nearest accommodation for Sant'Antonino is to be found in Pigna or Algajola. The Calvi tourist office (p106) may be able to advise you on a local *chambre d'hôte*.

For lunch, try **La Taverne Corse** (☎ 04 95 61 70 15; menu Corse €18, children's menu €8) for a substantial lunch, or nearby **La Voûte** (☎ 04 95 61 74 71; menus €16 & 20), a nice, airy place with great views from its panoramic terrace. They also offer more snack-style pizzas (€7 to €9).

For something lighter, climb through the village side streets to **A Stella** (☎ 04 95 61 33 74), a rustic little spot, for its salads (€8) and sandwiches (€4). There's a small adjoining shop where you can buy local produce.

MONTICELLO

postcode 20220 / pop 200 / elevation 150m

About 4km further along the D263 from the relatively deserted Santa Reparata di Balagne, the village of Monticello is a positive hive of activity compared with some of the other Balagne villages.

It's a small place but the main draw here is a bunch of sporting facilities, 1km from the village square with a small clubhouse/snack bar also on site.

Activities

Locals indicate that a swimming pool is also due to open – watch this space.

Horse-riding centre (☎ 04 95 60 05 71)
Tennis club (☎ 06 18 02 07 32; €10/hour)
Mini-golf (☎ 06 18 02 07 32 adult/child €4.5/3)

Sleeping & Eating

In the main square, **A Pasturella** (☎ 04 95 60 05 65; www.a-pasturella.com; d without/with half-board €76/125; **P**) is big on pomp but not particularly good on value. Rooms are spacious and come with balconies but the compulsory half-board regime in summer is pricey for what you get and feels rather constrictive in what is otherwise a pretty small place. The hotel's restaurant *menus* for lunch are from €24.

Also in the main square there's a little **grocery shop** (☺ 8am-1pm & 5-8pm Mon-Sat, 8am-1pm Sun) for snacks and drinks.

The West Coast

CONTENTS

In their numerous scalloped indentations, the great western gulfs of Porto, Sagone and Ajaccio shelter treasures such as the Réserve Naturelle de Scandola, home to a fantastic range of flora and fauna, and the awe-inspiring rock formations of Les Calanques de Piana. Little resort villages such as Sagone, the region's best-kept gastronomic secret, remote Girolata, playground of the jetset, and the laid-back Cargèse, high over the Golfe de Sagone, all have their own unique character. Breezy golden beaches flank virtually the whole coast and their clear aquamarine waters offer some of the best scuba diving and water-sport opportunities in the Mediterranean.

While mountain hamlets with long histories offer a taste of authentic, unhurried village life, the wonderful gorges of Spelunca and Prunelli in the green hinterland are a haven for hikers. Busy port town Ajaccio, the most populous town on the island, plays at being the working person's version of Nice.

HIGHLIGHTS

- **Chill-Out Spot**
  Watch the sun go down on the spectacular **Les Calanques** (p136) from the terrace of Piana's Hôtel des Roches Rouges

- **Wining & Dining**
  Savour delicious, inspired home cooking at **A Stonda** (p142) in Sagone

- **Beach Bum**
  Make a splash at one of **Golfe de Sagone**'s (p139) many gorgeous beaches

- **Au Naturel**
  Hike between Genoese bridges at the wonderful **Gorges de Spelunca** (p133)

- **Boating**
  Sail the beautiful coastal reserve of **Réserve Naturelle de Scandola** (p132)

- **Kid's Stuff**
  Enjoy a midnight stargaze at the **Centre Scientifique de Vignola** (p150) in Ajaccio

Girolata
Réserve Naturelle de Scandola
Gorges de Spelunca
Les Calanques
Plage d'Arone
A Stonda
Golfe de Sagone
Centre Scientifique de Vignola

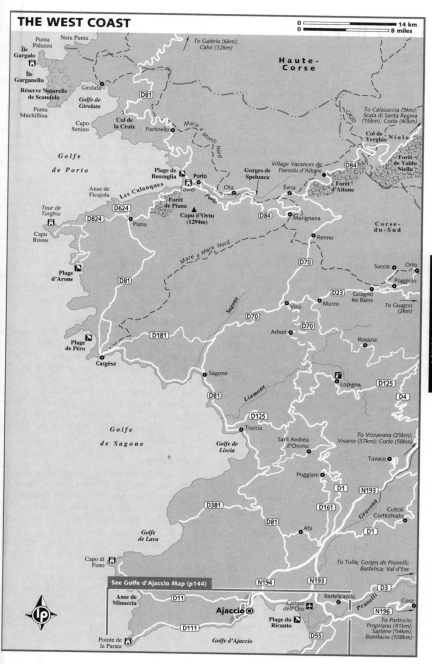

THE WEST COAST

0 — 14 km
0 — 8 miles

Punta Palazzu
Nera Punta
Île Gargalo
Île Garganellu
Réserve Naturelle de Scandola
Punta Muchillina
Girolata
Golfe de Girolata
D81
To Galéria (6km); Calvi (32km)
Haute-Corse

Capo Senino
Col de la Croix
Partinello
Mare e Monti Nord
To Calacuccia (9km); Scala di Santa Regina (16km); Corte (40km)
D220
Col de Verghio
Niolo
Forêt de Valdu Niellu

Golfe de Porto
Plage de Bussaglia
Porto
Tower
Porto
Ota
Gorges de Spelunca
Village Vacances de Paesolu d'Aitone
Évisa
D84
Forêt d'Aïtone

Anse de Ficajola
Les Calanques
Forêt de Piana
Capu d'Ortu (1294m)
D84
Marignana
Corse-du-Sud

Tour de Turghiu
D624
D824
Piana
Capu Rossu

Mare a Mare Nord
Renno
D70
Soccia
Orto
Poggiolo

Plage d'Arone
D81
Sagone
Vico
D70
Murzo
D23
Guagno les Bains
To Guagno (2km)

Plage de Péro
D181
Arbori
D70
Rosazia

Cargèse
Sagone
Liamone
Lopigna
D125
D4

D81
Golfe de Sagone
D125
Tiuccia
Golfe de Liscia
Sant Andréa d'Orcino
To Vizzavona (25km); Vivario (37km); Corte (58km)
Tavaco

Poggiare
D1
N193
Cuttoli Corticchiato

D381
D161
D1
Golfe de Lava
D81
Afa

Capo di Feno
To Tolla; Gorges de Prunelli; Bastelica; Val d'Ese

See Golfe d'Ajaccio Map (p144)
D3
Anse de Minaccia
D11
Campo dell'Oro
Bastelicaccia
Prunelli
Coro
N196
Ajaccio
Plage du Ricanto
N194
N193
To Porticcio; Propriano (41km); Sartène (54km); Bonifacio (108km)
Pointe de la Parata
D111
Golfe d'Ajaccio
D55

THE WEST COAST

GOLFE DE PORTO

PORTO

postcode 20150 / pop 300

Porto serves as the port for the mountain village of Ota, and the location is its main attraction. It is situated at the foot of a lovely square tower erected in the 16th century to protect the superb Golfe de Porto from incursions by the Saracens. This small seaside resort seems to have mushroomed somewhat too suddenly in recent years, yet it still retains a certain charm. Packed in summer but deserted in winter, it makes a good base for exploring the mountainous back country – as well as for getting a look at the exceptional wilderness along the coast of the Scandola nature reserve (p132).

Orientation

Porto's pharmacy is one of the few buildings visible from the D81, the main road through this part of the coast, and it is a useful landmark because it is at the intersection with the road that leads 1.5km down to the area around the harbour. Between the pharmacy and the harbour lies the quarter known as Vaïta, or Porto le Haut. The harbour area is divided by the River Porto, which is crossed by a footbridge. Those travelling by car to the southern side of the harbour area should take the road signposted 'Porto rive gauche' on the D81 towards Piana. Though the main cluster of accommodation and restaurants are found in the port area, the town proper is quite spread out and extends a good kilometre along the coastal route.

Information

Porto's only ATM (across from the Hôtel Cala di Sole in Vaïta) takes all major credit cards. The *bureau de change*, near the Spar supermarket on the D81, provides cash advances against credit cards.

L'Aiglon (☎ 04 95 26 10 46) Sells French and foreign newspapers, beach accessories and camera film, near the harbour. Newspapers are also available from Le Colombo in Vaïta.

Post office (☎ 04 95 26 10 26; ✆ 9am-12.30pm & 2-5pm Mon-Fri, 9-11.30am Sat) Is next to Hôtel Lonza in Vaïta; has a fax service and changes travellers cheques.

Tourist information (☎ 04 95 26 10 55; www.porto -tourisme.com; place de la Marine; ✆ 9am-6pm Jul & Aug, 9am-6pm Mon-Sat Apr-Jun & Sep; 9am-noon & 2-5pm Mon-Fri Oct-Mar) Mostly English-speaking staff can provide information on activities and walks in the area.

Sights & Activities

GENOESE TOWER

Standing guard over the entrance to the fishing harbour, the **Genoese tower** (adult/child under 12 €2.50/free; ✆ 11am-7pm, 9am-9pm Jul & Aug) is an ideal place to watch the sun set over the gulf. It was built in 1549, in the same period as the other 85 towers around the Corsican coast. Restored in 1993 it looks almost as good as new.

The tower is worth a visit for all the information you'll get about how this and the other towers were financed and about the hard life of the tower watchman. You reach the tower via a series of steps starting next to La Tour Génoise restaurant. From the top, in fine weather, you can see the tower on Capu Rossu (Capo Rosso, also often called the Tour de Piana because it was used to protect Piana) on the southern side of the gulf.

AQUARIUM DE LA POUDRIÈRE

Open since summer 2000 in the town's former powder magazine, this little **aquarium** (☎ 04 95 26 19 24; adult/child 7-12 €5.50/4; ✆ 8am-10pm Jun-Aug, 8am-7pm Sep-May) is worth a visit if you take the time and effort to read the accounts of the marine species in residence. There are about 500 fish in total and plenty of information on the flora and fauna of the gulf. It's adjacent to Hôtel Monte Rosso.

BOAT TRIPS

Two companies arrange boat trips out of Porto between April and October. **Nave Va** (info from Hôtel Le Cyrnée; ☎ 04 95 26 15 16; adult/child under 10 €36/18) runs trips twice a day to the coast of the Scandola nature reserve and Girolata in summer (two hours).

Porto Linea (tickets & info Hôtel Monte Rosso; ☎ 04 95 26 11 50) organises a similar excursion aboard a yellow 12-seat boat, *Le Mare Nostrum*, which is small enough to explore some tiny inlets. Trips to Scandola cost €40 and to Les Calanques, €20.

Those wishing to explore the Golfe de Porto on their own can hire inflatable motor dinghies from €75 for a half-day – ask at the harbour.

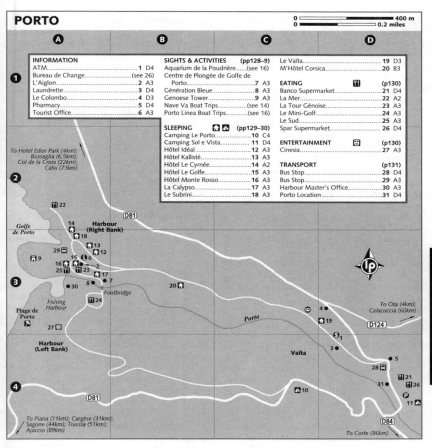

PORTO

BEACHES
It is not the most stunning beach in Corsica but the **Plage de Porto** should still content those keen on sunbathing and swimming. See also Bussaglia (p131).

DIVING
Centre de Plongée du Golfe de Porto (☎ 04 95 26 10 29; www.plongeeporto.com; ☼ Apr-Oct) is at the back of the Lannoy Sports store near the footbridge, close to the marina. Prices start at €36 for an introductory dive and €25 for an exploratory dive. There are various packages with several dive options.

Génération Bleue (☎ 04 95 26 24 88; www.generation-bleue.com; ☼ Apr-Oct) charges €40 for an introductory dive at Castagne or Capu Rossu,

€30 to €40 for an exploratory dive, and €140 to €190 for five dives depending on whether you have your own equipment.

The dive program of both dive centres is identical, and both tend to lower their fees as the season begins to wind down.

Sleeping
Like elsewhere in Corsica, it's a good idea to make reservations in advance particularly during the high season.

BUDGET
Hôtel Le Golfe (☎ 04 95 26 13 33; s/d/tw €38/50/60) With their thinning carpets, plastic flowers and towelling bedspreads you mightn't book one of the 10 rooms here for your

honeymoon. That said, they are generous in size, most have bathrooms and balconies and you can't beat the welcome or the harbour location.

M'Hotel Corsica (☎ 04 95 26 10 89; d from €60-83 P X ﹩) The unmissable pink M'Hotel Corsica, in Vaïta, 500m from the marina, is an airy Californian-style motel set in its own eucalyptus forest and garden. There are 30 simply furnished double rooms and studios with air-conditioning, just off the swimming pool. Beat that for value.

Camping Sol e Vista (☎ 04 95 26 15 71; adult/ tent/car €5.18/2.13/2.44; ☼ Apr-Oct) Near the Spar supermarket on the D81 above Porto, this is an attractive, three-star, shady campground with good facilities, including laundry, children's playground and wheelchair-accessible chalets.

Camping Le Porto (☎ 04 95 26 13 67; www.camping sporto.com; adult/tent/car €4.88/1.83/2.74; ☼ mid-Jun–Oct) On the D81 to Piana, before you come to the turn-off to 'Porto rive gauche', this campground is in a lovely, secluded spot in a grove of eucalyptus and has been recommended by readers.

MID-RANGE

Hôtel Idéal (☎ 04 95 26 10 07; ☼ Apr-Oct; P X) At the bottom of the slope that leads to the harbour, this child-friendly place has clean and pleasant, if somewhat small, double rooms with bathroom. Rooms overlooking the sea have terraces.

Le Subrini (☎ 04 95 26 14 94; d €90-132; ☼ Apr-Oct; P X) With its marble floors and chintz and wicker furniture a-go-go, the three-star Subrini, in the harbour area, feels like it hasn't left the '80s. It has 24 spacious and well-equipped rooms with tiled floors and large balconies overlooking the harbour.

Hôtel Kallisté (☎ 04 95 26 10 30; www.hotel -kalliste.com; d €76 Jul & Sep, €136 Aug; ☼ Mar-Oct; P X) This three-star place has 54 inoffensive, clean rooms with large bathrooms in need of a bit of sprucing up. Prices rocket in August, though if you stay three nights the rate goes down to (a still-steep) €106 per night.

TOP END

Hotel Eden Park (☎ 04 95 26 10 60; d €145; ☼ Apr-Oct; P X ﹩) This chi-chi pile set in the maquis 4km north of Porto on the D81, is the area's most swish hotel. It has 35 charming, bungalow-style rooms with satellite TV, spread around a tennis court, a nicely landscaped swimming pool, and a piano bar.

Eating

BUDGET

Lots of restaurants and hotels along the seafront serve pizzas and inexpensive, unsurprising *menus*.

La Tour Gén-oise (☎ 04 95 26 17 11; pizza €8-11, menus €16-20) With its 'surf' or 'turf' *menus* and shady terrace, this place perhaps stands out a bit from the others. Half-litre pitchers of local wine cost €6.

Le Mini-Golf (☎ 04 95 26 17 55) You'll get particularly generous pizzas in this restaurant in a little green area on the left bank.

Spar and **Banco** supermarkets on the D81, not far from the pharmacy, provide for self-caterers and there's also a little **grocery** by the harbour.

MID-RANGE & TOP END

Le Sud (☎ 04 95 26 14 11; mains €11-22, menus €25) With its hippy-chic-inspired décor, terracotta urns, sun mirrors and whitewashed walls, Le Sud epitomises Mediterranean cool. From its sweeping terrace you can enjoy some of Porto's finest and most imaginative dishes in a relaxed atmosphere and with the best view of the marina to boot. The refreshingly simple meat- or fish-based *menus* offer rarities (in these parts) such as sushi, fish korma or lamb lasagne, and vegetarians will relish the *assiette du sud* (€11) with minted cucumber, tapenade, roasted peppers and pea purée.

La Mer (☎ 04 95 26 11 27; menus €22) Down at the harbour, La Mer serves good fish dishes on its terrace overlooking the gulf and the Genoese tower, which is illuminated at night. The *menu* may include grilled snapper or fresh sardines.

Restaurant Eden Park (☎ 04 95 26 10 60; www .hotels-porto.com/edenpark; menus €22-38) is renowned for its gastronomic feasts. The refined *menus*, based on French and Corsican cuisine, include steaks, *charcuterie*, local fish and seafood, all presented with style.

Entertainment

Cinesia (☎ 04 95 26 10 49) screens films in the open air in a little eucalyptus forest by the harbour in July and August.

Getting There & Around

SAIB buses (☎ 04 95 22 41 99) stop in Porto between one and four times daily on their way back and forth between Ajaccio (€11) and Ota (€3). Frequency depends on the time of year and day of the week. Other towns served, in addition to Ota, are Piana, Cargèse, Sagone and Tiuccia. SAIB also connects Porto and Calvi (€16, 2½ hours), via Col de la Croix, once daily from 15 May to 10 October.

Autocars Mordiconi (☎ 04 95 48 00 04) runs buses from Porto to Calacuccia and Corte (€19, 2pm Monday to Saturday July to mid-September). This journey is spectacularly beautiful. Buses stop at the pharmacy and at the harbour; ask at the tourist office for further information.

Sailors should note that space for mooring in Porto harbour is limited due to its size and shallowness. Typically, yachts drop anchor just off the beach. Washroom facilities are at Camping Municipal, a 10-minute walk away. The little **harbour master's office** (☎ 04 95 26 14 90) is on the left bank of the river.

Porto Location (☎ /fax 04 95 26 10 13; www.porto-locations.com; ⏰ 8.30am-9pm Apr-Oct), opposite Spar supermarket on the D81, hires out cars for €60 per day, scooters for €46 per day and mountain bikes for €15 per day. Rates go down on rentals of two days or longer.

AROUND PORTO
Bussaglia

The nearest beach to Porto is about 6.5km northwest of town. From the D81 take a sharp left turn just after the Eden Park hotel down a narrow sheltered roadway that runs parallel to a stream to the gently curving Bussaglia beach with its dramatic backdrop facing Les Calanques. The coarsely pebbled beach is surprisingly quiet, given its proximity to Porto. The loose pebble bed makes it difficult to enter the water without footwear and this, combined with a relatively steep shelf and strong drag, make swimming here unsuitable for small children.

You can hire boats (€70 for a half day), *pedalos* (€5 for 30 minutes) and parasols from **Les Galets** (☎ 04 95 26 10 49), one of the two restaurants on the beach.

The lack of public transport to Bussaglia keeps the hordes away, but also means you'll need your own transport to get there.

SLEEPING & EATING

Résidence Marina Livia (☎ 04 95 26 12 60; 2-/3-/4-person chalets per wk €580/595/640) The nicest thing about this small *résidence* is its location – 200m from the beach in a eucalyptus grove bursting with colourful wildflowers. The wooden chalets are simply equipped with kitchenettes and bathrooms, but all have verandahs and the location is remarkably quiet and peaceful.

Hotel L'Aiglon (☎ 04 95 26 10 65; Serriera; s/d €30/60, with bath €50/100; ⏰ May-Nov) Not much has changed here since the 1950s, and charmingly so. This pretty stone house with blue shutters and wide terrace overlooking the maquis still feels like a family home. The 18 sparse rooms are surprisingly bright and simply decorated with colourful, museum-quality fabrics and quaint country furnishings. You can browse a dusty copy of a French *policier* novel or play chess in the cool shade of the foyer. Half board costs €45 per person and features a rustic Corsican menu that might include *terrine de sanglier* and delicious roast pork in port. The beach is 400m away.

Opposite Les Galets restaurant on the beach, the friendly **Mare Chiare** (☎ 04 95 26 11 86; pizza €7-9, salad €7, panini €5) serves filling snacks on its shaded terrace. It also runs karaoke nights on the beach on Friday evenings.

GIROLATA

Although not officially part of the Scandola nature reserve, Girolata and the surrounding area are outstanding. Girolata can be seen from many points on the drive between Calvi and Porto, but it can't be reached except by boat or on foot from Col de la Croix. The walk (about three hours) is described in the boxed text (p132).

Despite its inaccessibility, Girolata, between the Scandola peninsula and Capo Senino, gets quite busy in July and August. Private yachts carrying the kind of people who frequent end-of-the-world beaches pull in at the superb harbour, and some people complain that the beach gets dirty. But this jewel of the Corsican coast, with its Genoese fortress, is definitely worth a visit, especially out of high season.

COL DE LA CROIX TO GIROLATA WALK

The trail from the Col de la Croix (Bocca a Croce) sets off on a clear path down a gentle slope through dense maquis. After about 15 minutes you pass a pretty pebbled fountain. Fifteen minutes later you reach a fork; take the left path, which leads down to the **Tuara cove**. Theoretically, this cove should be idyllic, but the charm can sometimes be spoiled when the tide carries in gravel and rubbish. Don't spend too much time here; instead walk around to the northern end of the beach. In the maquis, you'll make out a path to the left that follows the line of the coast and a second, to the right, that heads up the hill. Take the path to the right; there's a 20-minute climb to the junction with the **Mare e Monti Nord** (p46; orange markings).

Once there, you have a stunning view over Girolata and the Baie de Girolata, havens of tranquillity guarded by a small Genoese fort. To the south-west is Capo Senino and on the other side, to the north-east, is Punta Muchillina (on the edge of the Réserve Naturelle de Scandola). Descending to Girolata from here takes about 30 minutes.

Girolata, unfortunately, tends to get overcrowded in summer, and the beach is disappointing. There are a few good restaurants on the seafront, though (see Eating below).

You can return by a slightly different route. Cross back over the beach in Girolata and follow the path you came on for about 20m. Then, instead of continuing up, take the path to the right, which follows a ledge around the coast as far as the Tuara cove.

On 19 March locals from the region descend on the village in small boats for the feast of St Joseph.

Sleeping

Girolata lies on the Mare e Monti Nord path and has two *gîtes d'étape*.

Le Cormoran Voyageur (☎ 04 95 20 15 55; half-board €35; ✆ Apr-Oct) This red stone house, where the village meets the beach, is lovingly tended by Joseph Ceccaldi (a sometime fisherman and one of Girolata's leading citizens). It has 20 beds divided among three reasonably comfortable rooms and half-board, with an emphasis on fish dishes, is obligatory; there are no self-catering facilities.

La Cabane du Berger (☎ 04 95 20 16 98; camp site €8, bunk without/half-board €15/30, d chalet €20/45; ✆ Apr-Oct) This place, on the beach, is primarily a bar and restaurant, but it has *gîte d'étape* facilities as well, all with shared toilet and shower.

Eating

There are several restaurants particularly well situated above the beach and beneath the Genoese fortress; they all have excellent fish-based *menus* and open daily in the high season for lunch and dinner.

Le Bel Ombra (☎ 04 95 20 15 67; menus €18-24; ✆ Apr-Oct) Just above Le Cormoran Voyageur, you can enjoy an unrestricted view over the cove from the teak armchairs on its terrace.

Le Bon Espoir (☎ 04 95 10 04 55) Next door offers the same great view, fish dishes and a Corsican *menu*. Both restaurants take credit cards.

There's a public telephone on the beach, and also a small grocery store.

RÉSERVE NATURELLE DE SCANDOLA

Created in 1975, the Scandola nature reserve at the northern end of the Golfe de Porto occupies 920 hectares of land and approximately 1000 hectares of sea. Owing its exceptional ecological richness to a varied geology as well as a particularly favourable climate and regular sunshine, it is home to a variety of plant and animal

---

THE KING OF THE SCANDOLA NATURE RESERVE

The Scandola peninsula was home to just three osprey pairs in 1973. Today there are about 20 pairs, which is more than one-third of the entire osprey population in the whole of the Mediterranean. A large bird of prey with a white body and brown wings, the osprey is a magnificent sight, especially when hunting. It soars in wide circles until it spots a fish moving just below the water's surface, then dives towards the waves. It extends its claws to grab the fish only at the very last moment.

---

species, including osprey, cormorant, puffin, coral and seaweed. Scientists come in droves to study this flora and fauna.

Although the reserve was established too late to save the last colonies of monk seal, and Corsican deer (now reintroduced around Quenza in the Alta Rocca), Scandola is a unique breeding ground for grouper and osprey (p132). Another of its curiosities is a type of calcareous seaweed that is so hard it forms pavements on the water's surface.

The reserve is bound in the north by Punta Palazzu and in the south by Punta Muchillina. **Île Gargalo**, with its tower, and **Île Garganellu** at the western edge of the reserve have won renown both for their wildlife and for their volcanic caves and faults. Bird-watchers are usually in luck until around the end of June.

The reserve is managed by the Parc Naturel Régional de Corse (PNRC), whose work the Council of Europe recognised with a special certificate in 1985. A portion of the coastline belongs to the Conservatoire du Littoral, and Scandola is also on the Unesco World Heritage list.

Getting There & Away
There is no motor-vehicle access or footpath to the Scandola nature reserve, which means that the only way to get close is by water. Companies organising boat trips to the reserve operate out of Porto (p128), Cargèse (p140), Sagone (p141) and Ajaccio (p149), and Calvi (p110).

PORTO TO COL DE VERGHIO
The D124 leads out of Porto and up through the mountains to Ota, renowned for its superb Genoese bridges. It then connects with the D84, which continues the climb to the marvellous Gorges de Spelunca in Évisa, the Forêt d'Aïtone and Col de Verghio (Bocca di Verghju), above which lies the Niolo (Niolu) region. From here you can continue on to the Forêt de Valdu Niellu, Calacuccia, the Scala di Santa Regina and Corte.

Ota
postcode 20150 / pop 152 / elevation 335m
The sleepy village of Ota, clinging to a mountainside 5km to the east of Porto, perches above the town's cemetery. The

---

---

ascending approach road from Porto is also dotted with a string of familial burial grounds and mausoleums, a measure of Ota's respect for its dead. Here you'll find terracotta-topped granite houses teetering in rows along the mountain slopes, a war memorial shaded by palm trees (opposite the village hall) and a genuinely peaceful atmosphere. Inexpensive *gîtes* signal the village's setting along the Mare e Monti Nord path.

The two **Genoese bridges**, about 2km beyond the village centre on the D124, merit a pitstop. The graceful Pont de Pianella to the south of the road forms a perfect arch. You can walk down to the river here and, if you wish, go for a swim. The second bridge, a few hundred metres beyond, is equally astonishing. It stands at the confluence of the rivers Aïtone and Tavulella. A footpath off to the right beyond this second bridge gets you back to Ota, following the river, in about 40 minutes.

GORGES DE SPELUNCA
A lovely walk from the Genoese bridges into the nearby Gorges de Spelunca also begins nearby (p134). It's an old mule track that runs up through the Défilé de la Spelunca to the Ponte Vecchju, then climbs up to the overgrown Ponte Zaglia and on to Évisa. It's a justifiably popular route for casual as well as more serious walkers and families who combine a leisurely hike with a dip in one of the many rocky river pools. The route is described in more detail in the boxed text on p134.

THE WEST COAST

PONTE VECCHJU TO PONTE ZAGLIA WALK

The path starts at the edge of the double bridge – on the left if you are coming from Ota, 2km past the village. It's a former mule track which links the villages of Ota and Évisa through the Spelunca canyon and, for at least part of the way, along the Porto stream. This is actually a section of the Mare e Monti Nord between Calenzana and Cargèse. It passes two outstanding Genoese bridges. Ponte Vecchju is the first of these, and it is about 300m downstream from the start of the path and can be seen from the D124.

The rocky path now climbs rapidly up the left face of the valley, but green oaks provide a substantial amount of shade. After 30 minutes you come to Ponte Zaglia, the second magnificent Genoese bridge, which is located in the depths of the vegetation. You can refresh yourself in any number of pools close by the bridge. It will take you an hour round trip to complete this easy walk but be warned there is a very steep section at the end of the walk.

It is worth noting that you can also start this walk in Ota (just past the Chez Felix restaurant), but it is not as interesting.

Sleeping & Eating

Chez Félix (☎ /fax 04 95 26 12 92; place de la Fontaine; dm/half-board €12/30) The dormitories here each have a bathroom and six bunk beds. There's a communal kitchen but half board is a good deal because of the home cooking. Non-guests can eat here for €25; the *menu* features rabbit 'the way grandma used to make it'. Chez Félix also rents private rooms and studios as well as operating the only local taxi service.

Chez Marie & Bar des Chasseurs (☎ 04 95 26 11 37; d/dm/half-board €12/29/29; mains €8-13) Down the road is this friendly place where you'll find local men convening for an afternoon's *pastis* and a game of cards on the terrace. Marie has absolutely spotless, modern tiled dorms and one double room, all with shared bathrooms. You can dine well on rustic food such as kid with butter bean (€13), the ubiquitous *cannelloni au brocciu* (€9) or opt for the four-course *menu* (€20). The terrace has wonderful views of the valley

The **grocery shop** (☑ 7am-12.30pm & 3-8pm Mon-Sat high season) is near the church. Hours are shorter at other times of the year.

Getting There & Away

SAIB (☎ 04 95 22 41 99) operates two buses to Ota daily except Sunday and public holidays from Porto, Piana, Cargèse, Sagone, Tiuccia and Ajaccio, and in the period from 1 July to 15 September there is a third bus and Sunday service as well. Buses leave Ota from place de la Fontaine, not far from Chez Félix.

Marignana

postcode 20141 / pop 90 / elevation 750m

This little village, on a mountainside between Ota and Évisa, was famous in the 19th century as the scene of a particularly prolonged and bloody vendetta and as the hideout of partisan *le maquis* during WWII. Now it's a stop for hikers on the Mare a Mare Nord trail.

At **Ustaria di a Rota** (☎ 04 95 26 21 21; dm €10; menu €16) traditional Corsican dishes are a speciality. Ustaria di a Rota also provides a home for Corsica Trek, which organises hikes and outdoor sports activities in the area. Studio apartments can be rented in the village as well.

ÉVISA

postcode 20126 / pop 196 / elevation 830m

The lively little village of Évisa, between the Gorges de Spelunca and the Forêt d'Aïtone, is popular with walkers because of its location at the junction of the Mare a Mare Nord and Mare e Monti Nord paths. Its fame, however, arises from its chestnut harvests. Évisa Chestnuts even have their own *appellation*, and a chestnut festival is held in the village every November.

There's a supermarket and a **post office** (☎ 04 95 26 20 43).

Sleeping & Eating

Gîte d'Étape d'Évisa (☎ 04 95 26 21 88; dm/half-board €12/27; ☑ Apr-Oct) This *gîte* is prized among walkers for its warm reception. It has one dormitory and is near the post office, at the end of a narrow street.

La Châtaigneraie (☎ 04 95 26 24 47; d/half-board €42/61; ☑ Apr-Nov) The quaint La Châtaigneraie (Chestnut Grove), at the entrance to the village as you come from Porto, is run by a friendly young Californian woman and her local husband. The 12 no-frills bedrooms are impeccably clean and the food is renowned locally. The €20 Corsican *menu* might feature wild boar, kid or pork with chestnut sauce. There are plenty of fresh fish options too.

U Pozzu (☎ 04 95 21 11 45; d/tr €46/70; 2-/4-bed apt per wk €305/427; ☒ May-Sep) U Pozzu is on the outskirts of Évisa as you head for the Forêt d'Aïtone, has comfortable doubles and apartments with simple rustic furnishings. It's a child-friendly place with tennis and board games.

L'Aïtone (☎ 04 95 26 20 04; www.hotel-aitone.com; d €36-100; ☒ ☒ ☒) Opposite U Pozzu, L'Ätone has spectacular views from its terrace and on a clear day you can see Porto. Rooms are comfortable if a little old-fashioned; more expensive options have baths, TV and balconies. There are two daily *menus* (€16 and €18) offering such dishes as roast pork or trout with almonds and half-board is available.

Several cafés in the village serve snacks and there are grocery shops as well as a supermarket that accepts credit cards.

Getting There & Away
Autocars Ceccaldi (☎ 04 95 20 29 76) operates a bus service from Ajaccio to Évisa via Vico (€12) daily except Sunday and public holidays.

AROUND ÉVISA
Forêt d'Aïtone
The Forêt d'Aïtone – 1670 hectares in area, 800m to 2000m high – begins a few kilometres outside Évisa and is one of the most beautiful forests on the island. In the 17th century the Genoese built a path through these trees to Sagone, from where timber from the forest was sent to shipyards in Genoa. Corsican laricio pine is the dominant species, covering around 800 hectares. Beech covers around 200 hectares and you'll also come across maritime pine, fir and larch. The forest has long been famous for its wealth of plant extracts.

Look out for the signs for a tiny waterfall and natural basin serving as a miniature swimming pool on the left-hand side of the road as you come from Évisa. The walk takes only about 10 minutes and the site

is cool and peaceful. The waterfall is about 4km from Évisa along a pleasant footpath.

Two kilometres above the waterfall is **Village Vacances de Paesolu d'Aïtone**, a holiday village, and a **PNRC information centre** (☎ 04 95 26 23 62). The information centre has an interesting exhibition on the fauna and flora of the forest. Unfortunately, it is often closed, but you may be able to borrow the key at the holiday village reception.

A few hundred metres away, the short **Sentier de la Sittelle** (Nuthatch Path) – watch for the image of the nuthatch on Office National des Forêts (ONF; National Office for Forests) signposts – offers an opportunity to explore the forest close up. The path follows the former Piste des Condamnés (Trail of the Condemned), named in memory of the prisoners who did forced labour in the forest in the 19th century.

There's no public transport service to the forest but you can take a taxi from Ota.

Col de Verghio
About 6km above the Village Vacances de Paesolu d'Aïtone, Col de Verghio (1467m) marks the boundary between Haute-Corse and Corse-du-Sud. As you cross this boundary you'll pass by the sculptor Bonardi; it represents Jesus in a long cloak, his arm outstretched, his palm turned upwards towards the heavens. A vendor of Corsican produce and drinks in the car park is his constant companion in summer.

There are a number of **walking paths** from Col de Verghio, which has unobstructed views over the Forêt d'Aïtone on one side and the Forêt de Valdu Niellu on the other. See p136 for details on the walk to the Bergeries de Radule on the GR20.

The Niolo region and the Forêt de Valdu Niellu stretch eastwards from Col de Verghio. A few parcels of forestry land are used to study the longevity of the Corsican laricio pine. Some of its trees are 300 years old and have grown to a height of 30m.

SLEEPING & EATING
Hôtel Castel di Verghio (☎ 04 95 48 00 01; camping €5; s/d/tr €43/49/61; half-board 55/80/117) This place, which caters mainly for walkers, has 29 basic rooms, each with a shower and sink (toilets on the landing). In the evening, the hotel's restaurant offers a €15 menu that

---

COL DE VERGHIO TO THE BERGERIES DE RADULE WALK

The path starts from behind the statue that, by tradition, marks the border between Haute-Corse and Corse-du-Sud 12km beyond Évisa on the D84. This walk, waymarked in yellow, is a spectacular one, among mountain-tops and forests, and it is not very difficult. The Bergeries de Radule are on the GR20; make sure on your way back that you follow the yellow markings, and not the red and white route of the GR20.

The bergeries are a few little stone shepherds' huts and sheep pens clinging to the side of the mountain and it is very difficult to make them out against their barren background. A shepherd lives here during the summer months. A few minutes' walk from here, where a natural stone basin catches water flowing over some small falls, you might think you have stumbled on heaven on earth. It will take you about 40 minutes to walk this easy route (one way).

---

attracts hordes of hungry walkers. The hotel bar sells a range of basic foodstuffs as well. Credit cards are not accepted.

Accommodation is also available in Calacuccia (p215), about 20km from Col de Verghio.

GETTING THERE & AWAY
A bus service linking Corte and Porto passes by Hôtel Castel di Verghio once daily in each direction.

LES CALANQUES (E CALANCHE)

The phantasmagorical rock formations, known as Les Calanques, which crop up from the sea in teetering columns, towers and irregularly shaped boulders are truly awe-inspiring and a highlight of any visit to Corsica.

As you follow the road, turning switchback after switchback, you are struck by breathtaking vistas, each more spectacular than the last. Gargantuan granite shapes, naturally coloured with iridescent shades of pink grapefruit, ochre and ginger, appear like the scene of a Dali painting. Guy de Maupassant, who visited Corsica in 1880, likened these strange geological formations to 'some fantastic fairy-tale race, petrified by an unknown supernatural force'. In fact, this amazing stone garden – which UNESCO has named a World Heritage site – was formed by wind and sea erosion. For a really stunning, full technicolour experience, Les Calanques should be savoured at sunset and on foot.

The D81 begins to wind its way through Les Calanques at a distance of about 1.5km from Piana, on the way to Porto; the route then twists and turns through the ochre-red rocks for several kilometres more.

Walks
You can explore the site and surrounding area of Les Calanques on foot. The first three of the routes described below start at the **Pont de Mezzanu**, approximately 1.5km from Piana towards Porto (halfway between the Chalet des Roches Bleues souvenir shop and Piana). A brochure and a map detailing the paths are available from the tourist office in Piana (p137).

- **Sentier Muletier** This route takes about an hour and follows the mule track that linked Piana and Ota before the D81 was built in 1850. It is signposted in blue.
- **Forêt de Piana** This comprises two alternative routes (round trip 2½ and three hours respectively) that pass through the pine forests and chestnut groves above Les Calanques.
- **Capu d'Ortu** This starts like the Forêt de Piana walk before ascending to a rocky spur. The walk takes six hours (round trip) and takes you to the Capu d'Ortu plateau (1294m).
- **Château Fort** Leading to a rocky promontory over the Golfe de Porto and Les Calanques, this walk takes about 40 minutes round-trip. See p137 for full details.
- **Sentier du Coeur** The name refers to the heart-shaped indentation in the rock to which it leads. The walk takes no more than 15 minutes and starts from Le Moulin des Calanques (p138) whose proprietors developed this walk.

Getting There & Away
It is easy to get to Les Calanques on foot from Piana. SAIB buses that run between Ajaccio and Porto can drop you off here or at the Chalet des Roches Bleues souvenir shop.

LES CALANQUES: A WALK TO THE CHÂTEAU FORT

This short path leads from the Tête de Chien (Dog's Head), which is a distinctively shaped rock signposted on a large bend in the D81, 3.5km from Piana on the way to Porto. (If you happen to be coming from Porto, the reason for the rock's name will actually make some sense.) The trail is roughly marked but you are unlikely to get lost because there are always lots of people around in the summer. Avoid wearing sandals because the path, although easy, is rocky.

Twenty to 30 minutes into the walk, you reach a natural platform known as the Château Fort from which the view over the Golfe de Porto and the deep rocky inlets of Les Calanques is stunning. It's even better at sunset. The whole walk is at most an hour's round trip.

PIANA

postcode 20115 / pop 500 / elevation 438m

Piana overlooks the Golfe de Porto from a small plateau, 68km from Ajaccio and 12km southwest of Porto. Les Calanques (E Calanche), Piana's famous rocky inlets, cast a golden shadow over the village. Many people just pass through Piana, but it is a pleasant village and definitely worth a stop.

In the 15th century Piana was ruled by the hot-headed *seigneurs de Leca*, who governed a vast area on the western coast of the island. Rebelling against Genoa, they were massacred alongside the defenders of the parish. The Genoese then banned anyone from living in Piana, which came to life again only after Genoese influence on the island had begun to wane.

The **Église Ste-Marie**, which contains several exceptional statues, was built between 1765 and 1772.

Orientation

Entering Piana from Porto, you'll first see Hôtel des Roches Rouges, then the path to the *gîte* d'Étape Giargalo on a bend in the road just before the Hôtel Mare e Monte. Following that you'll find the tourist office, post office and the village square with its church and restaurants. The Hôtel Continental and a supermarket are on the outskirts of Piana heading towards Cargèse.

Information

The **tourist office** (☎ 04 95 27 84 42; www.sipiana .com; ☺ 9am-6pm May–mid-Oct, 10am-3pm Mon-Fri mid-Oct–Apr) is on the main road next to the post office and has brochures and information on walks in the area.

There are no banks, *bureaux de change* or ATMs in Piana but you should be able to exchange your travellers cheques at the **post office** (☎ 04 95 27 89 29; ☺ 8am-noon & 1-5pm Mon-Fri) in the building next to the town hall.

Sleeping

Hôtel Mare e Monti (☎ 04 95 27 82 14; www.mare -e-monti.com; rte de Porto; s & d €78; P) This hotel has immaculate and comfortable, if somewhat fusty, rooms with bathroom, telephone and balcony.

Hôtel Continental (☎ 04 95 27 83 12; s/d from €28/34, s/d with bathroom from €43/57; ☺ Apr-Oct; P) This one-star hotel in an imposing townhouse just south of the main square offers simple but pleasant rooms with rustic wooden floorboards.

Le Scandola (☎ 04 95 27 80 07; infos@hotel scandola.com; rte d'Ajaccio; s/d €50/55, s/d with bathroom €83/89; ☺ Mar-Nov) Also situated at the southern end of the village, Le Scandola

THE AUTHOR'S CHOICE

Hôtel des Roches Rouges (☎ 04 95 27 81 81; fax 04 95 27 81 76; s & d €71; P) The terrace at the Roches Rouges, looking over Les Calanques at sunset, must offer one of the finest views on earth. Even if you don't stay here, stop in for a drink and savour the vista. Set up as a hotel in 1912, it looks like time has stood still in the house, with little changed except for the addition of a few telephones. The hotel oozes faded turn-of-the-century elegance with its grand, tall-windowed dining room and sweeping foyer where guests play chess and backgammon. Its 30 rooms are huge and sparsely furnished. But one of the hotel's most charming aspects is the lived-in, slightly dog-eared condition that gives it an authentic atmosphere. It goes without saying you should ask for a room with a sea view.

THE WEST COAST

has 17 modestly furnished rooms, some with fine views of the gulf. The reasonable price includes breakfast.

Mr Casanova (☎ 04 95 27 84 20) rents out rustic one- or two-room studios with sea views at the end of the village for €370/470 in high season.

Camping de la Plage d'Arone (☎ 04 95 20 64 54; adult/tent/car from €5/2/2; ☼ May-Sep) This lovely campground (but with little shade) is 11km from Piana and 600m from the Plage d'Arone.

Eating

Le Casanova (☎ 04 95 27 84 20; mains €4-10, pizza €7-9; ☼ Apr-Oct) The name refers, not to a philandering patron but to the owner's surname. In a pretty stone house on the square, run by the friendly Antoine Casanova and his children, Le Casanova serves large wood-fired pizzas and €15 *menus* featuring Corsican specialities such as *figarellu* (pork liver sausage) or pasta with prawns. The large terrace is normally packed at night.

The restaurant at the **Hôtel des Roches Rouges** (☎ 04 95 27 81 81; menu €22-32) gives you the opportunity to settle into a comfortable, cane armchair and enjoy superior nouvelle cuisine, superb décor and an exceptional panoramic view of the gulf. The *menu* is inventive and may include trio of fish on curried risotto but, be warned, portions are particularly small. There's a good selection of local wines by the half-bottle.

Le Phocea (☎ 04 95 27 80 98) whose name refers to the type of Brazilian tree, imported to the spot just outside this tiny *tabac-bar* almost 100 years ago, is a shady pit stop for a coffee and sandwich (€4).

Nicely located beside Les Calanques in an old chestnut flour mill **Le Moulin des Calanques** (☎ 04 95 27 84 80) is a kilometre outside of Piana on the way to Porto. It serves light snacks, sandwiches and panini. The proprietors are real enthusiasts of the area and will gladly provide advice on where to walk.

Getting There & Away

SAIB buses (☎ 04 95 22 41 99) stop in Piana on their way back and forth between Ajaccio and Porto. The buses run twice daily Monday to Saturday except public holidays. Between 1 July and 15 September they operate on Sundays as well.

AROUND PIANA

Les Calanques are just one of the interests of the area around Piana, but in order to explore further you may find it useful to have a car.

La Marine de Ficajola

From the church in Piana, follow the D824 towards the Plage d'Arone for 1km, then turn right onto the D624, which winds its way down through superb rocky red mountains for about 4km. Leave your vehicle and walk for about 10 minutes down a path to the marina. This is a spot where, in days gone by, lobster-fishing boats used to take shelter. Along the way you will have opportunities to admire the marvellous views over Les Calanques. At the marina there is a small snack bar in summer.

Plage d'Arone

This vast and exposed fine-sand beach is reached by following the D824 for 12km from the church in Piana. The drive takes you along a ridge offering wonderful views over the Golfe de Porto, then cuts through superb wild mountain scenery and maquis to end up south of Capu Rossu.

The beach itself has a special place in Corsican history as it was here that the first weapons for the Corsican resistance arrived on the submarine *Casabianca* in 1943, under the command of Captain L'Herminier (after whom several quays in Corsican harbours are named).

Le Casablanca (☎ 04 95 20 70 40; mains €9-24; ☼ Apr-Oct), with its shady terrace overlooking the beach, comes highly recommended by locals for its wood-fired pizzas and seafood specials such as turbot and prawn kebab.

Capu Rossu (Capo Rosso)

Between the Golfe de Porto and the Golfe de Sagone, this scrub-covered headland with pink-grey rock stands 300m high, and is crowned by the **Tour de Turghiu**. There is an excellent walk along the headland, and the view over the Golfe de Porto and the Plage d'Arone is breathtaking. To get to the headland, follow the D824 out of Piana towards Plage d'Arone. The 7km road that turns off to Capu Rossu cuts through a superb wilderness. The walk to Capu Rossu from the D824 is described in the boxed text on p139.

WALK TO CAPU ROSSU

A snack bar at the bend in the D824 just before Plage d'Arone marks the beginning of this breathtaking walk. From the road you can clearly make out the haughty silhouette of the **Tour de Turghiu** as it rises above Capu Rossu to the west. The pebbly path, lined initially with low stone walls, descends steadily through the maquis for 20 minutes to a point at which you will see a little *bergerie* to the left.

A bit further on, there's a spectacular view to the left over the cove and the white sand of **Plage d'Arone**. The path skirts around to the south of the rocky escarpment on which the Tour de Turghiu stands, before coming to a second *bergerie*. Note how the granite here takes on different shades of grey and pink. The path then turns right (northwards) to tackle the climb to the tower. Watch the small cairns that mark the tight bends up to the summit. Allow about 30 minutes. Though there's no shade whatsoever (wear a hat), the effort will seem worthwhile when you reach the Tour de Turghiu. At your feet, there's a 300m sheer cliff drop to the sea beneath. The views of the Golfe de Porto and the Golfe de Sagone are fantastic. Give yourself three hours for the round trip.

GOLFE DE SAGONE

CARGÈSE (CARGHJESE)

postcode 20130 / pop 1008

This sleepy little town, on a promontory over the sea, was founded in 1676 to house a community of 730 Greeks, who had appealed to Genoa for refuge from the conquering Turks (p141). There is no longer much to mark the town as Greek, however, other than the Greek Orthodox religious festivals celebrated in the Eastern Rite church (Église Catholique de Rite Grec). The immigrants' descendants are no longer in any significant way distinguishable from other Corsicans. Cargèse's history has created a unique atmosphere but its charm lies simply in its quiet streets and white façades. With five beaches in the vicinity, it's a great base for sun-worshippers .

Orientation

Most of the hotels and restaurants in Cargèse lie along the main road (D81) while the old town and the churches are to the right as you come from Piana. Several streets lead off the main road down to a small fishing harbour but it is not of great interest. The beautiful Plage du Péro, where much of the town's accommodation is based, is 1.5km north of Cargèse.

Information

Banque Populaire Provençale et Corse (☎ 04 95 26 40 43; ⏰ 8.30am-12.15pm & 1.30-4.50pm Mon-Fri Jun-Sep; 8.30am-12.15pm & 1.30-4.50pm Tue-Fri, 8.30am-noon Sat Oct-May) On the way into town from Piana, provides cash advances against credit cards; has an ATM. (Shopi supermarket also has an ATM.)

Crédit Agricole (☎ 04 95 26 41 75; rue Colonel Fieschi) Changes currency.

Post office (☎ 04 95 26 41 97; ⏰ 9am-12.30pm & 2-6.45pm Mon-Fri, 9-11.45am Sat) On the main road at the entrance to the old town; stays open during lunch in high season and has an ATM.

Tourist office (☎ 04 95 26 41 31; www.cargese.net; ⏰ 9am-7pm Mon-Sat, 9am-1.30pm Sun Jun-Sep; 9am-12.30pm & 2.30-6pm Mon-Sat Oct-May) Below the main road towards the old town.

Sights & Activities

ÉGLISE CATHOLIQUE DE RITE GREC

This white-fronted church, opposite the Église Latine Ste-Marie, is worth visiting for its icons (several of which were brought from Greece in 1676), its old paintings and for its interior staircase. The present church dates from 1852, when it replaced the original building, which was no longer large enough to accommodate the entire congregation. The new church took 20 years to build and the parishioners were themselves frequently enlisted to help. Like all Greek churches, this is above all distinguished by the richness of its ornamentation and its iconostasis (a traditional painted wooden partition separating the sanctuary from the nave).

ÉGLISE LATINE STE-MARIE

The history of this church goes back to 1817, when the town's non-Greek families decided that it was time to establish a fund

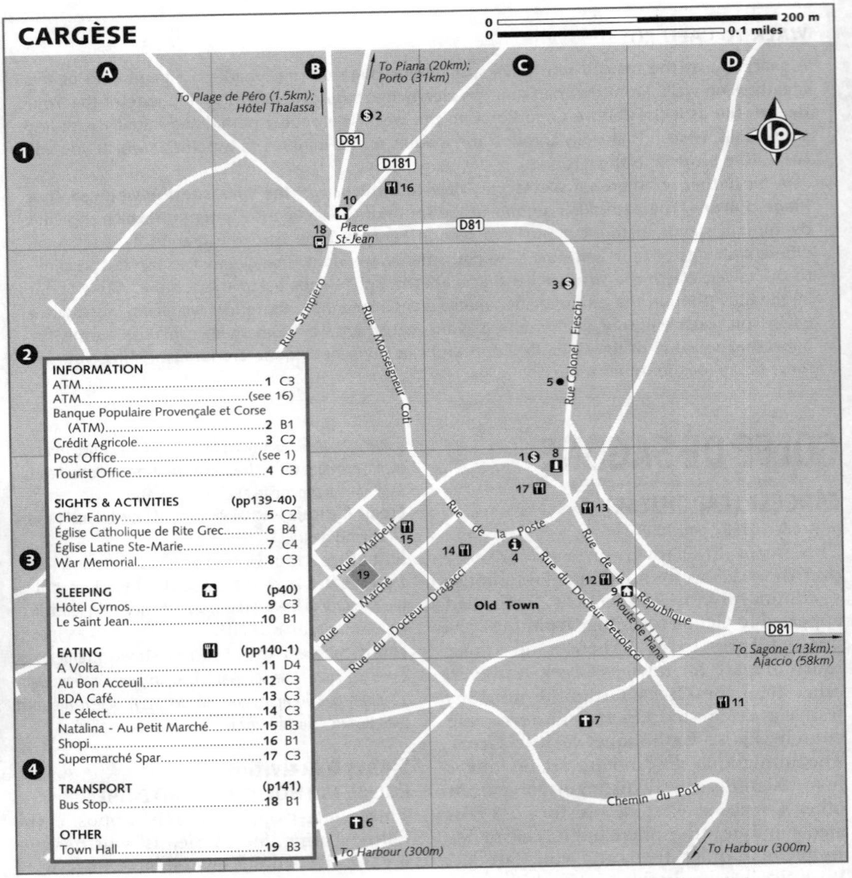

CARGÈSE
0 200 m
0 0.1 miles
A
B
C
D
1
2
3
4
To Plage de Péro (1.5km); Hôtel Thalassa
To Piana (20km); Porto (31km)
D81
D181
Place St-Jean
Rue Sampiero
Rue Monseigneur Coti
Rue Colonel Fieschi
Rue de la Poste
Rue Marbeuf
Rue du Marché
Rue du Docteur Dragacci
Rue du Docteur Petrolacci
Rue de la République
Route de Piana
Old Town
To Sagone (13km); Ajaccio (58km)
Chemin du Port
To Harbour (300m)
To Harbour (300m)
INFORMATION
ATM....1 C3
ATM....(see 16)
Banque Populaire Provençale et Corse (ATM)....2 B1
Crédit Agricole....3 C2
Post Office....(see 1)
Tourist Office....4 C3
SIGHTS & ACTIVITIES (pp139-40)
Chez Fanny....5 C2
Église Catholique de Rite Grec....6 B4
Église Latine Ste-Marie....7 C4
War Memorial....8 C3
SLEEPING (p40)
Hôtel Cyrnos....9 C3
Le Saint Jean....10 B1
EATING (pp140-1)
A Volta....11 D4
Au Bon Acceuil....12 C3
BDA Café....13 C3
Le Sélect....14 C3
Natalina - Au Petit Marché....15 B3
Shopi....16 B1
Supermarché Spar....17 C3
TRANSPORT (p141)
Bus Stop....18 B1
OTHER
Town Hall....19 B3

to build a Roman-Catholic sanctuary. Work, in the neo-classical style, began eight years later and continued until 1828. Wind blew the roof off in 1835 and there were no interior fittings until 1845. The square tower was added in 1847.

BOAT TRIPS

Nave Va (☎ 04 95 28 02 66; adult/child 5-10 years/child under 5 €40/20/free; May-Sep) organises boat trips to Capu Rossu, Les Calanques and the Scandola nature reserve. Boats leave the harbour at 9.30am and return at 4.30pm. The fare includes a two-hour stop at Girolata and a half-hour swim in an inlet. Tickets are sold at the shop **Chez Fanny** (☎ 04 95 26 44 43) on rue Colonel Fieschi. The tourist office also has information on two other local companies offering boat trips.

Sleeping

Hôtel Cyrnos (☎ 04 95 26 47 73, rte de Piana; d €40-60) This friendly two-star place has a handful of simple, bright, tile-floored rooms, some with views over the bay. The patron also has self-catering chalets that sleep four, 3km from town, for €400 per week.

Le Saint Jean (☎ 04 95 26 46 68; www.zanettacci.com; place St-Jean; d €60-73; P) Choose from newly renovated, very comfortable rooms with either maquis views or (marginally more expensive and slightly bigger) sea views. The hotel's restaurant, with a broad choice of *menus*, is the liveliest

FROM THE PELOPONNESE TO CARGÈSE

In 1663 some 800 Greeks from the southern Peloponnese fled their Ottoman-Turk conquerors and entered into talks with the Genoese authorities to find a new homeland. Twelve years later the Genoese granted them the territory of Paomia, just above what is now Cargèse, at a distance of about 50km north of Ajaccio. In March 1676 the surviving 730 émigrés – those who had not perished en route – set foot on Corsican soil for the first time. Their colony flourished. Some even gave up the 'akis' with which Greek names characteristically end and replaced it with a more Corsican-Italianate 'acci'. But then came the hitch. When the Corsicans rebelled against the Genoese in 1729, the Greeks, true to their pledge to their Genoese benefactors, sided with Genoa, and the Corsicans sacked Paomia. The Greek community moved to Ajaccio, where it then lived unobtrusively for about 40 years.

Relations between Greeks and Corsicans began to improve during the period of Corsican independence but it was only in the first decade of French rule that Cargèse itself was granted to them and they began to build new homes there. This time they were set upon by inhabitants of the neighbouring village of Vico and by Niolo shepherds who had been in the habit of wintering their flocks in the Cargèse area. Until around 1830, the Greeks shifted back and forth between Cargèse and relatively friendly Ajaccio but by then tempers had at last cooled and hostilities had gradually ceased. The Greeks installed themselves in Cargèse and for most of the past two centuries they and their Corsican neighbours have lived together in exemplary harmony – to the point at which nothing in particular distinguishes the two communities but the continuing allegiance of most of the Greeks to the Greek Orthodox church.

in town and there's Internet access available at the bar.

Hôtel Thalassa (☎ 04 95 26 40 08; fax 04 95 26 48 67; half-board s/d €100/140; ☿ May-Oct; ℗) You'll feel right at home here where the welcome is genuinely familial. The place has a real holiday feel to it, with a garden that leads right onto the beach and 26 airy rooms that are simply furnished, some with a terrace and some with wheelchair access. People come back here year after year so book well in advance.

Eating

Cargèse is no great gastronomic destination but there are many quite adequate restaurants along the main road and some pizzerias on the harbour.

BDA (☎ 04 95 26 43 37; rue de la République) In the old town, BDA is a funky new café with stressed metal front, low vaulted ceiling and sunny terrace. The friendly young brother-owners serve salads and panini all day.

Au Bon Acceuil (☎ 04 95 26 42 03; rue de la République) This bar in the centre of town is a traditional place with panelled walls and a lively terrace that serves good-value, hot snacks all day.

A Volta (☎ 04 95 26 41 96; mains €8-30) In a crumbling old cul-de-sac at the end of rue du Docteur Petrolacci in the old town, A Volta serves the best tucker in town. Try the Senegalese Yassa chicken (€13), hearty pastas (€9) or *bouillabaisse* (€30 for two) on the terrace with stunning views of the bay.

There are two supermarkets (Shopi on the D81 is one) for self-caterers, and Natalina – Au Petit Marché, a small grocery shop in the old town, sells Corsican delicacies.

Getting There & Away

SAIB buses (☎ 04 95 22 41 99) on their way to Ajaccio and Porto stop two or three times daily in place St-Jean or at the post office. The one-way fare from Ajaccio is €8.

SAGONE

postcode 20118 / pop 230

The seaside resort of Sagone to the south of Cargèse is renowned not only for its beautiful, steeply shelving beach but also for its fine cuisine, making it a great village for a stopover. An old Roman city, Sagone had a bishop's palace from the 6th to the 16th century, one of Corsica's oldest, but no trace of it remains today.

Crédit Agricole (☎ 04 95 28 19 00) has an ATM that accepts Visa, MasterCard and Cirrus.

You can do **Nave Va's** (☎ 04 95 26 41 31 in Cargèse) boat trips to Scandola and Girolata from Sagone. Tickets are sold at the souvenir shop next to Le Bowling (an ice-cream shop, not a bowling alley) in town.

Sleeping & Eating

There are a handful of good places to stay along the beach.

La Marine Hôtel & Restaurant (☎ 04 95 28 00 03; d/tr from €50/80; mains €7-30; ☒ Apr-Oct) This friendly hotel is in a great location right on the beach as you enter town from Ajaccio. Rooms are cheerily decorated in bright colours, and those with sea views (€20 extra) have breezy balconies from which to take in the glorious views of the gulf. Though it doesn't look much, the busy terrace restaurant overlooking the beach serves excellent fresh salads and outstanding seafood. Service can be slack, so take advantage and get a swim in after you order.

A Stonda (☎ 06 95 28 01 66; mains €8-15; ☒ Tue-Sun Dec-Oct) Locals travel for miles to get a table at A Stonda (across the road from La Marine), and for good reason. Under tiki paper lampshades and hanging baskets, in what looks no more than an open stone shed, you'll find some of the best food around. The simple *menu* of grilled meat, seafood and wood-fired pizza changes daily and uses organic and seasonal local produce to mouth-watering effect.

Getting There & Around

SAIB buses (☎ 04 95 22 41 99) operate between Ajaccio and Ota via Sagone two or three times daily.

You can hire boats or scooters from **Location 2000** (☎ 04 95 28 04 78) beside La Marine Hôtel.

TIUCCIA

postcode 20111 / pop 192

A small necklace of houses and shops around a crescent-shaped bay mark the village of Tiuccia, 7km south of Sagone, whose only real attraction is its proximity to the gently curving Plage du Stagnone and sweeping Plage de Liamone.

Sleeping & Eating

Though smaller than Sagone there are still a few places to comfortably bed down for the night, including a couple of campsites. One such option is **Les Flots Bleus** (☎ 04 95 52 21 65; s/d €51/62; half-board s/d €71.80/103.70; mains €8-16; P), as you enter the village. This small, friendly hotel and restaurant sits on the edge of what is effectively its own beach. It has simple white-washed rooms with tasteful,

rustic furnishings and terracotta floors. All rooms have showers and breakfast is included in the price. The busy restaurant, which serves Corsican dishes, seafood and salads, is particularly good value.

Getting There & Away

SAIB buses (☎ 04 95 22 41 99) operate between Ajaccio and Ota via Tiuccia two or three times daily.

LE LIAMONE

This mountainous green micro-region, also known as Les Deux Sorru, between Sagone and Col de Verghio takes its name from the river that flows through it to the Golfe de Sagone. Its largest villages are Renno (Rennu) and Vico (Vicu), which has an imposing convent. The villages detailed below lie along the Mare a Mare Nord path.

Vico

postcode 20160 / pop 450

Nestling in the mountains 14km from Sagone, the small town of Vico, with its narrow, tree-lined streets and tall townhouses offers welcome respite from the heat of the coast. A typical provincial town, Vico bustles during the day with local trade, ramblers stocking up on fresh produce and men playing *boules* on the place Padrona.

SLEEPING & EATING

Ferme-Auberge Pippa Minicale (☎ 04 95 26 61 51; d €40; ☒ year-round) The welcoming hostess of this *auberge* and her son offer five cosy rooms in a working farm on the outskirts of town. Savour the hearty home cooking, which uses the farm's own seasonal garden vegetables and farm produce such as herb-stuffed pork or *figatellu* cooked on a wood fire.

Café National (☎ 04 95 26 60 25; place Principale; mains €6-12) This stylish bar is beautifully situated in an old stone building in the corner of a small, elegant square. At a table under huge chestnut trees, you can sample fine crusty sandwiches with local *charcuterie* and cheeses, omelettes or wood-fired pizzas. There's singing on the square on Thursday evenings.

Guagno les Bains

The road that winds its way up beyond Vico leads to a picturesque cluster of villages

THE WEST COAST

perched on the mountainside. Guagno les Bains, the first village you come to, became a popular thermal spa in the 18th century, and after a major revamp in recent years visitors are once again flocking here in droves to experience the curative powers of Corsica's mineral waters.

SLEEPING & EATING
Established in the 19th century as a military hospital, **Hôtel des Thermes** (☎ 04 95 26 80 50; www.hotel-lesthermes.com; s/d €63/83; menus €17-28; ☺ Apr-Nov; ℗ ☎) is, thankfully, a far less austere place these days. The recently renovated hotel attracts punters from far and wide for its peaceful setting at an altitude of 480m, but more specifically for the adjoining hydrotherapy spa with its allegedly curative powers for respiratory and rheumatic ailments. Napoléon himself was a visitor to the spa, which offers baths of sulphurous water at a constant 61°C, saunas and a hamman. The hotel's no-frills rooms are comfortable, if a little dull, but residents will undoubtedly waste no time cashing in on the large, decked swimming pool, tennis courts, gourmet grub and idyllic surroundings.

Soccia & Orto
postcode 20125 / pop 126 & 54
Perched at an elevation of 700m, the pretty village of Soccia is set on mountainside terraces, 6.5km above Guagno les Bains. A great place to escape from the GR20, it is the starting point for the pleasant Lac de Creno walk (below). The **village church** (☺ 10am-noon & 4-7pm) dates from 1875 and contains a 15th-century triptych. The war memorial in the picturesque village square is testimony to the importance of local

---
SOCCIA TO LAC DE CRENO WALK

Visitors to the area may enjoy a little hike up to Lac de Creno (1310m). The lake is particularly pretty, set amid pine trees. Many travellers do it simply as a short stroll (about 30 minutes) down from the mountain village of Soccia. Hikers on the GR20 will turn west just before the Refuge de Manganu to make a detour to the lake; the descent takes about an hour.

---

involvement in WWI – it lists almost 50 names.

Orto, a few kilometres from Soccia, is even more remote, at the bottom of a narrow, steep valley where each house seems to overhang the one below. There is no public transport to the village. To get there you could get a bus to Vico and taxi from there.

Guagno
postcode 20160 / pop 130 / elevation 800m
From Guagno les Bains follow the winding road up the valley for 8.5km until you reach Guagno, only a three-hour walk from the GR20. There are several paths from Guagno to this walking route, which you can join either at Col de Soglia or just to the south of the Pietra Piana *refuge*. The village hosts a *gîte d'étape*, a small grocery shop and a public telephone.

GOLFE D'AJACCIO

AJACCIO (AJACCIU)
postcode 20000 / pop 60,000
Ajaccio is the largest town on the island, the capital of the French department of Corse-du-Sud, the site of the Assemblée Territoriale de la Corse, and famous as the birthplace of Napoleon Bonaparte. It even has a more lively side slightly reminiscent of Nice on the Côte d'Azur. But don't expect more of Ajaccio than it can deliver. Ajaccio is a provincial town with a limited bag of tricks and it also has a melancholic, or as the French might say *triste,* side.

Some of the town's museums, particularly Musée Fesch, contain collections whose quality cannot be faulted; but they are not guaranteed to appeal to all. The kitsch representation of native son Napoleon I may provoke second thoughts in those dreaming of world conquest and international fame. The more appealing of the two major shopping streets, rue du Cardinal Fesch, is a good place for a stroll.

History
Some sources attribute the town's origins to the mythical Greek hero Ajax, while others claim that its name derives, much more prosaically, from that of a Roman encampment. In fact, modern Ajaccio probably dates from no earlier than 1492, when

THE WEST COAST

GOLFE D'AJACCIO

Genoese families first began moving here from other less healthy spots on the island. Indigenous Corsicans were banned from living in the town until 1553, when it was seized by Sampiero Corso and his French allies, assisted by the Turkish privateer Dragut. Shortly afterwards a citadel was built on the foundations of a pre-existing Genoese

NAPOLEON'S CAPITAL

Ajaccio rose to fame under Napoleon, its most illustrious native son. In 1811 an imperial decree made Corsica a single department, and Ajaccio was made its capital. There was an outcry in Bastia, which lost its status as the island's principal town, but Napoleon justified his decision by asserting that Ajaccio 'should be the capital...since it is a natural harbour that lies across the water from Toulon and is thus the closest to France after St-Florent'. In accordance with the emperor's wishes, Ajaccio went on to spearhead the campaign to Gallicise the island.

castle. Recaptured in 1559 by the army of the Republic of Genoa, the town was not truly open to Corsicans until 1592.

The birth of Napoleon on 15 August 1769 was a turning point in the town's history. In accordance with the emperor's later decree, Ajaccio replaced Bastia as the island's capital in 1811 (see the boxed text, left). From that point on, the town's prosperity – or at least its relative prosperity – was a foregone conclusion.

Orientation

The main road through the town, cours Napoléon, links place de Gaulle (place du Diamant) with the train station. The old town is bordered by place de Gaulle, place Foch and the citadel. The route des Sanguinaires (D111), which leads to Pointe de la Parata, heads out of town, along the coast, to the west.

MAPS

The tourist office provides comprehensive, free Ajaccio street maps, with hotels and most attractions marked.

Information

BOOKSHOPS

Album (2 place Foch; 8.30am-noon & 2.30-7pm Mon-Sat, 8.30am-noon Sun Oct-May) Good selection of foreign-language books.

Stall (6am-8pm Mon-Sat) Sells local, national and foreign newspapers. There are two branches: cours Napoléon (opposite the main post office) and place Foch.

EMERGENCY

CROSS (04 95 20 13 63) Sea rescue.

Police (04 95 11 17 17; rue Général Fiorella)

INTERNET ACCESS

Tourist office (04 95 51 53 03; 3 blvd du Roi Jérôme) Has a computer where you can access the Internet at local call rates, by debiting your bank card.

Absolute Game (04 95 21 56 60; 1 cours Grandval, Diamante III; 15/30 min €2/3; 10-4am May-Oct, 9-2am Nov-Apr)

LEFT LUGGAGE

Bus station (04 95 51 55 45; quai l'Herminier; €1.50-5; 7am-7pm)

MEDICAL SERVICES

Hospital (04 95 29 90 90; 27 ave de l'Impératrice Eugénie) Has a 24-hour emergency department.

MONEY

Banque Populaire Provençale et Corse (04 95 21 49 85; 6 ave Antoine Serafini, place Foch) Has an ATM.

BNP (04 95 21 54 90; 33 cours Napoléon) Exchanges currency, Eurocheques and travellers cheques, and has an ATM.

Crédit Lyonnais (04 95 29 30 01; 59 cours Napoléon; 8.25am-12.20pm & 1.50-4.40pm Mon-Fri) Exchanges currency, Eurocheques and travellers cheques, and has an ATM.

POST

Main post office (04 95 51 84 75; 13 cours Napoléon; 8am-6.30pm Mon-Fri, 8am-noon Sat) Provides a fax and poste restante service. Post should be addressed: poste restante, poste principale d'Ajaccio, cours Napoléon, 20185 Ajaccio RT. Post is kept for two weeks and there must be a return address. You can also exchange travellers cheques here.

TOURIST INFORMATION

Tourist office (04 95 51 53 03; 3 blvd du Roi Jérôme; www.tourisme.fr/ajaccio; 8am-8.30pm Mon-Sat, 9am-1pm & 4-7pm Sun May-Oct; 8am-6pm Mon-Fri, 8am-noon & 2-6pm Sat Nov-Apr;) Large centre with numerous brochures and helpful, multilingual staff.

Bureau d'Information du Parc Naturel Régional de Corse (PNRC; 04 95 51 79 10; www.parc-naturel -corse.com; 2 rue Sergent Casalonga; 8am-7pm Mon-Fri, 8am-noon & 2-7pm Sat) The regional park office with all sorts of useful information on walking in Corsica.

Dangers & Annoyances

Ajaccio is a generally safe place to visit. Like anywhere else, you'd be foolish to leave valuables on display in vehicles, especially hire cars. One of the main problems you may encounter while driving is the difficulty in getting where you want to go in the one-way traffic system that seems to be almost permanently congested. Finding parking in the centre of Ajaccio is also a nightmare. To make matters worse, few hotels have their own parking facilities and public parking areas are small and fill up quickly. If you're staying in a centrally located hotel, your best bet is to drop off your luggage and then try to find a spot in the outlying streets. Cours Genérale Leclerc is a good option.

Sights

Ajaccio's main sights are all concentrated around the centre of town and are easily reached on foot. If you plan to visit a few of Ajaccio's museums during your stay, get your hands on a museum pass from the local tourist office. It will set you back €10 and allows access to six museums within a week.

MUSÉE FESCH

Built at the instigation of Cardinal Fesch (p148) to house a collection that he donated to the town in 1839, **Musée Fesch** (04 95 21 48 17; www.musee-fesch.com; 50 rue du Cardinal Fesch; adult/child €5.35/3.80; 1.30-6pm Mon, 9am-6.30pm Tue & Fri, plus 9pm-midnight Fri, 10.30am-6pm Sat & Sun, Jul & Aug; 1-5.15pm Mon, 9.15am-12.15pm & 2.15-5.15pm Tue & Sun, Apr & May, June & Sep; 9.15am-12.15pm & 2.15-5.15pm Tue-Sat Oct-Mar) has some outstanding 14th- to 19th-century Italian paintings by Titian, Fra Bartolomeo, Veronese, Botticelli and Bellini. On level 1 look out for *La Vierge à l'Enfant Soutenu par un Ange sous une Guirlande* (Mother & Child Supported by an Angel under a Garland), one of Botticelli's masterpieces. *Portrait de l'Homme au Gant* (Portrait of the Gloved Man) by Titian forms a matching set with another in the Louvre. Level 2 displays yet more Italian works. In

THE WEST COAST

THE WEST COAST

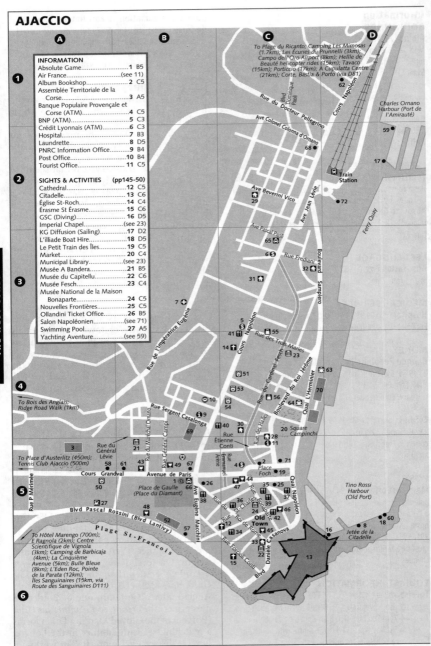

AJACCIO

INFORMATION
Absolute Game...........................1 B5
Air France...............................(see 11)
Album Bookshop......................2 C5
Assemblée Territoriale de la
  Corse.....................................3 A5
Banque Populaire Provençale et
  Corse (ATM)..........................4 C5
BNP (ATM)..............................5 C3
Crédit Lyonnais (ATM)............6 C3
Hospital...................................7 B3
Laundrette...............................8 D5
PNRC Information Office..........9 B4
Post Office.............................10 B4
Tourist Office.........................11 C5

SIGHTS & ACTIVITIES (pp145–50)
Cathedral................................12 C5
Citadelle.................................13 C6
Église St-Roch.........................14 C4
Érasme St Érasme....................15 C6
GSC (Diving)...........................16 D5
Imperial Chapel......................(see 23)
KG Diffusion (Sailing)..............17 D2
L'illiade Boat Hire....................18 D5
Le Petit Train des Îles..............19 C5
Market....................................20 C4
Municipal Library....................(see 23)
Musée A Bandera.....................21 B5
Musée du Capitellu..................22 C6
Musée Fesch...........................23 C4
Musée National de la Maison
  Bonaparte.............................24 C5
Nouvelles Frontières................25 C5
Ollandini Ticket Office.............26 B5
Salon Napoléonien.................(see 71)
Swimming Pool........................27 A5
Yachting Aventure..................(see 59)

To Plage du Ricanto; Camping Les Mimosas
(1.7km); Les Écuries du Prunnelli (3km);
Campo dell'Oro Airport (8km); Hélile de
Beauté helicopter rides (15km); Tavaco
(15km); Porticcio (17km); A Cupulatta Centre
(21km); Corte, Bastia & Porto (via D81)

Charles Ornano
Harbour (Port de
l'Amirauté)

Train
Station

Ferry Quay

Blvd Dominique Paoli

Rue du Docteur Pellegrino

Ave Colonel Colonna d'Ornano

Cours Napoléon

Ave Beverini Vico

Ave Jean Lévie

Ave Pascal Piot

Rue Frediani

Boulevard Sampiero

Rue des Trois Maries

Cours Napoléon

Rue du Cardinal Fesch

Boulevard du Roi Jérôme

Quai L'Herminier

Square
Campinchi

Place
Foch

Quai Napoléon

Tino Rossi
Harbour
(Old Port)

Old
Town

Rue de l'Impératrice Eugénie

To Bois des Anglais;
Ridge Road Walk (1km)

Rue Sergent Casalonga

Rue du Maréchal Ornano

Rue Général Campi

To Place d'Austerlitz (450m);
Tennis Club Ajaccio (500m)

Rue du
Général
Lévie

Cours Grandval

Avenue de Paris

Rue P Mérimée

Place de Gaulle
(Place du Diamant)

Blvd Pascal Rossini (Blvd Lantivy)

Plage St-François

To Hôtel Marengo (700m);
E Ragnola (2km); Centre
Scientifique de Vignola
(3km); Camping de Barbicaja
(4km); La Cinquième
Avenue (5km); Bulle Bleue
(8km); L'Eden Roc, Pointe
de la Parata (12km);
Îles Sanguinaires (15km, via
Route des Sanguinaires D111)

Ave Eugène Macchini

Ave Emmanuel Arène

Rue Fesch

Rue Forcioli Conti

Rue St-Charles

Rue du Roi de Rome

Rue Bonaparte

Rue Cardinal Fesch

Danièle Casanova

Jetée de la
Citadelle

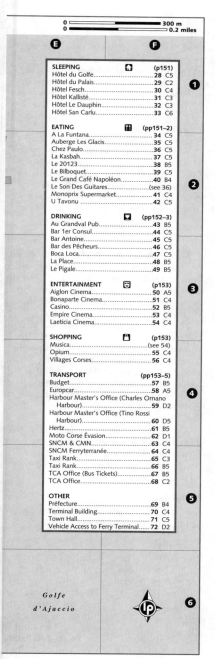

the basement there is a rather disappointing Napoleonic collection.

Admission to the **Imperial Chapel** next door, where the tombs of several members of the imperial family are found, costs €1.50. Don't expect, however, to find Napoleon's own remains here – he's buried in Les Invalides in Paris.

MUNICIPAL LIBRARY

Situated inside the Musée Fesch but with a separate entrance (not on the courtyard, but just to the left of it, as you face the courtyard), Ajaccio's **municipal library** (☎ 04 95 51 13 00; admission free; ☺ 9am-4.30pm Jun-Aug, 8.30am-noon & 2-6pm Mon-Fri Sep-May) merits a browse. The two lions decorating, or perhaps guarding, the entrance are modelled on the beasts that stand watch over the tomb of Pope Clement XIII at St Peter's in Rome; Cardinal Fesch donated them. Inside, uniform leather-bound volumes stretching to the ceiling, wooden ladders, and an 18m-long central table are altogether very impressive.

Napoleon's brother, Lucien Bonaparte, commissioned the library as early as 1801 to house the thousands of works piled up helter-skelter under the museum's gables. He added another 12,310 volumes confiscated during the French Revolution from *émigré* aristocrats and members of the religious orders. Cardinal Fesch made yet further contributions. The library was built in 1868, to plans by the architect Caseneuve.

MUSÉE A BANDERA

Tucked away on a little side street, the interesting **Musée A Bandera** (Flag Museum; ☎ 04 95 51 07 34; histoirecorse@wanadoo.fr; 1 rue du Général Lévie; adult/student €4/2.50; ☺ 9am-7pm Mon-Sat, 9am-noon Sun Jul–mid-Sep; 9am-noon & 2-6pm Mon-Sat mid-Sep–Jun), provides an overview of Corsican history from its origins until WWII. Among the highlights are a diorama of the 1769 battle of Ponte Novo that confirmed French conquest of the island, a model of the port of Ajaccio as it was in the same period, a coat of arms of the short-lived Anglo-Corsican kingdom, and some yellowing 19th-century pages from the *Petit Journal* and *L'Illustré*, recounting the arrest of famous Corsican bandits. Attention is also given to the role of women in Corsican society and in

THE WEST COAST

CARDINAL FESCH

Joseph Fesch (1763–1839) was Napoleon's mother's half-brother; his father was Swiss – a military man in the service of Genoa – which explains Joseph's un-Corsican name. His religious vocation was apparently genuine (he studied in the seminary at Aix and served as archdeacon of Ajaccio), but not his only interest. He left the church for a time to make himself rich and accompanied his warrior nephew to Italy as a super-glorified quartermaster. By 1800 Fesch was nevertheless back in clerical garb. In 1802 he was archbishop of Lyon, and, the following year, a cardinal, in which capacity Napoleon made him ambassador to Rome with the leading French Romantic literary figure François-Auguste-René Chateaubriand as his first secretary.

In Rome, Fesch's great achievement was to persuade the Pope to travel to Paris for the purpose of personally crowning Napoleon emperor – not that Napoleon allowed him to do so. Napoleon, the paradigm of the self-made man, took the crown from the Pope's hands and crowned himself. All of this, though, is only to scratch the surface of Fesch's complex career that moved alternately between the ecclesiastical and the secular. Fesch's very large responsibilities did not, moreover, preclude his finding time to amass the large collection of paintings and books that have made Ajaccio the art-pilgrimage town it certainly could never have become in any other way.

---

particular to the considerable power that they have sometimes wielded.

There are plans to move the museum to larger quarters on the route des Sanguinaires in 2005.

MUSÉE NATIONAL DE LA MAISON BONAPARTE

The chief interest of this **museum** (☎ 04 95 21 43 89; rue St-Charles; adult/18-25/under-18 €4/2.60/free; ⏰ 9am-noon & 2-6pm Apr-Oct; 10am-noon & 2-4.45pm Oct-Mar; closed Mon morning year-round), on one of the narrow streets of the old town, is that it contains the room in which the emperor was actually born. Visitors are asked to dress in a respectful manner.

SALON NAPOLÉONIEN

This **ceremonial room** (☎ 04 95 51 52 62; place Foch; adult/under-15 €2.30/free; ⏰ 9-11.45am & 2-5.45pm mid-Jun–mid-Sep, closed Sat & Sun mid-Sep–mid-Jun), just over the entrance chamber of the town hall on place Foch, contains sculptures and paintings of the imperial family, furniture from the 'return from Egypt' period, a Bohemian crystal light and numerous medals.

OTHER SIGHTS

The small, private **Musée du Capitellu** (☎ 04 95 21 50 57; 18 blvd Danièle Casanova; adult/under-10 €4/2; ⏰ 10am-noon & 2-6pm Mon-Sat, 10am-noon Sun Apr-Oct; open by appointment Nov-Mar) provides a fascinating glimpse into the town's history with its collection of 19th-century silverware and porcelain.

The 15th-century **citadel**, an imposing military fortress overlooking the sea, which housed a prison during WWII, is normally closed to the public but the tourist office organises two guided visits a week during summer.

The Venetian-style **cathedral** was built in the second half of the 16th century. Inside you can see the font used for Napoleon's baptism and Delacroix's painting of the *Vierge au Sacré Coeur*. The cathedral, which has an ochre façade and is in the shape of a Greek cross, stands in the old town at the corner of rue Forcioli Conti and rue St-Charles.

About 1km from place de Gaulle, **place d'Austerlitz** contains an immense statue of Napoleon. There's a suggestion that Napoleon may have played as a child in the adjacent grotto.

Activities

See p154 for details on hiring motorbikes, scooters and mountain bikes.

BEACHES

Not far from the city centre you can find a number of beaches, though unsurprisingly they tend to get a bit crowded in summer. The large **Plage du Ricanto** lies about 6km east of the town towards the airport. You can reach it on the No 1 bus. Smaller expanses of sand can be found in Ajaccio itself and around **Pointe de la Parata**, which you can reach on the No 5 bus.

The sprawling seaside resort of Porticcio (p155), south of the airport, prides itself on its long sandy beach, and there are yet more beaches south of Porticcio.

BOAT TRIPS

Nave Va (☎ 04 95 51 31 31; ☒ 7am-noon & 2-7pm) in the old port organises boat trips to the Îles Sanguinaires (€22), the Scandola nature reserve via Les Calanques, Piana and Girolata (€46) and Bonifacio (€55) from April to October (usually daily in high season). You must reserve your ticket in advance by phone and pay at the boat. Children under five go free, five to 10-year-olds are charged half-price.

DIVING

GSC (☎ 06 03 58 93 00; ☒ mid-May–Sep) is the only club in the centre of Ajaccio proper (specifically in the Tino Rossi marina). It's a small establishment that charges €35 for an introductory dive (children under 14, €27), and €20 to €32 for an exploratory dive. It offers various packages for multiple dives.

There are two trips at 8.30am and 2.30pm daily, and there may be a third, depending on demand.

E Ragnole (☎ 04 95 21 53 55; www.eragnole.com) is part of the Anthinéa fitness club, and the team of young instructors give it a particularly relaxed atmosphere. Look for it about 2km from the centre of Ajaccio on the beach side of the route des Sanguinaires, just after the Champion supermarket. Rates are €35 for an introductory dive in the sea, €30 to €35 for an exploratory dive, or €130 for five dives.

Bulle Bleue (☎ 04 95 52 01 68, 06 11 89 01 11; ☒ May-Oct), in the basement of the Hôtel Stella di Mare, on the route des Sanguinaires 8km from Ajaccio centre, offers introductory dives in front of the hotel for €37 or a beginners' course starting in the swimming pool and then moving out to sea. Exploratory dives cost €39; a six-dive package costs €206.

HORSE RIDING

Les Écuries du Prunelli (☎ 04 95 23 03 10; rte de Campo dell'Oro; adult/child per hr €18/16) on the Bastia road offers treks, lessons and a children's pony club during the summer.

SAILING

The friendly team at **Yachting Aventure** (☎ 04 95 10 26 25; www.yachting-aventure.com; port Charles

---

HIKING THE RIDGE ROAD

The walk starts just opposite the **Bois des Anglais** (English Woods) bus stop near Ajaccio. To walk there (15 minutes), follow cours Grandval and ave du Général Leclerc from town to the Grotte Napoléon, from where you veer to the right onto ave Piétri. There's a sign reminding you of the basic safety rules and telling you that the path is marked out with blue arrows – not that these arrows are really visible any more.

The dirt track quickly narrows and winds its way through an arid landscape of cactus and aloe. As the markings are almost nonexistent and there are numerous crossroads, the easiest thing to do is keep on climbing until you reach a wide forest track. Depending on how you go, this will take anywhere between 15 and 40 minutes.

The forest track is known as the **chemin des Crêtes** (Ridge road); it looks down over the town of Ajaccio and the Golfe d'Ajaccio, and it even affords an interesting perspective on Monte d'Oro, which begins to take shape inland at the bottom of the Vallée du Gravone. Follow this path away from the town centre as it snakes through the maquis and eucalyptus bushes and alongside large, eroded rock formations. You'll have wonderful views all the way over a whole string of beaches and inlets. After you've walked for about two hours, you'll clearly make out the Îles Sanguinaires.

The path then descends to the sunny resort of Vignola (about 30 minutes) and the route des Sanguinaires (D111), which goes along the coast to the west starting from the No 5 bus stop opposite the Hôtel Week-End.

At the end of this walk (allow three to four hours), the beaches, snack bars and restaurants are plentiful, and you can return to Ajaccio on the No 5 bus (hourly, 7.30am to 7.30pm, daily during high season).

Ornano), near the harbour master's office in the Charles Ornano harbour, hire out two-seater jet skis (from €300 per day) and six- or seven-seat motor boats (from €300 per day or €1900 per week).

KG Diffusion (☎ 04 95 20 51 05) and **L'illiade** (☎ 06 77 97 14 02), both near the Tino Rossi harbour master's office, hire out sailing dinghies.

There are several sailing schools in Ajaccio; the tourist office can provide you with a list.

TENNIS
Tennis Club Ajaccio (☎ 04 95 21 26 70; Le Casone) just beside the grotto at place d'Austerlitz, offers lessons at €25 per hour.

OTHER ACTIVITIES
For a special star-spangled night out you could head to the observatory at the **Centre Scientifique de Vignola** (☎ 04 95 21 22 01; rte des Sanguinaires; adult/child €2/free; ☾ 9.30pm Fri Sep–mid-Jun, 10pm Fri mid-June–late Aug), just past the Hôtel Week-End beach. There you'll discover the night sky, with fascinating commentary (in French) on the stars, planets and associated Greek mythology. You can stargaze up until about 1am.

Ajaccio for children
With its fairly compact centre, Ajaccio is easily navigable on little legs (or big ones pushing buggies) and there's enough to keep children of all ages happy during a visit. Most hotels will provide cots on request, but few offer a babysitting service. Providing you're happy to go out *en famille*, Ajaccio is a safe place to stroll around in the evening, and restaurants, unlike many in northern Europe, will accommodate children at any hour. On summer nights there are market stalls and funfair rides around the port area just south of place Foch.

Le Petit Train des Îles (☎ 04 95 51 13 69) is an old-fashioned electric train that runs on two circuits: one through the old town (€6, 45 minutes) and a longer one through the old town and onto the Îles Sanguinaires (€9, 90 minutes). They leave every half-hour from opposite the town hall on place Foch (10am to 6.30pm).

There are a several beaches (p148) to go for a picnic or swim but on cooler days young ones may prefer to splash about in

the **swimming pool** (Piscine Municipale; ☎ 04 95 50 41 51; Complexe Municipal, blvd Pascal Rossini; adult/child €4/2; ☾ 9am-noon & 2-6pm; closed Aug).

The **A Cupulatta Centre** (p155), a breeding centre for turtles, has over 3000 of the species on view.

Pony riding enthusiasts could head to **Les Écuries du Prunelli** (p149) for an afternoon's trek, followed by an evening under the stars at **Centre Scientifique de Vignola** (left).

Tours
Ajaccio Vision (☎ 06 20 17 50 33; ajaccio-vision@ tiscali.fr; adult/child 8-12/child under 8 €10/5/free; ☾ every 90 minutes 10am-4.30pm Apr-Oct) runs tours of the city's main sights in an open-top bus, stopping for a break at the Sanguinaire islands. Tours depart from opposite the town hall on place Foch, where you also buy your ticket.

Ollandini (☎ 04 95 21 10 12; autocars@ollondini.fr; 3 place de Gaulle; adults per day €27-55; ☾ 8.30am-12.30pm & 2-6pm Mon-Fri, 9am-11.45am Sat), runs six coach trips from Ajaccio to various spots around Corsica.

A fantastic way to see Ajaccio and its environs is from the air. **Hél'île de Beauté** (☎ 04 95 72 18 63; adult/child under 12 €100/free) runs helicopter tours of the Sanguinaire islands and Ajaccio bay and the beaches to the south (20 minutes), departing from its base about 15km from Ajaccio on the Bastia road. Discounts for groups of four or more apply.

The tourist office also organises daily walking tours of the old town and Ajaccio's main sights during summer.

Festivals & Events
A Madunuccia (18 Mar) A big religious procession files through town in honour of Our Lady of Misericorde who has allegedly protected Ajaccians from plague since 1656.

Festival of St Érasme (2 June) Nautically themed festivities, food stalls, boat rides and amusements in the harbour celebrating the patron saint of fishermen.

Bastille Day (14 July) Fireworks and amusements.

Fêtes Napoléoniennes (15 Aug) Napoleon's birthday is celebrated with a parade, music, fireworks and amusements.

Shopping de Nuit (July & Aug) Shops open late and there's live music and street entertainment organised by the tourist office from 9pm-midnight on Fridays.

La Tour de Corse (mid-Oct) French rallying championships.

Sleeping

The tourist office can help you reserve accommodation and provide a free brochure listing most of the town's options, including self-catering rentals. If you plan to use Ajaccio as a base for exploring over a week or so the latter may well suit best.

BUDGET

Cheap accommodation in high season is thin on the ground in Ajaccio. Campers may be better heading south to Porticcio or north to Sagone.

Camping de Barbicaja (☎ 04 95 52 01 17; rte des Sanguinaires; adult/tent/car €5.70/2.30/2.30; ❧ Apr-Oct) The best thing about this campsite, around 4.5km from the town centre, is its location, on a shady site overlooking the sea. It tends to get very crowded in the high season. To get there catch the No 5 bus.

Camping les Mimosas (☎ 04 95 20 99 85; rte d'Alata; adult/tent/car €4.80/2/2; ❧ Apr-Nov) Three kilometres from the town centre, on a busy main road, Les Mimosas won't win any awards for its location but offers shade under its eucalyptus trees and enough facilities to merit a stopover. The No 4 bus comes within 900m of the site.

MID-RANGE

Hôtel du Palais (☎ 04 95 22 73 68; hoteldupalais@ wanadoo.fr; 5 ave Beverini Vico; s/d €70/80; ❧ Mar-Jan) This two star hotel offers eight simple, comfortable rooms with TV. Be warned though, in summer you may be required to book for three nights.

Hôtel Kallisté (☎ 04 95 51 34 45; www.cyrnos.net; 51 cours Napoléon; s/d €56/69; P ☒) Kallisté, on the main street, has 29 clean, comfortable rooms with bathroom, satellite TV. The owner speaks English.

Hôtel Marengo (☎ 04 95 21 43 66; fax 04 95 21 51 26; 2 rue Marengo; s & d €59; ❧ Mar-Nov; P ☒) This great hotel, just outside the town centre, will appeal to those in search of sun, sand and relaxation. Its 16 lovely rooms have TVs, telephones and balconies.

Hôtel Le Dauphin (☎ 04 95 21 12 94; fax 04 95 21 88 69; 11 blvd Sampiero; s/d €54/60; P) If you arrive late, Le Dauphin, opposite the ferry terminal, is a good choice. It offers 39 simple, though in some instances rather grim, rooms with bathroom, TV and telephone. With breakfast included, this is probably the best value, of its kind, in town.

Hôtel San Carlu (☎ 04 95 21 13 84; fax 04 95 21 09 99; 8 blvd Danièle Casanova; s/d from €72/79) This place, with its pastel and chrome décor, will make '80s aficionados feel right at home. Rooms are compact and clean, the service is friendly and you can't beat its central old town location.

TOP END

Hôtel Fesch (☎ 04 95 51 62 62; 7 rue Cardinal Fesch; s/d with shower €69/78; ☒) Right in town, the historic Hôtel Fesch has 77 pretty spacious and spotless rooms, decorated with rustic wooden furniture. The lift, bizarrely, is on the first-floor landing which won't do wheelchair-users or those toting heavy bags any favours. Rooms with a balcony cost up to €20 more.

Hôtel du Golfe (☎ 04 95 21 47 64; www.hotel dugolfe.com; 5 blvd du Roi Jérôme; s/d standard €72/88, with sea view €83/94 ☒) This friendly hotel is nicely located next to the port with a view over the bay. Rooms are rather small for the price and have bathrooms that are so small you nearly have to leave your washbag outside the door. It's worth paying a bit extra for a terrace and sea view.

L'Eden Roc (☎ 04 95 51 56 00; www.edenroc -corsica.fr; rte des Sanguinaires; half-board s/d from €232/ 343; P ☒ 🖳 🖳) L'Eden Roc is a swish, modern, four-star hotel, 8km from the town centre towards Pointe de la Parata. Indulge yourself in the elaborate thalassic fitness centre, spa and sauna. Half-board is obligatory in July and August.

Eating
BUDGET

Le Pigale (☎ 04 95 21 20 46; 6 ave de Paris; mains €6-10; ❧ Mon-Sat; ☒) This is a busy, friendly bar that serves hearty salads (€9), omelettes (€6 to €9) or a plate of cheeses and crusty bread for €4. There's outdoor seating.

Chez Paulo (☎ 04 95 51 16 47; 7 rue du Roi de Rome; mains €6-11, 3-course menu €15) There's always a crowd at Chez Paulo and for good reason. Visitors and locals alike watch life go by from its busy terrace and if you've had your fill of *aubergines farcies*, you can feast on a good selection of fresh pasta and pizza at prices that won't break the bank. There's live Corsican music each night after 10pm at the adjoining Le Son Des Guitares.

Auberge Les Glacis (☎ 04 95 21 18 70; rue des Glacis; 3-course menu €16-18) This place in a busy little

THE WEST COAST

alleyway stuffed with tables has a small but decent selection of *menus*. Try the Corsican, with its delicious roast lamb and potatoes with rosemary (€18).

There's also no lack of supermarkets in Ajaccio. **Monoprix** (cours Napoléon; ⏰ 8.30am-7.15pm Mon-Sat, to 7.45pm in summer) is well stocked.

MID-RANGE

Le 20123 (☎ 04 95 21 50 05; 2 rue du Roi de Rome; 3-course menu €26) The 20123 takes its unlikely name from the postal code of the village of its owner, Monsieur Habane. Inside it looks more like a mini-Corsican theme park than a restaurant. Life-sized dolls in traditional dress, a washing line sagging with pantaloons, and a hotch-potch of 1940s country paraphernalia shouldn't detract from its well-cooked, rustic dishes that use local produce.

U Tavonu (☎ 04 95 50 02 50; 3 rue Pozzo di Borgo; mains €10-14) U Tavonu, on a narrow laneway in the old port, serves Corsican specialities, wood-fired pizzas or great fish and seafood dishes, including the *pièce de resistènce*, a selection of langoustine, prawn and lobster flambéed with cognac (€23).

Le Bilboquet (☎ 04 95 51 35 40; 2 rue des Glacis; 3-course menu €21) This colourful little place on a bustling laneway specialises in inventive fish and seafood dishes, as well as finely prepared regulars such as *bouillabaisse* and grilled dorada.

Le Kasbah (☎ 04 95 50 57 97; 7 rue des Anciens Fossés; mains €11-19) Le Kasbah is a dark and cosy Moroccan place with richly coloured silk drapes and cushions, sumptuous *tagines* (meat stew), a selection of couscous and pungent mint teas.

Top End

Le Grand Café Napoléon (☎ 04 95 21 42 54; 10 cours Napoléon; 3-course menu €27-43; ⏰ closed Sun) This local institution, in a balmy plant-filled room with high ceilings, grand piano and elegant turn-of-the-century atmosphere, is a romantic spot for a special evening's dining. Despite the classical surroundings, the menu is surprisingly modern, featuring dishes like monkfish on wild rice with marinated butter beans.

A La Funtana (☎ 04 95 21 78 04; 9 rue Notre Dame; ⏰ closed Mon evening) This snazzy joint with white-washed walls adorned with abstract artwork is reputedly the best restaurant in town. It has an ambitious wine cellar and traditionally French cuisine; a six-course *menu* will set you back €46.

Drinking

For a town its size, Ajaccio has its fair share of bars, but, as party-loving destinations go, Ibiza will have nothing to worry about. Most of Ajaccio's action happens with knives and forks rather than cocktail glasses. The bars on cours Napoléon cater mainly for the tourist trade of the town with few exceptions so you'll need to sniff around to find the locals' hang-outs. There are a number of options, with terraces, on ave de Paris. Opening hours can be erratic though, and tend to follow demand, so don't be surprised to find the shutters down on all but the busiest spots on any given night.

Le Pigale (☎ 04 95 21 20 46; 6 ave de Paris) This friendly bar has plenty of terraced seating to keep its young crowd happy.

Au Grandval (☎ 04 95 21 13 15; 2 cours Grandval; ⏰ 6am-9pm) A charming little watering hole and one of Ajaccio's oldest bars. Opened in 1892, little has changed in Monsieur Fleschi's bar except for the addition of a formica bar counter thirty years ago. Archive photographs of Ajaccio streets cover the walls and outside you can sit by the palm tree, planted by the patron's grandfather on the 100th anniversary of Napoléon's death, and listen to the amusing chatter of the resident parakeet.

Bar des Pêcheurs (1 rue Pozzo di Borgo) Bar des Pêcheurs is just that – a tiny little mosaic-tiled room with plastic-framed fishy pictures where local fishermen quaff *pastis* after the day's haul.

Bar 1er Consul (☎ 04 95 21 36 16; 2 rue Bonaparte) A good spot to stop for a morning coffee on the terrace overlooking busy place Foch. Brown leather banquettes and smoke-stained walls add to the laid-back atmosphere.

Boca Loca (☎ rue de la Porta; ⏰ closed Sun & Mon) This Spanish joint is a small grungy cave-like place, up a laneway, that is open late. Its cocktails, tapas and live music (most evenings) are the main draw.

Bar Antoine (☎ 04 95 21 39 17; 15 rue du Roi de Rome) A long bar in an old building with sagging ceiling beams and fishing-inspired paraphernalia on the walls. Locals and visitors alike spill out from the terrace onto lively rue du Roi de Rome on warm evenings.

La Place (☎ 04 95 51 09 10; blvd Lantivy; ☽ 11pm-3am) Next to the casino, La Place is the only disco in Ajaccio proper and is an older person's pick-up joint. Expect to pay in excess of €7 for drinks.

La Cinquieme Avenue (☎ 04 95 52 09 77; rte des Sanguinaires; ☽ 12-5am) This *discoteque*, 5km from town, plays tinny French pop and chart hits to a young crowd. Good for anthropologists.

Entertainment

The municipal **casino** (☎ 04 95 50 40 60; blvd Lantivy; ☽ 1pm-4am) is rather on the plush side but fun anyway. Its slot machines, *bureau de change*, restaurant and bar are open to anyone over the age of 18. The more serious gaming room, with roulette and blackjack, opens at 9.30pm. Visitors are expected to dress 'appropriately'.

The **Empire** (☎ 04 95 21 21 00), **Laeticia** (☎ 04 95 21 07 24) and **Bonaparte** (☎ 04 95 51 26 46) cinemas on cours Napoléon all screen new releases, while **Aiglon** (☎ 04 95 51 29 46; 14 cours Grandval) shows independent French and foreign films. Tickets cost around €7. Programmes generally begin at 9.30pm but the Bonaparte also has screenings at 2.30pm and 6.30pm.

The tourist office runs a summer **concert programme** of traditional polyphonic singing throughout the summer on Wednesday evenings in St Érasme's church (adult/child €8/5, 7pm).

Shopping

There is a farmer's market in **square Campinchi** (☽ 8am-noon; Tue-Sun). On weekends stalls of clothing and crafts join those of fruit, vegetables, and Corsican cheeses and meat products.

Villages Corses (☎ 04 95 51 08 05; 44 rue du Cardinal Fesch; ☽ 8am-12.30pm & 2.30-7.30pm Mon-Sat) This shop is packed with Corsican delicacies, including *charcuterie*, cheeses, liqueurs, wine, chestnut flour and honey.

Opium (☎ 04 95 21 12 17; 6 rue des Trois Maries; ☽ 9.30am-12.30pm & 2.30-8pm) This shop offers no Corsican products at all. The owner, herself a victim of the travel bug, instead sells magnificent jewellery and crafts, for the most part from Africa and Asia.

Musica (☎ 04 95 21 00 59; 26 cours Napoléon) This music shop has a small selection of Corsican music and film on VHS.

Getting There & Away

Further information is contained in the Transport chapter (p233).

AIR

The small modern terminal building at **Campo dell'Oro airport** (☎ 04 95 23 56 56), 8km east of town, boasts a bar, souvenir and craft shops, a bookshop and an ATM machine.

Air France (reservations & general info ☎ 08 02 80 28 02; www.airfrance.com; 3 blvd du Roi Jérôme; ☽ 8.30am-noon Mon-Sat & 2-6pm Mon-Fri) Other airline offices can be found in the airport itself.

Nouvelles Frontières (☎ 04 95 21 55 55; www .nouvelles-frontieres.com; 12 place Foch; ☽ 9am-noon Mon-Sat & 2-6pm Mon-Fri)

BOAT

Ferry

Ferries leave from the modern **terminal building** (☎ 04 95 51 55 45; quai L'Herminier; ☽ 6am-8pm) which also houses the ticket windows for intercity buses.

SNCM **Ferryterranée** (☎ 04 95 29 66 99, 04 08 36 67 95 00; www.sncm.fr; ☽ 8.15-11.45am Mon-Sat & 2-6pm Mon-Fri) has two offices in the harbour. The office next to the Compagnie Méridionale de Navigation (CMN) sells tickets for same-day travel; the other, opposite the terminal building, handles reservations. **CMN** (☎ 08 10 20 13 20; www.cmn.fr; blvd Sampiero; ☽ 8am-7.30pm Mon-Fri, 9am-noon Sat) also runs crossings. For more information on ferry crossings, see the Transport chapter (p235).

In summer you can get a boat from Tino Rossi harbour to Porticcio (p157).

Yacht

Ajaccio has two yacht harbours; the Charles Ornano is bigger but sailors prefer the Tino Rossi. At the Charles Ornano harbour the **harbour master's office** (☎ 04 95 22 31 98, fax 04 95 20 98 08, VHF channel 9; ☽ 7am-9pm Jun-Oct, 8.30am-noon & 2-5pm Nov-May) is helpful. There are almost 1000 berths, 30 of which are reserved for visitors, and water, fuel, shower and toilet facilities as well as weather reports, a careening area and a chandlery. The daily rate for a 12m boat varies from €10 to €49

THE WEST COAST

per night depending on the month. Multi-hull vessels are charged an additional 50%. The harbour used to be known as the Port de l'Amirauté until it was renamed after a former mayor but most of the town's inhabitants use the old name.

At the Tino Rossi harbour (old port), the **harbour master's office** (☎ 04 95 51 22 72; fax 04 95 21 93 28; ☺ 8am-8pm Jun-Sep, 8am-noon & 2-6pm Oct-May) has washroom facilities, showers, shops, a laundrette, a ship's chandler, weather reports, restaurants, mechanics and a sail-repair shop, among other services. The harbour makes more berths available to visitors than the Charles Ornano, even though it is smaller. Expect to pay between about €15 and €50 daily depending on the size of your boat and the season. The high season runs from 1 June to 30 September.

BUS

A number of bus companies have offices in the modern ferry terminal on quai L'Herminier and, together, they provide service from Ajaccio to most other parts of the island. **Eurocorse** (☎ 04 95 21 06 30) goes to Bonifacio (€19.50, four hours, four daily Monday to Saturday, two Sunday). In summer there are buses Monday to Saturday to Sartène (€11.50, four hours, four daily) and to Zonza (€16.50, 3½ hours, twice daily). Buses leave for Bastia twice daily (€18). It is faster and cheaper to get to Calvi (€23, one daily, 3½ hours) by bus than by train. Baggage carriage costs an extra €1.

Bus companies are as follows:
SAIB (☎ 04 95 22 41 99) Goes to Porto (€11, two hours, two daily).
Casanova Buses (☎ 04 95 25 40 37) Has several daily departures between Ajaccio and Porticcio (€3, 20 minutes).
Autocars Ceccaldi (☎ 04 95 20 29 76) Operates a service from Ajaccio to Évisa via Vico (€12, daily except Sunday and public holidays).

TRAIN

Four trains daily leave **Ajaccio station** (☎ 04 95 23 11 03) for Vizzavona (€8.40, 30% cheaper in winter), Vivario (€9.20) and Corte (€12.50). There are four trains daily to Bastia (€23.50) and two to Île Rousse (€20.80) and Calvi (€27.30, five hours). There's no longer a left luggage facility at the station.

Getting Around

TO/FROM THE AIRPORT

TCA bus No 8 (€4, 16 daily 6.40am to 11.10pm, 20 minutes) runs between the airport and the town centre 8km away. Buses leave the airport from the car park at the far end of the air terminal on the departures side and make stops at the train and bus stations and ferry terminal. They leave the ferry terminal every day approximately hourly from 6.20am to 7.25pm.

A taxi from the airport to the town centre during the day costs around €20; between 7pm and 7am and on Sunday and public holidays the fare will be closer to €25. Ask whether the €2.16 airport tax is included or supplementary.

BUS

TCA (☎ 04 95 21 62 22; ave de Paris; ☺ 8am-noon & 2.15-7.30pm) runs buses within Ajaccio. You must buy five tickets at a time (€9) but they're valid for 10 journeys. You can get timetables and a network map from the office. The main lines are as follows:
No 4 Budiccione – town centre – Hôpital de la Miséricorde
No 5 Town centre – Pointe de la Parata (rte des Sanguinaires)
No 8 Bus station – airport

CAR

At the airport there are car-hire firms in the car park across from the terminal. Theoretically they open 9am to about 11pm in summer and 9.30am to 9pm the rest of the year. Rates differ considerably; it's worth the trouble to compare. Their contact details are as follows:
Ada (☎ 04 95 23 56 57; www.ada-en-corse.com)
Avis (☎ 04 95 23 56 90; www.avis.fr)
Budget (☎ 04 95 23 57 21/22; www.budget-en-corse.com)
Castellani Sixt (☎ 04 95 23 57 00; www.sixt-castellani-auto.com)
Citer (☎ 04 95 23 57 15; www.corse-auto-rent.fr)
Europcar (☎ 04 95 23 57 01; www.europcar.fr)
Hertz (☎ 04 95 23 57 04/05; www.hertz-en-corse.com)

A small, five-door car with air-conditioning (mileage included) costs about €180 for one week from Europcar.

MOTORCYCLE & BICYCLE

Moto Corse Évasion (☎ 04 95 20 52 05; www.corsica moto.com; montée St Jean; ☺ 8.30am-12.30pm & 2.30-6.30pm, Mon-Fri only Oct-Apr) hires out 125cc motorbikes (per day/week in summer €58/321), mountain or city bikes (€13/76) and 4WD vehicles (€107/442). It also organises biking and 4WD mountain trips.

TAXI

There is a **taxi** (☎ 06 03 69 42 20) rank on the corner of cours Napoléon and ave Pascal Paoli and another on the place de Gaulle.

AROUND AJACCIO
Îles Sanguinaires

These four small islands with their jagged coastlines take their name – meaning 'bloody' – from their distinctive red rock. They lie 12km off Pointe de la Parata at the mouth of the Golfe d'Ajaccio and they are a good place for a walk.

Nave Va (☎ 04 95 51 31 31; ✆ 7am-noon & 2-7pm; adult/child over 5/under 5 €22/11/free) organises boat trips to the islands from Tino Rossi harbour in town. The No 5 bus will take you as far as Pointe de la Parata.

A Cupulatta Centre

A Cupulatta (☎ 04 95 52 82 34; www.acupulatta.com; Vignola, Vero; adult/child 4-11/under 4 €7/3.50/free), 21km from Ajaccio towards Corte on the N193, is Europe's largest centre for the breeding and preservation of tortoises. It was opened in 1998 thanks to the enthusiasm of Philippe Magnan and his team of volunteers and today shelters approximately 3000 representatives of more than 150 species from all over the world, some of them in danger of extinction.

PORTICCIO
postcode 20166 / pop 2200

Porticcio could best be described as one long, string of hotels, burger joints and tourist shops selling tacky souvenirs, sprawled along its best asset, a long sandy beach. In summer Porticcio's main street is bumper to bumper with holiday traffic, consisting mostly of Ajaccians in search of a quick fix of sun, sand and surf. For some, its jolly seaside atmosphere, water-sports facilities and convenience to Ajaccio make up for the crowds and tailor-made development. Porticcio is just south of Campo dell'Oro airport.

Orientation

The town stretches along the length of its beach. A series of uninspiring modern commercial developments known as La Viva, Les Marines and Les Marines 2 on either side of the D55 are the focal points. Les Marines has a tourist office, bookshop, cinema, the Blue Moon disco and a landing stage. Across the road, Les Marines 2 has a petrol station, a taxi rank, banks, a post office and a Champion supermarket.

The Golfe d'Ajaccio south of Porticcio is composed of three beaches: Plage d'Agosta, Plage de Ruppione and Plage de Mare e Sole.

Information

Crédit Agricole (☎ 04 95 25 29 90; ✆ 8am-noon & 2-5.10pm) Changes currency and has an ATM.
Newsagent (☎ 04 95 25 08 41; ✆ 7am-9pm Jul & Aug, 7am-12.30pm & 2.30-7.30pm Mon-Sat, 8am-12.30pm Sun) In Les Marines; sells French and foreign newspapers and a small selection of books; look for the sign that reads 'tabac-presse-lotto'.
Post office (☎ 04 95 25 01 92; ✆ 8.30am-5.30pm Mon-Fri, 9am-noon Sat May-Oct) Behind the Elf petrol station in Les Marines 2. Hours are shorter outside high season.
Tourist office (☎ 04 95 25 01 01; www.porticcio.org; ✆ 8.30am-7pm Apr-Oct) A small white kiosk in Les Marines; opens shorter hours the rest of the year.
Société Générale (☎ 04 95 53 80 90; ✆ 8.10am-12.15 pm & 1.10-7pm Tue-Fri, 8.15am-12.15pm Sat) Next to the post office; changes currency and has an ATM.

Activities

You don't come to Porticcio for its sights; its beautiful **Plage de La Viva** fringing the town is the real draw and it has enough bars and restaurants as well as stalls that hire out sailboards and deck-chairs to keep most punters happy. Plage d'Agosta, Plage de Ruppione and Plage de Mare e Sole, further south, are less popular, less crowded and often more pleasant.

BOAT TRIPS

Nave Va (☎ 04 95 51 31 31; ✆ Apr-Oct) has a kiosk near the tourist office in Les Marines selling tickets for boat trips to the Scandola nature reserve (€26), Bonifacio (€55) and the Îles Sanguinaires (€22). Children between the age of five and 10 are half-price.

CYCLING

The **Shell station** (☎ 04 95 25 06 64) rents out mountain bikes at €13/60 per day/week against a €150 deposit.

THE WEST COAST

DIVING

For scuba diving try **Maeva** (☎ 04 95 25 02 40; www.maeva-plongee.com; Marines de Porticcio; ☺ Apr–Oct), opposite the Elf garage. You'll pay €38 for an introductory dive on the beach, €42 for a boat dive, €33 to €42 for an exploratory dive or €155 to €200 for five dives, depending on whether you use your own equipment or not.

Alternatively, try **Corse Plongée** (☎ 04 95 25 50 08, 06 07 55 67 25; www.corseplongee.fr.st; ☺ Apr–Nov or on request), on the Isolella peninsula just south of Porticcio. An introductory dive costs €40, an exploratory dive €26 to €38, and six dives go for €148 to €219. Corse Plongée's itinerary includes all of the famous sites – the wreck of the *Meulière*, the Tête de Mort and the Grotte à Corail – but Nicolas Caprili, director, diver and skipper, prides himself on having several other 'private' sites up his sleeve.

WATER SPORTS

Porticcio Nautical Centre (☎ 04 95 25 01 06; plage de la Viva) is a reputable company that rents windsurfing equipment (€13 to €16 per hour), kayaks (€10 to €14 per hour) and Hobie Cat 16 catamarans (€28 to €36 per hour). Beginners and advanced classes in windsurfing are available for children and adults (€14 per hour).

Ski Nautique Viva (☎ 04 95 25 17 93; ☺ 7.30am-noon & 2.15-7pm Jun-Sep), near the Maeva Diving Centre, offers water-skiing (€22 for a 10-minute spin) as well as beginner- or advanced-level instruction.

Rive Sud Nautique (☎ 04 95 25 19 89, 06 09 98 87 56; Plage de La Viva; ☺ Jun-Sep) hires out jet skis and organises jet-ski outings.

Loca-Nautic (☎ 04 95 25 17 85; www.loca-nautic .com; Plage de La Viva) hires out Zodiac boats (no permit required), dinghies and water skis.

Sleeping

BUDGET

Porticcio has plenty of accommodation for the independent traveller. **Camping U Prunelli** (☎ 04 95 25 19 23; pont de Pisciatello; adult/tent/car €7/3/3; ☺ Apr-Nov; P ☒) This is a lovely, shady, three-star site, 2km from the centre of Porticcio on the banks of the Prunelli river. There's a swimming pool, pizzeria and little shop selling basics on site. It also has wheelchair-accessible chalets for hire (2/4 beds per week from €420/500).

Camping Les Marines de Porticcio (☎ 04 95 25 09 35; adult/tent/car €6/2/2.50; ☺ Jun-Sep) Near the beach and the town centre, behind the Elf petrol station, this campground has the virtue of being fairly quiet. It has a children's playground and some small chalets available too, but these get booked up fast.

MID-RANGE

Les Flots Bleus (☎ 04 95 25 49 57; www.flotsbleus.com; d €115; ☺ Apr-Nov; P ☒) You'll really feel like you're at the seaside here, up the road at Agosta beach, with 33 bright rooms decorated in blue and white and terraces overlooking the beach. With a sauna, gym and tennis facilities, this place is hard to beat for value. It also has equipped apartments to rent that get snapped up early.

Acqua Dolce (☎ 04 95 25 19 62; www.hotel -acquadolce.com; s/d from €49/67; half-board s/d €71/110, 2-/4-bed studios per wk €590/785; rte de Sartène, Pisciatello; P ☒) Beside the river Prunelli, 3km from town in a lovely oak grove, Acqua Dolce is a good place to get away from the hustle and bustle of Porticcio. Rooms are simply furnished but clean and there are some lovely walks in the area. The studios have rustic wood-panelled walls, kitchenettes, showers and terraces.

Eating & Drinking

Porticcio is not one of Corsica's great eating destinations. Fare at its snack bars and restaurants is unremarkable but, on the plus side, nearly all the restaurants have wide terraces overlooking the sea and tables on the beach. So feast on the atmosphere (if not the food) because you'll be paying through the nose for it.

Le Sextant (☎ 04 95 25 54 07; mains €6-12; closed Mon; P), right on the Viva beach, is a reliable option. This friendly bar serves a good selection of mostly meat-based tapas in the evening. There's live Cuban music most evenings till 2am. **A Merendella** (☎ 04 95 25 08 27; mains €3-8) serves good savoury and sweet crêpes.

For self-caterers, there is a Champion **supermarket** at Les Marines 2.

Getting There & Around

BUS

There is a **bus service** (☎ 04 95 25 40 37) between Ajaccio and Plage de Mare e Sole Monday to Saturday from 1 July to 15 September.

THE WEST COAST

Buses leave approximately every 90 minutes from 9am until 7pm from Ajaccio, and from 7.30am until 6pm from Mare e Sole. They stop at Porticcio (€3) and Isolella. There is a morning and evening shuttle in winter.

BOAT

In summer, **boat trips** (☎ 04 95 25 94 14) run from the Tino Rossi harbour in Ajaccio to Porticcio (one-way/return, €5/7, 20 minutes). The first of five daily departures leaves at 8am and the last at 6.30pm. Call ahead to make sure they're not taking the day off.

There is a taxi rank in the Elf garage car park in Les Marines 2.

AROUND PORTICCIO
Forêt de Chiavari

A peaceful place for a picnic and some welcome respite from the heat is under the cork and eucalyptus groves of the Forêt de Chiavari. Just off the D55, easily accessible from the Plage de Verghia, follow the windy road, with stunning views of the bay, up towards the mountain-top village of Coti-Chiavari. On your left-hand side you will pass several huge, dilapidated buildings, the curious remains of the prison l'Ancien Pénitencier de Chiavari used during the late 19th century and again during WWII.

Capo di Muro

A walk to the cliff-top tower of Capo di Muro on the southernmost tip of the Golfe d'Ajaccio will reward you with outstanding panoramic views of the bay. It's possible to climb a small metal staircase to the 1st floor of the solid watchtower for even better viewing. To get there, follow the D155 south, taking a small road right, just after the village of Acqua Doria, as far as it goes. From here, you'll need to walk the final 800m or so to the tower.

Bastelica
pop 400

After leaving Ajaccio the D3 winds its way up into the mountains for about 25km until it reaches the village of **Tolla** on a perch over a lake. The road then continues along the **Gorges du Prunelli**, which can be seen lower down, at bends in the road, until it gets to Bastelica.

This rustic mountain village is famous for its *charcuterie*, made from local *cochons*

PIGS ON THE RUN

There are no longer any wild pigs (except wild boar) in Corsica: pigs seen at the sides of mountain roads are domestic animals known as *cochons coureurs*, or free-ranging pigs. It is estimated that there are 15,000 free-ranging pigs in Haute-Corse and 30,000 in Corse-du-Sud.

Corsican pork derives its flavour from the free-ranging pigs' diet of acorns and chestnuts (supplemented with other food at certain times of the year). The *charcuterie* produced in Corsica is excellent but expensive and some of the specialities sold on the island are actually made from imported pork meat.

coureurs (above), and also as the home town of Sampiero Corso (see the boxed text, p22). Visitors are greeted by a statue of Corso. A curious plaque, contributed by William Bonaparte Wyse (Napoleon's Irish grand-nephew), on the site of the house in which Corso was born, announces the hero as 'the most Corsican of all Corsicans'.

The **Val d'Ese** ski resort is a further 16km away along an unimproved road through beautiful mountain scenery. The ski resort (at an elevation of 1700m) has little impact on the environment: there are only two buildings and no hotel or restaurant. You can hire ski equipment in Bastelica.

SLEEPING & EATING

Chez Paul (☎ 04 95 28 71 59; half-board s/d €32/64) offers clean, no-fuss rooms in the house or adjacent apartments, and a warm welcome. Half board is obligatory in July and August, which shouldn't pose a problem as the food is legendary in these parts. After a hearty supper of *cannelloni au brocciu*, slow roasted lamb and their own cured *charcuterie*, washed down with the local *vin de myrte*, you should sleep like a baby. It's open all year.

GETTING THERE & AWAY

Bernardi (☎ 04 95 20 06 00) buses connect Ajaccio and Bastelica on Monday, Wednesday and Friday at 4.45pm (Monday to Saturday July and August). Buses leave Ajaccio from the car park at Charles Ornano harbour.

THE WEST COAST

The South

CONTENTS

Southern Corsica, in the area south of east-coast Porto Vecchio and west-coast Propriano, manages to line up an astonishing variety of human cultures and landscapes, despite tightly cramped quarters. Porto Vecchio and Propriano are the lively nerve-centres of increasingly sprawling beach resorts. In the hills behind Port Vecchio, Alta Rocca harbours fascinating little villages, ancient archaeological sites and numerous footpaths. The cool, mountaintop Fôret de L'Ospedale offers plenty of opportunities for wonderful hikes, rock climbing and canyoning away from the heat and bustle of Porto Vecchio. The proud old walled town of Sartène, with its narrow streets and tall elegant houses perched high over the valley, exudes a sense of history and is considered the most Corsican of all towns.

The Sartenais, the area around Sartène, is home to many of the island's most celebrated complexes of menhirs (standing stones), dolmens (standing stones capped by a horizontal stone) and *torri* (circular stone formations or towers). The very southernmost tip of the island, meanwhile, boasts a wonderful coastline with a dozen or so of undoubtedly Corsica's best beaches, a countryside of handsome cork oaks and the cliff-top, fairy-tale town of Bonifacio that looks across the straits to Italian Sardinia. Although the south was initially slower to capitalise on tourism than other parts of the island, it is now quickly catching up.

HIGHLIGHTS

- **Chill-Out Spot**
  Get the best views of wonderful **Bouches de Bonifacio** (p181) from a boat

- **Prehistoric**
  Wander the mystical prehistoric remains of **Filitosa** (p164)

- **Kid's Stuff**
  Take an action-packed activity break at **Porto Pollo** (p166)

- **Beach Bum**
  Snorkel in the clear aquamarine waters of the sweeping **Plage de Portigliolo** (p167)

- **Culture Vulture**
  Wonder at the identity of the cross-bearer in the **Procession du Catenacciu** (p170)

- **Au Naturel**
  Take a hike to the **Piscia de Gallo waterfall** (p190) in the cool Fôret de L'Ospedale or take a look at the unusual mountain peaks of **Aiguilles de Bavella** (p192)

THE SOUTH

PROPRIANO & FILITOSA

PROPRIANO (PRUPIŔ)
postcode 20110 / pop 3500

Founded by the Genoese as early as 1640, for a long time Propriano remained a modest hamlet in the shadow of the village of Fozzano.

The town is at the eastern end of the Golfe de Valinco, from where Sampiero Corso led an attempt to liberate the island in 1594. Its belated growth was largely a result of the construction of port facilities early in the 20th century, which made Propriano the centre of maritime activity for the Sartenais region. The arrival of tourists to the Golfe de Valinco's shores did the rest, and Propriano is now a popular and unpretentious, though somewhat unattractive seaside resort. Although the surrounding hills and commercial area around the harbour has a string of restaurants and hotels to its name, the feeling that Propriano is a working port town scantily clad in ribbons and bows to entice visitors, is inescapable. Propriano, however, with all its amenities is useful for a stopover and as a base for water-sports enthusiasts.

Orientation

Ave Napoléon, which runs alongside the harbour, and rue du Général de Gaulle, which veers off to the southeast, are the

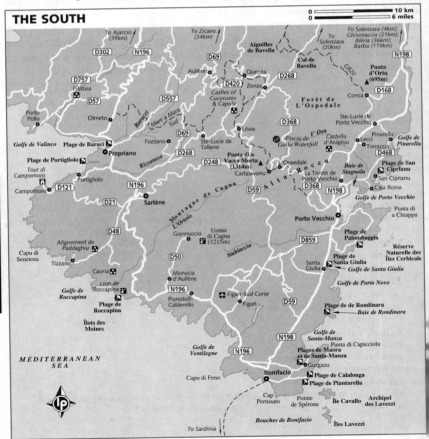

THE SOUTH

THE SOUTH

main thoroughfares of the town centre and the focus of most activity. If you arrive from the north, you'll come into Propriano along rue de 9 Septembre (the wide coastal road), which comes out at the junction of the above two roads.

Information

BOOKSHOPS

La Maison de la Presse (☎ 04 95 76 06 77; cnr ave Napoléon & rue du Général de Gaulle; ⏳ 7.30am-8pm Jun–mid-Sep; 7.30am-12.30pm & 2.30-730pm Mon-Sat, 7.30am-12.30pm Sun mid-Sep–May) Stocks a large range of paperbacks and books about Corsica, as well as French and foreign newspapers.

MONEY

Société Générale (☎ 04 95 76 05 44;1 rue du Général de Gaulle; ⏳ 8.15am-noon & 1.45-5pm Mon-Fri) Changes foreign-currency travellers cheques and cash; has an ATM.
Crédit Agricole (rue du Général de Gaulle) Has an ATM.

POST

Post office (☎ 04 95 76 73 00; quartier de la Plaine; ⏳ 9am-6pm Mon-Fri, 9am-noon Sat Jul & Aug; 9am-noon & 2.30-5.30pm Mon-Fri, 9am-noon Sat Sep-Jun) It's a short walk from the harbour.

TOURIST INFORMATION

Tourist office (☎ 04 95 76 01 49; www.propriano.net; ⏳ 8am-8pm Mon-Sat, 9am-1pm & 4-8pm Sun Jul & Aug; 8am-12.30pm & 2.30-7pm Mon-Sat Sep & Oct; 9am-noon & 2-6pm Mon-Fri Nov-Apr) It's at the marina.

Activities

BEACHES

The best of the little beaches in town are **Plage du Lido**, west of the lighthouse, and its extension, **Plage du Corsaire**. There are better places to swim in the Golfe de Valinco, especially at the fantastic Plage de Portigliolo, 7km south of town.

BOAT TRIPS

Boat excursions in the Golfe de Valinco, almost two hours long, in groups of up to 12 people, are organised by the **École de Voile de Propriano** (☎ 04 95 76 04 26; adult/child aged 6-12 €28/12) aboard a sightseeing vessel or a catamaran. The boat stops at an inlet for swimming and, thanks to an innovative sound system, you can actually listen to music underwater.

I Paesi di u Valincu (☎ 04 95 76 16 78), close to the tourist office at the harbour, organises outings in a 150-seat boat specially fitted for close observation of the underwater world. One route, southerly, takes in Bonifacio by way of the Lion de Roccapina (p172) and Figari Bay (departs 8.30am, returns 6pm, €40). Another route heads north for the Réserve Naturelle de Scandola via Les Calanques de Piana, the Golfe de Porto and the Îles Sanguinaires (departs 7.15am, returns 7pm, €50). The company also offers a two-hour excursion around the Golfe de Valinco, and Corsica-by-night excursions (9pm to 10.30pm), both for €17. Children aged six to 12 pay half-price.

DIVING

The Golfe de Valinco is treasured by divers for its underwater relief – even more dramatic than that of other parts of the western coast – with depths of up to 800m. The most appealing dives are over rocky mounts close to the shore at the northern and southern entrances to the gulf, but for beginners there are sheltered inlets closer to Propriano. **Valinco Plongée** (☎ 04 95 76 31 01; www.valinco-plongee.com; ⏳ Apr-Oct) charges €40 for an introductory dive, €35 for a dive with equipment hire, or €115 for five self-equipped dives.

HORSE RIDING

The reputable **Ferme Équestre de Baracci** (☎ 04 95 76 08 02; www.corse-equitation.com; rte de Baracci), about 2km north of Propriano, stables 20 Corsican horses, which you can take out riding or trekking with a guide or qualified supervisor. A two-hour ride in the maquis and along the coast will set you back €35 though the centre's main business is week-long treks along the sea (€640) and outings of up to 17 days to cross the whole island (€1067), with a guide, with nights spent either camping out or in *bergeries* (shepherds' huts).

MOUNTAIN BIKING

Ventura Location (☎ 04 95 76 11 84; 25 ave Napoléon; ⏳ 9am-noon & 2-7pm, closed Sun Oct-Apr), near the ferry quay, hires out good mountain bikes for €13 per day (with a €200 deposit) and 125cc trail bikes for €58 per day. It also organises motorcycle trips in the winter.

WATER SPORTS

The **École de Voile de Propriano** (☎ 04 95 76 04 26; perso.wanadoo.fr/propriano/nautic; ⏳ 8am-7pm Jul & Aug,

THE SOUTH

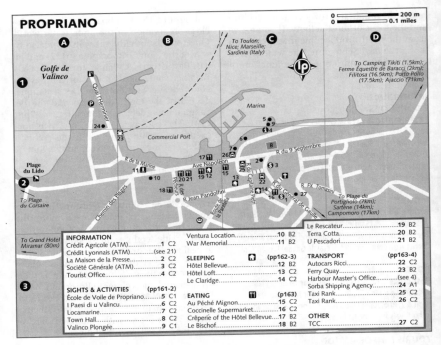

PROPRIANO

INFORMATION		Ventura Location	10 B2	Le Rescateur	19 B2
Crédit Agricole (ATM)	1 C2	War Memorial	11 B2	Terra Cotta	20 B2
Crédit Lyonnais (ATM)	(see 21)			U Pescadori	21 B2
La Maison de la Presse	3 C2	SLEEPING 🛏 (pp162-3)			
Société Générale (ATM)	4 C2	Hôtel Bellevue	12 B2	TRANSPORT (pp163-4)	
Tourist Office	4 C2	Hôtel Loft	13 C2	Autocars Ricci	22 B2
		Le Claridge	14 C2	Ferry Quay	23 B2
SIGHTS & ACTIVITIES (pp161-2)				Harbour Master's Office	(see 4)
École de Voile de Propriano	5 C1	EATING 🍴 (p163)		Sorba Shipping Agency	24 A1
I Paesi di u Valincu	6 C2	Au Péché Mignon	15 C2	Taxi Rank	25 C2
Locamarine	7 C2	Coccinelle Supermarket	16 C2	Taxi Rank	26 C2
Town Hall	8 C2	Crêperie of the Hôtel Bellevue	17 C2		
Valinco Plongée	9 C1	Le Bischof	18 B2	OTHER	
				TCC	27 C2

9am-12.30pm & 4-7pm Jun & Sep) is on the wharf 100m beyond the tourist office. It offers private and group lessons in sailing both catamarans and Optimists, and in windsurfing for adults and children at all skill levels. Also available for rental are surfboards (€11 to €18), catamarans (€22 to €40), and canoes (€6 or €9 for a single/double) at hourly rates.

Locamarine (☎ 04 95 76 11 32; www.locamarine .com), in the harbour, rents boats with or without a captain. Expect to pay €1760 for a seven-seat Ultramars boat or €320 for a four-seat dinghy per week.

Sleeping
BUDGET
Ferme Équestre de Baracci (☎ 04 95 76 08 02; d from €50; ☸ Apr-Oct) You can rent one of six double rooms some with an optional evening meal (€14 extra). The rooms are simple, a little on the small side, but clean.

Camping Tikiti (☎ 04 95 76 08 32; www.camping tikiti.fr.st; adult/tent/car €6/2/2) This site, about 1.5km north of Propriano, overlooks the main road towards Ajaccio. The site is huge, and covered with flowers and greenery; it's not built up like many of the other camp sites in the area. It has spotless facilities, and, above all, plenty of space. The beach is within walking distance.

MID-RANGE
Hôtel Bellevue (☎ 04 95 76 01 86; www.hotels-prop riano.com; Port de Plaisance; s/d €58/65; Ⓟ) This hotel, near the harbour, has an eye-catching, pink façade and blue shutters. It's pleasant, all rooms have a private bathroom and some have a view over the harbour. Try to book the rooms with balconies (€5 more).

Le Claridge (☎ 04 95 76 05 54; www.hotels-prop riano.com; rue Bonaparte; s/d €49/56; Ⓟ) Under the same ownership as Bellevue, Le Claridge is an ochre-coloured building a few streets back from the harbour. Though the setting is somewhat less inspiring than that of the Bellevue, if you ignore the busy furnishings, the Claridge's rooms with private bathroom are spacious and comfortable.

Hôtel Loft (☎ 04 95 76 17 48; fax 04 95 76 22 04; 3 rue Jean-Paul Pandolfi; s/d from €52/54; Ⓟ) Though the hotel is family owned, its décor looks strangely like that of an '80s chain hotel. Its 25 rooms are ultra-clean and spacious if a little charmless.

TOP END

Grand Hôtel Miramar (☎ 04 95 76 06 13; www.miramar corse.com; rte de la Corniche; d €305-646; ⊗ Apr–mid-Oct; P ⊠ ⊠ ⊒) This four-star place is the top hotel in town. It's a villa-style hotel that feels more like an opulent family home than a hotel. In lovely landscaped grounds right next to the beach, its 28 bright rooms and suites, with whitewashed walls and earthy furnishings, let you get away from it all in comfort and style.

Eating

There are lots of cafés and restaurants scattered along the marina and, if you enjoy fish, you're in luck.

BUDGET

A **Coccinelle supermarket** is situated on rue du Général de Gaulle.

Au Péché Mignon (☎ 04 95 76 01 71) This *patisserie* by the harbour has a few tables, and is ideal for a breakfast of hot drinks and pastries.

The **Hôtel Bellevue Crêperie** (☎ 04 95 76 01 86; www.hotels-propriano.com; Port de Plaisance; crêpes €3-9; P) serves sweet and savoury crêpes, plus ice creams and cocktails, on a terrace with a good view of the harbour.

MID-RANGE

U Pescadori (☎ 04 95 76 42 95; 13 ave Napoléon; mains €6-16) Listen to salty seadog stories here in a cavernous room, decked out with lobster pots, nets and fishing paraphernalia. You'll find good-value fresh fish that's simply cooked. It's normally packed to the gunwales, but the service is smart.

Le Bischof (☎ 04 95 76 30 00; rue des Pêcheurs; mains €10-18) If you want a break from a seafood diet this is where you should head. Bonefide carnivores will delight in delicacies such as tripe, snails or liver in Roquefort, sourced from the patron's family butcher next door.

Le Rescateur (☎ 04 95 76 08 46; ave Napoléon; mains €11-18) This restaurant takes its name from the pirate in a 1960s French TV show and continues the seafaring theme in its menu of fresh local fish and seafood. The choice

here is a notch above the rest though, with aromatic herbs from the owner's garden used to stuff simply grilled or roasted fish on the bone. Try the mixed seafood plate for €21 between two.

Terra Cotta (☎ 04 95 74 23 80; ave Napoléon; mains €9-18) This funky little café with a terrace and warm Mediterranean coloured décor, serves a mix of French and Italian dishes, such as Provençal prawns with butter beans or wild mushroom risotto with parmesan. There's a three-course *menu* (€14 at lunch, €24 at dinner) and vegetarians, who dine here, will relish the rare chance to expand their holiday diet on the island beyond stuffed aubergine or omelette.

Getting There & Away

BOAT

Ferries link Propriano with Nice, Toulon and Marseille as well as with Sardinia. You can buy tickets at **Sorba** (☎ 04 95 76 04 36; voyages -sorba@wanadoo.fr; quai L'Herminier; ⊗ 8-11.30am & 2-5.30pm Mon-Thu, 8-11.30am & 2-4.30pm Fri), a shipping agency which represents all the lines. For more information on ferry crossings, see the Transport chapter (p235).

The yacht basin's **harbour master** (☎ 04 95 76 10 40; ⊗ 8am-noon & 2-6pm) shares space with the tourist office. In season, allow €30 to €40 to tie up a craft of 9m to 11m. Multi-hulls pay a 50% premium. In the marina you'll find hot showers for €2 and also electricity, mechanical help, fuel and supplies.

BUS

Autocars Ricci (☎ 04 95 76 25 59; 6 rue du Général de Gaulle) runs buses from Ajaccio (€9.99, 80 minutes) at 4pm Monday to Saturday year-round and at also 3pm daily in summer. The return service to Ajaccio is at 5.15pm daily except Sunday year-round and at 9am daily in summer. Buses leave from in front of the Autocars Ricci office.

CAR & MOTORCYCLE

Ventura Location (☎ 04 95 76 11 84; 25 ave Napoléon; ⊗ 9am-noon & 2-7pm; closed Sun Oct-Apr) represents Citer car hire. A small car costs €75/270 per day/week.

Scooters can be rented from **TTC** (☎ 04 95 76 15 32; www.ttcmoto.fr; 25 rue Général de Gaulle) for €36/196 a day/week.

THE SOUTH

Getting Around

There is a taxi rank on rue du Capitaine Pietri, which is often called rue des Taxis. Some drivers organise excursions in the summer; ask at the tourist office for details. Otherwise, **Taxis Bartaccia** (☎ 04 95 76 11 03) operates a 24-hour service in town.

FILITOSA

Even though it's the most celebrated prehistoric site in Corsica, there are still many unsolved mysteries connected with **Filitosa** (☎ 04 95 74 00 91; adult/child €5/free; ☼ 8am-8pm Apr-Oct). The site was discovered in 1946 by the owner of the land, Charles-Antoine Césari (whose family still runs the reception area), and owes a great deal to the archaeologist Roger Grosjean, who supervised the excavations. What is special about Filitosa is that some of its many monuments date from as far back as the early Neolithic era; others from as relatively recently as Roman times.

The oldest findings on the site suggest a human population living in caves, and remnants of pottery, arrow heads and farming tools point to fixed settlements beginning as early as 3300 BC.

The menhir statues of the megalithic period are even more impressive; the fact that they were erected at all marks a major human advancement. What the purpose was of these granite monoliths 2m to 3m high and carved to represent human faces or entire human figures armed with weapons, is not clear. It's unknown whether they are phallic symbols to encourage the fertility of the land, representations of local

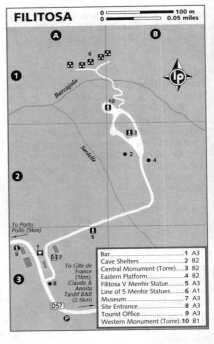

Bar	1	A3
Cave Shelters	2	B2
Central Monument (Torre)	3	B2
Eastern Platform	4	B2
Filitosa V Menhir Statue	5	A3
Line of 5 Menhir Statues	6	A1
Museum	7	A3
Site Entrance	8	A3
Tourist Office	9	A3
Western Monument (Torre)	10	B1

horsemen (the Paladini) or monuments to ward off the threat of the Torréen invaders (see boxed text below).

Researchers are at least agreed that the Torréens arrived at the peak of the megalithic period. The Torréens were more advanced and better armed than the then indigenous communities on the island, and they seem to have driven the creators

MYSTERIOUS PEOPLE OF THE SEA

Who were the Torréens, those people who appeared on Corsican shores around 1100 BC, drove out the settled inhabitants of Filitosa, destroyed many of their statues and built the *torri* (circular monuments) in their place? The traces they left are very faint indeed.

According to Roger Grosjean, the archaeological authority on Filitosa, they could actually have been Shardanes, the people enigmatically known to historians as 'sea people', who battled with the pharaoh Ramses III. They probably originated from Anatolia, from Crete or from along the coast of the Aegean Sea.

The Shardanes are first mentioned in around 1200 BC. They were allied with the Libyans and planned to attack the prosperous civilisation in the Nile Valley. It was a mistake: Ramses III succeeded in blocking their advance and sinking the Shardanes' fleet during a battle that is recorded in hieroglyphics carved into the wall of the Medinat Habu temple in Luxor, Egypt. After this defeat, the vanquished Shardanes made their way to Corsica and then to Sardinia, before disappearing back into obscurity.

of the menhirs from Filitosa around 1500 BC. Apparently, they destroyed some of the menhirs and buried others face down. In their place they erected circular structures, now known as *torri*, of which the central and western monuments in Filitosa are examples. The purpose of the torri is as mysterious as that of the menhirs.

Filitosa is worth a one-hour visit. You have to go through the little museum (better visited on the way out) to get to the menhir statue known as Filitosa V. This has a distinctive, rectangular head, and is the largest and 'best-armed' statue in Corsica; a sword and a dagger are both clearly visible.

If you continue along the path you come to some caves and the foundations of some huts before you get to the central torre with its six little statues, including the one known as Filitosa IX, the face of which is considered one of the masterpieces of megalithic art.

The western monument, where a pile of stones marks the perimeter of a torre, is a few metres farther on, and then the path goes down towards the highlight of the visit: five menhir statues lined up in an arc around the foot of a 1200-year-old olive tree. Behind them is a little granite quarry, from where it's thought the ancient sculptors got their materials.

Visitors who aren't archaeology buffs might want some help from the little €5 guide, but experts and casual visitors alike will be struck by the peaceful stillness of the atmosphere, especially at the end of the day, and the impressive geometry of the last five statues as seen from the west monument.

It's worth spending a few minutes in the museum before you leave. It houses three more menhir statues, some pottery, some human remains, a few stone tools and information about the Torréens-Shardanes. There is also a bar and a souvenir shop on the site.

The Filitosa **tourist office** (9.30am-6pm May-Oct), 100m from the entrance to the site, in the village, is particularly helpful at supplying information on accommodation.

Sleeping

The nearest campgrounds and hotels are in Porto Pollo (p166). To get there by car from Filitosa, take the D57 towards Propriano

---

PONT DI CALZOLA

All that walking around the sites of Filitosa is bound to make you hungry. A short detour from the site will take you 8km north along the D757 to the tiny crossroad hamlet of Calzola from where you hang a right onto the tiny D302 over a precarious and extremely narrow stone bridge, Pont di Calzola, over the river Tavola. Just to your left, you'll spot an old mill in the trees, home to **U Molinu di Calzola** (☎ 04 95 24 32 14; s/d/t €31/43/56; P ⊠), a gorgeous riverside inn, in a beautiful setting, surrounded by fragrant eucalyptus and fig trees and a garden that leads down to the river. Stop for a dip, or a delicious lunch (*menus* €14.50 to €27.50) in the rustic dining room with its whitewashed walls and beamed ceiling or on the terrace where you can feast on French cuisine or an array of refined Corsican dishes. Its 14 immaculate rooms are modernistically decorated, with tiled floors and colourful bedspreads, and the welcome is hearty.

From here you can follow the D302 back down to **Propriano via Olmeto**, a small tree-lined granite village whose main point of interest is its spectacular views down to the Golfe de Valinco

---

for 4.5km, then turn right onto the D157 for the same distance.

You can find B&B accommodation and *gîtes* closer to Filitosa.

The B&B belonging to **Claude & Annita Tardif** (☎ 04 95 74 29 48, 06 62 43 13 69; d €60) has magnificent ocean view and offers three clean and pleasant rooms with bathrooms. The price includes breakfast, and residents may use the excellent, outdoor cooking facilities. It is 2.5km east of Filitosa along a small side road; it's well signposted.

Paul Luccioni's **Gîte de France** (☎ 04 95 74 00 98; €400-510), 1km east of Filitosa to the left of the main road, has well-appointed apartments that sleep four.

Getting There & Away

There are no real bus services to Filitosa, but **Autocars Ricci** (☎ 04 95 51 08 19), on its Ajaccio to Porto Pollo line, passes 2km from the site.

GOLFE DE VALINCO

This bay, all the more magical if you approach it for the first time from the open sea, has some of the wildest and most rugged coastal scenery of the island. It has a little seaside resort on each side of its open mouth – on the north side is Porto Pollo, and on the south is Campomoro, both good diving spots. Public transport to both villages is limited.

NORTH OF THE BAY

To the north of the bay, **Plage de Baraci** is just one of the beaches you come across before you reach Porto Pollo, the closest village to the megalithic site at Filitosa.

Porto Pollo

postcode 20140 / pop 359

The busy resort of Porto Pollo, 18km from Propriano, in a protected inlet to the north of the Golfe de Valinco, sits on a horseshoe-shaped bay, bordered by a lively **marina** and sheltered sandy **beach**. Its small size and the accessibility of water sports make it popular with young people and families who flock to it in high season for activity-based holidays. Despite its popularity Porto Pollo retains the atmosphere of a small fishing village and is a great base from which to explore the surrounding countryside. Some of the best diving in the region is close by.

ACTIVITIES
Beaches

The 900m long sandy beach in the village slopes gently into the water and is sheltered from the wind, making it safe for children. There are plenty of more remote sandy coves south of town or 14km to the north is the glorious crescent-shaped **Plage de Cupabia**, which until 2002 when an asphalt road off the D155 was built, was only accessible by foot. Despite the new road, it rarely gets crowded. You'll need to bring your own snacks and drinks as there are no facilities yet.

Diving

In a prefab overlooking the marina, **Porto Pollo Plongée** (☎ 04 95 74 07 46; perso.wanadoo.fr/portopolloplongee) has a relaxed family atmosphere. An introductory dive in an inlet at the mouth of the Baie de Porto Pollo costs €34, an exploratory dive €22 to €34, or six dives will set you back €123 or €195 including equipment.

Horse Riding

Jacques Abatucci (☎ 04 95 74 08 08; Fil di Rosa) has about 20 horses and offers treks of one (€20) or two hours (€34) with the option of going for a gallop on a local beach.

Water Sports

The sailing school of **Club Mer et Vent** (☎ 04 95 74 08 25), on the beach, offers sailing and kiteboarding tuition and hires catamarans.

SLEEPING & EATING

There are no shortage of hotels, bars and restaurants in town.

Valinco Village Hôtel (☎ 04 95 74 02 78; half-board s per wk €273; P 🐕) This *résidence* provides '70s-style bungalow accommodation, in a sheltered garden, just off Porto Pollo's main drag. The modest bungalows, which come in doubles, triples or family units with bunk beds, have their own bathrooms and terraces and, most attractively, lead onto a virtually private strip of beach. There's a games area, snack bar and antiquated disco on site.

Hôtel du Golfe (☎ 04 95 74 01 66; s/d €50; half-board d €120; 🕑 mid-Apr–Oct) This hotel, in a charming old house at the end of town, is only a stone's throw from the beach. It has clean, simple rooms with quaint furniture, terrazzo floors and showers, and the price includes breakfast. The half-board option includes a choice of meals and wine from the co-owned **Pizzeria du Golfe** next door.

Hôtel Kallisté (☎ 04 95 74 02 38; half-board s/d €66/122; mains €11-22; 🕑 mid-Apr–Nov) The modern Kallisté, Porto Pollo's best, has comfortable, spotless rooms with bathroom. It's on the main strip and its restaurant has good *menus* for €23 with Corsican staples and excellent desserts.

Le Pirate (☎ 04 95 74 08 74; mains €9-16) This restaurant on the beach serves delicious seafood kebabs and salads on its terrace.

There are three campgrounds in town.

ENTERTAINMENT

An **open-air cinema**, in a field just off the main street, screens current releases on summer nights.

GETTING THERE & AWAY
Autocars Ricci (☎ 04 95 51 08 19) runs a bus service that departs Ajaccio for Porto Pollo on Monday and Wednesday (4pm, €8.38, 1¼ hours) and Saturday (12.30pm). It leaves Porto Pollo on the same days at 7am.

Serra-di-Ferro
The tiny hill-top village of Serra-di-Ferro, perched 4km above Porto Pollo overlooking the beautiful **Baie de Cupabia** may be a quieter alternative to Porto Pollo for self-caterers. At the entrance to the village, the small **U Turracconu** (☎ 04 95 74 00 57; adult/tent/car €7/3/3, bungalows €695 per week; P 😃) is a popular camp site set in a pine grove with a children's play area. The modest bungalows, around the swimming pool, sleep four. From here it's a 20-minute, cross-country walk down to the Plage de Culpabia. There are two good pizzerias in the village **U San Petru** (☎ 06 19 94 79 95) and **San Mateo** (☎ 04 95 74 07 81) opposite, that serve wood-fired pizzas as well as grilled meats.

SOUTH OF THE BAY
Plage de Portigliolo
Seven kilometres south of Propriano, the beautiful Plage de Portigliolo, stretches out on either side of a little airfield that manages not to spoil the coastline. The beach is an incredible 4km long and, with its fine, white sand and lack of development, is by far the nicest in the area. The beach, cut in two by the River Rizzanese, is not to be confused with another Portigliolo further north in the Golfe d'Ajaccio.

There's a sailing school on the beach, **Club Vela e Ventu** (☎ 06 09 52 24 20), which offers tuition to beginners and hires catamarans and surfboards. There's little or no shade on the beach so bring your own as well as plenty of water.

South of Portigliolo, the road climbs a little before reaching Belvédère. The coast is magnificent and still wild; it is under the protection of the Conservatoire du Littoral and the views back to the beach at Portigliolo are breathtaking. At the end of the road is the pretty little seaside resort of Campomoro.

SLEEPING & EATING
U Livanti (☎ 04 95 76 08 06; livanti@club-internet.fr; 😃 Apr-Nov) This is a fully-equipped holiday village in a lovely shady location, right on the edge of the beach. Simple bungalows with kitchenettes, that sleep four or five, cost €680 per week in high season. Fresh bread and basic provisions are available at the shop, or there's a restaurant and snack bar on site. The kids' club, and games like ping-pong, tennis and bowling, should please young ones.

Campomoro
postcode 20110 / pop 150
The pretty little village of Campomoro marks the southernmost tip of the gulf. Reached by a twisting, coastal road inhabited by only a few peripatetic sheep and goats, it really feels like the end of the line. Though there is only a handful of accommodation options and restaurants dotted around its small sandy beach, its popularity as a sailing and diving location gives it an attractive holiday atmosphere. Be warned: the place becomes packed in high season. During this period you'll have trouble finding both a bed for the night and a parking space in town.

At the end of the beach you'll find the **Tour di Campomoro**. Built in the 16th century by the Genoese, the tower is one of Corsica's largest, and it is also the only one on the island to have been fortified with a star-shaped surrounding wall. It was lovingly restored in 1986.

There's a post office in the village and a small shop in the village.

Campomoro Plongée (☎ 04 95 74 23 29; www .campomoro-plongee.com), a small, friendly establishment on the beach opposite the church, offers introductory dives for €37, an exploratory dive for €28, or four dives for €92.

SLEEPING & EATING
Hôtel Le Ressac (☎ 04 95 74 22 25; hotelressac@aol .com; half-board s/d from €88/102; mains €7-19; 😃 Apr-Nov) At the end of a little laneway leading up past the church, the quiet two-star hotel is a friendly place with comfortable rooms (with bathroom); some have terraces overlooking the bay. There's a three-course Corsican *menu* (€19) and a separate *menu* available for children (€9). Half board is obligatory in July and August.

Don't leave yourself stuck in search of a late lunch – most eateries on the beach stop serving between 2.30pm or 3pm until evening time. Of the few snack-bars along the beach **U Spuntinu**, near Campomoro Plongée, is the best. Ignore its cartoon-adorned *menu*, it turns out surprisingly good fresh salads (€7) and sandwiches (€6).

GETTING THERE & AWAY
Autocars Ricci (☎ 04 95 51 08 19) goes to Porto Pollo from Ajaccio at 4pm on Monday, Wednesday and at 12.30pm on Saturday. Buses return from Porto Pollo at 7am on the same days.

THE SARTENAIS

In more ways than one, the Sartenais is a reminder of what the whole of Corsica used to be like. The town of Sartène itself fervently perpetuates traditions going back to the Middle Ages, while to the south of the town there are prehistoric remains that bear witness to the way of life of the island's very first inhabitants.

SARTÈNE (SARTÈ)
postcode 20100 / pop 2500
'The whole place breathes war and vengeance', the poet Paul Valéry said about Sartène, and the shadowy town's gaze out over the Rizzanese valley from its high granite walls does seem quite ferocious. Within its walls, however, you'll find a charming, well-preserved town whose narrow streets, plane trees and tall, granite townhouses exude a sense of history and integrity. Unlike Propriano, its more commercially minded counterpart down the mountain, the Sartenais treat visitors with a healthy degree of nonchalance. This gives the town an attractive authenticity that is ironically appealing.

In earlier times, Sartène was a bastion for great families of nobles who didn't want anyone meddling in their business, and even today Sartène seems reluctant to reveal very much about either its past or its present. Nevertheless, history tells that the town was subject to repeated Saracen raids in the 15th and 16th centuries, and pirates from Algiers took 400 of its inhabitants into slavery in 1583.

Danger for Sartène didn't always come from the outside, either. The town enjoys pride of place in the chronicles of Corsica's long tradition of vendetta. In the course of the Colomba Carabelli vendetta, a curate protagonist is said to have remained shut up for nine years in his home in the Borgo quarter for fear of reprisals. Colomba Carabelli was the principal inspiration for Prosper Mérimée's romantic tale of Corsican vendetta, *Colomba*. Another famous 19th-century rivalry pitted one family from the Borgo quarter against another from Santa Anna. What was in effect a small-scale civil war ended only with the ratification of a peace treaty in the Église Ste-Marie. And some suggest that all of the bloody confrontations leading up to the treaty of peace were provoked by nothing more than a dispute over a dog.

Undoubtedly, it was the tradition of the vendetta and other related exotica that inspired Mérimée's comment that Sartène was the 'most Corsican of all Corsican towns'.

In recent years, the Catenacciu procession (p170), dating from the Middle Ages, has been exploited to attract tourists, so perhaps the town is at last emerging from its immemorial introversion.

Orientation
Sartène is built around place de la Libération, from which cours Sœur Amélie and cours Général de Gaulle, the town's main streets, lead off.

The old quarter of Santa Anna stretches out to the north of place de la Libération. Many of its little streets have more than one name and just as many signs.

Information
Crédit Agricole (cours Sœur Amélie) Near the petrol station; has an ATM.
Crédit Lyonnais (cours Général de Gaulle) Has an ATM.
Cyber Café (☎ 04 95 73 28 70; place Porta; per 15/30 min €2/3; ⏱ 6.30am-2am Mon-Sat) A little space at the back of Le Cyrnos bar.
Post office (☎ 04 95 77 70 72; rue du Marché; ⏱ 8.30am-noon & 2-5.30pm Mon-Fri, 8.30am-noon Sat) It's near place de la Libération; also an ATM here.
Tourist Office (☎ 04 95 77 15 40; perso.wanadoo.fr /ot-sartene; cours Sœur Amélie; ⏱ 9am-2pm & 3-8pm Jun-Oct, 9am-noon & 2-6pm Mon-Fri Nov-May) It's not far from place de la Libération.

Sights
The old town is a labyrinth of stone stairways and little streets and alleyways, some

of them so narrow that two people can barely pass through. Yet a virtue of these corridors, particularly on hot summer days, is that they provide the pedestrian with some welcome shade.

The bell tower of the **Église Ste-Marie** rises above place de la Libération, which is still sometimes called place Porta. The church was built in 1766 on the site of an older building that collapsed not long after it was erected. It boasts a superb altarpiece of polychrome marble (formerly in the Couvent St-François) and canvasses of the Stations of the Cross dating from 1843. The chains and cross used during the Catenacciu procession are also on display.

Next to Église Ste-Marie is the building that now houses the **town hall** (admission free; 8.30am-noon & 2-6pm Mon-Fri), but which, in the 16th century, was the palace of the Genoese lieutenants. Sadly, the anonymous Italian canvasses it shelters have not been maintained properly. If you go through the gateway below this former palace, you will come out on the narrow streets of the **Santa Anna quarter**, which is the real jewel of the old town.

An *échauguette*, or watchtower, to the right of the post office, bears witness to the importance the people of Sartène gave to keeping a lookout around the city. It is not open to visitors.

Activities
HORSE RIDING
The friendly, multilingual Claudine and Christian Perrier at **Le Domaine de Croccano** (04 95 77 11 37; www.corsenature.com) offer an hour's trek (€20) on Corsican horses in beautiful open countryside or week-long outings year-round (€640 to €700) along the still rather wild coastline. Accommodation, evening meal and picnic lunch are included. It's 3.5km out of town on the road to Granace.

WALKING
The **Association Nature et Sentiers du Sartenais** (04 95 77 18 21; rando.sartene@libertysurf.fr), the nature and trails association, organises theme walks around Sartène and in southern Corsica.

Sleeping
Hôtel des Roches (04 95 77 07 61; d €57-75, half-board s/d €75-80/107-113; P) This hotel, at the

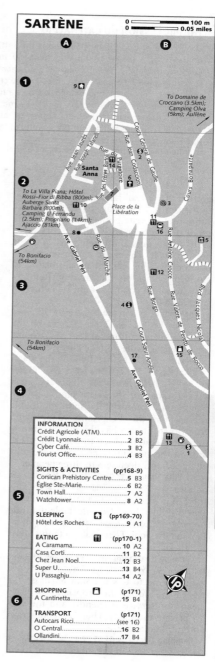

SARTÈNE

0   100 m
0   0.05 miles

INFORMATION
Crédit Agricole (ATM)...............1 B5
Crédit Lyonnais.........................2 B2
Cyber Café................................3 B2
Tourist Office............................4 B3

SIGHTS & ACTIVITIES   (pp168-9)
Corsican Prehistory Centre........5 B3
Église Ste-Marie.......................6 B2
Town Hall.................................7 A2
Watchtower..............................8 A2

SLEEPING   (pp169-70)
Hôtel des Roches......................9 A1

EATING   (pp170-1)
A Caramama............................10 A2
Casa Corti...............................11 B2
Chez Jean Noel.......................12 B3
Super U..................................13 B4
U Passaghju...........................14 A2

SHOPPING   (p171)
A Cantinetta...........................15 B4

TRANSPORT   (p171)
Autocars Ricci.....................(see 16)
O Central................................16 B2
Ollandini................................17 B4

THE SOUTH

THE PROCESSION DU CATENACCIU

On the eve of Good Friday, Sartène is the setting for one of the oldest religious traditions on the island – the Procession du Catenacciu. In a colourful re-enactment of the Passion, the Catenacciu (literally, 'the chained one'), an anonymous, barefoot penitent, covered from head to foot in a red robe and cowl, carries a huge cross through the town, dragging heavy chains at his feet. The Catenacciu is followed by a procession of other penitents (eight dressed in black, one in white), members of the clergy and local notables. As the chains clatter by on the cobblestones, spectators look on in great (if rather humourless) excitement. Needless to say, everyone is curious to find out the identity of the penitent, selected by the parish priest from applicants seeking to expiate a grave sin.

When they are not in use, the chains and cross of the Catenacciu can be seen in the Église Ste-Marie.

---

bottom of ave Jean Jaurès, is the only hotel in the centre of Sartène. Though the foyer is nothing to write home about, the newly renovated rooms with tiled floors, spacious bathrooms and bright, stylish décor are top class. The more expensive rooms overlooking the valley have terraces and stunning views on a clear day. Renovations to all 66 rooms should be complete by mid-2004.

Le Domaine de Croccano (☎ 04 95 77 11 37; www .corsenature.com; s/d €36/72, half-board s/d €61/122) Here you can rent one of four cosy rooms in a pretty granite cottage surrounded by cork and olive trees, overlooking the sea.

Hôtel Rossi – Fior di Ribba (☎ 04 95 77 01 80; r €59-72; ⊗ mid-Mar–Nov; P ⓡ) This is a great place to stay for its warm, family atmosphere and comfortable, spotless double rooms. On the Propriano road, 800m from town, it also has three new, prettily decorated studios (€520 to €600 per week) around the swimming pool, that are fully equipped and sleep two to three people.

La Villa Piana (☎ 04 95 77 07 04; www.lavilla piana.com; r €95; ⊗ Apr–mid-Sep; P ⓡ) This three-star place, next to the Hôtel Rossi – Fior di Ribba, has 31 comfortable if a little homely doubles, some with terrace, overlooking the pool. There's also a tennis court for guests' use.

Camping U Farrandu (☎ 04 95 73 41 69; adult with tent & car €5.50; ⊗ Apr–mid-Sep) This is the closest campground to town, 2.5km north on the right-hand side of the Propriano road. It's clean, the service is friendly and the sites are private and shady. There's a tennis court and mini-golf course.

Camping Olva (☎ 04 95 77 11 58; adult/tent/car €6/3/3; ⊗ Apr–Oct) On the other side of town,

5km out on the D69 towards Aullène, is a quiet, eight-hectare park shaded by eucalyptus trees. Its amenities include a good tennis court, a swimming pool and a little supermarket. If you are on foot, call from Sartène and someone will pick you up.

Eating
BUDGET & MID-RANGE
Super U (⊗ 8.30am-7.45pm Mon-Sat) If you are self-catering, head to this supermarket at the bottom end of cours Sœur Amélie near the petrol station.

Casa Corti (☎ 04 95 73 40 85; rue Borgo) Grab a bar stool and a coffee at this congenial, little, no-frills bar, where the charming Jeanot Corti will gladly give you a rundown on the town's history and lore.

Chez Jean Noel (☎ 06 12 77 75 70; 8 rue Borgo; ⊗ Feb-Dec) A bright little café, Jean Noel's is popular with Sartène's young people, on the quiet rue Borgo. Choose from a simple *menu* (€17) of *lasagne au brocciu*, local sausage or gratin potato.

A Caramama (☎ 04 95 77 07 84; mains €7-15; ⊗ May-Oct) Nicely located in the old town, this family restaurant serves good pizzas with local toppings, salads or *menus* (€19 to €23) featuring Corsican delicacies such as tripe or spinach cannelloni. Whatever you do, leave some room for the divine chestnut cheesecake, made with local *brocciu*.

TOP END
Auberge Santa Barbara (☎ 04 95 77 09 06), Set in a palm-fringed garden opposite La Villa Piana and with a panoramic view of the valley, it deserves its reputation as one of the region's best restaurants. The familial Corsican *menu* (€25) uses fresh local

produce in an imaginative way and features a generous selection of local wines.

Shopping

Have a look at the wine, the liqueurs and the honey at **A Cantinetta** (☎ 04 95 77 08 75; rue Borgo). Marie-Dominique Bartoli will welcome you warmly to the family cellar, established in 1902. The wines here are the Sartenais' best, and the *charcuterie* and the cheeses can make an exceptionally good meal.

Getting There & Away

Autocars Ricci (☎ 04 95 51 08 19) buses leave Sartène for Ajaccio at 7am daily (€10.50, 1¾ hours). The service is via Propriano, Olmeto and St-Georges. There are also departures at 7.30pm for Ste-Lucie de Tallano, Lévie and Zonza and in summer to the Col de Bavella. The Autocars Ricci base in Sartène is the O Central bar, on place de la Libération.

Ollandini (☎ 04 95 77 18 41; ave Gabriel Péri; 9am-noon & 2.30-6.30pm Mon-Fri, 9am-noon Sat), the representative for Eurocorse, has buses leaving for Ajaccio at 8am and 4pm daily (€11.50). There are also two buses daily to Bonifacio, Porto Vecchio and (at 11.45am and 7pm, €10) via Zonza (€7.65).

PREHISTORIC SITES OF THE SARTENAIS

Corsica's dolmens and menhirs remain shrouded in considerable mystery. Archaeologists and historians seem to agree at least that the dolmens mark burial sites. But what of the menhirs? Were they meant to represent divinities, or deceased elders, or were they sculpted as a means of stripping enemies of their power? The answers are elusive, and the diversity of the evidence only complicates the problem.

Some of the menhirs are extremely crude, but on others, human faces and weapons can clearly be made out. Yet there are others, as at Filitosa, so phallic that they're thought to have been fertility symbols for the land.

In the absence of any conclusive scientific answers, many visitors will be happy simply to let the dolmens and menhirs serve as a rather mystical backdrop to their walks.

The sites of Cauria and Paddaghiu, to the south of Sartène, are not only among the most interesting on the island, but also stand as they have for thousands of years, unfenced, untended, unprotected by guards, and unmediated by guides. Such remoteness means that you will have a hard time getting to them without a vehicle.

Cauria

The desolate and beautiful Cauria plateau, about 15km south of Sartène, is home to three megalithic curiosities: the *alignements* (lines) of menhirs of Stantari and Rinaghiu, and the Funtanaccia dolmen.

To get to the sites, you will have to climb over some barriers designed to keep animals from straying, and this makes the walk somewhat challenging for people with reduced mobility. In any event, do not expect to do this visit in less than an hour.

No admission is charged for any of these sites, and there are no facilities.

From Sartène, follow the road to Bonifacio for 2km before turning off onto the winding D48, on the right. The megalithic site at Cauria is signposted off to the left after another 8km. The next leg, 4.5km along a road that is only casually maintained, leads to a sign riddled with bullet holes. The sign points to the menhirs and the dolmens, along a driveable track to the right, but you can leave your car in the shade here and undertake the last 700m to the **Alignement de Stantari** on foot.

The Alignement de Stantari consists of nine stones: the fourth from the left represents a sword, and its next two neighbours represent faces with their mouths open in muted cry. The **Alignement de Rinaghiu** is larger, slightly less orderly and 300m further on, at the edge of a little wood that some say may once have been sacred.

If you retrace your steps to the Alignement de Stantari, you can climb over a barrier made from the two main branches of a cork oak, then follow the path another 350m to the **Funtanaccia dolmen**. This megalithic monument is the largest of its type in Corsica, and is more worth the effort than the lines of menhirs.

Alignement de Paddaghiu

With nearly 260 menhirs, some standing, others lying, the Alignement de Paddaghiu is the largest collection of megalithic statuary in the Mediterranean. Four distinct *alignements*, each of them four to eight menhirs long, are the highlight.

To get there by car from Cauria, drive the 4.5km back to the D48 and turn left towards Tizzano. The entrance to the site is on the right, 1.3km beyond the Mosconi vintners' wine-tasting facility. Follow the arrows for about 1.2km before coming to the car park. Admission is free.

PROTECTED COASTLINE
Marine de Tizzano

This charming little cove, formerly protected by a fort that is now in ruins, lies approximately 5km southwest of the Alignement de Paddaghiu. You'll find a beach, a few little inlets, a grocery, a hotel and restaurants. It is an ideal spot to spend a few nights.

At the tranquil **Hôtel-Restaurant du Golfe** (☎ 04 95 77 14 76; s/d €150; ☷ Mar-Oct), take advantage of the bright and airy rooms with terraces which provide wonderful views over the sea. You'll pay €20 extra for a room with a bath. The delicious *menus* at the restaurant start at €25 where seafood and fish straight from the boat are served.

Roccapina

The landmark Roccapina site, 20km from Sartène and 30km from Bonifacio, is famous for a geological curiosity: a lion sculpted by nature out of the rock. It really is a mere curiosity though and whether it even resembles a lion is debatable. However, with children on board you might fancy a moment's pitstop. To find it, look out in the direction of the sea from the neighbourhood of the Auberge la Corralli, on the N196. Two enormous blocks of rock on top of a ridge crowned by a Genoese tower define the basic shape; a few standing rocks suggest the mane. The lion is not the only curiosity at the site. From the snack bar 2km beyond Auberge la Corralli in the direction of Bonifacio, armed with a vivid imagination, you may see another rocky configuration whose shape suggests a gorilla's head. You may also be able to make out the shape of an elephant in the rocks; it's recognisable by its trunk.

The view down to the shimmering waters of Rocapina beach from the R196 is seductive. To get to the beach, take the potholed track, leading off the main road

next to Auberge la Corralli, and follow it downhill for 2km. A handful of boats moor in the calm, aquamarine water and the beach itself is fine and sandy making it particularly suitable for children. There aren't any facilities or much shade on the beach itself though, so you'll need to bring your own supplies and umbrella. The juniper-covered dunes, damaged by campers in the years prior to 1985, are now protected by the Conservatoire du Littoral. Limpets are also protected. The larger females used to be eaten by mollusc-fanciers, and the species was in danger of extinction before it was added to the protected list.

A footpath connects it to the lion rock.

SLEEPING & EATING

If you don't mind feeling a little cut off, there are a few places to stay in the area.

Auberge la Corralli (☎ 04 95 77 05 94; d per week €567-686; ☷ Apr-Nov) You'll find this auberge on the main road. It has eight good rooms with shower, balcony and TV, or more expensive options with bath and air-conditioning. Rooms are rented by the week. Seafood *menus* are offered for €20.

Camping Rocapina (☎ 04 95 71 01 55; adult plus a tent & car from €10; ☷ May-Sep) This site at the bottom of the path has few amenities but is very close to the beach.

GETTING THERE & AWAY

Eurocorse buses (☎ 04 95 21 06 30) stop at Roccapina on the route between Ajaccio and Bonifacio.

Pianottoli-Caldarello
postcode 20131 / pop 700

Some 20km from Bonifacio on the N196, the small hamlet of Pianottoli-Caldarello is made up of two villages, over a kilometre apart. There's a post office, supermarket, petrol station and a couple of pleasant cafés here.

SLEEPING & EATING

Hôtel Le Libecciu (☎ 04 95 71 87 93; s/d €160, s half-board €110; ☷ Dec-Oct; **P** ☒ ☐) Overlooking the Baie de Figari, 3km from the village, this modernist, three-star hotel has spacious rooms and large bathrooms. Though it gets packed with French visitors in high season, it's a good place to bring children. It has its own small, gently-shelving beach, kids' club, play area and water sports on site. You could take or leave the restaurant though. To get there, follow signs to Camping Le Damier in the village.

Chez Matthieu (☎ 04 95 71 86 61) Back in Pianottoli-Caldarello, drop in to Chez Matthieu, on the main drag, for a coffee. It's a spit-on-the-floor local bar where men smoke Gauloise, surrounded by pictures of Che Guevara, Mauré and Grand Prix winners.

Boulangerie Artisanale (☎ 04 95 71 80 35) Join the queues for mouth-watering crusty breads, sandwiches and fine cakes at this excellent bakery.

Restaurant Florida (☎ 04 95 71 09 38) The fancy Florida, in an intimate dining room on the village's main street, features a decent *menu* (€21) centred, unsurprisingly, on local fish and seafood.

THE FAR SOUTH

A narrow plain separating the coast from the island's rocky foothills, along with abundant cork oaks, gives the extreme southern end of the island its special rugged look. Parts of its terrain resemble the rocky plains of Arizona, but the extraordinary town of Bonifacio is the principal reason for coming to the area. You'll undoubtedly have come across postcards of Bonifacio at souvenir shops and stalls the length and breadth of the country, but they really don't do the place justice. To best appreciate the town's strikingly unique position, carved into the cliff face, approach Bonifacio by boat, or at least take an unmissable boat trip around the cliffs during your stay.

BONIFACIO (BUNIFAZIU)
postcode 20169 / pop 2800
The incredible town of Bonifacio sits on two levels. The citadel, with its ancient buildings and its narrow, twisting streets sits up at cloud level. Its walls and buildings are constructed so they appear to be a continuation of the sheer, chalky cliffs on which they're perched. Down below, an inlet, or fjord, about 100m wide, plunges in behind the great cliffs to form the town's fine natural harbour, home to a buzzing port. The whole town with its crumbling buildings and the comings and goings of

people at the port retains a pleasantly unpolished, unpretentious atmosphere. The place heaves with visitors in high season though, so do yourself a favour and visit in the quieter months.

This 'Corsican Gibraltar', as Bonifacio is sometimes called, looks across a mere 12km of water to the Italian island of Sardinia.

History
The discovery of the *Dame de Bonifacio* (Lady of Bonifacio), the remains of a young woman who lived near the present town about 8500 years ago, proves that the area was inhabited as far back as the Neolithic period. There is no doubt that there was a sizeable population here in the period that we now think of as Classical Antiquity. Some people even suggest that the episode of the *Odyssey* in which Ulysses meets the Laestrygonians (a race of giant cannibals), at the foot of 'sheer cliffs on either side', could well have taken place at the entrance to the Goulet de Bonifacio (Bonifacio Narrows). The town as we know it today was probably founded by the Marquis de Toscane Boniface, who gave it its name, in 828.

A few hundred years later, in 1187, the town was taken by Genoa, supposedly while the locals were busy celebrating a wedding. Genoa sent in colonisers, who prospered, and, true to form, Genoa drove the previous inhabitants out.

Genoese Bonifacio nevertheless had to fight for its life on two separate occasions. The first came in 1420, when Alphonse V of Aragon laid siege to the town for five months on the grounds that Pope Boniface VIII had given Corsica to Spain; according to legend, the Escalier du Roi d'Aragon (King of Aragon's Stairway) was carved at this point. Ultimately, a Genoese squadron was dispatched to assist the colony and Alphonse was obliged to retreat.

The second siege took place in 1553. This time it was an alliance between French troops, followers of Sampiero Corso and the Turkish pirate Dragut, which aimed to liberate the town. Bonifacio resisted the attack for 18 days, then surrendered on the heels of double-dealing by one of its inhabitants. Together with the rest of the island, it was returned to the Genoese in 1559, however, under the terms of the treaty of Cateau-Cambrésis.

BONIFACIO

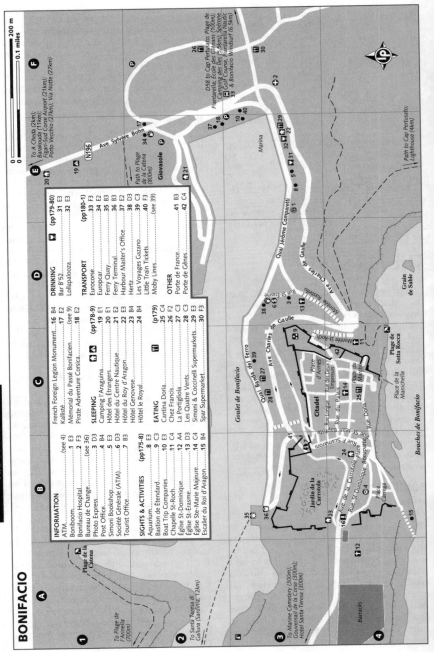

INFORMATION		
ATM.............................(see 4)	
Boniboom.........................	1	E3
Bonifacio Hospital.............	2	F3
Bureau de Change............(see 36)	
Photo Express...................	3	D3
Post Office......................	4	B4
Simoni Bookshop..............	5	B4
Société Générale (ATM).....	6	D3
Tourist Office..................	7	B3

SIGHTS & ACTIVITIES	(pp175–8)
Aquarium.........................	8	C3
Bastion de Étendard.........	9	C3
Boat Trip Companies.........	10	C4
Chapelle St-Roch.............	11	C4
Église St-Dominique.........	12	A4
Église St-Erasme.............	13	D3
Église Ste-Marie Majeure..	14	C4
Escalier du Roi d'Aragon...	15	B4

French Foreign Legion Monument..16	B4
Kalliste..........................	17	E3
Mémorial du Passé Bonifacien....(see 9)
Pirate Adventure Corsica...	18	E2

SLEEPING	🛏 🛏	(pp178–9)
Camping l'Araguina.........	19	E1
Hôtel des Étrangers.........	20	E1
Hôtel du Centre Nautique..	21	E2
Hôtel du Roy d'Aragon.....	22	E3
Hôtel Genovese..............	23	B4
Hôtel le Royal................	24	B4

EATING	🍴	(p179)
Cantina Doria.................	25	C4
Chez Francis...................	26	F2
La Portigliola.................	27	C3
Les Quatre Vents............	28	C3
Simoni & Coccinelli Supermarkets..	29	E3
Spar Supermarket............	30	F3

DRINKING	🍷	(pp179–80)
Bar B'52.......................	31	E3
Lollapalooza..................	32	E3

TRANSPORT	(pp180–1)
Eurocorse.....................	33	F3
Europcar......................	34	E2
Ferry Quay....................	35	B3
Ferry Terminal...............	36	B3
Harbour Master's Office...	37	E2
Hertz..........................	38	D3
Les Voyages Gazano........	39	C3
Little Train Tickets..........	40	F3

OTHER	
Porte de France.............	41	B3
Porte de Gênes..............	42	C4

To A Cheda (2km);
Barakouda (11km);
Figari-Sud Corse Airport (21km);
Porto Vecchio (27km); Via Notte (27km)

To Plage de
l'Arinella
(700m)

To Santa Teresa di
Gallura (Sardinia, 12km)

To Marine Cemetery (300m);
Gouvernail de la Corse (300m);
Hôtel Santa Teresa (800m)

Plage de la
Catena

Path to Plage de
la Catena
(800m)

Giovasole

Ave Sylvère Bohn

N196

Marina

D58 to Cap Pertusato; Plage de
Piantarella; École des Glénans (100m);
Camping des Îles (5.5km); Spérone
Golf Course, Piantarella Nautic
& Bonifacio Windsurf (6.5km)

Path to Cap Pertusato;
Lighthouse (4km)

Quai Jérôme Comparetti

Ave Charles de Gaulle

Montée Rastello

Rue St-Érasme

Ave Charles de Gaulle

Place
d'Armes

Citadel

Rue des Deux
Empereurs

Rue du Palais

Rue Doria

Montée St-Roch

Plage de
Sotta Rocca

Place de
la Manichella

Goulet de Bonifacio

Quai Banda del Ferro

Rue F. Scamaroni

Rue Longue

Rue St-Jean Baptiste

Place F.
Scamaroni

Place
Carrega

Rue de la Carrotola

Ave St-Dominique Bonaparte

Jardin de la
Carrotola

Barracks

Bouches de Bonifacio

Grain
de Sable

THE SOUTH

200 m
0.1 miles

Orientation

Bonifacio can be separated into two main sections: the marina at the bottom of the Goulet de Bonifacio, and the Genoese-built citadel – also known as the *vieille ville* (old town) or *ville haute* (upper town) – perched on the cliff top between the inlet and the sea. There are two ways into the citadel: by the handsome Porte de Gênes (Genoa Gate; pedestrian access only) at the top of montée St-Roch, and the Porte de France (France Gate; vehicle access), which overlooks the ferry terminal.

Information

BOOKSHOPS

Simoni (☎ 04 95 73 02 63; ☒ 8-12am Jul & Aug; 8am-noon & 3.45-7pm Mon-Sat, 8am-noon Sun Sep-Jun; closed 1-4pm Sun) Stocks a wide range of French and foreign newspapers and books in the summer. It's on the harbour near the aquarium.

EMERGENCY

Bonifacio Hospital (☎ 04 95 73 95 73) On the marina; 24-hour emergency unit.
Ambulance (☎ 04 95 73 06 95)
Police (☎ 04 95 73 00 17)

INTERNET ACCESS

Boniboom (☎ 04 95 73 05 89; www.boniboom.com; ☒ 6am-2am) It's a superior Internet café, built into the cliff under the Upper Town on the quai Jérôme Comparetti; charges €2 for 15 minutes or €3 for 30 minutes Internet access.

MONEY

Société Générale (☎ 04 95 73 02 49; 7 rue St-Érasme; ☒ 8.15am-noon & 2-4.50pm Mon-Fri) The only bank in town. On the south side of the harbour, is it has an outdoor ATM. A second ATM can be found at the post office.

PHOTOGRAPHY

Photo Express (☎ 04 95 73 58 87; 5 place St-Érasme) The prices are reasonable here all year-round. A 100 ASA film costs about €7.

POST

Post office (☎ 04 95 73 73 73; ☒ 8.30am-6pm Mon-Fri, 8.30am-noon Sat Jul & Aug; 9am-noon & 2-5.30pm Mon-Fri, 9am-noon Sat Sep-Jun) It's rather hidden in place Carrega in the citadel.

TOURIST INFORMATION

Tourist office (☎ 04 95 73 11 88; www.bonifacio.fr; 2 rue Fred Scamaroni; ☒ 9am-8pm May–mid-Oct, 9am-noon & 2-6pm Mon-Fri mid-Oct–Apr) It's next to the Porte de France and has multilingual brochures on local sights and activities.

Sights

CITADEL & UPPER TOWN

There are two sets of stairs from the harbour to the citadel. **Montée St-Roch**, which starts as montée Rastello, links rue St-Érasme to the Porte de Gênes. The second set ascends to the Porte de France from quai Banda del Ferro, not far from the ferry quay. The montée St-Roch and Porte de Gênes route is undoubtedly the best way to enter the citadel.

Porte de Gênes, which was fitted with a drawbridge in the last years of the 16th century, was the only way of getting into the citadel until the Porte de France was built in 1854. To the north is the **Bastion de l'Étendard**, a remnant of the fortifications built in the aftermath of the siege in 1553. It is home to the **Mémorial du Passé Bonifacien** (Memorial to Bonifacio's Past) where various episodes in the town's history have been recreated. To the south of the bastion are **place du Marché** and **place de la Manichella**, with their splendid views over the Bouches de Bonifacio (p181). The street that under Genoese supremacy was the citadel's main thoroughfare now bears the name **rue des Deux Empereurs**. The emperors alluded to are Charles V and Napoleon I, both of whom lodged in the town, the former on his way to Algiers in 1541, the latter in 1793 on his way to conquer Sardinia. Commemorative plaques at Nos 4 and 7 indicate the houses the two men stayed in, but neither house opens to the public.

The **Église Ste-Marie Majeure** was built by the Pisans and completed in the 14th century. Although it has been modified on numerous occasions and has gradually lost its original style, it retains its main feature, the loggia, under the arches of which the notables of the town used to gather. Opposite it is the old cistern, in which the town formerly collected rainwater from the many aqueducts running above the streets of the Old Town. Much of the citadel's stonework was erected for the purpose of solving the town's water-supply problem, and for a long time water supply was by means of mule-powered scoop wheels.

Even the **Escalier du Roi d'Aragon** (€2) may have been connected with water provision.

THE SOUTH

Legend has it that the 187 steps down from the southwestern corner of the citadel to the sea 60m below were carved in a single night by the King of Aragon's troops during the 1420 siege. It is more likely that this impressive scar down the side of the cliff was carved to allow access to a spring discovered by monks.

To the west of the citadel is the **Église St-Dominique**, one of the few Gothic churches in Corsica. It houses an altarpiece made of polychrome marble that dates back to the mid-18th century, as well as the reliquaries carried in processions through the town during a number of religious festivals. The church was closed to the public in 2003 but was due to reopen in the near future.

The marine cemetery, with its immaculate lines of tombs, stretches out to the sea a few hundred metres farther to the west. Although the surroundings are far from seductive, there is a spectacular view over the Sardinian coast, about 12km away. An underground passage dug by hand during WWII leads to the **Gouvernail de la Corse** (Rudder of Corsica), a rock about a dozen metres from the shore with a shape reminiscent of the rudder of a ship. The passage opens to the public until around 6pm in the summer.

The tourist office offers a group ticket, allowing entry to four attractions for €5.

THE SAD END OF THE SÉMILLANTE

The line of graves in the Achiarino cemetery on Île Lavezzi is a reminder of the tragic events of the night of 15 February 1855. The *Sémillante* had left Toulon the night before with more than 350 crew and 400 soldiers on board. She was bound for Sebastopol with reinforcements for the Crimean War. Heading out through the poorly marked Bouches de Bonifacio in heavy fog, the three-mast frigate caught a sudden gust of wind and ran aground on Île Lavezzi. For weeks, nightmarishly mangled naked bodies washed up onto the shore. The only one who could be identified was the captain; the other victims of the tragedy were buried anonymously. It is still the worst shipping disaster ever in the Mediterranean.

MARINA

The **Église St-Érasme**, dedicated to the patron saint of fishers, was built in the 13th century. The church is at the foot of montée Rastello.

The **Aquarium** (☎ 04 95 73 03 69; quai Jérôme Comparetti; adult/student/child under 14 €3.80/2.70/1.90; ☑ 9am-midnight Apr-Oct) is in a natural cave and features the marine flora and fauna of the Bouches de Bonifacio.

BEACHES

A very steep path leads down from the bottom of the montée St-Roch to **Plage de Sotta Rocca**, which nestles at the foot of the cliffs across from the so-called Grain de Sable (Grain of Sand); this is a section of cliff that seems to have escaped erosion a few dozen metres out to sea.

The little **Plage de la Catena** and **Plage de l'Arinella** stretch out at the back of the coves of the same name, on the north side of the *goulet*. There is a path leading to them from the corner of the U Veni snack bar on ave Sylvère Bohn. Unfortunately, both of these beaches tend to collect the rubbish from the *goulet*. With a car you can reach the beaches at Piantarella, Calalonga and Santa-Manza in the Bouches de Bonifacio (p181).

Activities

ADVENTURE SPORTS

Pirate Adventure Corsica (☎ 06 73 48 53 80; Les Palmiers bldg), just to the right of the harbour master's office in the pleasure port, offers jet skiing (€70 for 30 minutes), quad biking (€45 for two hours), bungy jumping and abseiling (€5 for 10 minutes) or mountain bike trekking (€10 for two hours).

BOAT TRIPS

Don't leave Bonifacio without taking a boat trip around its extraordinary coastline where you'll get the best perspective of the town's precarious position on top of the magnificent chalky cliffs. There are two basic itineraries. The first includes the *goulet* (narrow harbour entrance), the *calanques* (deep rocky inlets; *calanche* in Corsican) with their clear aquamarine waters and the magical Grotte du Sdragonato (Little Dragon Cave) with its gloriously multicoloured sea bed, referred to as the Persian Carpet. A 50-minute tour costs

---

WALK TO PERTUSATO LIGHTHOUSE

As long as you don't suffer from vertigo, there's a fantastic breezy walk you can take along the cliffs of Bonifacio to the Pertusato lighthouse, east of town. From the signposted starting point, which is just to the left of the sharp bend on the hill up to the Old Town, turn left and a ramp of paving stones climbs to the top of the cliffs. When you get there, follow the path along the cliffs towards the southeast. There is low-growing maquis on your left; to the right, a sheer drop down to the sea.

After around 30 minutes the path joins the D260, which leads to the signal station and light-house. Follow this little road as it veers away from the cliff edge for a short distance. The path passes a farm, then curves around low and then starts back up again past some old military bunkers to the signal station. The walk to this point takes about 45 minutes.

After the signal station, the road follows a long hairpin-shaped indentation in the coast to the lighthouse. Notice that, 50m before the lighthouse, a path leads down to a cove edged with golden sand and to Île St-Antoine.

On the way out, your view is dominated by chalk cliffs shaped and eroded by the sea, while on the return journey you'll be able to admire the Old Town of Bonifacio balanced atop its promontory. You'll also have excellent views over the spectacular Bouches de Bonifacio (Straits of Bonifacio) to Sardinia to the south. But it's wise to avoid the hotter parts of the day, as there is no shade and nowhere to get water. Allow 2½ hours for the walk.

---

about €12. The second (around €18) puts emphasis on the Îles Lavezzi and boats are operated shuttle-fashion, so you can linger on the islands. But, if you do, take your own food and drink since you won't find any there. On the way back, the boats pass close to Île Cavallo, the Pointe de Spérone, the calanche and the cliffs. Both trips are well worth taking.

Numerous companies vie for customers at the pleasure port in summer (9am to 7pm), all offering pretty much the same deal. Ignore touts offering free parking with a ticket. It's free anyway in the port.

DIVING

Bonifacio's magnificent underwater king-dom has been remarkably well preserved thanks to: the careful management of an internationally renowned marine nature reserve (Réserve Naturelle des Bouches de Bonifacio); the absence of an inten-sive, commercial fishing industry; and an almost total lack of polluters and pollu-tion. For these reasons the waters around Bonifacio are the most dived in Corsica. The turquoise-green water, among chis-elled granite rocks, is reminiscent of more tropical climes. The small inlets seem to have been designed for novice divers, and the more renowned sites – some of them quite famous – provide thrills for more experienced divers.

Dive Centres

The friendly, PADI-approved **Atoll** (☎ 04 95 73 02 83; www.atoll-diving.com; ☯ Apr-Oct), prob-ably the most famous in Corsica, is part of the Hôtel A Cheda (p179). It operates a welcome centre on the marina itself, close to the terminal for ferries to Sardinia. Introductory dives in the Îles Lavezzi or at Cap Pertusato will set you back €69, an exploratory dive costs from €37. Six dives cost €185.

The informal **Barakouda** (☎ 04 95 73 13 02; www.club.barakouda.free.fr; ☯ year-round) is 1km before Atoll on the road from Bonifacio to Porto Vecchio, on the left. Prices are reasonable: an introductory dive costs €37, an exploratory dive between €28 and €37 and a set of five dives from €110 to €160 depending on whether or not you have your own equipment.

The beautifully maintained **Kallisté** (☎ 04 95 73 53 66; www.corsicadiving.com; ave Sylvère Bohn; ☯ Apr-Oct), a few metres back from the harbour just opposite the Esso station, charges €44 for an introductory dive and from €36 to €44 thereafter. For a package of six dives you'll pay €205 with your own equipment or €248 without.

GOLF

Spérone Golf (☎ 04 95 73 17 13; www.sperone.net), on the seaside before Piantarella beach, is a beautiful, 18-hole course. Green fees are

THE SOUTH

€80 per day in high season. Golf lessons are available and equipment can be rented.

WALKING
There is a sign describing the footpaths along the coast at the foot of montée St-Roch. Don't miss the one that goes to the Pertusato lighthouse (see boxed text p177).

WATER SPORTS
A branch of the reputable **École des Glénans** (☎ 04 95 73 03 85; www.glenans.asso.fr), on the Santa-Manza road 300m from the port, offers sailing courses for adults and for children aged 13 or over. Beginners learn on a 5.7m boat in the inlets near Bonifacio. More advanced learners take a 13m boat out onto the open sea. One-week programmes in high season cost between €370 and €460, two weeks cost around €690 for advanced learners (with lunch); beginners start at €375 per week.

Windsurfing and kayaking fans should head for the magnificent Pointe de Spérone. On the Plage de Piantarella, **Bonifacio Windsurf** (☎ 04 95 73 52 04) rents standard/fun boards for €18/12 an hour, as well as one-/two-person kayaks for €5/8 per hour. Private lessons are given for beginners (€23 an hour) and for those who want to hone their skills (€45 for two hours). A five-day package of group lessons is also available (from €90).

Piantarella Nautic (☎ 04 95 73 51 64), on the same beach, rents Zodiacs (permit required) for €200 to €320 per day (depending on its horsepower) or €61 per half-day or €92 per day for a boat without a permit.

Sleeping
The majority of the hotels in Bonifacio have three stars; however, it is possible to find more reasonable accommodation options nearby.

BUDGET
Hôtel des Étrangers (☎ 04 95 73 01 09, fax 04 95 73 16 97; ave Sylvère Bohn; r €50-72; ☼ mid-Mar–Oct; P ☒) A few hundred metres north of the marina, this is an olde worlde hotel at the entrance to town. Rooms are simple but comfortable, all have private bathroom, and the welcome is friendly. Prices vary according to the season, room size and appointments. The choicest rooms, cool and quiet, are at the rear.

Camping l'Araguina (☎ 04 95 73 02 96; ave Sylvère Bohn; adult/tent/car €5.50/1.70/0.60; ☼ mid-Mar–mid-Oct; P) Tightly packed, but close to town, this one-star campground north of the marina is clean and shady, and there's a snack bar and laundrette.

Camping des Îles (☎ 04 95 73 11 89, fax 04 95 73 18 77; adult/tent/car €6.70/2.50/3.40; ☼ Apr–mid-Oct; P ☒) Camping des Îles, 5.5km from town on the road to Cap Pertusato, is in a glorious setting and has enough amenities to make some hotels envious. Plage de Piantarella is about 1km away; the Spérone golf course is across the way. The only downside is that there isn't any shade.

MID-RANGE
Hôtel du Roy d'Aragon (☎ 04 95 73 03 99; 13 quai J Comparetti; r €87-130; ☒) This newly renovated hotel is undoubtedly the best value place to stay in the town centre, in this category. Rooms are stylishly decorated with subtle furnishings and lighting and some make a nice feature of the exposed stone arches and brickwork of the original building. Bag room 403 or 405 on the top floor if you can; they have wide terraces overlooking the whole port and are great for people-watching at sunset.

Hôtel Santa Teresa (☎ 04 95 73 11 32; hotel-santa teresa.com; quartier St-Francois; s/d/tr €126/137/200; ☼ Apr-Oct; P) Right at the cliff's edge, in a converted police station, Santa Teresa has 48 very comfortable bright rooms with balconies – somewhat ironic given their provenance. Rooms with a sea view have smaller bathrooms, but more than make up for it with their wonderful views across the Bouches de Bonifacio to Sardinia.

Hôtel Le Royal (☎ 04 95 73 00 51; 8 rue Fred Scamaroni; r €69-99; ☒) The best thing about this little place is its location, right in the heart of the citadel. It has 14 large, slightly antiquated double rooms with bathroom. Those with a sea view are more expensive.

TOP END
Hôtel Genovese (☎ 04 95 73 12 34; hotel-genovese .com; quartier de la Citadelle; r €230-350; ☒ P ☒) The ultra-hip Genovese, built within the town's original ramparts at the top of the old town, epitomises style and sophistication. Its 15 luxurious rooms are extremely comfortable and equipped with understated modern furnishings, including minibars

and plasma TVs. The gracious, decked swimming-pool area, hidden inside the city walls even has steps up to an original sentry tower, overlooking the fjord.

Hôtel du Centre Nautique (☎ 04 95 73 02 11; www.centre-nautique.com; quai Nord; r €140-190; ⊠ P) This modern hotel is in a beautifully renovated, old building by the port. It has 10 spacious, duplex rooms which are effectively suites, with tasteful, nautically themed sitting rooms and teak winding stairways up to a cosy sleeping area on the mezzanine.

Hôtel A Cheda (☎ 04 95 73 02 83; www.acheda -hotel.com; Cavallo Morto; r €144-269; P ⊠ ▱ ▣) This charming, small hotel is set in lovely landscaped gardens 2km from Bonifacio in the direction of Porto Vecchio. Its 13 newly renovated rooms, in little private bungalows dotted around the garden, are all individually decorated in a Mediterranean style using imaginative natural furnishings. The owners also operate a dive school from here and offer a 10% discount on diving to residents.

Eating
BUDGET
There are many shops and cafés by the harbour where you can get sandwiches, pizzas and panini.

Simoni (☑ 7am-8pm Jul & Aug; 8am-12.30pm & 3.30-7.30pm Mon-Sat, 8am-12.30pm Sun Sep-Jun) This well-stocked supermarket is on the south side of the marina. **Coccinelli supermarket** is next door.

Cantina Dora (☎ 04 95 73 50 49; 27 rue Doria; mains €6-11) is a buzzing, little, no-nonsense joint in the Old Town with long wooden tables and rustic hunting rifles and blades on the walls. It serves hearty Corsican *menus* (from €11 to €14) or à la carte dishes such as the carb-fest *lasagne au brocciu* (€8) or *aubergine à la bonifacienne* (€9.50). There's no air-conditioning so in summer sweat it out inside or try to reserve one of the few tables on the street.

La Portigliola (☎ 04 95 73 55 63; 11 quai Banda del Ferro; mains €5-11) In an intimate, little cave in the cliffs that was once a donkey shed, this vibrant crêperie-restaurant, with bench seating and a handful of tables, overlooks the port. Everything is homemade and tastes it, from the huge salads to the char-grilled meats, pasta dishes and sinful crêpes

(€3 to €5). Vegetarians will be well looked after here.

MID-RANGE
Chez Francis (☎ 04 95 73 05 45; mains €6-17; ☑ Apr-Oct) Near the port, this kooky joint with colourful tiki tables is set in a garden of palm trees, cacti and rockery. Choose from large salads or a selection of meats and fish whipped up on the barbeque.

Les Quatre Vents (☎ 04 95 73 07 50; quai Banda del Ferro; mains €12-30; ☑ closed Tue Nov-Apr) This restaurant, near the ferry quay, is popular for its fish in summer, its Alsatian specialities in winter, and for its warm welcome year-round. The €19 *menu* may feature *coq au vin* or fondue.

TOP END
Hôtel du Centre Nautique (☎ 04 95 73 02 11; www .centre-nautique.com; quai Nord; seafood mains €15-32; ⊠ P) The hotel's restaurant on the north side of the harbour, opposite most of the other restaurants, is probably the town's most hip eatery. With its loosely nautical décor, it attracts the well-heeled boating set, for its first-rate pasta dishes as well as its seafood.

Restaurant A Cheda (☎ 04 95 73 02 83; www .acheda-hotel.com; Cavallo Morto; menu €32-39; P ⊠) Just out of town, this is the perfect spot for an intimate, gourmet dinner in the stylish surroundings of an Indonesian-style terrace overlooking a tropical garden and decked swimming pool. The daily *menu* here is traditionally French using Corsican produce, with an emphasis on fresh fish (€18 to €27). There's a simplified children's *menu* (€12) too which will appeal to junior gourmands.

Drinking
If it's Ibiza-style nightlife you're after, you're barking up the wrong tree. In fact, even in mid-summer, you could hear a pin drop on the streets after midnight. The only place you'll find some action, unsurprisingly, is the port area where a handful of bars stay open until the small hours.

Bar B'52 (quai Jérôme Comparetti) This bar stays open until 3am. You can watch teens snog on the terrace or dance to French chart-driven, poptastic tunes in the grotto-like room carved into the rock. **Lollapalooza** (25 quai Comparetti) 100m away, Lollapalooza, with its buzzing balcony area and terrace, is the better of the two. It plays a good blend of hip-hop, soul and indie music but only really gets going around midnight and stays open till 4am.

The nearest club proper is **Via Notte**, at the south end of Porto Vecchio (p187). It's not that far if you're willing and able.

Entertainment

For those in favour of more genteel pursuits, there are occasional classical concerts in the normally closed **Église St-Dominique**; check with the tourist office for details.

Getting There & Away

AIR

Figari-Sud Corse airport (☎ 04 95 71 10 10) is in the middle of the maquis, 21km north of Bonifacio, near the village of Figari. Daily flights from Marseille, Nice and Paris, plus charter flights in summer from London and Geneva, serve both Bonifacio and Porto Vecchio.

Like most airports in Corsica, this one has neither an ATM or a *bureau de change*, despite its having been renovated as recently as 1996.

BOAT

Ferries operated by the Italian Moby Lines sail between Bonifacio and Santa Teresa di Gallura in Sardinia. Moby Lines is represented in Bonifacio by **Les Voyages Gazano** (☎ 04 95 73 00 29/02 47, fax 04 95 73 05 50; ☻ 9am-noon & 3-6.30pm Mon-Fri, 9am-noon Sat). In summer Moby Lines provides 10 daily return services from 7.45am to 10pm, with a last return from Sardinia at 9.20pm. Tickets cost €11/22 per person (one way/return) and a car costs from €22.50 to €27.50.

Another company, **Saremar** (☎ 04 95 73 00 96; www.traghettiservice.com/saremar; ☻ 8.30am-8.30pm Jul & Aug; 8.30am-6.30pm Sep-Jun), also at the ferry terminal and cheaper than Moby Lines, operates four crossings daily (€11.70 per person, cars €21 to €25.60) to Santa Teresa di Gallura in summer and three crossings daily the rest of the year.

The Bonifacio **harbour master's office** (☎ 04 95 73 10 07, fax 04 95 73 18 73; ☻ 7am-10pm Jul & Aug, 7am-9pm Jun, 7am-9.30pm Sep, 7am-noon & 2-6pm Oct-May) is by the marina. Chandlers, fuel, water and showers are all available. The charge for mooring a 9m to 10m boat ranges between €20 and €43, depending on the season.

BUS

Eurocorse (☎ 04 95 21 06 30, 04 95 70 13 83; ☻ 8am-7pm), whose offices are at the harbour, operates services between Bonifacio and Porto Vecchio, Roccapina, Sartène, Propriano, Olmeto, Ste-Marie Sicche and Ajaccio. There are up to four departures daily during the high season, though only two on Sundays and public holidays. There are two departures daily in the low season. The journey to Ajaccio takes 3½ hours and costs €19.50.

CAR

There is a **Europcar agency** (☎ 04 95 73 10 99; ☻ 8am-noon & 2-7pm) on the way into town, near the petrol station.

Hertz cars can be rented at the Elf petrol station at the corner of rue St-Érasme and the quai Banda del Ferro.

The airport has the widest choice of car rental companies, many of which, however, open only when flights are arriving and departing. The main ones are:

Avis (☎ 04 95 71 00 01)
Budget (☎ 04 95 71 04 18)
Citer (☎ 04 95 71 02 00)
Europcar (☎ 04 95 71 01 41)
Hertz (☎ 04 95 71 04 16)

Getting Around

Bonifacio is such a popular destination – because it is in a sense the end of the line, and for half a dozen other reasons – that it does to cars what a spider's web does to flies. In summer, traffic sometimes backs up all the way from the town centre to the roundabout on the main road – no short distance. Nor are matters helped by the scarcity of car parks. Your best bet, particularly in the high season, is to find a hotel that provides a parking space and get around on foot or arrive early and try for a spot in the port.

TO/FROM THE AIRPORT

Transports Rossi (☎ 04 95 71 00 11) provides a shuttle service between the airport and Bonifacio from the end of June to the beginning of September. The departure times correspond to the arrivals and departures of the flights. The journey to Bonifacio costs €8 and takes about half an hour. The departures for the airport leave from the harbour car park.

By **taxi** (☎ 04 95 73 19 08), the trip from the airport to Bonifacio centre costs a about €35.

There's a little **train** (☎ 04 95 73 15 07; €5) that runs from the port up to the Old Town (every half hour from 9am to 12am in high season). The price is as steep as the route, but you may be doing your legs a favour by hopping on. Tickets are available from a kiosk in the port car park.

BOUCHES DE BONIFACIO

This is the name for the narrow stretch of sea that separates the southern tip of Corsica from Italian Sardinia. It is home to several of the island's natural treasures, and is a protected area (known as Les Réserves Naturelles des Bouches de Bonifacio).

Archipel des Lavezzi

The Archipel des Lavezzi (Lavezzi Archipelago) is a group of about 10 main islands, a protected paradise between sky and sea. The islands' beauty owes a great deal to the colour palette from which they have been decorated – the turquoise and ultramarine of the water complementing the bright hues of the granite. The islands' strangeness owes much to the way the rocks have been sculpted by the forces of sand and sea so that, while some have a polished, sensual roundness, others seem reminiscent of the scales of a fabulous sea monster.

The 65-hectare **Île Lavezzi**, which gives its name to the whole archipelago, is the most accessible of the islands. It is the southernmost point of Corsica, and signal-station keepers are its only inhabitants.

The island's savage beauty aside, its superb natural pools make good swimming holes, and the island also has the cemetery for the victims who perished on board the Sémillante (p176). In high season, the tour boat operators at Bonifacio harbour make it easy to get to; for details see p176.

Île Cavallo, just north of the Îles Lavezzi, is a paradise frequented by the very rich and protected from outsiders. Though it is almost twice the size of Île Lavezzi and even has a small landing strip, it is inaccessible except by private boat.

Cap Pertusato

Recognisable by its resemblance to a sinking ship, Cap Pertusato (also called Pointe St-Antoine) makes a good destination for walkers from Bonifacio. By car, take the D58, by the hospital. It would be difficult to describe the panoramic view of cliffs, open water, the Îles Lavezzi and the high citadel. Suffice it to say that the cape is the best place you'll find for a fantastic view of the town without stepping onto a boat.

Pointe de Spérone

Among other things, Pointe de Spérone has become a destination for international celebrities. The golf course that overlooks it was created by importing the fertile soil needed to grow the grass for perfect greens. The course is now one of the most celebrated in Europe. To the north is the little **Plage de Piantarella**, which opens to the public. You can rent boats, kayaks and windsurfing gear. There is also a snack bar.

BONIFACIO TO PORTO VECCHIO

The stretch of road between Bonifacio and Porto Vecchio is one of the best and, noticeably straightest in the country! Between the Golfe de Pinarellu and the Golfe de Santa-Manza the jagged coastline is regularly punctuated by stretches of gorgeous, white-sand beach. Sadly, these beaches are no longer a secret; at the peak of the summer tourist season, they are frequently very crowded.

Plage de Palombaggia

The Plage de Palombaggia is certainly the most famous beach in south Corsica, and it may be the most beautiful, too. It is a long ribbon of sand edged with pine trees and with a view of the Réserve Naturelle des Îles Cerbicale a short distance offshore.

The road to this beach is well marked, off the N198 just south of town; it is 14km from the turn-off to the beach.

Kallisté Plongée (☎ 04 95 72 07 63, 06 80 11 71 54; www.corsicadiving.com), on the beach, offers introductory **dives** (in an inlet in the Îles Cerbicale) from €23 to €54. Thereafter single dives cost from €36. A package of 10 dives will set you back €320 or more. Advance booking is a must. It's open year-round.

Jet Liberté (☎ 04 95 70 03 92, 06 81 02 40 90; www.jetliberty.com), on the beach, rents jet skis from €68 for 30 minutes. A one-hour rental costs from €110 to €125.

SLEEPING & EATING

There's a string of camp sites along the road to Palombaggia, and during the high season bars and restaurants open along the edge of the beach.

Camping U Pirellu (☎ 04 95 70 23 44; www.u -pirellu.com; adult/tent/car €7.70/3.05/4; ☼ Apr-Oct; P ☼) You need never leave this three-star site, about 4km from the Plage de Palombaggia, with all the facilities it has on site; tennis, mini-golf, jacuzzi, supermarket and pizzeria.

Hôtel Ranch Campo (☎ 04 95 70 13 27; www.ranch campo.com; rte de Palombaggia; d €90-116; ☼ May-Oct; P ☼) Ranch Campo has 10 charming, simply furnished rooms, with terracotta floors and big pine beds housed in rustic stone buildings in a shady garden. There are also a few secluded bungalows to rent (€780 per week for two in high season), on the grounds, 900m from the beach. There's a small restaurant on a rustic, Mexican-style terrace that serves good wood-fired pizzas and grilled meats (€7 to €15).

Plage de Calalonga

The little shale-covered plage de Calalonga doesn't get too crowded and is popular with **snorkellers**. To get there follow the D58 east of Bonifacio for 6km, from where you'll need to walk a further 200m down a sandy track to the beach. There's usually a little van selling ice-cream and cold drinks, but you'll need to bring more substantial snacks yourself.

Golfe de Santa-Manza

Just 7km east of Bonifacio, you'll find the windswept and virtually empty **Plages de Maora et de Santa-Manza**, a windsurfer's paradise. All around the gulf you can stop and make your way down to the many little rocky coves or rough sandy inlets, with, if you're lucky, only stray wild goats (and a bunch of windsurfers) for company. To get there follow the D60, just off the main Bonifacio–Bastia road.

Tam Tam Windsurf (☎ 04 95 73 11 59; www.tam -tam.fr; ☼ Jun-Sep) offers an hour's windsurfing tuition for €45 or €30 with your own board. It also offers lessons on funboards (€22 an hour) and rents kayaks (€8/10 for a single/double), water skis (€30 per day) and mountain bikes (€15 per day).

La Cabane du Pecheur (☎ 04 95 73 06 27; rte de Santa-Manza) is a little restaurant, where you can eat from the simple but excellent menu of fresh grilled fish (€18) or seafood risotto (€20) under the shade of a few palm trees and a gigantic willow.

Plage de Rondinara

The beautiful 300-degree horseshoe-shaped **Baie de Rondinara**, home to the fine sandy Plage de Rondinara, is one you'll certainly write home about. Flanked by pines on one side and a protected nature reserve, the beach, with its calm, turquoise water almost resembles a lagoon. To find it from Bonifacio, take the Bastia road for about 16km where you'll see a small turn to the right, in the direction of Suartone. The winding, switchback D158 takes you a further 3km through the maquis and cork trees, down to the beach. Access to the beach is via a narrow track that takes you over some precarious rocks, which won't suit the elderly or wheelchair-users. There's a holiday village and camp site nearby.

Plage de Santa Giulia

Only 7km south of Porto Vecchio, the gently curving, long, white, sandy beach of Santa Giulia is idyllic with its shallow, aquamarine waters and maquis fringe which offers some welcome shade. It's a popular spot for water sports, so it might be best to visit early in the morning or in low season. It is accessible from the N198 about 3km south of the turn-off to Palombaggia. Santa Giulia is another contender for honours as the most beautiful beach in south Corsica.

Blue Marine (☎ 04 95 70 04 44; fax 04 95 70 11 34; bungalows for 2-3 people Jul & Aug €833-1075; P ☼) On the edge of the beach, this holiday village offers spacious, comfortable bungalows of different sizes with fully equipped kitchens, set in nicely landscaped gardens.

WATER SPORTS

Club Nautique Santa Giulia (☎ 04 95 70 58 62; ☼ 9am-7pm), right on the beach, offers surfboard (€14 per hour), funboard (€18 per hour) and catamaran (€29 to €40) rentals or surfboard (€17 per hour) and sailing (€20 per hour) lessons.

With **Sud Corse Loisirs** (☎ 04 95 70 22 67), also on the beach, you can take an introductory scuba dive for €32 or take four dives for €115. It also does night dives and offers PADI training.

Try your hand at water-skiing with **Santa Giulia Ski Club** (☎ 06 14 23 59 99; www.santagiulia-skiclub.com; ☘ 8am-7pm) for €29 for an introductory ski or €22 thereafter.

You can also parasail and hire jet-skis and motor boats on the beach.

PORTO VECCHIO (PORTIVECCHJU)

postcode 20137 / pop 12,000

Porto Vecchio's appeal is centred not so much on what's left of its citadel but on the beautiful coastline stretching both north and south from this old 'city of salt'. Everything in town, in summer especially, seems to be geared towards the incessant stream of (mostly Italian) visitors. While this is good for local business, prices can rocket to above reasonable levels, and the presence of so many visitors contributes to Porto Vecchio's vaguely unreal, Disney-like atmosphere. Provided you can find accommodation, the town could be used as a base if you want to discover the highlights of the Alta Rocca region, the Forêt de l'Ospedale, the Col de Bavella and Aiguilles de Bavella, and the surrounding villages.

History

In a bid to establish itself on the eastern coast of the island, the Genoese republic set its sights on Porto Vecchio in the 15th century. This site, which was inhabited in ancient times, is set at the back of a deep bay, and provided the best shelter between the fortified towns of Bonifacio and Bastia. The Genoese settled on the heights over the bay, where they created what is now called the *ville haute* (upper town), which they fortified with thick ramparts.

Their attempt to wall themselves off from danger did not prove successful; the malaria prevalent along the coast decimated the Genoese settlers.

A few years later a second attempt to populate the town, this time with forcibly recruited Corsicans, was no more successful. Porto Vecchio was essentially abandoned before re-emerging in 1564, when Sampiero Corso chose it as base for his renewed efforts to liberate the island. The town was besieged and forced to capitulate a few months later.

The town did not really begin to thrive until the malaria-infested swamps around it were transformed into salt marshes. With the health threat removed, the town blossomed. The beauty of the beaches stretching away on either side of the bay helped to make it the popular and lively tourist town that it is today.

Orientation

Porto Vecchio is quite spread out and divided into two parts. There is the Upper Town with its little streets and the ruins of the citadel, and below this the more modern harbour, which stretches along ave Georges Pompidou. Rue de Cavasina, which leads off the first roundabout to the north of the marina, links the two parts. The carrefour des Quatre Chemins, to the north, is the focus for much of the activity in the town.

Information

BOOKSHOPS

Librairie-Papeterie-Presse (☎ 04 95 70 07 71; 12 rue Pasteur; ☘ 7am-9pm Jul & Aug, 8am-7pm Jun & Sep, 8am-noon & 2-7pm Mon-Sat Oct-May) It stocks a range of French and foreign newspapers, books and stationery.

EMERGENCY

24-hour emergency (☎ 04 95 72 09 76) Clinique de l'Ospedale, between the Hyper U supermarket and the stadium, close to the carrefour des Quatre Chemins. The nearest hospital is in Bonifacio.

INTERNET ACCESS

Cyberlink (☎ 04 95 70 69 64; 4 rue Jean Jaurès; ☘ 9am-12am) Charges €2.50 for a half hour, €4 an hour's Internet access.

Cyrnocom (☎ 04 95 72 06 98; www.cyrno.com; ☘ 9am-noon & 2-7pm Mon-Sat) Charges €3 for a half hour or €5 for an hour's Internet access. It's near the Hyper U supermarket.

MONEY

Crédit Lyonnais (☎ 04 95 70 94 81) On the corner of rue du Général Leclerc and rue Scamaroni, not far from the post office. It has an ATM but doesn't change travellers cheques.

Société Générale (☎ 04 95 70 10 15; rue du Général Leclerc; ☘ 8.15am-noon & 1.45-4.50pm Mon-Fri) Changes foreign currencies.

There is an ATM at the post office which also will change travellers cheques for you. It has better exchange rates than the banks.

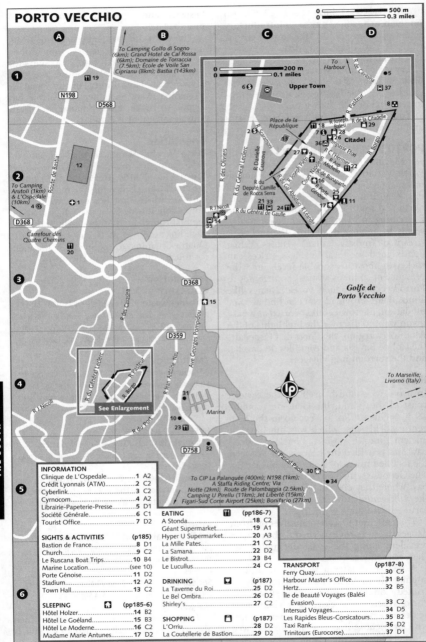

PORTO VECCHIO

THE SOUTH

INFORMATION
Clinique de L'Ospedale	1	A2
Crédit Lyonnais (ATM)	2	C2
Cyberlink	3	C2
Cyrnocom	4	A2
Librairie-Papeterie-Presse	5	D1
Société Générale	6	C1
Tourist Office	7	D2

SIGHTS & ACTIVITIES (p185)
Bastion de France	8	D1
Church	9	C2
Le Ruscana Boat Trips	10	B4
Marine Location	(see 10)	
Porte Génoise	11	D2
Stadium	12	A2
Town Hall	13	C2

SLEEPING (pp185-6)
Hôtel Holzer	14	B2
Hôtel Le Goéland	15	B3
Hôtel Le Moderne	16	C2
Madame Marie Antunes	17	D2

EATING (pp186-7)
A Stonda	18	C2
Géant Supermarket	19	A1
Hyper U Supermarket	20	A3
La Mille Pates	21	C2
La Samana	22	D2
Le Bistrot	23	B4
Le Lucullus	24	C2

DRINKING (p187)
La Taverne du Roi	25	D2
Le Bel Ombra	26	D2
Shirley's	27	C2

SHOPPING (p187)
L'Orriu	28	D2
La Coutellerie de Bastion	29	D2

TRANSPORT (pp187-8)
Ferry Quay	30	C5
Harbour Master's Office	31	B4
Hertz	32	B5
Île de Beauté Voyages (Balési Évasion)	33	C2
Intersud Voyages	34	D5
Les Rapides Bleus-Corsicatours	35	B2
Taxi Rank	36	D2
Trinitours (Eurocorse)	37	D1

Upper Town

Place de la République

Citadel

Golfe de Porto Vecchio

Marina

See Enlargement

To Marseille; Livorno (Italy)

To Harbour

To Camping Golfo di Sogno (6km); Grand Hotel de Cal Rossa (6km); Domaine de Torraccia (7.5km); École de Voile San Ciprianu (8km); Bastia (143km)

To Camping Arutoli (1km) & L'Ospedale (10km)

Carrefour des Quatre Chemins

To CIP La Palanquée (400m); N198 (1km); A Staffa Riding Centre; Via Notte (2km); Route de Palombaggia (2.5km); Camping U Pirellu (11km); Jet Liberté (15km); Figari-Sud Corse Airport (25km); Bonifácio (27km)

POST
Post office (☎ 04 95 70 95 00; rue du Général Leclerc; ⊙ 8.30am-6 pm Mon-Fri, 8.30am-noon Sat) It's centrally located.

TOURIST INFORMATION
Tourist office (☎ 04 95 70 09 58; rue du Deputé Camille de Rocca Serra; ⊙ 9am-8pm Mon-Sat, 9am-1pm Sun May-Sep; 9am-12.30pm & 2-6.30pm Mon-Fri, 9am-12.30pm Sat Oct-Apr). The English-speaking staff are helpful and are happy to provide information on gîtes and B&Bs. A small 'learning garden' in front identifies many of the maquis plants.

Sights
UPPER TOWN
There are still a few vestiges of the old Genoese citadel here, notably the Porte Génoise and the Bastion de France (closed to the public). The beautiful rue Borgo gives a glimpse of what the city was like in earlier days.

BEACHES
Although there is no beach in the town proper, some of the island's best, and most famous, beaches are close by. For details see p188.

Activities
BOAT TRIPS
Le Ruscana is an old fishing boat aboard which you can explore the coast as far as Bonifacio. Its **ticket office** (☎ 04 95 70 33 67/71 41 50; adult/child €55/25; ⊙ 8am-noon & 4-7.30pm May-Oct) is opposite the harbour master's house at the marina. The excursion, which takes a whole day, passes along the Réserve Naturelle des Îles Cerbicale and the beaches to the south of Porto Vecchio before reaching the Îles Lavezzi, Île Cavallo, the Pointe de Spérone and Bonifacio (weather permitting). The congenial crew provides commentary, and there is a stop for a swim in a lovely little cove. The ticket price includes a picnic.

Kallisté Plongée (☎ 04 95 72 07 63, 06 80 11 71 54; www.corsicadiving.com), based at Palombaggia (p181), runs glass-bottom boat excursions. You'll be taken to see the Pecorella shipwreck site and the depths of Cerbicale.

Marine Location (☎ 04 95 70 58 92; www.marine-location.fr), next to the Ruscana ticket window, offers a good selection of motorboats for hire.

DIVING
CIP La Palanquée (☎ 04 95 70 16 53, 06 07 49 4 04; aldeso@club-internet.fr; ⊙ Mar-Dec), with more than 20 years of service, is 400m from the town harbour on the road to Bonifacio, in a large building on the right, 100m before you get to the Casino supermarket. Exploratory dives start at €27.

The small **Hippocampe** (☎ 04 95 70 56 54; www.hippocampe.de; ⊙ May-Oct) links diving with naturism. It's owned by a German couple, and its headquarters are on naturist beach La Chiappa, south of the Golfe de Porto Vecchio. Follow the main road towards Bonifacio and, as you leave Porto Vecchio, turn left towards Palombaggia. Continue on this road for 7km, then bear left towards Chiappa, 2.5km away. The drive from the town centre takes roughly 20 minutes. After you leave your vehicle in the car park, you will hand over some ID at the reception desk. But divers get in free.

An introductory dive off the beach costs €40, exploratory dives go from €22.

HORSE RIDING
The **A Staffa riding centre** (☎ 04 95 70 47 51, 06 16 56 73 60) opens year-round and offers pony games, polo and obstacle courses (€8.50 to €16 per hour). To get there, take the N198 south and turn off onto route de Palombaggia; the centre will be on your right after about 400m. Rides in the maquis and along the seafront are organised both early in the morning and in the evening. Advance booking is necessary.

WATER SPORTS
The **École de Voile San Ciprianu** (☎ 04 95 71 00 48, 06 14 67 91 55), 8km north of Porto Vecchio right on the beach, is without doubt the best place for all water sports. You can rent windsurfing equipment (€13 per hour, €16 for a funboard), catamarans (€32 per hour, €16 for a Hobie Cat), canoes (€11), kayaks (€10) and pedal boats (€15). Private and group sailing and windsurfing lessons are offered at reasonable prices.

Sleeping
BUDGET
Madame Marie Antunes (☎ 04 95 70 37 31; 55 rue Borgo; €55) For B&B accommodation, Mme Antunes in the citadel, rents two rooms, one with a balcony and a pretty view of

THE SOUTH

the gulf and the other with a kitchen for €10 more.

Houses with patios, for four persons, adjacent to the harbour, can be rented for about €600 to €800 per week; ask at the tourist office.

Camping Arutoli (☎ 04 95 70 12 73; www.arutoli .com; rte de l'Ospedale; adult/tent/car €5.90/3.05/3.25; ✹ Apr-Oct; ℗ ☒ ⬚ ⬚) This three-star camp site, 1km from the carrefour des Quatre Chemins on the road towards L'Ospedale and Zonza, is the closest to the town centre. Watch for the signposts to the site from the D368. The pitches are quiet and shaded, the site is clean, and there is a restaurant, laundrette and extensive games. The site also rents out bungalows sleeping up to four people for €547 to €644 per week in high season.

There are plenty of other camp sites in the vicinity, but you will need a car to get to them. For details see p189.

MID-RANGE

Hôtel Holzer (☎ 04 95 70 05 93; fax 04 95 70 47 82; 12 rue Jean Jaurès; s/d/tr €61/91/118; half-board s/d/tr per person €75/59.50/53.40; ℗ ☒) This two-star hotel near the centre of the Upper Town (it also has a door on rue Jean Nicoli) offers comfortable, spotless rooms with air-conditioning, satellite TV and telephone. Half-board is mandatory in August.

Hôtel Le Moderne (☎ 04 95 70 06 36; 10 cours Napoléon; d/tr €61-110/80-120; ✹ Apr-Oct) Set in a pretty white building with blue shutters across from the church, the interior doesn't really live up to the promise of the facade. Its 20 modest rooms are clean but in need of a lick of paint, though you won't beat the price in this extremely central location. Rooms 20 and 21 on the roof, have open showers in the room and a large terrace overlooking the town and the harbour.

Hôtel Le Goéland (☎ 04 95 70 14 15; ave Georges Pompidou; s/d €87/150; ✹ Mar-Nov; ℗) Family-run, two-star Le Goéland owes a great deal of its charm to its waterside location, between the harbour and the roundabout before the carrefour des Quatre Chemins. The atmosphere is relaxed and quiet, and there's a garden. English and Spanish are also spoken.

TOP END

Grand Hôtel de Cala Rossa (☎ 04 95 71 61 51; www .relaischateaux.com/calarossa; Cala Rossa; half-board r €716-838; ✹ Apr-Jan; ℗ ☒ ⬚ ⬚) Situated 6km north of Porto Vecchio, this is the area's – and possibly the country's – top hotel. Part of the Relais & Chateaux group, its 48 rooms with terrace, while not enormous, are stylishly decorated in Mediterranean colours with terracotta floors, whitewashed walls and ethnic furnishings. Every conceivable amenity is available, from a top-notch spa and fitness centre to its own private white sandy beach. While you'll pay through the nose to stay here in high season, special offers are available off season, such as the attractive package offering a night's accommodation, plus dinner and breakfast for two people for €310.

Eating
BUDGET & MID-RANGE

The **Hyper U supermarket** (carrefour des Quatre Chemins) and the **Géant supermarket** on the next roundabout to the north stock everything self-caterers will need. Both are in large shopping complexes with lots of other shops.

La Samana (☎ 04 95 70 45 31; rue Asp Michelin; mains €8-15; ✹ May-Sep) In the Upper Town, this place is a bustling little restaurant-crêperie with a terrace that has tasty *menus* (€13) which might include mussels with chips or stuffed aubergine The savoury and sweet crêpes (the chocolate and cream one is particularly good) go from €3 to €5.

A Stonda (☎ 04 95 70 15 51; 6 rue Camille de Rocca Serra; mains €4-12) The little familial restaurant, A Stonda, packs local workers in at lunchtime for its *menu* of salads, savoury tarts and crêpes. It's a friendly, down-to-earth place with a shady terrace near place de la République that opens year round.

La Mille Pates (☎ 04 95 70 63 63; 3 rue du Général de Gaulle; mains €5-10) Set in a cosy room with a handful of tables, it serves generous portions of pasta just like mamma used to make, and light salads to boot. There's a choice of a good €16 Italian or €15 Corsican *menu*.

Le Bistrot (☎ 04 95 70 22 96; ave Georges Pompidou; mains €12-26) Le Bistrot, in the port, has a good reputation for its fish and for its €17 lunch *menu*, or €30 dinner *menu*. The setting is pleasant and the décor nautical.

In the Upper Town, rue Borgo is home to a number of restaurants that back onto the ramparts and have attractive terraces facing out over the sea.

TOP END

Le Lucullus (☎ 04 95 70 10 17; rue du Général de Gaulle; mains €19-27) What makes Le Lucullus Porto Vecchio's hippest restaurant is its stylishly understated room with pannelled walls and big table lamps, and a well-heeled upmarket clientele – not to mention the beautiful waiting staff. Steaks and seafood dominate the *menu* which has both Corsican and French influences.

Drinking

Shirley's (☎ 06 85 91 75 25; 4 rue Joseph Pietri; mains €3-10) It's Hawaii forever in Shirley's, a funky little bar in a laneway behind the church with an eccentric, day-glow tiki décor and killer cocktails. It's a gay-friendly place that draws an up-for-it young crowd to its tiny terrace. They also serve exotic salads and great snacks (€3 to €8) throughout the day.

La Taverne du Roi (Cnr Porte Génoise & rue Borgo) Most nights this intimate, inviting place features traditional Corsican singing with guitar accompaniment.

Le Bel Ombra Café (☎ 04 95 70 52 21; place de la République) In an old stone building with a magnificent medieval door, this busy bar has a wide terrace from which to nurse a beer and watch life on the square go by.

Via Notte (☎ 04 95 72 02 12; www.vianotte.com; ☾ 11pm-5am) Via Notte, on the road out of Porto Vecchio in the direction of Bonifacio, is *the* club in Corsica. It's big. It's in the open air and there's even a swimming pool. Bring plenty of dosh if you want to drink.

Shopping

L'Orriu (☎ 04 95 70 26 21; cours Napoléon; ☾ 9am-12am Mon-Sat, 9am-1pm & 6pm-12am Sun mid-Mar–Oct & Dec–mid-Feb) This Porto Vecchio institution is fragrant with hams hanging from the ceiling, cheeses sitting on the shelves amidst wines and spirits, and jams and pâtés.

La Coutellerie du Bastion (☎ 04 95 72 06 02; 14 rue de la Citadelle) This cutler's shop offers a broad selection of Corsican knives (*coutellerie* is akin to cutlery) from a shepherd's knife to a stiletto to a knife identified somewhat chillingly as a Vendetta. The craftsman whose store this is makes some of the knives he sells himself, and he also offers items from his outstanding collection of antique knives.

Getting There & Away

AIR

Figari Sud-Corse airport is about 20km from Porto Vecchio. For details see p180.

BOAT

The *Monte d'Oro*, with capacity for over 500 passengers, links Porto Vecchio with Marseille on behalf of SNCM, and with Livorno in Italy on behalf of the SNCM subsidiary, Corsica Marittima.

SNCM and Corsica Marittima are both represented by **Intersud Voyages** (☎ 04 95 70 06 03; ☾ 8.45am-11.45am & 2.30-5.30pm), whose offices are in the tinted-glass building with the red metal column on top, opposite the ferry quay. For more information on ferry crossings, see the Transport chapter (p235).

About 100 moorings in the Porto Vecchio marina are reserved for visitors. Look for the **harbour master's office** (☎ 04 95 70 17 93; ave Georges Pompidou; ☾ 8am-9pm May-Oct; 8.30am-noon & 2-6.30pm Nov-Apr). Showers, fuel, water and chandlers are all available. It costs between €18 and €40, depending on the season, to moor a 9m to 10m boat.

BUS

Les Rapides Bleus-Corsicatours (☎ 04 95 31 03 70; 16 rue Jean Jaurès; 8.30am-noon & 2.30-6pm Mon-Fri), operates a service twice a day (daily except Sunday and public holidays in winter) to Bastia via Ste-Lucie de Porto Vecchio, Solenzara and Ghisonaccia (€18.60, departures at 8am and 1.30pm). It also operates a shuttle service to Santa Giulia in the summer, via Camping Arutoli (€5.10, four shuttles daily).

Île de Beauté Voyages (☎ 04 95 70 12 31; 13 rue du Général de Gaulle; ☾ 8.30am-noon & 2.30-6.30pm Mon-Fri, 9am-noon Sat), represents Balési Évasion, whose buses go to Ajaccio via the mountain towns of Zonza, Bavella, Aullène and so on. Buses depart daily in July and August, and on Monday and Friday only in winter (€19.90 to Ajaccio, €6.10 to Zonza).

Eurocorse, represented by **Trinitours** (☎ 04 95 70 13 83; rue Pasteur; ☾ 8.30am-noon & 2-6.30pm Mon-Fri, 8.30am-noon Sat), at the Cavasina junction on the way into the citadel, operates a service to Ajaccio along the coast via Sartène and Propriano. In summer there are three departures daily Monday to Saturday and two on Sunday and public holidays. There are also two departures daily in winter, and in summer there is a further bus to Ajaccio via the mountain route through Ospedale, Zonza, Bavella and Quenza. It costs €19.50 to Ajaccio. Buses depart from in front of the offices.

CAR

Europcar (☎ 04 95 72 13 10) and **Citer** (☎ 04 95 70 16 96) have car-hire facilities in the building housing the harbour master's office on ave Georges Pompidou; it opens in the summer. Hertz is on the quai Pascal Paoli towards the ferries. For details of car-hire companies at Figari-Sud airport see p180.

Getting Around
TO/FROM THE AIRPORT

Transports Rossi (☎ 04 95 71 00 11) operates a shuttle service between Figari-Sud Corse airport and Porto Vecchio (€8, 30 minutes) in July and August. The times of buses correspond to flight arrival and departure times; they depart from in front of the Bar de la Marine by the harbour.

For a taxi, allow about €45 (€55 on Sunday, on public holidays and at night).

TAXI

There is a **taxi rank** (☎ 04 95 70 08 49) on cours Napoléon.

NORTH OF PORTO VECCHIO

At La Trinité de Porto Vecchio, a few kilometres north of Porto Vecchio proper on the N198, you can turn east onto the D468 towards the popular beaches at **Cala Rossa** and the **Baie de San Cipriano**. Farther to the north is the stunning peninsula of **Pinarellu** (Pinaraddu) with its Genoese tower and yet more beautiful stretches of sand.

When the white sand, turquoise sea, warm sun and shady pine trees get to be too much, head for the village of **Lecci**, just before Ste-Lucie de Porto Vecchio on the main road. As you enter the village you will see a sign for the **Domaine de Torraccia** (☎ 04 95 71 43 50; 8am-7pm Mon-Sat Jul & Aug, 8am-noon & 2-6pm Sep-Jun), 1.5km away in the direction of the sea. The owners of this 43-hectare estate produce sweet wines, marc brandy, olives and olive oil, but the estate is best known for its red, rosé and white table wines, costing between €6 and €8 per bottle.

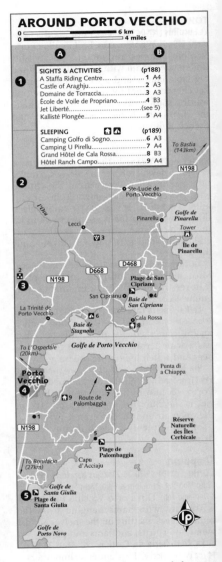

AROUND PORTO VECCHIO

0 — 6 km
0 — 4 miles

SIGHTS & ACTIVITIES	(p188)
A Staffa Riding Centre	1 A4
Castle of Araghju	2 A3
Domaine de Torraccia	3 A3
École de Voile de Propriano	4 B3
Jet Liberté	(see 5)
Kallisté Plongée	5 A4

SLEEPING	(p189)
Camping Golfo di Sogno	6 A3
Camping U Pirellu	7 A4
Grand Hôtel de Cala Rossa	8 B3
Hôtel Ranch Campo	9 A4

To Bastia (143km)

Ste-Lucie de Porto Vecchio

Lecci — Pinarellu — Golfe de Pinarellu — Tower — Île de Pinarellu

D668 — D468 — Plage de San Cipriano

San Cipriano — Baie de San Cipriano

La Trinité de Porto Vecchio — Baie de Stagnolu — Cala Rossa

To L'Ospedale (20km) — Golfe de Porto Vecchio — Punta di a Chiappa

Porto Vecchio — Route de Palombaggia — Réserve Naturelle des Îles Cerbicale

To Bonifacio (27km) — Capu d'Acciaju — Plage de Palombaggia

Golfe de Santa Giulia — Plage de Santa Giulia

Golfe de Porto Novo

Higher up the scale, the vineyard also produces some magnificent reds. Its Domaine de Toraccia really is outstanding, and l'Orriu, a 'prestige' vintage red, is unquestionably one of the best reds produced in all of Corsica. In fact, Torraccia is one of the few wine-producers on the island to age its reds at all.

Sleeping & Eating

Camping Golfo di Sogno (☎ 04 95 70 08 98; www
.golfo-di-sogno.fr; adult, tent & car €22; ☼ May-Oct; **P**)
If there's such a thing as a luxurious camp
site, this is it. Pitches are large and green,
and there's a bar, a restaurant, direct access to the beach, two tarmac tennis courts
and facilities for hiring mountain bikes
or windsurfing equipment. The camp site
also rents basic bungalows for up to eight
people (€397 for two per week). It is about
6km northeast of Porto Vecchio via the
N198 and then the D468 in the Baie de
Stagnolu.

There are plenty of touristy places to eat
along the beach during the high season.

Le 37°2 (☎ 04 95 71 70 24; rte du Benedettu, plage
de Cala Rossa; mains €8-15; ☼ May-Sep) is a busy
eaterie right on the beach and one of the
few with prices that won't burn a hole in
your pocket. Have a salad or panini or
choose from the decent €15 lunch or €20
dinner menu.

ALTA ROCCA

Alta Rocca is the name given to one of the
regions of foothills to the great mountain
range that constitutes the long dorsal spine
of the island; it is the region specifically
that looks out towards the Golfe de Porto
Vecchio. The tranquillity of L'Ospedale,
the prehistoric remains in Lévie and the
surrounding countryside, the beauty of
the little villages clinging to the rocks and the
stunning Bavella massif all combine to make
Alta Rocca a region not to be missed.

The **tourist office** (☎ 04 95 78 56 33; alta-rocca@
wanadoo.fr; ☼ 8.30am-noon & 2-5.30pm Mon-Fri) for
the Alta Rocca region is in Lévie.

GETTING THERE & AWAY

Autocars Ricci (☎ 04 95 51 08 19) runs a daily
bus service between Ajaccio and Zonza
(€15.43, two hours 50 minutes) via Propriano, Sartène, Ste-Lucie de Tallano and
Lévie. Buses depart from Ajaccio at 4pm
(also at 3pm in July and August), Propriano, Sartène and Ste-Lucie de Tallano; they
arrive in Zonza at about 7pm. In the other
direction, buses leave Zonza at 6am (and
8am in July and August). In summer, the
service extends beyond Zonza to the Col
de Bavella.

Balési Évasion (☎ 04 95 70 15 55) operates
buses that link Zonza (and Bavella in
summer) to L'Ospedale, Porto Vecchio,
Quenza and Ajaccio. In summer, buses run
daily Monday to Saturday, and on Monday
and Friday only the rest of the year. Buses
from Porto Vecchio leave from the offices
of Île de Beauté Voyages. The fare from
Porto Vecchio to Zonza is €11.43.

L'OSPEDALE

postcode 20137

L'Ospedale holds a special place in the
hearts of the good people of Porto Vecchio.
The place takes its name from a former
'hospital', or health spa, and has long been
synonymous with relief from the oppressive
heat of summer at sea level. While there's
not much to detain you in L'Ospedale itself,
you might stop for a coffee en route to the
Forêt de l'Ospedale.

Sights & Activities

The beautiful **Forêt de l'Ospedale** starts about
1km up from the village of L'Ospedale. It
covers vast plains above Porto Vecchio,
and still bears the scars of fires in 1990
and 1994.

A short way into the forest on the D368
from L'Ospedale, a road branches off to the
left for the hamlet of Cartalavonu. After
about 2km on this you can turn off onto
the **Sentiers des Rochers** (Rock Paths), also
known as the Sentier des Tafoni.

The path has been well marked out by
the ONF and is a good place for an easy,
mainly flat walk among the laricio pines
and the cavities formed in the rocks by
erosion (p35). These cavities are the *tafoni*
that give the walking trail one of its names.
After about 30 minutes you come to a little
grassy plain littered with rocks. The Mare
a Mare Sud walk crosses here, too, and the
view is wonderful.

If you're feeling energetic you can continue along the path (which is now not as
well marked) to the left towards **Punta di a
Vacca Morta** (1314m), from where you can
look down over the Golfe de Porto Vecchio and the Lac de l'Ospedale. You can
also start the walk at the Refuge de Cartalavonu or the Col de Melu on the Mare
a Mare Sud.

The walk from there to the **Piscia de Gallo**
waterfall is described on p190.

THE SOUTH

WALK TO PISCIA DE GALLO

If the heat and crowds of Porto Vecchio get too much for you, escape to the cool, calm surroundings of the Forêt de l'Ospedale, 25km above town, where you can take a 90-minute walk to the Piscia de Gallo waterfall and back. The start of the walk, marked by a signpost, is near a couple of snack bars beside the D368, 1km on from the Barrage de l'Ospedale. The first part of the route slopes down gently through the middle of a splendid forest of maritime pines. The path then fords two streams before ascending to a bald little plateau, where the coast becomes visible to the west. Next, the trail follows along a ridge that overhangs a steep-sided canyon with a fast-flowing stream running through it to the right; it's the same one that will flow over the falls somewhat farther on. You arrive at a little pass with panoramic views over the coast and the Golfe de Porto Vecchio. The pink granite massifs, left and right, form a gorge that appears to narrow in the direction of the coast.

The path then descends across the maquis, here consisting chiefly of arbutus and heather, and winds between massive lumps of rock. You can clearly hear the sound of the waterfall at this stage, and a sign informs you of the end of the trail markings and warns of danger. If you want to see the Cascade de Piscia de Gallo (Chicken Piss Waterfall!), you have to descend through a very steep rocky gully and use your hands to steady yourself until you reach a little ledge. This perch gives a good view of the water crashing down onto a rocky outcrop and dividing into two streams. But this last section is not advisable if you have small children with you or if there's wet weather – you risk slipping.

Although you cannot bathe under the waterfall, on the way back up you'll come to a pine tree beside which, on the left, a path leads down to some inviting pools.

The **Castellu d'Araghju** is less visited than the castles of Cucuruzzu and Capula, but it is better preserved and, though it dates from the 2nd millennium BC, the entrance allows you to guess at the importance the stronghold must once have had. Follow the corridor a dozen metres long to the interior rooms. Then climb to the top of the thick walls for a magnificent view over the Golfe de Porto Vecchio and the mountains. It takes about 25 minutes to get up from the village of Araghju; be sure to carry water and wear a sturdy pair of shoes. Admission is free. The village snack bar, L'Orée du Site, is a good spot for a drink and stocks brochures explaining the site.

The road that leads into Araghju is the D759, 12km from the village of L'Ospedale off the D368.

Xtrem Parc (☎ 04 95 72 12 31; www.xtremsud.com; ⏰ 9am-9pm) is an adventure centre set in the forest near Barrage de L'Ospedale. It has two types of obstacle courses on site for different levels of physical ability (adult/child €25/22 per 90 minutes). It also organises climbing hikes (€30 per half-day, €60 per day) or canyoning (€50 for five hours) in the Aiguilles de Bavella (p192), canyoning at the Piscia de Gallo (€50 for five hours), hiking the Bavella massif (€20 per day) or for beginners, an easy riverside hike through the Purcaraccia area (€20 per half-day) which includes swimming in rock pools.

Sleeping & Eating

Le Refuge (☎ 04 95 70 00 39) Le Refuge, in Cartalavonu, is popular with walkers tackling the Mare a Mare Sud. It opens year-round and has good dormitories (with bathroom) sleeping six people, as well as a large common room, for €31 per night half-board. There are also three lovely double rooms costing €62. The restaurant serves good home-cooked food. The refuge is in a pretty stone building right at the edge of the village. By road, leave the D368 before the lake of L'Ospedale and head 3km in the direction of Cartalavonu.

Bar Restaurant U Funtanonu (☎ 04 95 70 47 11; mains €6-15) On the road just as you enter Ospedale from Porto Vecchio, this is a classy little restaurant and deli serving simple but top-quality salad and *charcuterie* plates, fine savoury tarts and delicious desserts.

ZONZA

postcode 20124 / pop 300

This granite mountain village was briefly home to the exiled Mohammed V of Morocco in 1953 before he moved on to

Île Rousse; it's now frequented by walkers and those heading for the famous peaks of Bavella by car. Its excellent location, with views overlooking the Forêt de L'Ospedale, goes some way towards explaining the village's better than average hotels. There's an information stand at the town hall and a bookshop, open daily, that sells detailed IGN (National Geographic Institute) maps, guides and film. The village has several grocery stores. The best one, at the village exit going towards L'Ospedale, sells good Corsican products that are often cheaper than in the centre of town.

Should the stultifying heat make you want to take a dip, head 2.5km towards Ajaccio and Quenza on the D420, park your car just before the bridge and head down towards the river, where a beautiful pool awaits you.

Sleeping & Eating

Camping Municipal de Zonza (☎ 04 95 78 62 74; adult/tent/car €3/2.15/2.15; ☒ May-Oct) This place is a haven of tranquility in the depths of the forest, 3km east of the village on the D368. Few camper vans come this way.

On the main street, funky **Le Zampa** is a snack bar with Mexican influences. It dishes up excellent omelettes (€4 to €7), crêpes (€1.50 to €3) and panini (€4), with imaginative fillings, such as mince meat, peppers and chillis.

Hôtel Clair de Lune (☎ 04 95 78 56 79; d €61-76; ☐ ☒) The two-star Clair de Lune on the road to Levie, has 18 bright, spacious, tastefully renovated rooms, one of which is wheelchair accessible, and is open year-round. The patron also owns **Auberge du Sanglier** (☎ 04 95 78 67 18), on the main street, which offers an authentic Corsican country *menu du Berger* (€20) featuring *charcuterie*, sausage and local meats. It has a simplified children's *menu* (€9) and a great terrace with views over Les Aiguilles de Bavella.

Hôtel-Restaurant l'Incudine (☎ 04 95 78 67 71/71 43 11; r €60, half-board r €108; ☒ Apr-Oct; ☐) L'Incundine has 18 cosy double rooms with bathroom. Its restaurant, which offers a traditional *menu* (€15 at lunch, €25 at dinner) of meats cooked over a wood-fire, has a nice terrace that gets packed out with walkers at lunchtime.

Hôtel-Restaurant Le Tourisme (☎ 04 95 78 67 72; www.hoteldutourisme.fr; r €85, with half-board €140;

☒ Mar-Nov; ☐ ☒) Le Tourisme has 14 recently modernised, spacious rooms with all the mod-cons you'd expect of a three-star country hotel. Half-board is obligatory in August which may suit tired walkers who don't want to budge by evening time. The food is traditional and of a standard well above usual hotel fodder.

QUENZA
postcode 20122 / pop 218
This little gem of a village is high up in the mountains a few kilometres northwest of Zonza along the D420, on the way to Aullène. At an altitude of 813m, Quenza is no farther than a four-hour walk from the GR20 and lies square on the Mare a Mare Sud trail, thus attracting its fair share of walkers. The village, with its own unique character, has an excellent reputation as a base for leisure pursuits such as walking, horse riding and canyoning.

It has a post office and two telephone boxes.

BARRAGE DE L'OSPEDALE

This is only a detour if you weren't heading to Zonza, but is a route that will send a shiver down your spine! If you continue on the D368 towards Zonza, you will come to the pretty chocolate-box lake formed by the Barrage de l'Ospedale, a reservoir supplying water to the area. About 2km north of L'Ospedale, keep your eye out to the left of the road, from where, through a thin curtain of pines, you will come upon a most bizarre vista that will stop you in your tracks.

A vast lunar landscape of scorched, sandy earth studded with the burnt remains of pines tree trunks which crop up like carbonised standing stones, leads down to the shimmering lake. Granite boulders in strange teetering columns and the rocky mountain backdrop add to a truly apocalyptic scene.

This spectacular Daliesque setting is best appreciated in summer when, as the lake partially dries up, its exposed bed becomes a plain of hard rippled ground that catches the striking shadows of the stumps in stark relief. Walk among the stumps to fully experience this manifestation of the force of nature.

Sleeping & Eating

Corse Odysée (☎ 04 95 78 64 05; www.corseodyssee.com; half-board s €31; ☼ Apr-Oct) Just to the north of the village, this place operates as a *gîte d'étape* in chalets that sleep between five and seven people with obligatory half-board. The establishment also provides qualified guides for day-long walks (€31), canyoning (€55 per person) in the massif de Bavella.

Hôtel Sole e Monte (☎ 04 95 78 62 53; sole.e .monti@wanadoo.fr; half-board d €95-105) If you prefer more luxurious accommodation, head for this place at the eastern end of the village, on the main road from Porto Vecchio and Zonza (D420). Rooms are modest but comfortable and the owners are welcoming. It has a large garden and its restaurant is renowned locally and offers a variety of menus (from €25) and an extensive game-oriented à la carte menu.

The village has two groceries where you can stock up.

In the tourist season, Autocars Balesi buses stop once daily, except Sunday, in each direction, on their Ajaccio to Porto Vecchio line.

CONCA

postcode 20135 / pop 300

Backing onto the mountains but still close to the coast (6km as the crow flies), Conca is a little town nestling at the foot of Punta d'Ortu (695m) and best known to walkers as the end (or start) of the GR20. There is a post office here.

La Tonnelle (☎ 04 95 71 46 55; dm/d €17/34; dinner €17) La Tonnelle is a *gîte d'étape* on the road into the village just opposite the cemetery. Accommodation is in dorms and each room has its own bathroom. There's also a large common room and a kitchenette. It's possible to camp here for about €5. The *gîte* will provide transportation down to Porto Vecchio or to Ste-Lucie de Porto Vecchio for a small fee, where it's possible to catch the bus to Porto Vecchio proper.

There's a choice of snack bars and restaurants in the centre of the village. Conca also has a well stocked grocery, open daily in summer.

In the absence of public transport services to Conca, ask at La Tonnelle. They'll help you to get around on an informal basis.

AIGUILLES DE BAVELLA

The Col de Bavella (Bavella Pass; 1218m), about 8km northeast of Zonza, is overlooked by the imposing silhouette of one of the most beautiful landscape features in the south of Corsica: the Aiguilles de Bavella. These peaks, which rise to a height of more than 1600m and which are also known as the Cornes d'Asinao (Asinao Horns), are jagged points whose colour ranges from ochre to golden depending on the position of the sun in the sky. Behind these stone 'needles' looms the profile of Monte Incudine (2134m), which the GR20 links to the Col de Bavella. From the pass you can see the statue of Notre Dame des Neiges (Our Lady of the Snows). You may also spot more than a few of the *mouflons* that frequent the area.

The Bavella massif is a wonderful place for climbing, canyoning and walking. There is indeed a high mountain spur of the GR20, which splits off beyond Notre Dame des Neiges and allows you to approach the peaks. Bear in mind that the pass is not always open in winter. Some of the guides in the area meet at the **Auberge du Col de Bavella** (☎ 04 95 57 43 87).

The D268, which descends in the direction of Solenzara via the Col de Larone, is also worth a look. Crossing the Bavella forest, replanted after the 1960 fire, the road scoots along between tall peaks and tall pine. You can also explore the forest with an ONF guide who organises three-hour walks (€7). Just turn up at 9.30am on a Thursday in July and August at the **Arza Forest Lodge** (☎ 04 95 23 78 21), 6km beyond the pass.

The challenge of driving here does not take much away, though, from what is in every respect an astonishing 30km descent to Solenzara. About 12km before you reach the coast the D268 begins to run along the wide stony bed of the River Solenzara, which is particularly good for swimming in the summer.

ARCHAEOLOGICAL SITES OF PIANA DE LÉVIE

The *piana* (Corsican for the French commune, a small administrative area) of Lévie is home to two remarkable archaeological sites: the *castelli* (castles) of **Cucuruzzu** and **Capula**. The Cucuruzzu site was discovered in 1963 and is an interesting example of Bronze Age monumental architecture. Set in a granite wilderness, the remains indicate that this was the site of an enduring and organised community whose activities were originally based on agriculture and animal husbandry but then broadened during the later Bronze Age (1200 to 900 BC) to include milling, pottery and weaving. The Castellu de Capula is somewhat more recent, although it is likely that Cucuruzzu was still in business when it was founded; Capula, it is believed, continued to be inhabited into the Middle Ages.

Besides the wonderful view they provide over the Aiguilles de Bavella, these two castles are worth a detour for the way they've been packaged for consumption by visitors. Individual stereo kits are provided at the entrance to the site, with a recorded commentary backed by traditional Corsican polyphonic chants (p32). The commentary brings the castles to life with mini-lectures on, for example, curiosities of Corsican nature such as the tafoni (big rock blocks into which erosion has dug deep cavities) and the ubiquitous chestnut tree.

The **archaeological sites** (☎ 04 95 78 48 21; www.parc-naturel-corse.com; adult/child under 6 €5/2.50; ☒ 9.30am-8pm Jul & Aug, 9.30am-7pm Jun & Sep, 9.30am-6pm Apr-May & Oct) are on the right-hand side of the D268, 3.5km after the village of Lévie in the direction of Ste-Lucie de Tallano; the sites are about 4km after the turn-off. Admission includes the use of an audioguide. Be prepared to spend a good 1½ hours here. Wear sturdy shoes and carry water.

LÉVIE (LIVIA)
postcode 20170 / pop 712

The peaceful little village of Lévie was a bastion of Corsican resistance during WWII and is now frequented by walkers on the Mare a Mare Sud route. You'll find bars, restaurants, a post office and a tourist office here. You'll also find a very impressive little archaeological museum, **Musée de l'Alta Rocca** (☎ 04 95 78 47 98), which was closed at the time of writing. It was due to move premises and reopen soon after.

The museum does a good job of elucidating Corsican geology, climate, flora and fauna. You can see Bonifacio Woman, the oldest human remains ever unearthed on the island; she is thought to have lived on the island about 8500 years ago.

The museum also displays cutting tools made of obsidian, flint and rhyolite, arrow heads, Neolithic vases and some wonderful Bronze Age pottery. The Iron Age is represented by a woman's skeleton that was found at the Capula site, and textiles and jewellery with some remarkable craftwork.

The museum has a scientific seriousness which, in regards to prehistoric times, frequently seems to be in much shorter supply elsewhere on the island; photography is not permitted.

Activities

La Ferme Auberge A Pignata organises half-day horse rides for €39 or full day's treks for €65. You can also rent mountain bikes for either of two well marked circuits of 11km and 25km. Advance booking is a must.

Based in Lévie, **Christophe Pigeault** (☎ 04 95 78 58 25, 06 20 61 76 81; www.aqa-canyon.com) organises beginner and advanced canyoning outings. This certified mountain guide will show you magnificent, little-known, wilderness canyons around the Bavella massif. It helps to be in good shape physically. It costs €50 to €70 for a full day; groups consist of up to 12 people.

Sleeping & Eating

Gîte d'Étape de Lévie (☎ 04 95 78 46 41; s €14, half-board s €28; ☒ Apr-Nov) This gîte offers five clean, four-bed dorms in a new stone building above the police station. You can eat a €13 Corsican menu.

La Ferme Auberge A Pignata (☎ 04 95 78 49 81; half-board s €58-64) On the road leading to the Cucuruzzu and Capula archaeological sites, this auberge enjoys a loyal following for its excellent home cooking; the €30 menu is perfect. You can also rent one of the spacious rooms at a half-board rate. Advance booking is recommended. To get there, travel 1.4km after the turn-off from the D268 and then take the first left in the direction of the stables.

STE-LUCIE DE TALLANO (SANTA LUCIA DI TALLA)
postcode 20112 / pop 404

Ste-Lucie de Tallano would definitely be a contender if anyone decided to award a prize for the prettiest village in Corsica.

Although time has robbed the hamlet of many of its inhabitants, it has taken away none of the charm of its little houses, with their reddish-orange tiled roofs, which nestle tightly together against the deep green, verdant backdrop of the surrounding forest and maquis.

Information

There's a **post office** (☎ 04 95 78 81 59; ☽ 9am-2pm Mon-Fri, 9am-noon Sat Jul & Aug; 9am-noon & 2-4pm Mon-Fri Sep-Jun) on the square. A **welcome centre** (☎ 04 95 78 80 13; www.sainteluciedetallano.com; ☽ 9am-noon & 2-5pm Mon-Fri Jul & Aug) is in the village hall and provides a wealth of information.

Sights

The **moulin à huile** (oil mill; adult/child €2/1; ☽ 10am-noon & 3.30-6.30pm Mon-Sat May-Oct) illustrates the importance of olive culture in the history of the village. Ste-Lucie enjoys a reputation not just for its olive oil, but also for its deposits of orbicular diorite. This is a rare igneous rock with distinctive grey cavities; see it close up on the pedestal of the war memorial in the village square.

The **Église Ste-Lucie** is also worth a visit, as is the Renaissance-style **Couvent St-François**. This is an imposing building, which sometimes stages theatrical events. It's at the edge of the village on the road to Lévie. If it's closed, ask for the key at one of the eateries in the village square.

Another regional curiosity is the **Bains de Caldane** (☎ 04 95 77 00 34; adult/child €3.50/1.67; ☽ 9.30am-12am Jul & Aug; 9.30am-8.30pm Sep, Oct, May & Jun; 10.30am-6pm Sat & Sun Nov-Apr), a 38°C sulphur spring that's said to have health benefits. The bathing area accommodates 20 people. To get there, head south out of Ste-Lucie for 5km, then turn left onto the D148 for 2.2km more.

Festivals & Events

In the spring, a carnival and a masked ball take place after the **Festa de l'Olio Novu** (New Olive Festival), and a craft fair takes place in July. There are also feasts in the nearby hamlets of Bizé and Chialza in August.

Sleeping & Eating

Gîte d'Étape U Fragnonu (☎ 04 95 78 82 56; www .lacorsemysterieuse.com/fragnonu.htm; half-board s €31; ☽ Apr-Nov) In a massive, old mill building about 300m from the main square in the direction of Zonza, U Fragnonu has nine spacious dormitories, each with four beds and their own spotless bathroom. The common room is large and pleasant and the overall level of comfort is – for a *gîte* – exceptional. Half-board is obligatory but the food is outstanding.

Two Ste-Lucie restaurants serve Corsican specialities: the **Santa-Lucia**, with its terrace on the square, and the **Sporting Bar**, which serves pizzas as well as Corsican specialities, on the way out of the village.

MONTAGNE DE CAGNA

This isolated massif overlooks Figari, and is famous for the **Uomo di Cagna**, a huge rock balanced on a block of granite at the summit. Many people think they can make out a human profile in it. The Cagna mountain, with its wonderful views, is a popular place for walking. The climb starts just above the highest house in Giannuccio, a village at the end of the D50 north of Monacia d'Aullène. The path, roughly marked out with cairns, passes through an impressive granite landscape. Make sure you take some water with you if you plan to go as far as the hamlet of Uomo di Cagna; it takes about three hours.

The Eastern Plain

CONTENTS

The east of Corsica remains, by far, the area least explored by travellers, partly because of the lack of public transport, and partly because it lacks the obvious attractions of the other regions. The three main areas of interest are anchored around Aléria, La Castagniccia and La Casinca.

Aléria makes for a surprisingly small regional hub with little to divert you outside the Roman ruins. Meanwhile, much of the nearby Costa Serena is given over to huge, toy-town-like beach developments visited by coach-loads of Germans or Scandinavians who stay for a fortnight and rarely speak a word of French. Moving inland, La Castagniccia is a deeply traditional area with a predominantly agrarian economy. It is here that the production of chestnut flower, one of Corsica's most famous cottage industries, finds its spiritual home. La Casinca, meanwhile, is also home to cottage industries, local produce and rural farmsteads.

Tourists rarely stray into some of the smaller villages in this region and those that do often find a pretty cool reception from the locals. This makes for a bizarre contrast with the flip-flop brigade basting like Christmas turkeys on the beaches of the Costa Serena, less than half an hour's drive away.

HIGHLIGHTS

- **Dining**
  Eat healthy at **L'Ortu** (p204), Corsica's first dedicated vegetarian/organic restaurant

- **Chill-Out Spot**
  Enjoy a sundowner on the patio at **A Stella Serena** (p204), La Casinca's best *chambre d'hôte*

- **Living History**
  Take a peek behind the Paoli legend with a visit to **La Maison de Pascal Paoli** (p200) in Morosaglia

- **Gastro Trails**
  Take a drive through the villages of **La Casinca** (p203), stopping en route to stock up on excellent local wine and cheese

- **Off the Beaten Track**
  Drive the switchbacks through the remote hamlets of **La Castagniccia** (p199)

La Casinca Region
A Stella Serena ★
★ L'Ortu
★ La Maison de Pascal Paoli
★ La Castagniccia Region

ALÉRIA

postcode 20270 / pop 2000

In ancient times, the region that today forms Aléria – first known as Alalia (p21) – was Corsica's capital. Today the main activity is clustered around Caterragio, a regional hub that most travellers pass through on their way between Bastia and Porto Vecchio on the N198. The main points of interest in these parts are the Roman ruins and the archaeological museum at Caterragio.

The area bordering the lakes **L'Étang de Diane** and **L'Étang d'Urbino** to the north and south of Caterragio respectively, are good spots for walkers, as are the banks of the River Tavignano, which connects Aléria to Corte.

ORIENTATION

Most of the facilities are grouped around the intersection of the N198, running from Bastia to Port Vecchio, with the N200, heading west towards Corte. The Roman ruins and the archaelogical museum are a few blocks south of the intersection, following the N198.

INFORMATION

There is no laundry or Internet access in the immediate area.

Money

There are a number of banks with ATMs on the main road; you can change money only at **Crédit Agricole** (8.15-11.55am & 1.30-4.45pm Mon-Fri); it's next to the Super U supermarket on the main drag.

Tourist Information

The **tourist office** (☎ 04 95 57 01 51; officetourisme aleria@wanadoo.fr;   9am-7pm Mon-Sat, 9am-noon Sun), on the main road in Casa Luciani, offers guided group tours to the archaeological site every Thursday (€8); staff speak English and Italian.

SIGHTS

The main reason why people stop in Caterragio is to visit the museum and Roman ruins illustrating 8,000 years of history of Corsica's erstwhile capital. This is really one for the history buffs.

Musée Archéologique Jérôme Carcopino & Fort de Matra

The Jérôme Carcopino Archaeological Museum, named after the distinguished historian of ancient Rome, is inside the **Fort de Matra** (admission to museum & ruins €2). Built by the Genoese in 1484, this edifice towers over the Vallée du Tavignano and L'Étang de Diane.

The objects on display were unearthed at the former site of Alalia and bear witness to the town's Etruscan, Phocaean and Roman past. The **exhibition rooms** (☎ 04 95 57 00 92; www.cg2b.fr;   8am-noon & 2-7pm Mon-Fri) have moderately interesting displays of historical artefacts.

The archaeological site is a 300m walk southwest of the fort. Excavations started in 1921 but were only organised in a methodical way in 1958. The site now boasts the remains of a forum, a citadel, some temples and part of the centre of the Roman town, but the largest part of the city is still to be unearthed.

The **Association Alalia** (☎ 04 95 57 11 18; maison Matra;   9am-noon & 2-6pm Mon-Fri, 9am-noon weekends) welcomes free group visits to the site.

ACTIVITIES

There are six tennis courts at **Marina d'Aléria** (☎ 04 95 57 06 24; €8 per hr;   7am-10pm); lessons are also available.

The **Centre de Tourisme Équestre de Bravone** (☎ 04 95 38 91 90; half-/full-day €38/64;   8.30am-noon & 4-8pm), 7km north of Aléria along the N198 near Linguizzetta, offers trail riding in the maquis and rides by the ocean.

SLEEPING

L'Hôtel Atrachjata (☎ 04 95 57 03 93; www.hotel-atrachjata.net; s/d €80/105; P X), next to the tourist office, is an above-average, three-star property with all mod cons and a nice terrace restaurant. If it's full, **L'Empereur** (☎ 04 95 57 02 13; s/d €70/76; P X R) is less plush but has a swimming pool.

The cheapest hotel in the area is **L'Hôtel les Orangers** (☎ 04 95 57 00 13; s/d/tr €39/46/55), a basic one-star, 50m from the tourist office heading east towards the beach. **Chambre d'Hôte di U Fiume** (☎ 04 95 57 02 89; s/d/tr €40/45/60) in Caterragio has simple but functional rooms with breakfast included in the price.

For campers, the four-star **Marina d'Aléria** (☎ 04 95 57 01 42, www.marina-aleria.com camping/

THE EASTERN PLAIN

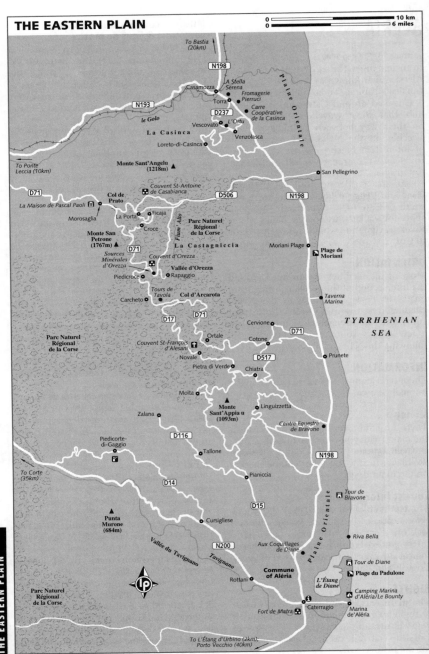

THE EASTERN PLAIN

0 |—————————| 10 km
0 |—————————| 6 miles

To Bastia
(20km)

N198

N193

le Golo

Casamozza

A Stella
Serena

Fromagerie
Pierruci

Torra

D237

Carre
Coopérative
de la Casinca

Vescovato   L'Ortu

La Casinca

Venzolasca

Loreto-di-Casinca

To Ponte
Leccia (10km)

Plaine Orientale

San Pellegrino

Monte Sant'Angelu
(1218m)

D71

Col de
Prato

Couvent St-Antoine
de Casabianca

D506

N198

La Maison de Pascal Paoli

Morosaglia

La Porta   Ficaja

Croce

Parc Naturel
Régional
de la Corse

Monte San
Petrone
(1767m)

D71

Flum'Alto

La Castagniccia

Sources
Minérales
d'Orezza

Couvent d'Orezza

Vallée d'Orezza

Morani Plage

Plage de
Moriani

Piedicroce   Rapaggio

Carcheto

Tours de
Tavola

Col d'Arcarota

D71

Taverna
Marina

D17

D71

Ortale

Cervione

Cotone

D71

TYRRHENIAN
SEA

Parc Naturel
Régional
de la Corse

Couvent St-François
d'Alesani

Novale

Pietra di Verde

Chiatra

D517

Prunete

Moïta

Zalana

Monte
Sant'Appia u
(1093m)

Linguizzetta

Centre Équestre
de Bravone

Piedicorte-
di-Gaggio

D116

Tallone

N198

To Corte
(35km)

D14

Pianiccia

D15

Tour de
Bravone

Punta
Murone
(684m)

Vallée du Tavignano

Cursigliese

N200

Aux Coquillages
de Diane

Plaine Orientale

Riva Bella

Commune
of Aléria

Tour de Diane

Plage du Padulone

Parc Naturel
Régional
de la Corse

Tavignano

Rottani

L'Étang
de Diane

Camping Marina
d'Aléria/Le Bounty

Fort de Matra

Caterragio

Marina
de'Aléria

To L'Étang d'Urbino (2km);
Porto Vecchio (40km)

KIT-OFF CORSICA

If you've come to Corsica to lose your inhibitions then Alérie is a good place to start. There are 20km of naturist resorts and villas in a, ahem, strip, heading south along the N198 between the turn-off for the D71 (towards Cervione) and the tourist office at Caterrragio. No sniggering at the back now.

The pick of the bunch is **Riva Bella** (☎ 04 95 38 81 10; www.rivabella-corsica.com; treatments 9am-1pm & 3-8pm daily), which has comfortable bungalows on the beach and specialises in massage and hypoallergenic treatments. A black soap body exfoliation and seaweed wrap costs €74.70. Anti-cellulite treatment weighs in at a hefty €89.94.

bungalow per wk €12/680) is the best bet in the area. Stretching 500m along the edge of the long sandy beach at the eastern end of the N200, it has excellent facilities for families, with a kid's club and children's entertainment, as well as tennis, mini-golf and water sports. Bookings are highly recommended in summer.

EATING

For eating options, your best bet is to run the gauntlet of the bars and restaurants that line the N198 or the seafront at Plage de Padulone.

The pick of the bunch is **Aux Coquillages de Diana** (☎ 04 95 57 04 55; menus €16), a wood-frame, seafood establishment with a terrace overlooking L'Étang de Diane. It's very popular with coach parties.

Also worth a try is **Le Bounty** (☎ 04 95 57 00 50; pizza & fish dishes €8-14), on Plage de Padulone, with a terrace facing the open sea. You will get over the slightly tacky décor.

GETTING THERE & AWAY

Les Rapides Bleus (☎ 04 95 31 03 79) runs two buses daily in summer from Bastia to Porto Vecchio, stopping in Caterragio outside l'Empereur (€11, plus €1 baggage, 1½ hours). See Bastia's intercity bus connections, p88.

In summer only, **Autocars Cortenais** (☎ 04 95 46 02 12) operates a service to Aléria from Corte (€10, 40 minutes) on Tuesday, Thursday and Saturday. Buses depart from Corte

train station at 11am and from the car park opposite the tourist office in Aléria at 2.50pm.

AROUND ALÉRIA

Stretching nearly 70km from Bastia in the north to Aléria in the south, the Plaine Orientale alluvial coastal plain and the narrow ribbon of sandy beach parallel to it, constitute the only real flatlands in all of Corsica. Until WWII, malaria made the region effectively uninhabitable, and it was not until the 1960s that repatriates from Algeria introduced modern farming techniques and viticulture. Wine co-operatives were developed with the encouragement of the government, and dams were built to improve irrigation (see boxed text, p200). Today, farmers here also grow citrus fruits such as clementines, citrons and kiwis.

Between Bastia and Aléria there's really very little to distract you from the N198, apart from a clutch of fairly uninviting resort complexes and a handful of naturist colonies (see boxed text above).

TAVERNA MARINA

One place worth a stop, however, is the new Taverna Marina development at Santa Maria Poghju; the turn-off is marked on the N198 by a large, blue anchor.

The marina has a slew of brand, spanking new tourist facilities. These include a **tourist office** (☎ 04 95 59 05 48; 🕙 10am-noon & 5-9pm Mon, Tue, Thu, 5-9pm Wed & Fri, 6-9pm Sat) and, in the same building, the **Point Multimedia** (P@M; ☎ 04 95 59 05 48; 🕙 9am-noon & 5-9pm, Sat 2-6pm; 🖥) with free Internet access.

There are also shops, showers and weather advice at the **harbour master's office** (☎ 04 95 38 07 61; 🕙 6am-10pm), and a **laundry** (🕙 9am-8pm; €6). For a snack try **Le Bistro du Port** (☎ 04 95 38 40 70) for its giant salads (€10).

Taverna Marina is 25km from Aléria and 40km from Bastia.

LA CASTAGNICCIA

Bordered by the River Golo to the north, the River Tavignano to the south and the central mountains to the west, La Castagniccia owes its name to the Genoese, who planted its first chestnut trees in the 16th century (see boxed text, p201). The region's hills and mountains are shot through with streams and rivulets, and the whole area is blanketed with dense vegetation, out of which emerges a village here and there. The villages are linked by small, winding roads and dozens of footpaths. There is no public transport.

La Castagniccia was one of the main bastions of Corsican nationalism in the 18th century, and feelings still run high today. In the 19th century, with its inhabitants numbering more than 50,000, it was both the most populous and the most prosperous of the island's several regions. After WWI it suffered severe depopulation and today many of its villages are almost deserted, while others are less than welcoming to outsiders.

Accommodation in the area is also extremely limited but the area makes for an easy day trip from Bastia – if you have your own car and steely nerves to tackle the switchback roads.

Ponte Leccia
postcode 20218 / pop 1200 / elevation 120m

Bizarrely, while Ponte Leccia is the major train interchange for the Chemins de Fer de la Corse (p241), it's also one of the most barren little settlements on the island. Given that most train travellers will often end up spending at last some time hanging around Ponte Leccia, the station itself has absolutely zero facilities – no toilets, no

---

SIMEONI'S STAND

On 21 August 1975 Edmond Simeoni and 20 followers barricaded themselves in a wine cellar in Aléria to protest against the French government's financial support of refugees from Algeria. Simeoni alleged that Algerian wine growers were muscling in on the territory of native Corsicans.

The following day, in an extraordinary show of force, the Interior Ministry sent eight squadrons of crack law- enforcement officers from Paris and assaulted Simeoni's redoubt. Two of the policemen lost their lives. The sequence of events was not only a first warning to France that it had a serious ' Corsica problem', it was also the beginning of a full quarter-century of separatist agitation.

---

water, no coffee. Nothing, despite the fact that huge numbers of people change trains here daily in summer. The only options are a couple of cafés running south along the main drag and a large Super U supermarket 100m south of the train station.

There are, however, two things in deserted Ponte Leccia worth seeking out. The first, right next door to the ramshackle station building, is **In Terra Corsa** (☎ 04 95 47 69 48; www.interracorsa.fr; 9am-7pm), one of Corsica's leading adventure activity organisers. Activities range from canyoning (€35) to abseiling in the Asco Valley (€17). Multi-adventure activity packages start from €68.

The second point of interest is **Lana Corsa** (☎ 04 95 48 43 79; www.corsicata.com; 9am-7pm), a cottage-industry-style wool producer with a little shopfront 1km east of the train station. The owner heads up a local artisan's association, and the shop sells everything from winter ponchos (€74) to summer walking socks (€14). They are planning to open a visitor's centre here and move production to a new building for next season.

Despite its interchange status, sleeping and eating options in Ponte Leccia are severely limited.

Morosaglia
postcode 20218 / pop 120 / elevation 650m

Morosaglia, 15km northwest of Ponte Leccia along the D71 (towards La Porta) is known primarily as the birthplace of Pascal Paoli. There's little to distract you in the village itself but the small museum in Paoli's honour – and converted from the house where he lived as a boy – is well worth a look.

La Maison de Pascal Paoli (☎ 04 95 61 04 97; 9am-noon & 2.30-7.30pm Wed-Mon; adult/child €2/1) makes for a worthwhile 30-minute visit and offers an insight into the man known as the father of the nation (p24). The tour starts with a 10-minute video (available in English), after which you take a quick whiz around the exhibits, before heading downstairs to the chapel where his remains are kept. While Napoleon hogs the publicity in Corsica, Paoli is a far more important figure to Corsicans. When his remains were returned to his home village on 3 September 1889, villagers lined the route to pay their respects. The floral tributes from that ceremony are still preserved to this day in the chapel.

CORSICAN MANNA

Pascal Paoli said, 'As long as we have chestnuts, we'll have bread'. For Corsicans, the chestnut tree was for many long centuries 'the bread tree'. Indeed, the French had no sooner conquered the island in 1771, than the king's council of state recommended restricting the plantation of the tree, and even considered destroying them, for fear it made the Corsicans lazy.

'They dry it, they mill it, even their horses feed on it. The result is that the land is otherwise neglected.'

In the glory days of Corsican chestnut culture, a Corsican wedding dinner typically required 22 different chestnut delicacies. In the region of La Castagniccia (from *castagnu*, meaning 'chestnut') a single chestnut tree kept a family for a month. The people of La Castagniccia, once the single most prosperous and most populous of the island's many regions, traded their chestnuts with the Balagne for olive oil, with the Niolo for cheese, and with Porto Vecchio for salt. Chestnuts and chestnut meal were frequently all that was needed in the way of exchange currency, and casual agricultural labourers were paid in chestnuts.

Chestnut culture began to decline after WWI as the result of massive depopulation, fungal diseases and an infant chemical industry that used the chestnut wood, and just the wood, for the production of cellulose and tannin.

In the 1880s Corsica harvested some 150,000 tonnes of chestnuts. By the 1990s the chestnut harvest was down to a mere 2000 tonnes.

Heading east along the D71 from Morosaglia, the **Col de Prato** (985m) is a centre for hikers with dozens of footpaths spreading out in all directions. One, signposted, leads to **Monte San Petrone** (1767m), the highest point in La Castagniccia. Allow two to three hours to reach the peak and as many again for the return journey.

A place for a stop around here is **L'Hôtel San Petrone** (☎ 04 95 39 20 19; d/tr €39/54), a family-run hotel, restaurant and museum. It has clean, quiet rooms and you can also pitch a tent in the grounds outside (€7 per person). The restaurant is à la carte only (no *menus*) but serves hearty fare. Most interesting of all, however, is the little ethnographical museum (admission €1). The owner's father has spent 40 years ferreting out local antiques to build an amazing collection of old Corsican furniture, pottery, weapons and tools.

La Porta
postcode 20237 / pop 100 / elevation 800m
Accessed via winding roads through the chestnut groves, La Porta has dual claims to fame as both the former capital of La Castagniccia and as one of the highest villages in Corsica.

Its focal point, at the entrance to the town, is the **Église St-Jean Baptiste**, with its impressive five-storey, 45m-high bell tower. Built between 1664 and 1707, it is among the most beautiful Baroque buildings on the island. Its hand-crafted organ, which dates back to 1780, was originally destined for the Couvent St-Antoine de Casabianca, 8km north of La Porta on the D515, where Pascal Paoli was proclaimed general of the nation (p24). Instead it was offered to the church at the time of the French Revolution by the Bonapartist commissioner Antoine-Christophe Salicetti, who closed the convent. A concert of Corsican organ music is held here every August.

There are no facilities in town aside from a **post office/tabac** (9-11.30am & 2-4pm Mon-Fri, 9-11.30am Sat, closed Wed afternoon).

SLEEPING & EATING
In the absence of any hotels, the only accommodation option in La Porta itself is a *chambre d'hôte*. Try Monsieur **Felix Taddei** (☎ 04 95 39 20 51) or Monsieur **Claude Vittiri** (☎ 04 95 39 21 32), who both rent out rooms for about €40 per night.

The best eating option is **Restaurant L'Ampugnani** (Chez Élisabeth; ☎ 04 95 39 22 00; menu Corse €14.50-22.90) right on the main drag. Ask for a table in the large dining room with bay windows overlooking the gardens of surrounding houses, rather than the terrace across the road – it's rather noisy. And try to dodge the tour parties, if possible, by arriving after the lunch or dinner rush. The owners make their own industrial strength *eau de vie* from clementines, and are planning to open La Porta's first hotel – watch this space.

Next door, **Bar Le Kallisté** (☎ 04 95 39 23 03) has simple snacks and drinks if you're just passing through.

Piedicroce

postcode 20229 / pop 100 / elevation 625m

From La Porta the D515 trundles through the tiny hamlets of Ficaja and Croce before rejoining the D71 as it heads towards the **Vallée d'Orezza**. Here the natural springs in the hamlet of Rappagio have recently been restored to proper working order (see boxed text, below). Not so long ago, the quarries in this area were mined for Vert d'Orezza, a hard emerald-green stone that polishes up almost like marble – it's the stone from which the magnificent Medici Chapel in Florence was constructed.

The area around the tiny hamlet of Piedicroce is also the hub for a number of **walking trails** across the heights of La Castagniccia. Suitable for walkers of most abilities, many of these trails start in La Porta and radiate across the region, passing Col de Prato, Ficaja and Croce. The village **information kiosk** (☎ 04 95 35 82 54; ⏲ 9am-noon & 2-5pm) is the best place for guidance on walks in the area.

The area is best known for its Baroque 17th-century church **L'Église Saintes Pierre et Paul**; there's also a little **post office** (⏲ 8.30am-noon & 1.30-3.30pm Mon-Fri, 8.30-11.30am, closed Wed afternoon).

On leaving Piedicroce, the D71 winds its way through the chestnut groves of the **Col d'Arcarota**, after which the road drops down via the hamlet of Carcheto towards Cervione. This is a spectacular drive but there is no real reason to stop the car.

SLEEPING & EATING

Hôtel Le Refuge (☎ 04 95 35 82 65; s/d €46/49, half-board s/d €66/91) is the only accommodation in the area and offers a decent welcome in an otherwise characterless, modern building. All rooms are simply furnished, and numbers 11 and 12 have the best views across the region. The in-house restaurant offers a good *menu* (€16) year-round; the hotel closes 15 November to Easter.

At the **Piedicroce town hall** (☎ 04 95 35 86 37), walkers can rent *refuge* space (€7 for two people) in the heart of the village.

Cervione

postcode 20221 / pop 1200 / elevation 350m

This mountainous settlement is the largest community in La Castagniccia and has the most facilities in the region. It's

---

THE WATERS OF OREZZA

Although the English did not discover Orezza until the beginning of the 20th century, Pascal Paoli came 'to take the cure' here every year, as did much of 18th-century polite society. Orezza spring waters were discovered early on to be very rich in iron and calcium, while enthusiasts claimed that they were useful in combating a raft of ailments and in improving the digestive, circulatory and nervous systems.

In April 1856 the water was bottled and distributed both locally and on the French mainland, and in 1896 a thermal spa centre with massage rooms, showers and baths was built.

Despite the competition from mainland spas, Orezza developed rapidly until 1934, at which time a violent storm destroyed the pipework. During WWII the occupying Germans came to believe in the curative properties of the water and set up a small bottling plant. After the war the property changed hands numerous times, but the little bottles with green caps continued to be sold.

Production at the plant was rudely stopped in 1995 but, rather than let the complex fall into disrepair, the springs were bought by the Conseil Général de Haute Corse in collaboration with a new manager, la Société Nouvelle d'Exploitation des Eaux Minérales d'Orezza (SNEEMO). After a complete overhaul, the spring was back in business again.

Today it remains one of the most popular mineral waters in Corsica, with the factory producing 6000 bottles per hour in two sets of eight-hour shifts.

The **Orezza Complex** (☎ 04 95 39 10 00; ⏲ 8am-8pm Mon-Sat, 9am-6pm Sun) opens to visitors by appointment only; **La Boutique** (⏲ 10am-6pm, summer only) is a gift shop and café next to the main gates.

TOWERING ABOVE THE REST

For an extended stay in this charming but very remote and poorly serviced area, the best option is **Tours de Tavola** (☎ 04 95 35 82 03; http://perso.wanadoo.fr/les-tours-de-travola; 4-bed gîte per night/wk €50/340), 30km along the D71 from Cervione in an isolated spot near the hamlet of Carcheto.

The towers formed part of a 13th-century building, the erstwhile home of a Corsican countess, and have been converted into seven quiet, self-contained *gîtes* by Jean-Claude Rogliano, a local man who also just happens to be one of Corsica's best known writers. There's also a small house for five or six people (€450).

Rogliano is continually tinkering with the properties; the most welcome, latest addition is a communal swimming pool. It's a lovely, quiet spot, and all properties have kitchenettes and great views. Just don't expect much action.

Rogliano was born in the area and has used his earnings from writing to rebuild the towers and foster the sense of community that has all too often died out in rural Corsica.

'I had a dream as a child to bring these towers back to life', he says, sipping coffee and looking out across the chestnut groves from his lounge window. 'I've invested my life savings in these buildings and have done much of the work myself. You could say it's more of a love story than a commercial venture.'

Families staying in the gîtes are encouraged to spend their money in local shops, restaurants and buying the work of local artisans, providing a major boost to the flagging local economy. On Sundays, Rogliano often leads guests to the local produce market at the **Col de Arcarota** (☯ 10am-4pm), 3km from the gîtes, to stock up on local goods.

'The kind of people who tend to come here are of a certain mentality,' says Rogliano. 'We swap stories, we become friends. I like to tell them local legends and folk tales from Corsican history. It's all about keeping a tradition alive.'

---

not the most touristed village, however, so people are not particularly used to seeing foreigners on their doorsteps.

The action is split between the upper and lower village. The former is home to the **Musée de L'Adecec** (☎ 04 95 38 12 83; ☯ 9am-12.30pm & 2-7pm Mon-Sat), a converted monastery that has a fairly standard collection of Corsican folk traditions ranging from agriculture to early industrialisation. Overall it's one for the real history boffins, although some of the exhibits relating to Corsica's King Theodore (p23) are worth a look.

More interesting is the **community centre** (www.adecec.net) in an adjoining building that works to promote Corsican language, culture and the arts. There's a radio station here, and a real community focus. However, it's aimed primarily at locals, not tourists.

The lower town is focused around the main drag, A Traversa, where you'll find a **Spar supermarket** (☯ 9am-noon & 3.30-7.30pm Mon-Sat) and a **post office** (☯ 9am-noon & 2.30-5pm Mon-Fri, 9am-noon Sat). Walking uphill towards the museum, you pass a small **tourist office** (☎ 04 95 38 09 04; ☯ 9.30am-noon & 4-7pm).

SLEEPING & EATING

There's not much by way of accommodation around these parts but there is a brand, spanking new *chambre d'hôte*, **Vallee di Campolaro** (☎ 04 95 38 19 79; d €60), at the bottom of the village, just off the D71. Don't be put off by the fact that you enter via the family's garage. Inside it's studio-style with a well-equipped kitchenette (there's a microwave and coffee maker). Though there's only the one room, it's fine for a couple, and bright and modern inside.

The local pizzeria, **Les Trois Fourchettes** (☎ 04 95 38 14 86; menu €14), a few doors down from the tourist office, is a pleasant enough place for a bite to eat. The set menu comes with a free *pichet* of house wine. Also worth a look for a meal is **U Casone** (☎ 04 95 38 10 47; pizzas/mains €7/12), a reliable little place set behind place de l'Église through an archway.

LA CASINCA

Five kilometres southwest of Bastia-Poretta airport lies the start of La Casinca, a small, rural region along the eastern side of Monte Sant'Angelu (1218m), bordered by the Golo and Fium'Alto Rivers. It

---

THE AUTHOR'S CHOICE

Exiting Vescovato past the cemetery on the D237, there's a little garden restaurant, tucked-away on the left-hand side of the road, which is, in fact, Corsica's only organic and vegetarian eatery. **L'Ortu** (☎ 04 95 36 64 69; route de Venzolasca; ⏲ lunch & dinner Wed-Sun, Jun-Sep) is a hidden gem and, for vegetarians, a blessed relief from the charcuterie-dominated *menu Corse* served up by most restaurants.

All the produce used in meals is grown in the restaurant's garden, and the couple who run it go to a lot of trouble to present the food nicely, putting flowers in the salads and ice in the drinks. Meals are served on a terrace with world and jazz music gently drifting around the allotments. The best options are large salads (€7 to €10), omelettes (€8) and home-made ratatouille crepes (€10).

The owners plan to open *gîte*-style accommodation in tepees in the garden from the next season. L'Ortu is one of the few places in the area that is open in winter (by reservation only).

'We started the restaurant as part of a project to foster organic farming in Corsica, but people still tend to think that eating organic food means eating poorly', says co-owner, Swiss-born Madame Gigon. 'We're trying to encourage people to overcome that fear.'

They also sell home-made jams and honeys, and offer advice on where to find other organic producers across Corsica.

---

comprises a slew of tiny, hillside villages, set among forests of chestnut and olive trees, with tall, stone houses looking out over the Eastern Plain.

La Casinca has no public transport but, if you have a car, it makes for a pleasant day trip, winding your way through the rural mountain villages. The area's transport hub is Casamozza, on the suburban train line running out of Bastia.

The only suitable accommodation in the immediate area is a *chambre d'hôte* just off the Torra roundabout at the intersection of the N198 and the D237. **A Stella Serena** (☎ 04 95 36 65 29; s/d with breakfast €30/40) has three homely rooms with a shared bathroom and a shady patio terrace. The owners previously lived in Morocco, and have designed the house with a strong feel of the kasbah, plus they are very knowledgeable about excursions in the area. Call ahead for a pick-up from Casamozza train station.

This region has traditionally been associated with shepherds herding their flock, and today remains a major centre for cheese production. A well-known producer, **Fromagerie Pierucci** (☎ 04 95 36 72 74), offers visits to its production facility near the Torra roundabout by appointment only. The family-run business produces a total of 3000 cheeses per day, using one million litres of milk, and has plans to set up a cheese-tasting and vending area in the factory grounds.

Wine fans will want to make a stop at the **Cave Coopérative de la Casinca** (☎ 04 95 36 99 52; RN198, Torra; ⏲ 8.30am-noon & 2-7pm Mon-Sat) where tastings are available and a range of local wines and fruit liqueurs are for sale. Their gift packs of local fruit *digestifs* and apéritifs make for good presents; count on paying about €1.50 per litre for local AOC wines.

Vescovato

postcode 20215 / pop 300 / elevation 150m

Formerly a fortified town, hilltop **Vescovato** (the de-facto capital of La Casinca) got its name from the word *vescovo* (bishop); it was the site of the bishop's palace in the 15th century, before the bishop's seat was relocated to Bastia.

Heading west along the D237 from Torra, the road climbs steeply to the village square. It's best to leave the car here and explore the little alleyways and stairways between the high houses on foot. Vescovato is very much a living village with strong connections to Bastia.

The square is home to a **post office** (⏲ 9am-noon & 2.30-4.45pm, Sat 9am-noon) and, on its eastern side, a group of café-brasseries with tables spilling onto the shady square. Try **Café Funtanona** (☎ 04 95 36 61 05) for panini (€3.50) and crepes (€2.50), or **U Bel Fiuritu** (☎ 04 95 36 70 15) for salads (€7.50) and pizzas (€9). The western side of the square has a grocery shop, a butcher's shop and a *boulangerie*.

The adjacent Baroque **Église San Martino**, on a small terrace overlooking the roofs of neighbouring houses, was one of the first buildings in Corsica to be deemed of historical interest. The church is the scene of a large religious procession on 15 August each year. If you want to look inside, ask in cafés in the main square for the keys.

Venzolasca

postcode 20215 / pop 500 / elevation 380m

Further along the D237, the village of Venzolasca has the picturesque restaurant **Ferme-Auberge U Frangnu** (☎ 04 95 36 62 33; all-inclusive menu Corse €32), built around an old olive press. The views from its terrace remain superb, but the welcome and standards of service have rather slipped of late. It's open for dinner only; bookings recommended.

Loreto-di-Casinca

postcode 20215 / pop 180 / elevation 780m

Turning off the D237 onto the D6 will take you to the village of Loreta-di-Casinca. This quiet little spot has a **post office** (☒ 9.30-11.30am & 2-3.30pm) in the town hall building and a couple of café-brasseries built around the fringe of the shady village square. Try **Bar Jean-François** (☎ 04 95 36 09 84) for coffee and ice creams, or **Bar Ind'é Tittinu** (☎ 04 95 36 30 25) for snacks.

Visitors are welcome to pop into **Charcuterie Fieschi** (☎ 04 95 36 30 18), a family-run butcher's shop off the main square by the church. Here they prepare typical Corsican *charcuterie* by traditional means, using a *fucone* (a room with a large fire used to smoke the meat for up to 20 days at a time). Tastings are available; count on paying €14 per kg if you want to buy direct.

EATING

Loreta-di-Casinca also boasts a couple of decent restaurants. **U Campanile** (☎ 04 95 36 31 19; menu €25), next to the village's Baroque church, has hearty, traditional food and fantastic panoramic views across the region from its all-glass eagle's nest dining room.

U Rataghju (☎ 04 95 36 30 66; menu €20), at the bottom end of the village down the steps from the church, is a friendly, welcoming place with traditional village décor. The set *menu* (dinner only) is a hearty affair with five generous courses and unlimited house wine; there's also a good-value children's *menu* (€10).

The Central Mountains

CONTENTS

The Centru de Corsica is the umbrella name used to denote the grouping of highly disparate mountain communities radiating out from around Corte – principally the Niolo and the Vénachese. Corte, the area's hub, was the capital of Pascal Paoli's short-lived Corsican nation and remains, even today, very much the mountain redoubt – a symbol of the island's distinct and separate cultural identity. To appreciate the spectacular mountain scenery you'll really need to head out of town and get among the picturesque rural villages, particularly to the south, where islanders attempt to preserve a traditional way of life.

The trailheads for the Restonica and Tavignanu valleys are easily accessible from the centre of Corte. These two hikes make for ideal day excursions for those seeking to stretch their legs without tackling the gruelling GR20.

Overall, this area is one of the less developed for tourism in Corsica and its country folk can tend to be rather wary of outsiders. Its rough and ready nature will appeal to hikers, but those used to international standards may find facilities rather lacking.

HIGHLIGHTS

■ **Dining**
Enjoy a hearty Corsican dinner at **U Museu** (p213), or tapas at **La Riviére des Vins** (p213) in Corte

■ **Walking**
Blow away the cobwebs with a day's hiking through the **Valée de la Restonica** (p214)

■ **All Aboard**
Check out Gustave Eiffel's handiwork riding the narrow-gauge train across the **Pont de Vecchiu** (p218)

■ **Step Back in Time**
Spend a night soaking up the old-world atmosphere at the gloriously retro **Hôtel Monte D'Oro** (p218)

■ **Take the Air**
Breathe the cool mountain air in walks around **Vizzavona** (p219) in the Vénachese

THE CENTRAL MOUNTAINS

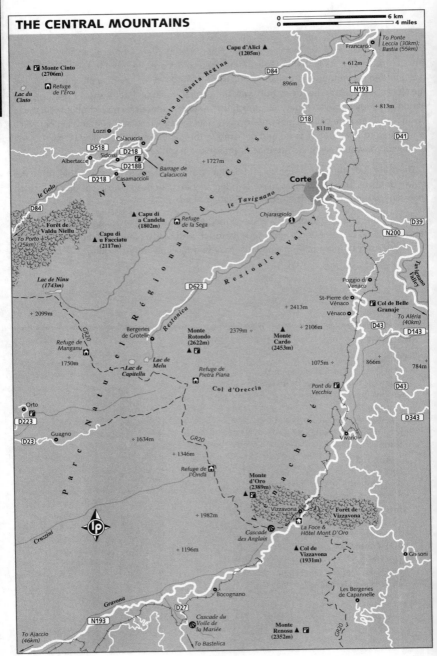

0 — 6 km
0 — 4 miles

Capu d'Alici ▲ (1205m)

To Ponte Leccia (30km); Bastia (55km)

Francardo

+ 612m

▲ Monte Cinto (2706m)

🏠 Refuge de l'Erco

Lac du Cinto

D84

+ 896m

+ 813m

N193

D18

+ 811m

D41

Lozzi

Scala di Santa Regina

Calacuccia

D518

D218

Sidossi

Albertacce

D218B

D218

Casamaccioli

Barrage de Calacuccia

+ 1727m

Niolo

N i o l o R e g i o n a l d e C o r s e

le Golo

Corte

le Tavignano

Chjarasgiolo

D39

N200

▲ Capu di a Candela (1802m)

🏠 Refuge de la Sega

Forêt de Valdu Niellu

To Porto (25km)

D84

Capu di ▲ u Facciatu (2117m)

Restonica Valley

Tavignano Valley

Lac de Ninu (1743m)

+ 2099m

Restonica

D623

+ 2413m

Poggio di Venaco

St-Pierre de Vénaco

🏠 Col de Belle Granaje

Vénaco

To Aléria (40km)

D43

D143

P a r c   N a t u r e l   R é g i o n a l   d e   C o r s e

GR20

Refuge de Manganu

+ 1750m

Bergeries de Grotelle

Monte Rotondo (2622m) ▲ 🏠

2379m +

▲ Monte Cardo (2453m)

+ 2106m

1075m +

866m

784m

Lac de Capitellu

Lac de Melu

Refuge de Pietra Piana

Col d'Oreccia

Pont du Vecchiu 🏠

D43

D343

Orto

D223

+ 1634m

GR20

V a c h e s é

Vivario

Guagno

D23

+ 1346m

Refuge de l'Onda 🏠

Monte d'Oro (2389m) ▲ 🏠

Vizzavona

Forêt de Vizzavona

La Foce & Hôtel Mont D'Oro

🏠

LP

Cruzzini

+ 1982m

Cascade des Anglais

▲ Col de Vizzavona (1931m)

+ 1196m

Ghisoni

Gravona

Bocognano

Les Bergeries de Capannelle

N193

D27

Cascade du Voile de la Mariée

GR20

To Ajaccio (46km)

To Bastelica

Monte Renosu ▲ 🏠 (2352m)

GETTING AROUND

Corte and the Vénachese are linked from Bastia and Calvi by the Chemins de Fer de la Corse (CFC; p241), Corsica's metre-gauge, single-track railway, which winds lazily through forests and around mountains. Outside of this track, however, there is scant public transport so, without your own car, either walking or hitching are the only options.

The Niolo, on the other hand, has hardly any transport connections at all, aside from a solitary bus connection in summer (p216). As such it remains remote and closed off from much of the island, let alone outside influences.

CORTE (CORTI)

postcode 20250 / pop 6693 / elevation 400m

At the mouth of the Restonica and Tavignano valleys, and surrounded by the mountainous countryscape of the Parc Naturel Régional de Corse, the town of Corte is the area hub.

It is best known for its ancient citadel, which looks as if it is clinging to the rocky headland. The town is also home to Corsica's only university, a venerable old educational institution founded in 1765. Today, the university boasts 3500 students and, during term time, when students crowd the local cafés, the town has a very different feel. During the summer season, on the other hand, the town is simply packed with tourists (many on walking holidays), swelteringly hot and grossly overpriced.

For all its historical importance, however, Corte is rather devoid of charm. There is talk of grand projects to foster the town's position as Corsica's cultural and spiritual heartland, but nothing concrete has, as yet, been finalised.

Between 1755 and 1769 Pascal Paoli founded the first independent Corsican government in the town and established one of the world's first democratic constitutions – the Couvent d'Orezza (p24). Corte remains a nationalist stronghold, so much so that even today it has a slightly uneasy relationship with tourism.

ORIENTATION

The main shopping and café drag, cours Paoli, divides the town centre in two halves, with steps to the west of the main street leading to the upper town and the citadel. To the east, steps descend steeply towards the train station. The citadel quarter dominates the upper town (*haute ville*), and the university district is the focus of the lower town (*basse ville*).

INFORMATION

Bookshops

Maison de la Presse (☎ 04 95 46 01 38; 24 cours Paoli; ⏰ 7am-12.30pm & 3-7.30pm Mon-Sat, 8am-noon Sun) Has a good range of guides, maps and foreign-language newspapers – the latter during summer only.

Emergency

The **police station** (☎ 04 95 46 04 81; ave Xavier-Zuciani) is on the outskirts of town, on the N200 heading towards Aléria.

Internet Access

Grand Café du Cours (☎ 04 95 46 00 33; 22 cours Paoli; €3 per hr; ⏰ year-round) Has a raft of Internet terminals available in its back room.
Café de l'Orient (☎ 04 95 61 11 77; 5 ave Jean Nicoli) Opposite the university; opens only during term time.

Laundry

Speed Laverie (⏰ 8am-9pm; €5) Next to the Casino supermarket on the southern edge of town.

Medical Services

Santos Manfredi Hospital (☎ 04 95 45 05 00; allée du 9 Septembre) Opposite the Casino supermarket. After 8pm ring the night bell.

Money

Caisse d'Épargne (cours Paoli; ⏰ 8am-noon & 1.30-5pm Mon-Fri, 8am-noon Sat) ATM.
Crédit Lyonnais (cours Paoli; ⏰ 8.20am-noon & 1.40-5pm Mon-Fri, 8am-noon Sat) ATM.
Société Générale (cours Paoli; ⏰ 8.15am-noon & 1.50-4.45pm Mon-Fri, 8am-noon Sat) ATM.

Post

Main post office (ave du Baron Mariani; ⏰ 8am-12.30pm & 1.30-5pm Mon-Fri, 8am-noon Sat) Also has an ATM.

Tourist Information

Tourist office (☎ 04 95 46 26 70; www.corte -tourisme.com; ⏰ 9am-8pm Jul & Aug, 9am-6pm Mon-Sat Jun & Sep, 9am-noon & 2-6pm Mon-Fri low season) Housed in the Padoue barracks at the entrance to the citadel; has town maps and accommodation guides.

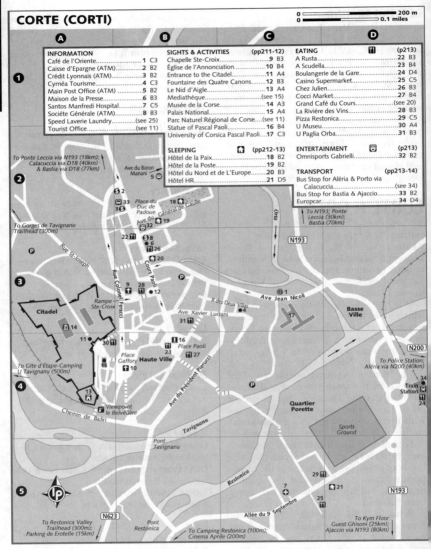

CORTE (CORTI)

0 — 200 m
0 — 0.1 miles

INFORMATION
Café de l'Oriente.....................1	C3
Caisse d'Epargne (ATM)...........2	B2
Crédit Lyonnais (ATM)............3	B2
Cyrnéa Tourisme....................4	C3
Main Post Office (ATM)..........5	B2
Maison de la Presse...............6	B3
Santos Manfredi Hospital........7	C5
Société Générale (ATM)..........8	B3
Speed Laverie Laundry........(see 25)	
Tourist Office....................(see 11)	

SIGHTS & ACTIVITIES   (pp211-12)
Chapelle Ste-Croix....................9	B3
Église de l'Annonciation............10	B4
Entrance to the Citadel.............11	A4
Fountaine des Quatre Canons.....12	B3
Le Nid d'Aigle........................13	A4
Mediathéque......................(see 15)	
Musée de la Corse...................14	A3
Palais National........................15	A4
Parc Naturel Régional de Corse...(see 11)	
Statue of Pascal Paoli...............16	B4
University of Corsica Pascal Paoli....17	C3

SLEEPING   (pp212-13)
Hôtel de la Paix.....................18	B2
Hôtel de la Poste...................19	B2
Hôtel du Nord et de L'Europe......20	B2
Hôtel HR..............................21	D5

EATING   (p213)
A Rusta.................................22	B3
A Scudella.............................23	B4
Boulangerie de la Gare..............24	D4
Casino Supermarket..................25	C5
Chez Julien...........................26	B3
Cocci Market..........................27	B4
Grand Café du Cours............(see 20)	
La Rivière des Vins..................28	B3
Pizza Restonica......................29	C5
U Museu..............................30	A4
U Paglia Orba.........................31	B3

ENTERTAINMENT   (p213)
Omnisports Gabrielli.................32	B2

TRANSPORT   (pp213-14)
Bus Stop for Aléria & Porto via Calacuccia..................(see 34)	
Bus Stop for Bastia & Ajaccio......33	B2
Europcar..............................34	D4

Also available is the useful pamphlet *Parcours Patrimonial*, published by the local historical society (free), which lists the main points of interest in the town, and the pamphlet *26 Detailed Hiking and Riding Trails* (€5). Staff will try to give advice on accommodation and sightseeing options but the office can get very busy in high season.

Parc Naturel Régional de Corse (PNRC; ☎ 04 95 46 27 44; ✆ same as tourist office) Has advice on walking

trails and offers hiking maps of the Restonica Valley. Access is through a connecting door from the tourist office.

Travel Agency
Cyrnéa Tourisme (☎ 04 95 45 25 10; www.cyrnea tourisme.com; 9 ave Xavier Luciani; ✆ 9am-noon & 2.30-6.30pm Mon-Fri, 9am-noon Sat) Acts as the local agent for air and ferry tickets, plus tour excursions.

SIGHTS & ACTIVITIES
Citadel

Corte's high-perched and roughly triangular citadel remains the only such inland structure in Corsica. The heart of the citadel was founded in 1419 by the Corsican viceroy, Vincentello d'Istria. He built a small fort that, due to its position on the rocky headland, became known as **Le Nid d'Aigle** (Eagle's Nest). This structure, complete with its own dungeon, still remains today. Given its position 100m higher than the town, it affords great views across the surrounding Restonica and Tavignanu valleys. This section of the citadel grounds close at 7pm each night.

The rest of the citadel complex, built at a lower level, was extended by the French in the 18th and 19th centuries. From place Paoli, climb the flight of stairs cut from Restonica marble to reach the fortifications at the citadel's southerly entrance. From here there are two large buildings facing one another, the **Caserne Serrurier** and **Caserne Padoue** (Padua or Barracks). Built under Louis-Philippe, they have been used for a variety of purposes, including as a prison and later, from 1962 to 1983, as housing for elements of the French Foreign Legion.

Today, the Caserne Serrurier houses the Musée de la Corse (below). Since 1981 the Caserne Padoue was used by the university and now provides space for the tourist office and the PNRC (p210).

The **Fonds Régional d'Art Contemporain** (FRAC; ☎ 04 95 46 22 18; ⏰ 2-6pm Mon-Sat), also in the Caserne Padoue, organises four exhibitions per year, one of which is usually dedicated to a Corsican artist.

Just outside the citadel ramparts, a staircase leads down from **le Belvédère**, a small viewing platform, to the riverside area.

Musée de la Corse (Museu di a Corsica)

Corsica's **National Museum** (☎ 04 95 45 25 45; adult/concession €5.30/3; ⏰ 10am-8pm, closed Mon out of season) inaugurated in December 1997, is also known as Musée Régional d'Anthropologie. The building had been restored prior to reopening by the Italian architect, Andrea Bruno, who kept the building's long façade and enlarged the windows to allow more light to enter the rooms.

The museum has nowhere to leave bags, nor a café, but does offer access to toilets

and lifts for those with disabilites. All signs are marked only in French and Corsican, not English. If you want English-language explanations you'll need to hire one of the audio guides (€1.50).

The building comprises two main galleries with a third space allocated to temporary exhibits. On the 1st floor the **Galerie Doazan** traces the history of the island through a permanent collection of approximately 3 traditional Corsican craft objects. With the focus solidly on Corsica's industrial heritage, this section is pretty standard museum fare; the gallery is named after the priest who assembled the collection over nearly three decades, from 1951 to 1978.

On the next level, the **Musée en Train de se Faire** (Museum under Construction) is a more compelling affair. This permanent gallery covers more contemporary subjects such as industry, tourism and music. Some of the best exhibits are based on case studies of Mattei, the spirit maker whose Bastia shop (p87) remains a piece of living history. Also good is the exhibit that traces the early tourism of Corsica, and the room full of sound effects that examines Corsica's rich heritage of polyphonic singing (p32).

Overall, a visit to the museum makes for a worthy two-hour addition to any Corte itinerary, though you can't help but come away feeling that it leaves out as much as it includes. Corsica's rich history of vendettas and blood feuds (p26) are particularly conspicuous by their absence.

Palais National (Palazzu Naziunale)

The large rectangular building to the left of the citadel entrance was once the palace of the local Genoese government, and it subsequently housed Paoli's first and only independent Corsican government (p24). Paoli lived here in this palace, which was simultaneously the principal university facility. Now the building houses some departments of the 20th-century university, as well as a library.

The ground floor serves as home to the new **Mediathéque** (Espace Culturel Municipal; ☎ 04 95 47 08 23; adult/concession €8/4; ⏰ 10am-noon & 3-6pm, closed Tue, Thu & Fri morning, Sat & Sun). This gallery space hosts regular talks, exhibitions and cultural events, and is the first of the plans to build on Corte's position as Corsica's cultural heartland to come to fruition.

The university library in the **Centre de Recherches Corses** annexe contains everything that has ever been written on Corsica in areas ranging from history to flora and fauna. This is also a good place to have a look at the nationalist press, including the famous *Il Ribombu*, the official publication of A Cuncolta Naziunalista (Nationalist Assembly) party. It only opens, however, during term time.

Below the palace on place Gaffory is the **Église de l'Annonciation**, built in the mid-15th century. It was transformed and enlarged in the 17th century.

University of Corsica Pascale Paoli

The main building of the university is on ave Jean Nicoli near the entrance to the lower town. One of the demands of the nationalists in the 1960s was that Corsica should have its own university. In 1975, the French government acceded to the demand, and in October 1981, nearly two centuries after Paoli founded the university, doors here were once again opened to students, establishing Corte as the island's centre of learning once more.

Walking

Trekking along the Vallée de la Restonica (p214) makes for an easy day's hiking from Corte. Several companies offer organised hiking tours:

Valle e Cime (☎ 04 95 48 69 29; www.vallecime.com)
In Terra Corsa (☎ 04 95 47 69 48; www.interracorsa.fr)
Compagnie Régionale des Guides et Accompagnateurs de Corse (☎ 04 95 48 10 43)

For walking and sports equipment, **Omnisports Gabrielli** (☎ 04 95 46 09 35; cours Paoli; ☼ 9am-1pm & 2.30-8pm) has all the bases covered.

FESTIVALS & EVENTS

Corte is the centre for Corsica's burgeoning hiking industry and plays host each July to the gruelling **Inter-Lacs** (www.interlacs.com), a cross-country marathon that makes walking the GR20 look like a summer afternoon stroll in the park.

SLEEPING
Budget

Hôtel HR (☎ 04 95 45 11 11; 6 allée du 9 Septembre; r with washbasin/bathroom €25/39; P) This hotel feels very institutional, like a student hall of residence, but remains by far the best budget option in town. There are no frills, but rooms are functional and good value. The hotel is 200m south of the train station and next to the commercial centre with the Casino supermarket (p213). It is a bit of a way from the action – such as it is – but the hotel does offer a sauna room (€4) and a fitness room (free), as well as a laundry service (€5), and a garden area where the breakfast buffet (€5) is served. Make sure you book ahead, even during the low season.

If it's full, **Hôtel de la Poste** (☎ 04 95 46 01 37; 2 place du Duc de Padoue; d/qd with bathroom €42.50/57) is a suitable stop-gap with 12 rather basic rooms in an old building. Room Nos 5 and 6 have balconies while rooms 9 and 10 share a wide terrace.

Gîte d'Étape-Camping U Tavignanu (☎ 04 95 46 16 85; camping €6, dm with breakfast/half-board €15/29) is a favourite with walkers for its rustic feel and great location just five minutes from the GR20 trailhead. The site is on the western side of the citadel, at the end of a narrow road 500m beyond the bridge from the chemin de Baliri. Facilities are above average and you can even hire tents (€15) for the in-house campground.

For the cheapest option in Corte, head to **Camping Restonica** (☎ 04 95 46 11 59; sites €11; reception ☼ 8am-noon & 2-11pm). Just 100m from the Casino supermarket (p213), it's the closest campground to the town centre. It's not the most welcoming place but there is a café-bar with a shady terrace and a decent range of facilities.

Mid-Range

Hôtel du Nord et de l'Europe (☎ 04 95 46 00 68, 22 cours Paoli; www.hoteldunord-corte.com; d/qd €55/85; ☐) This all-in-one hotel-café is the favoured spot for walkers and travellers coming to town. Deservedly so, as it has the best facilities and the owners also let you leave your cases for free in the absence of any luggage-storage facilities in town. This is also one of the few places in town open outside the tourist season. The only disadvantage is that it's quite a hike from the station, especially with heavy bags. The hotel rooms are spacious and comfortable with satellite TV but try to avoid rooms overlooking the street below if you want a good night's sleep. Add €23 per person for half-board (see p213 for eating options).

Other mid-range options pale by comparison. In a quiet location at the end of a short street just off cours Paoli, **Hôtel de la Paix** (☎ 04 95 46 06 72; ave du Général de Gaulle; **P**)) is a decent two-star place with simple rooms. It tends to get booked up in advance with tour groups. The hotel offers half-board for an extra €13.

EATING
Budget
In the evenings, the **Pizza Restonica** van (☎ 04 95 61 13 91; pizzas €5.50-9) opens opposite the Hôtel HR (p212) on allée du 9 Septembre for eat-in or takeaway pizza. The **Boulangerie de la Gare**, at the train station, offers better value for a morning croissant than any of the hotel breakfasts and is a useful place to stock up on supplies before catching the train.

For self-caterers, there's a large **Casino supermarket** (⏱ 8.30am-7.45pm Mon-Sat) next to the Hôtel HR on the southern edge of town, and a small **Cocci Market** (⏱ 7am-8pm) on place Paoli.

Mid-Range
U Museu (☎ 04 95 61 08 36, rampe Ribanelle; menu Corse €15) By far the best place to eat in Corte is this homely, terrace-style eatery, just before the entrance to the citadel in the upper town. Consistently popular, the menu covers all the local favourites and, unlike many places in town, actually does them rather well. Try the wild boar stew with wild myrtle (€10.70), *tripettes à la Cortenaise* (tripe with red wine sauce and shallots, € 8.40) or the *brocciu* and mint omelette (€7.30). Reservations are not accepted, and it's closed Sundays in low season.

La Riviére des Vins (☎ 04 95 46 37 04; 5 rampe Sainte-Croix; menus €9-15) This is a nice little spot for an outdoor candlelit dinner and boasts a great vantage point looking across the steps down to the Fountaine des Quatre Canons. La Riviére offers a series of tapas-style menus with an emphasis on local *charcuterie*, cheese and wine. Expect friendly service and a really cosy ambience.

A Scudella (☎ 04 95 46 25 31, 2 place Paoli; menu Corse €16) This innovative restaurant has had the bright idea of offering a mix 'n' match menu where you can choose a double starter and dessert for €9.10, or any two courses for €11.50. It's far better value than

the Plat d'Or opposite, however, the service can be very patchy and waiting staff are rather intolerant of non-French speakers.

U Paglia Orba (☎ 04 95 61 07 89, ave Xavier Luciani; mains €15-20) is a fairly simple eatery, but the one place in town with a few good vegetarian options. **A Rusta** (☎ 04 95 46 28 56; 19 cours Paoli; menus €12-19) is a suitably rustic spot on the main drag. Try the Corsican soup served in a huge tureen (€8).

Downstairs in the Hôtel du Nord et de l'Europe, **Le Grand Café du Cours** (☎ 04 95 46 00 33; 22 cours Paoli) has a huge *menu* of drinks and snacks. The hotel's half-board is available in conjunction with the restaurant **Chez Julian** next door; ask about the kid's and vegetarian *menus*.

ENTERTAINMENT
Cinema Aprile, Corte's only cinema, is about 100m southwest of Camping Restonica (p212).

GETTING THERE & AWAY
Bus
Eurocorse (☎ 04 95 21 06 30) run two buses a day Monday to Friday to Bastia (€10, 1¼ hours) and Ajaccio (€10.50, 1¾ hours); buses leave from in front of the Brasserie Le Majestic (19 cours Paoli).

Autocars Cortenais (☎ 04 95 46 02 12) runs one bus to Bastia (€10, 1½ hours) via Ponte Leccia on Monday, Wednesday and Friday; buses leave from in front of the Brasserie Le Majestic. From July to September it also runs buses to Aléria (€10, one hour) on Tuesday, Thursday and Saturday; buses leave from in front of the train station.

From July to September, **Autocars Mordiconi** (☎ 04 95 48 00 04) runs buses to Porto (€19, 2¾ hours) via Calacuccia (€10, one hour) and Évisa (€15, two hours); buses leave Monday to Saturday from in front of the train station.

Train
From the **train station** (☎ 04 95 46 00 97; ⏱ 6.30am-8.30pm Mon-Sat, 7.45am-8.30pm Sun & public holidays) there are trains to Ajaccio (€12.50, two hours, four daily), Bastia (€8.30, 1½ hours, five daily) and Calvi (€14.90, two hours, three daily) via Île Rousse (€11.80, 1½ hours) with a change at Ponte Leccia.

To take your bicycle on the train costs an additional €12.90.

GETTING AROUND

The centre of Corte is easily navigable on foot.

Europcar (☎ 04 95 46 08 02) runs a hole-in-the-wall kiosk at the train station.

Rinieri Minibus (☎ 04 95 46 02 12; min 20 people, per person €13) offers group excursions to the Restonica valley. A taxi costs about €35. For drivers, contact **Michel Balvani** (☎ 04 95 46 04 88) or **Taxi Francois** (☎ 04 95 61 01 17).

AROUND CORTE

VALLÉE DE LA RESTONICA

Despite some overcrowding during the summer months, the Vallée de la Restonica hike is certainly the one trail that every visitor to the area should tackle for a true glimpse of Corsica's rural heartland. Better still, it makes for an easy day trip – not to mention a welcome escape – from the pressure cooker atmosphere of Corte in high season. Be sure to wear good walking shoes, take plenty of water and avoid the midday sun. The mountains are often snowcapped, even in May.

The river, rising in the grey-green mountains, has hollowed out pretty little basins in the rock, and these provide numerous sheltered settings for bathing and sunbathing alike. From Corte, the D623 winds its way through the gorges of the valley for 15km to the **Bergeries de Grotelle**, where a car park (€5) marks the end of the road before trails, climbing onto the twin lakes, continue onwards and upwards.

The huge number of tourists in the Vallée de la Restonica in summer has led to the imposition of new parking regulations. Fires, bivouacs, unauthorised camping and the dumping of waste in or near the river – Corte's drinking water – are also strictly forbidden.

Caravans and camper vans are halted at **Tuani**, 7km from Corte, and not even cars are allowed to pass after 2.30pm. Instead, a free shuttle bus service operates in summer. It starts 3km into the valley from outside the tourist information kiosk and runs to the parking de Grotelle. It leaves every 30 minutes from 8am to 1.30pm with return journeys every 30 minutes from 2.30pm until 5pm.

Information

There's a kiosk-style **tourist information office** (☎ 04 95 46 33 92; ☾ 8am-5pm, summer only) at Chjarasgiolu, 2km along the Restonica gorge from the Corte trailhead. Beware that its opening hours have a tendency to vary rather randomly.

The **Corte tourist office** (☎ 04 95 46 26 70; www .corte -tourisme.com), see p209, can also help advise on Restonica valley hiking excursions.

Walking

Walks are signposted along the road. Two of the most popular destinations for walkers are **Lac de Melu** (1711m), an hour's hike, and the **Lac de Capitellu** (1930m), about 1¾ hours away on foot. The path to the lakes is signposted in yellow from the Bergeries de Grotelle car park (1370m).

The path to Lac de Melu follows the right-hand bank of the Restonica for most of the way, before branching into two tracks. The track that continues along the bank is harder going than the one that crosses the river, but you are less likely to come across snow in winter and spring. A circuit around the lakes takes about four hours, returning to the Bergeries de Grotelle car park.

Sleeping & Eating

Hôtel de la Restonica (☎ 04 95 45 25 25; d/with half-board €69/81; P ☒) This rustic place is in an old stone house about 1.5km from Corte. Facilities are above-average for the area and there's a decent restaurant next door. The pleasant setting boasts a waterfall and natural pools close by.

Hôtel Dominique Colonna (☎ 04 95 45 25 65, www .dominique-colonna.com; d/with half-board €94/114; P ☒ ☒) This hotel is a notch above the Hôtel de la Restonica directly opposite (and owned by the same family). It is named after the current owner's father, a former professional football player, and has decent-sized rooms with a bath, balcony and some homely touches. The hotel shares the same swimming pool with the Hôtel de la Restonica.

Camping Tuani (☎ 04 95 46 11 65; €11), halfway along the Restonica gorge, is a shaded campground with 90 sites, fairly basic facilities and a pretty ordinary café-bar. It's about 6km from Corte town centre and 5km before the Parking de Grotelle.

Getting There & Away
In summer **Rinieri Minibuses** (☎ 04 95 46 02 12) offers group excursions to the Restonica valley (p214). The minibus will arrange to pick up from your hotel, although this entails a higher charge.

VALLÉE DU TAVIGNANO WALK
Corsica's deepest gorge makes for a classic, day-long walk from the centre of Corte. Unlike the Restonica valley hike, however, this track has no facilities en route for walkers. Stock up on everything you will need before setting off and be sure to have strong shoes, a sun hat and plenty of water.

From Corte, the track climbs through the maquis and scrubland, hugging the river as it climbs. About 5km from Corte the gorge walk really kicks in and the scenery becomes increasingly dramatic. If you're planning to push onwards towards the **Lac de Nino** (1743m), a key point on the GR20 walking route (p58), there's a small walkers' *refuge*, **Refuge de la Sega**, roughly about halfway long the Tavignano valley.

THE NIOLO
The Niolo is the traditional sheep- and goat-herding district of Corsica, a tough place where lonely shepherds have eked out a stark, rural existence for centuries. Today it remains isolated from the rest of the island, not helped by a solitary bus service in summer only (p216) and a long, hard winter. This isolation means that the people of the Niolo are amongst the least used to foreigners on the island.

This is a quiet and secluded place – good for walkers or those seeking solitude, but not everyone's cup of tea.

Scala di Santa Regina
This awesome mountain pass northwest of Corte was, for years, the only way of getting into or out of Calacuccia and the villages of the Niolo region. The deep granite gorges that plunge down to the bed of the **River Golo** make this one of the island's most dramatic mountain landscapes – and all the more so because of the rock's other-worldly, reddish rust colour.

The D84, a narrow road that sometimes seems to be hardly more than a ledge with reinforced verges supported by arches,

winds its way through the pass for around 20km, from the outskirts of Calacuccia to close to the junction with the N193. The only blot on the landscape is the chain of rusty electricity pylons following the line of the river.

A dam and hydroelectric power station, which can dramatically alter the water levels without warning, make any descent into the gorges perilous. It's possible to go down a narrow walkway 4km from Calacuccia, but the view from the road is just as stunning.

You need a car to traverse the Scala di Santa Regina. From Corte, head north along the N193 as far as Francardo, then take the turning west onto the D84 (in the direction of Calacuccia).

Calacuccia
postcode 20224 / pop 350 / elevation 820m
Rising above the lake at its heart, the quiet little village Calacuccia is a haunt for hikers and has a handful of facilities. The town lies in the shadow of **Monte Cinto** (2706m; see boxed text, p216) and affords good views of **Les Cinq Moines** (The Five Monks), a series of five jagged peaks that glower on the rural community below. After a long day's walking, the locals tend to cool off with a swim among the mountain streams found between Casamaccioli and Albertacce. Visitors tend to take a dip in the lake, but boating is not allowed.

There are plans afoot to open an ethnology museum in Calacuccia but no date has been fixed as yet.

Calacuccia has a couple of pretty ordinary bars, a petrol station and a **pharmacy** (9am-noon & 2-6pm Mon-Fri, 9am-noon Sat), just before the Église St-Pierre. There's also a **grocery shop** (9am-noon & 3-7pm Mon-Sat, 9am-1pm Sun) and a **post office** (9am-noon & 2-4.40pm Mon-Fri, 9-11.40am Sat), down a series of winding side streets behind the town hall.

The **tourist office** (☎ 04 95 48 05 22; 9am-noon & 3-7pm) is 100m east of the Hôtel des Touristes (p216) on the main drag; it produces a booklet *Randonner dans le Niolu*.

The Compagnie Régionale des Guides et Accompagnateurs en Montagne de Corse can be contacted through the tourist office for details of hiking, climbing and canyoning excursions; count on prices starting from €45 per person.

CLIMBING MONTE CINTO

About 80% of visitors to Calacuccia come to climb Monte Cinto (2710m), Corsica's highest peak. It's a six-hour climb from Calacuccia so, if you're planning to tackle the summit, get an early start and take plenty of water.

From the trailhead at Lozzi, the path is signposted by bright orange signs and climbs gently towards the **Refuge de l'Ecru** (1650m; €6 overnight), in about three hours. From here the climbing really starts with the summit another three hours away.

For more details, contact the Compagnie Régionale des Guides et Accompagnateurs en Montagne de Corse via the Calacuccia tourist office (p215).

SLEEPING

Hôtel des Touristes (☎ 04 95 48 00 04; s/d with basin €31/37, with bath €49/54) Located at the very heart of the village, the rooms here are rather old fashioned but reasonably priced. The hotel also offers dorm beds (€12) and *gîte* rooms (€17) for hikers in the nearby annexe. The owners run the local bus service as well, and are very knowledgable about the region's walking trails.

Hôtel Acqua-Viva (☎ 04 95 48 06 90; d/tw €62/66; P) This is a more modern and much brighter affair than some other places, with prices to match. It's alongside a petrol station 300m to the west as you head out of Calacuccia towards Albertacce. Rooms are comfortable with pleasant furnishings and satellite TV; the best ones also have a garden view. There's a popular little café-bar downstairs where the locals congregate to play cards. At the time of writing the owners were hatching plans to open a campground opposite the hotel.

Casa Balduina (☎ 04 95 48 08 57; d without/with half-board €62/112), on the Albertacce road, used to be a restaurant but has recently been converted to a seven-room boutique-style hotel. Rooms are well equipped and the owner, having previously lived in London, speaks English very well. This is a new place and, as such, is finding its feet, but the welcome is genuine.

Gîte d'Étape du Couvent Saint Francoiş (☎ 04 95 48 00 11; dm/d/tr €13/39/53) A kilometre south of Calacuccia on the road to Albertacce, this converted Franciscan monastery is a useful port of call for walkers. The brothers have long since moved on but their rather spartan way of life remains a central motif – it's one for the converted.

EATING

Opposite the Hôtel des Touristes, **U Valduniellu** (☎ 04 95 48 06 92; pizzas/mains €8/15) is the village pizzeria with local favourites, wood-fired pizzas and friendly service.

To splash out, **Le Restaurant du Lac** (☎ 04 95 48 02 73; menus €13.20-20.50) at Sidossi, 2km west of Calacuccia and right on the edge of the lake, has a strong reputation as a beacon of *haute cuisine* in a culinary wilderness. The *menu* makes good use of fresh, local produce. There are two *menus* available for both lunch and dinner: a light three-course *formule* and a gourmet four-course version.

For a quick snack, **Bar des Platanes** has simple sandwiches (€4) and salads (€8). It's just after the *mairie* building as you head east out of Calacuccia along the main drag.

GETTING THERE & AWAY

Autocars Mordiconi (☎ 04 95 48 00 04) runs bus services from July to mid-September between Corte and Porto via Calacuccia. One bus leaves Calacuccia daily at 9am for Porto (€14, 1½ hours) and at 3.45pm for Corte (€8, one hour). Services operate Monday to Saturday only.

To explore the other parts of the Niolo, a car is mandatory – unless you enjoy really long walks.

Albertacce

postcode 20224 / pop 250 / elevation 860m

The D84 leads east out of Calacuccia towards the tiny hamlet of Albertacce, with a bar, two eateries and an archaeology museum, **Licninoi** (🕙 10.30am-12.30pm & 3.30-6.30pm Mon-Sat, 10.30am-12.30pm Sun; €2).

En route, you can take a detour via the D518 to **Lozzi**, the trailhead for climbing Monte Cinto (see boxed text above), and visit **U Mulinu** (☎ 04 95 48 09 08; adult/child €5/free; 🕙 10am-7pm), a restored old chestnut flour mill in the shadow of Monte Cinto.

SLEEPING & EATING

Gîte d'Étape d'Albertacce (☎ 04 95 48 05 60; dm €15), 2.5km south of Calacuccia on the outskirts of Albertacce, is a rough stone house with very basic dormitories for up to 20 people, a communal sitting room, a kitchen and clean bathrooms. It's a hard-core hikers hang-out.

Virtually opposite the *gîte*, **Paglio Orba** (☎ 04 95 48 01 13; menu €16) may not look much but, in fact, offers very authentic countryside cooking at reasonable prices – especially if you opt for the daily *menu*. The selection doesn't change from lunch to dinner but there is a children's *menu* (€8).

A local favourite **U Cintu** (Chez JoJo; ☎ 04 95 48 06 87; menus €12-17) has become besieged by the passing coach party brigade in high season and, as such, has rather gone off the boil. During the off-season, however, the owners will have more time for chatting with customers.

Casamaccioli
postcode 20224 / pop 50 / elevation 860m
If you thought Albertacce was quiet, just wait until you reach Casamaccioli, on the southern side of the lake and across the Golo river from Calacuccia.

The only attraction of note here is the statue of the Madonna, **Santa Maria della Stella**. The statue is paraded through the village each September, attracting thousands of pilgrims to one of Corsica's most venerated religious festivals. Once the event has passed, the village returns to its idle slumbers.

The only café open year-round is the local's hang-out, Bar de la Santa, opposite the church on the chestnut tree-fringed village square.

THE VÉNACHESE
This mountainous area to the south of Corte provides blessed relief in summer from Corte's sweltering pressure-cooker atmosphere. With its cooler, fresher mountain air, spectacular scenery and abundant hiking trails, the area has always been popular with European travellers in the tradition of the grand tour – especially those seeking to take the air.

The Vénachese is also well served by transport connections, with the N193 cutting a swathe through the mountains, and trains on the Corte–Ajaccio route offering daily connections. As such, the area makes a good base for an excursion into the heart of the Corsican mountains.

Vénaco
postcode 20231 /pop 620 /elevation 610m
Vénaco, overlooking the Tavignano valley, is best known for the quality and variety of its local produce – from fresh trout to ewe's milk cheese. Like any number of Corsica's mountain hamlets, this once-bustling village is now rather subdued as the population has moved to the cities in search of new employment. Today it is more of a place to stop for a coffee or a chance to stock up on supplies than a place to visit in its own right.

Vénaco has a **post office** (☒ 9am-noon & 1.50-4.30pm Mon-Fri, 9m-noon Sun) at the bottom of the village in a building shared with the town hall, school and fire service (that's multitasking for you!).

There's also a *tabac*, a pharmacy, two small grocery shops and a simple café-bar, **Restaurant de la Place** (☎ 04 95 47 01 30; menu €13), right on the main square, that does a passable job of preparing simple snacks for the passing trade.

From the train station at the foot of the village, it's a steep 600m climb up to the main road – especially in the summer heat. There is no left-luggage, nor indeed any facilities at all, at the train station.

SLEEPING & EATING
Vénaco is not the best place to overnight in the area given the limited options – consider pushing onto nearby Vizzavona.

Hôtel U Frascone (☎ 04 95 47 00 85; r without/with half-board €50/58) at the southern limit of the village is the only hotel in town. Rooms come with few frills and standard fittings. The adjoining terrace restaurant has more going for it with *menus* at €12.80 and €21.80, and giant salads for €7 to €9.

Camping-style accommodation is available in the tiny hamlet of St-Pierre de Vénaco (Santo Pietro di Venaco), north of Vénaco proper. Try **Gîte d'Étape de St-Pierre de Vénaco** (☎ 04 95 47 07 29; dm/r with half-board €27/60), a favourite stopover for hikers walking the Mare a Mare Nord hiking trail (p47). This handsome stone house, built in the traditional Corsican style, has spic-and-span four-person dormitories, and the owner is very knowledgable about walks in the area. To get to the *gîte*, go up to the top of the village, passing behind the church, then follow the signs. Beware: this place is popular with walkers so book well ahead in summer.

THE CENTRAL MOUNTAINS

THE AUTHOR'S CHOICE

If you feel like stepping back in time to a more genteel era then Vizzavona boasts a classic old hotel that, with its turn-of-the-century furniture and lost-in-time feel, is the perfect antidote to Corsica's vast swathe of mediocre places to stay.

The **Hôtel Monte D'Oro** (☎ 04 95 47 21 06; www.monte-oro.com; Col de Vizzavona; s/d € 51/69, half-board s/d €73/132; P 💻) is a huge complex with several accommodation annexes, its own tennis courts and a serene little chapel in the grounds. There's also a roadside café for snacks and drinks that is popular with passing hikers.

Built in 1880 to house workers on the first railway track from Ajaccio to Corte, it has been in the same family, the Plaisants, since 1904. The current owner, Madame Sicurani, has ensured the hotel has scarcely changed during its long history, retaining a strong family atmosphere. Even in 2004, when the hotel celebrates its 100th birthday, Madame Sicurani insists that there are no plans for a refit: 'My hope is that the hotel remains authentic, lively and a little living piece of history.'

The rooms are not flash (there's no air-con or satellite TV) but, if you take the half-board option that includes a hearty dinner – just like your grandma used to make – then it's a good-value proposition.

It's also mercifully cool here during the summer, with plenty of walking and nature trails to help you take the mountain air. That's why the hotel was so popular with Dorothy Carrington, the venerable grand dame who penned *Granite Island* (p10), still the best known literary work about Corsica.

'Madame Carrington used to come here when she was an old lady to enjoy the cool mountain air,' says Madame Sicurani, who remembers Corsica's best-known adopted daughter visiting the hotel in the 1980s. 'She was very elegant and always had a lot of dignity. I remember her as someone who was very polite and discreet. She never played the big star.'

The hotel is 3km south of Vizzavona in the hamlet of La Foce. A free shuttle bus will collect and drop off guests at Vizzavona train station if you call ahead.

On the D143, 3.5km from Vénaco, **Camping-Auberge de la Ferme de Peridundellu** (☎ 04 95 47 09 89; sites €9) is a small and friendly, family-run campground on a headland facing the valley. Meals are available (*menu* €14).

Vivario

postcode 20219 /pop 400/ elevation 696m

Like Vénaco, Vivario is more of a place for a stopover than a place to stay overnight. About 9km from Vénaco along the N193, it nestles among the mountains and provides an alternative route for walkers along the Mare a Mare Nord (p47).

Vivario has a handful of facilities. There's a **post office** (🕙 9am-noon & 2-4.30pm Mon-Tue & Thu-Fri, 9-11.40am Wed & Sat) on the 1st floor of the tiny *mairie* building, a couple of bar-restaurants – try **Bar La Cremerie** (☎ 04 95 47 20 11) for snacks and sandwiches – and two little grocery shops. The train station is about 500m north of the village.

The **train journey** via Vivario is famous for offering a chance to witness the handiwork of Gustave Eiffel (that's him of Eiffel Tower fame). The famous **Pont de Vecchiu** is a huge, graceful railway viaduct to the south of Vénaco that spans the countryside like a colossus of industrial revolution engineering. Unfortunately the adjacent, unsightly, concrete road bridge, built apparently to avoid a bend in the road and opened in 1999, rather spoils the view.

SLEEPING & EATING

Le Macchje Monti (☎ 04 95 47 22 00; s/d €42/50, half-board s/d €55/90), near the church, is the only hotel in town. Rooms are passable in a simple, don't-expect-too-much kind of way, while the adjoining restaurant, Chez Anne Marie, is a simple place with a decent set *menu* (€13).

Vivario is noteworthy in that it does have the pick of the local campgrounds. **Camping Savaggio** (☎ 04 95 47 22 14; tent site/gite €7.30/9), 3km south of the village along the N193, is handy for walkers following the Mare e Mare Nord trail. There's space to pitch tents, a small, walker's *refuge* and basic facilities.

Ghisoni

pop 180 / elevation 650m

Ghisoni is a tiny mountain hamlet on the D69 about 17km from the junction of the N197.

Before WWWII, Ghisoni boasted three dance halls, 12 cafés and 1800 inhabitants, but its population has since dwindled to about 180 people. Today the village lies peacefully at the foot of Punta Kyrie Eleïson, a mountain southeast of Vivario. Robert Colonna d'Istria, in his *L'Histoire de la Corse*, explains where its unusual name came from: in the 14th century members of the Giovannali sect, who were of Franciscan origin but equally resentful of secular and church authorities, were burnt alive on the mountain. Legend has it that as the flames rose and the priest sang the prayer of the Kyrie Eleïson, a white dove began to wheel above the burning woodpiles.

Ghisoni has a little **tourist office** (☎ 04 95 62 02 27; 9.30am-12.30pm & 5-7.30pm Mon-Fri) and a rather unspectacular hotel, **Hôtel Kyrié** (☎ 04 95 57 60 33; r with shower/bath €46/71).

There are no connections to Ghisoni by public transport – a car is the only answer.

Vizzavona

postcode 20219 /pop 30/ elevation 1200m

The N193 climbs steeply in the shadow of Mont d'Oro (2389m), the fifth-highest peak on the island, before arriving at the cool mountain hamlet of Vizzavona. This small village consists of a mere cluster of houses and hotels around a train station 700m from the main road, but is a major hub for the huge number of walkers who congregate here in high season to start or end their GR20 trek (p51).

The nearby **Forêt de Vizzavona**, where bandits routinely held travellers to ransom right up until the 19th century, is now a peaceful haven. It covers 1633 hectares and consists mainly of beech and laricio pine trees – some, it is said, more than 800 years old. There are over 25 hiking trails in the area but many are blighted by forest fires in summer (p40). Always check on conditions before setting out and be sure to stock up on bottled water.

SLEEPING & EATING

The hub of activity facilities-wise is the area around the train station. **Hôtel I Lericci** (☎ 04 95 47 21 22; s/d €55/70, half-board s/d €58/75),

---

WALKS AROUND VIZZAVONA

Two-and-a-half kilometres from the spot where the road from Ajaccio branches off towards the train station, a signpost indicates a short, gentle path that meanders down through a superb forest of pine and beech to **Cascades des Anglais**, a sequence of gleaming waterfalls.

After about 15 minutes on foot you come to the GR20 trailhead (p60), with its small refreshment stall (open in summer only). The path to the waterfalls continues to the left while the right fork leads back to Vizzavona train station (30 minutes).

In summer, there is a series of clear pools that are ideal for swimming. You can also sunbathe on the smooth rocks. The pools extend up the mountain for a distance best measured as a relatively easy 15-minute climb.

The attraction owes its name to the British holidaymakers who used to flock to Vizzavona, undeterred by the cold water, during the era of the grand tour.

Continuing southwest along the N193 for a few kilometres brings you get to the village of **Bocognano**. From here the road to the **Cascade du Voile de la Mariée** (Bridal Veil Falls) is on the left as you leave the village.

The narrow road passes a railway bridge, then comes up on a second bridge, recognisable by its iron guard-rails, 3.5km from the main road. A small wooden ladder on the left allows you to get over the fence. Continue along the path that climbs through the undergrowth, roughly marked out with lengths of rope tied between the trees. After around 10 minutes of rather difficult terrain you come to a tall, broad waterfall.

Fast-flowing in winter, it is rather disappointing in summer but allows you to freshen up.

East of here at **Les Bergeries de Capannelle** is a major winter sports resort for skiers, and a stopover on the GR20 trail (p61).

the best address in the area, is set in an old house and boasts comfortable rooms. The more expensive rooms are well worth the additional cost for their private bathrooms and mountain views. The owners also serve a range of snacks and drinks on the sunny terrace downstairs – try the house speciality mint tea (€2.50).

If you're on a tight budget, **Le Refuge GR20** (☎ 04 95 47 20 20) offers the €32 all-in walker's special: a place to crash, a hot shower and a simple dinner.

Right in front of the train station, **Restaurant du chef de la Gare** (☎ 04 95 47 24 41; menus €12-15) has simple but satisfying *menus*.

GETTING THERE & AWAY

Eurocorse Voyages (☎ 04 95 21 06 30) runs buses twice daily between Ajaccio and Bastia Monday to Saturday, stopping at Vizzavona (€8.50, one hour), Vivario (€9.50, 1¼ hours), Vénaco (€10, 1½ hours) and Corte (€10.50, 1¾ hours). Buses leave both Ajaccio and Bastia at 7.45am and 3pm (€18, three hours).

Chemins de Fer de la Corse (☎ 04 95 23 11 03) runs four trains daily from Ajaccio, stopping at Vizzavona (€8.40, 1¼ hours), Vivario (€9.20, 1½ hours), Vénaco (€10.70, 1¾ hours), Corte (€12.50, 2¼ hours), Ponte Leccia (€16.50, 2¾ hours) and Bastia (€23.50, 3¾ hours).

Directory

CONTENTS

ACCOMMODATION

There is very little luxurious, but a great deal of adequate and even comfortable, accommodation in Corsica. In most instances you could nearly deduct a star from the accommodation rating to bring it in line with mainland European standards. The majority of the clientele are French, whose main concern is often the quality of food available.

You are seriously advised to book a room in advance during July and August, especially if you're watching your pocket. The whole of France and half of Italy seem to descend onto the island during the holiday period and most reasonable accommodation gets snapped up fast. You can book by phone, fax or email in advance but many operators will take a substantial non-refundable deposit off your credit card to guarantee you show and penalise you if you don't.

Camping

Corsica has dozens, maybe even hundreds, of campgrounds, ranging in quality from extremely basic (electricity and hot showers) to deluxe – with restaurants, bars, mini-golf courses and swimming pools. Most sites fall somewhere in between the two extremes.

The majority of campgrounds in Corsica open only from June to September. *Camping sauvage* (literally 'wild camping', or camping outside recognised campgrounds) is prohibited; this is largely to reduce the chances of forest fires (especially in the maquis). In remote areas walkers can bivouac in *refuge* (mountain shelter) grounds for a nominal fee.

Chambres d'Hôtes

Chambres d'hôtes are the French equivalent of B&Bs, where, for marginally less than the price of a two-star hotel you can stay as a paying guest in somebody's house. Some may prefer the relative anonymity of a hotel and facilities will naturally vary but what you're sure to find is a far more familial and perhaps welcoming atmosphere than a hotel. With a willing host, it also affords you the opportunity to catch up on local lore and get a real feel for the locality. Half-board may be an option, especially in *fermes auberges* (farm guesthouses) where food comes from the land and garden and is probably very good traditional fare.

Hostels

There is one Hostelling International (HI) *auberge de jeunesse* (youth hostel) in Corsica at Poggio Mezzana, and another non-HI-affiliated youth hostel at Calvi, though you will find dorm accommodation in many of the *gîtes d'étapes*.

Hotels

For a directory listing of approximately 20 distinctly superior Corsican hotels, contact

Logis de France (☎ 01 45 84 70 00; www.logis-de-france .fr; 83 ave d'Italie, 75013 Paris).

The majority of Corsica's hotels are small and independent, and often family-run. Rooms are impressively clean and frequently have balconies or a terrace with views of mountains or of the sea. At the budget level, Corsica's hotels are said to be more expensive than budget hotels on the mainland, but in low season they are frequently discounted.

Refuges & Gîtes d'Étape

Refuges, located in the remote mountain areas of Corsica, offer basic dormitory accommodation exclusively to walkers. *Gîtes*, similarly located, offer dormitory accommodation and shared bathroom facilities mainly to walkers; but, because they are not only close to walking routes but to roads as well, these facilities also open to non-walkers, who will normally have to opt for half board. The Maison d'Informations Randonnées of the Parc Naturel Régional de Corse provides lists of refuges and *gîtes d'étape* along the GR20 and other walking trails.

A night's accommodation in one of the park *refuges* costs €9. Nightly rates in a *gîte d'étape* may be slightly lower or slightly higher, while half board is likely to cost up to €35.

Rental Accommodation

You can enjoy anything from a bargain-basement to an ultra-luxurious Corsican holiday by renting by the week or by the month. Several companies rent villas. One of them, **Maison des Îles** (☎ 04 95 28 44 00; www.maisons-des-iles.com), offers about 40 different luxury villas in the Porto Vecchio area, mostly with swimming pools, for €800 to €3000 per week in July or August. Several other agencies offer villas at various (but invariably expensive) rates around the country (see Internet Resources below).

A more economical option is to rent out a simple but comfortable *gîte rural* (a self-catering cottage in the country), at a price as low as €180 to €400 per week in low season. For €8, you can buy a brochure detailing all the *gîtes ruraux* in Corsica from the Ajaccio branch of **Gîtes de France** (☎ 04 95 51 72 82; www.gites-de-france.fr; rue du Général Fiorella, BP 10, 20181 Ajaccio Cedex 01). For summer accommodation by the week or month, in a villa or in a *gîte*, advance booking is essential.

PRACTICALITIES

- Use the metric system for weights and measures.

- Use the SECAM (*système électronique couleur avec mémoire*) system for video recorders and players.

- Old-type wall sockets, often rated at 600W, take two round pins. New sockets take fatter pins with a protruding earth (ground) pin.

- For numbers with four or more digits, use full stops or spaces, rather than commas: one million therefore appears as 1.000.000 or 1 000 000.

- For decimals, on the other hand, use commas, so 1.75 appears as 1,75.

- The two main daily newspapers are *Corse Matin*, based on *Nice Matin*, and *La Corse*.

- Catch up on nationalist news with one of the three weekly papers: *Le Journal de la Corse*, *U Ribombu* and *Arriti*.

- Tune into France Info at 105.5MHz FM.

- Pick up the Voice of America in the Ajaccio area at 96MHz FM.

- Corsicans measure road distances by time, not length because roads are so twisty.

Other appealing options for one-week-minimum rentals can be found through tour operators in your own country or by searching 'village vacances corse' on a good Internet search-engine such as Google. Other sites to try include the following:

Agence Conseil Immobilier (www.agenceaci.com) Contains pictures and descriptions of properties.

Particulier a Particulier (www.pap.fr) This French small ads paper is the best option for low-budget villas and apartments. Descriptions and photos can be a bit sparse.

Villas du Sud (www.villas-du-sud.com) Has some beautiful properties in all areas.

Resorts

Holiday villages or *résidences de vacances* are dotted all around the coast. Standards and prices vary but most have bungalow-type self-catering accommodation, which you can rent on a weekly basis (from €600 to €2500 a week for two), with laundry facilities, restaurants, swimming pool and children's play area. Often the best thing about these villages is their location right next to the beach. Tourist offices can give you details.

BUSINESS HOURS

Many businesses remain open continuously between 8am and 8pm – and sometimes even later – for every last one of the seven days of the week in July and August. Others, despite the once-a-year opportunity to replenish the till, continue to close for a couple of hours in the early afternoon, not for a siesta, but because the owners and the staff believe in their God-given right to eat a proper lunch, and frankly they cannot believe that anyone can fail to want to spend an hour or two over lunch. Ring a business between noon and 2pm at your peril; either you won't get an answer or, if you do, the reception will be anywhere between cool and hostile.

In other months of the year, businesses tend to open between 8am and noon and between 2pm and 6pm from Monday to Friday or Saturday. Many food businesses such as bakeries, pastry shops, butchers and greengrocers shut down between these hours as well.

Bars open daily from 7pm to 2am or 3am the following morning. Café opening hours generally run along the lines of other businesses, from 8am to 7pm or 8pm. During the tourist season (April or May to September or October), restaurants open seven days a week for lunch and dinner. Lunch is between noon and 2pm or 3pm; dinner, any time between 6.30pm and 11pm or midnight. The majority of restaurants in tourist-populated areas shut up shop in the off season.

The opening times displayed outside shops are not always adhered to.

CHILDREN

Corsica has a relatively low birth rate, but the family is highly valued and young children are often cooed over. There are no particular dangers on the island to watch out for, and there is a wide range of sporting activities to occupy kids on the water, the shore (schools for diving, windsurfing and so on) and in the mountains.

In summer, you should make sure that children are not overexposed to the sun: you should use a high-protection sunscreen and reapply it several times daily, and make sure that they wear a hat. Try to ensure that they drink lots of water as well. The Lonely Planet title *Travel with Children* gives plenty of other tips.

Practicalities

Many hotels provide cots for free and additional beds for children at a small extra cost. Car-hire companies can provide you with child seats for between €15 and €30 per hire period.

Most restaurants will provide high chairs willingly but nappy changing facilities are a rarity outside airports or large museums. Change mats are handy if you have to whip a nappy off on the floor or on a toilet lid, as may be the case! Nappies, formula for babies up to 12 months of age, mineral water and a range of medicines are also readily available at pharmacies. Of course, it's possible (and necessary with the dearth of baby-care facilities) to breastfeed anywhere in public: where and how discreetly you do it is up to your own sensitivity. Discounts for children are common at attractions and toddlers, in general, go free.

Sights & Activities

A trip to the beach is a sure-fire way of entertaining kids of all ages, at least for a few hours; and wherever you are in Corsica, you'll never be far from one. Armed with a picnic, plenty of sun cream, a bucket and spade (and a handful of newspapers) you can all enjoy a cheap, fun, and easy day out. See p16 for a list of the best beaches. Ajaccio, in particular, has plenty of sights and activities to keep children happy, from horse riding or water sports to its planetarium or turtle park. See Ajaccio for Kids (p150) and also Tot's Tour (p16) for ideas on the best activities for children around the island.

CLIMATE CHARTS

The Mediterranean climate, characterised by its summer droughts and abundant sunshine, gives Corsica an average annual temperature of 12°C. The mountains are cooler, however, and the temperature drops significantly as you climb. Snow can be seen above 1600m

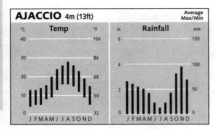

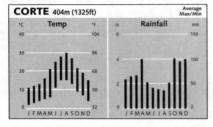

from October to June. This means that some skiing is feasible, but visitors to Corsica are usually sun- rather than snow-seekers.

On average, the island has 2700 hours of sunshine each year. This is one and a half times the sun that Paris sees. Between June and September, average temperatures often exceed 25°C; in July and August temperatures can sizzle above 35°C. According to the French meteorological office in Ajaccio, temperatures climb over 30°C on average 12 days a year in Ajaccio and 32 days in Corte.

Spring and autumn are both fine, with average temperatures of around 15°C and maximum temperatures of around 20°C. Rainfall is highest during the last three months of the year, when there are often severe storms and flooding. In high summer, precipitation is minimal. The mountains often experience severe winters and some of the island's peaks are snowcapped year-round. Corte has, on average, 30 days of frost per year, compared with 11 in Ajaccio and three in Bastia. Corsica's climate is typically slightly warmer in the north than in the south.

The prevailing winds are the dry, gentle *libecci*, especially in Haute-Corse, and the *tramontane*, which comes down from the north in winter. The warm, moisture-bearing *sirocco* occasionally blows up from the south-east. Cap Corse and the Bouches de Bonifacio are the windiest points (in 1965 wind speeds hit 288km/h). See also p9.

CUSTOMS

The following items can be brought into France, hence into Corsica, duty-free from non-EU countries: 200 cigarettes, 50 cigars or 250g of loose tobacco; 1L of strong liquor or 2L of liquor which is less than 22% alcohol by volume; 2L of wine; 500g of coffee or 200g of extracts; 50g of perfume and 0.25L of *eau de toilette*.

Do not confuse duty-free allowances with duty-paid items (including alcohol and tobacco) bought at normal shops and supermarkets in another EU country and brought into France, where certain goods might be more expensive. Then the allowances are more generous: 800 cigarettes, 200 cigars or 1kg of loose tobacco; and 10L of spirits (more than 22% alcohol by volume), 20L of fortified wine or apéritif, 90L of wine or 110L of beer. There are no duty-free shopping facilities in Corsican airports.

Note that your home country may have strict regulations regarding the import of meat, dairy products or plants.

In the unlikely event that you will be arriving on the island by boat from outside the EU – few visitors do – you must present yourself to the port authorities when you disembark. Customs authorities will usually want to board the boat.

DANGERS & ANNOYANCES

When Corsica makes the headlines, it's often because nationalist militants seeking Corsican independence have engaged in some act of violence, such as bombing a public building, robbing a bank or murdering the prefect. But the violence has never been targeted at tourists, and there's no reason for visitors to fear for their safety from this particular quarter.

The main peril in Corsica is the winding roads which follow narrow precipices and the sometimes blind turnings, combined with the impatience of Corsican drivers, and the tendency for livestock and other animals to appear suddenly and without warning in the right of way.

The majority of motor vehicle accidents appear to involve local young people on their way home from clubs in the early morning. Keep your eyes on the road. If you want to admire the scenery, stop at a lay-by. And if you do happen to pass a bunch of stray wild pigs, don't try to feed them or allow children to pet them. They may be cute but they are unpredictable and may bite.

Bring repellent and antihistamine cream with you if you're prone to insect bites, particularly mosquitoes, though both are available from pharmacies there.

DISABLED TRAVELLERS

France and especially Corsica could not be considered progressive in terms of its facilities for disabled people. However, the situation is changing, albeit slowly. Hotels and restaurants are modernising and adding wheelchair-accessible rooms and toilet facilities. The Ajaccio branch of the **Association des Paralysés de France** (☎ /fax 04 95 20 75 33; ave du Maréchal Lyautey, 20090 Ajaccio) publishes the details of places in Corsica (hotels, restaurants, cultural sites and so on) that are accessible to disabled people. These details can also be obtained from Ajaccio's **tourist office** in (☎ 04 95 51 53 03; www.tourisme.fr/ajaccio; 3 blvd du Roi Jérôme).

Airlines ensure that there are no access problems for disabled travellers on aeroplanes or at the airports. The traditional ferries *Napoléon Bonaparte*, *Île-de-Beauté*, *Danièle Casanova*, *Monte d'Oro* and *Paglia Orba* all have some cabins that are accessible to wheelchair users, as do the NGVs (the new high-speed ferries). However, in all cases you must contact the companies in question before travelling; see p235.

The town centres of Bastia, Ajaccio, Bonifacio, Porto Vecchio, Propriano and, to a lesser extent, Sartène are completely accessible, as are most of Corsica's museums.

See the destination chapters for details of wheelchair-accessible hotels, or check out the Association des Paralysés de France (above).

DISCOUNT CARDS
Senior Cards

Senior cards entitling those aged over 60 to 25% discount on train travel in high season or 50% discount in low season are available from **CFC** (☎ 04 95 32 80 60; www.membres.lycos.fr/traincorse/).

Student & Youth cards

A **Carte Jeunes** (☎ 01 43 43 89 97; Minitel 3615 CARTE JEUNES; €12 for one year) is available to anyone under 26 who has been in France for at least six months. It gets you discounts on things like air tickets, car hire, sports events, concerts and movies.

A Carte Zoom (€47), available from train stations, allows you unlimited travel over a week.

Hostel Cards

There is one Hostelling International (HI) *auberge de jeunesse* (youth hostel) in Corsica at Poggio Mezzana, and another non-HI-affiliated youth hostel at Calvi. An HI card is necessary at the Poggio Mezzana hostel. If you don't pick one up at home, you can buy one at official French hostels or buy guest membership for between €7.35 and €12.70 per night. With six stamps you get full membership for a year.

EMBASSIES & CONSULATES
French Embassies & Consulates

Australia Canberra (Embassy ☎ 02-6216 0100; embassy@france.net.au; 6 Perth Ave, Yarralumla, ACT 2600); Melbourne (Consulate ☎ 03-9820 0944/0921; cgmelb@france.net.au; Level 4, 492 St Kilda Rd, Melbourne, VIC 3004); Sydney (Consulate ☎ 02-9262 5779; cgsydney@france.net.au; St Martin's Tower, 31 Market St, Sydney, NSW 2000)

Canada Ottawa (Embassy ☎ 613-789 1795; www.ambafrance-ca.org; 42 Sussex Drive, Ottawa, Ont K1M 2C9); Montreal (Consulate ☎ 514-878 4385;

YOUR OWN EMBASSY

It's important to realise what your embassy can and can't do to help you if you get into trouble. Generally speaking, it won't be much help in emergencies if the trouble you're in is remotely your own fault. Remember that you are bound by the laws of the country you are in. Your embassy will not be sympathetic if you end up in jail after committing a crime locally, even if such actions are legal in your own country.

In genuine emergencies you might get some assistance, but only if other channels have been exhausted. For example, if you need to get home urgently, a free ticket home is exceedingly unlikely – the embassy would expect you to have insurance. If you have all your money and documents stolen, it might assist with getting a new passport, but a loan for onward travel is out of the question.

www.ambafrance-ca.org; 26th fl, 1 place Ville Marie, Montreal, Que H3B 4S3); Toronto (Consulate ☎ 416-925 8041; www.ambafrance-ca.org;130 Bloor St West,Ste 400, Toronto, Ont M5S 1N5)

Germany Berlin (Embassy ☎ 030-206 39000; www .botschaft-frankreich.de; Kochstrasse 6-7, D-10969 Berlin; Consulate ☎ 030-885 90243; www.consulfrance-munich .de; Kurfürstendamm 211, 10719 Berlin); Munich (Consulate ☎ 089-419 4110; www.consulfrance-munich.de; Möhlstrasse 5, D-81675 Munich)

Ireland (Embassy ☎ 01-260 1666; www.ambafrance.ie; 36 Ailesbury Rd, Ballsbridge, Dublin 4)

Italy Rome (Embassy ☎ 06 686 011; france-italia@france -italia.it; Piazza Farnese 67, 00186 Rome; Consulate ☎ 06-6880 6437; www.france-italia.it; Via Giulia 251, 00186 Rome)

Netherlands The Hague (Embassy ☎ 070-312 5800; www .ambafrance.nl; Smidsplein 1, 2514 BT The Hague); Amsterdam (Consulate ☎ 020-530 6969; www.consulfrance -amsterdam.org; Eertse Weteringdwars-straat 107, 1000 HA Amsterdam)

New Zealand (Embassy ☎ 04-384 2555; consul.france@ actrix.gen.nz; 34-42 Manners St, Wellington)

Spain Madrid (Embassy ☎ 91 423 8900; Calle de Salustiano Olozaga 9, 28001 Madrid; Consulate ☎ 91 700 7800; Calle Marqués de la Enseñada 10-3, 28004 Madrid); Barcelona (Consulate ☎ 93 270 3000; Ronda Universitat 22, 08007 Barcelona)

UK London (Embassy ☎ 020-7201 1000; www.amba france.org.uk; 58 Knightsbridge, London SW1X 7JT; Consulate ☎ 020-7838 2000; www.ambafrance.org.uk; 21 Cromwell Rd, London SW7 2EN; Visa section ☎ 020-7838 2051, recorded information 09065 508940; 6A Cromwell Place, London SW7 2EW)

USA Washington (Embassy ☎ 202-944 6000; visas -washington@amb-wash.fr; 4101 Reservoir Rd NW, Washington, DC 20007); New York (Consulate ☎ 212-606 3600; www.consulfrance-newyork.org; 934 Fifth Ave, New York, NY 10021; Visa section ☎ 212-606 3680; visa@france consulatny.org; 10 East 74th St, New York, NY 10021); Los Angeles (Consulate ☎ 310-235 3200, fax 312 0704; 10990 Wilshire Blvd, Los Angeles, CA 90024); other consulates are located in Atlanta, Boston, Chicago, Houston, Miami, New Orleans and San Francisco.

Embassies & Consulates in France

All foreign embassies can be found in Paris, although some countries also have consulates in other major French cities.

Only a few countries, Italy among them, have any kind of diplomatic representation in Corsica. Check with individual offices for opening hours.

Australia (Embassy ☎ 01 40 59 33 00; 4 rue Jean Rey, 15e, Paris)

Canada (Embassy ☎ 01 44 43 29 00; 35 ave Montaigne, 8e, Paris)

Germany (Embassy ☎ 01 53 83 45 00; ambassade@ amb-allemagne.fr; 3-15 ave Franklin D Roosevelt, 8e Paris; Consulate ☎ 01 53 83 45 00; 34 ave d'Iéna, 16e, Paris)

Ireland (Embassy ☎ 01 44 17 67 00, 01 44 17 67 67 after hours; Minitel 3615 IRLANDE; 4 rue Rude, 16e, Paris)

Italy Paris (Embassy ☎ 01 49 54 03 00; 51 rue de Varenne, 7e, Paris; Consulate ☎ 01 44 30 47 00; 5 blvd Émile Augier, 16e, Paris); Bastia (Consulate ☎ 04 95 31 01 52; fax 04 95 32 56 72; rue St-François Prolongée, 20200 Bastia)

Netherlands (Embassy ☎ 01 40 62 33 00; 7 rue Eblé, 7e, Paris)

New Zealand (Embassy ☎ 01 45 01 43 43; 7 ter rue Léonard de Vinci, 16e, Paris)

Spain (Embassy ☎ 01 44 43 18 00; 22 ave Marceau, 8e, Paris)

UK (Embassy ☎ 01 44 51 31 00, 01 42 66 29 79 for emergencies; ambassade@amb-grandebretagne.fr; 35 rue du Faubourg St-Honoré, 8e, Paris; Consulate ☎ 01 44 51 31 02; 8 bis rue d'Anjou, 8e, Paris)

USA (Embassy ☎ 01 43 12 22 22; ambassade@amb-usa .fr; 2 ave Gabriel, 8e, Paris; Consulate ☎ 01 43 12 23 47, 01 43 12 49 48 for emergencies; Minitel 3614 ETATS-UNIS; 2 rue St-Florentin, 1er, Paris)

The following countries are represented on Corsica by honorary consulates:

Belgium & the Netherlands (☎ 04 95 20 89 99; fax 04 95 23 56 44; c/o Air Fret Service, aéroport Campo dell'Oro, 20090 Ajaccio)

Germany (☎ 04 95 33 03 56; RN 193, zone industrielle Furiani, 20600 Bastia)

Switzerland (☎ /fax 04 95 20 80 34; 2 ave Pascal Paoli, 20000 Ajaccio)

FESTIVALS & EVENTS

Corsicans love to celebrate. For local festivals and events, see Festivals & Events in the destination chapters. For food- and drink-related festivals see p70, and for the author's favourite festivals and events see p10. Local tourist offices also have details.

FOOD

Food listings throughout the book appear in order of author preference beginning with budget, mid-range and then top end. This hierarchy is not written in stone, though, because authors, like you readers, can prefer caviar on a Monday and cod and chips on a Friday! The price ranges for an average main course in the budget category is from €3 to €10, mid-range €10 to €20, and top end over €20.

GAY & LESBIAN TRAVELLERS

Contrary to what you might expect, homosexuality does not seem to pose a problem to this conservative and traditional society, in theory at least. When it comes to being 'out' in public, the adage 'out of sight, out of mind' seems to apply. What you do behind closed doors may be perfectly acceptable to most Corsicans but open displays of affection, especially between men, will be frowned upon at the very least. Discretion is advisable. That said, few hoteliers will bat an eyelid if a same sex couple book into a room. There are no openly gay bars in Corsica but you may find information on gay-friendly hotels and businesses, as well as travel information on one of the following websites:

International Gay & Lesbian Travel Organisation (www.iglta.org) Founded in 1983, IGLTA is a worldwide umbrella group for the travel industry.
Gay Friendly France (www.francetourism.com/gayguide) A magazine site featuring gaycentric travel articles and pink pages for France.

HOLIDAYS

The following are public holidays in Corsica, during which most businesses close:

New Year's Day 1 January
Easter Sunday & Monday March or April
Labour Day 1 May
Victoire 1945 (VE) Day 8 May
Ascension 40th day after Easter
Pentecost/Whit Sunday & Monday 8th Sunday & Monday after Easter
Bastille Day 14 July
Assumption Day (Napoleon's birthday) 15 August
All Saints' Day 1 November
Armistice Day 11 November
Christmas 25 December

Corsica tends to get crowded with French families during the French school holidays (the last fortnight of July and August), so if you want to avoid *du monde* you may be better visiting outside this period.

INSURANCE

Travel insurance can protect you against not only emergency medical and repatriation costs, but also forced cancellations, forced curtailments, delays, lost tickets and luggage. Cover depends on your insurance and type of airline ticket.

Remember that airlines will themselves compensate you to a limited extent should *they* be responsible for losing your luggage. Paying for an airline ticket with a credit card will often provide some additional protection; for example, it may make it possible for you to get reimbursed if an operator fails to deliver. In the UK, institutions issuing credit cards are required by law to reimburse consumers if a company goes into liquidation and the amount in dispute is more than UK£100. Credit card issuers may also cover expensive car hire insurance. If you are in doubt as to what your credit card issuer provides, ask.

EU citizens are eligible for free emergency medical treatment if they have an E111 certificate (p243).

INTERNET ACCESS

Corsica is not the most Internet-friendly place – probably due to the lack of international business travel to the island. Aside from those at the top end, hotel rooms are not really geared towards travellers seeking to connect to the Internet and usually don't have the necessary plugs and sockets.

You will have more luck with Internet cafés, however, which are now slowly spreading across the island – perhaps helped by low levels of household computer ownership. Currently, however, cybercafés tend to be found only in bigger towns and resort areas such Calvi, Bastia and Corte. The connection is generally reliable and rates are fairly standard at around €3 per hour.

LEGAL MATTERS

Thanks to the Napoleonic Code (on which the French legal system is based), the police can pretty much search anyone they want to at any time – whether or not there is probable cause. If you are stopped, they will expect you to be carrying your passport.

If asked a question, the police are likely to be correct and helpful but no more than that (though you may get a salute). If the police stop you for any reason, be polite and remain calm. They have wide powers of search and seizure and, if they take a dislike to you, they may well choose to use them.

As elsewhere in the EU, the laws are very tough when it comes to drinking and driving. The acceptable blood-alcohol limit is 0.05%, and drivers exceeding this amount

DIRECTORY

face fines of around €4500, plus several years in jail. Licences can also be immediately suspended. The import or export of drugs can lead to a jail sentence of up to 30 years. The fine for possession of drugs for personal use can be as high as €70,000. The fine for littering starts from about €150.

Eighteen is the legal age for voting, driving and for heterosexual/homosexual sex.

MAPS

The maps available from local tourist offices are extremely poor quality so a good map is an essential before-you-go purchase. The Michelin road map No 90, at a scale of 1:200,000 (1cm = 2km) and the two IGN 'green series' maps (No 73 for the north and No 74 for the south) at a scale of 1:100,000 (1cm = 1km) are excellent for motoring. The AA Road Map France Series 16 is good for an overview.

Travellers intending to do lots of hiking should consult a specialist map retailer before departure. For those planning to walk the GR20 trail, see the map information on p53. Lonely Planet's *Walking in France* is also a useful reference.

MONEY

The euro has now been firmly established across France and, despite some initial reservations, is now the national currency. For information about euro exchange rates, see inside back cover.

For information on costs in Corsica, see p9.

ATMs

Known in French as Distributeurs Automatiques de Billets (DABs) or *points d'argent*, ATMs (Automated Teller Machines) are the easiest way to access funds while in Corsica. Visa, MasterCard and Cirrus are accepted widely. Most of the larger Corsican towns now have an ATM machine and many post offices – even in the country areas – also offer ATM service. However, the ATM is still not nearly as widespread in Corsica as it is in mainland France, and areas such as Cap Corse have only two in the whole region.

Cash

Hard cash, despite its advantages, is generally not a very good way to carry money. Not only can it be stolen, but also in France

you don't get an optimal exchange rate. Nevertheless, it can be a good idea to bring around €100 in low-denomination notes to get you started upon arrival. Travellers will also find it useful to have a ready supply of €1 coins for use in laundrettes, vending machines and parking meters.

Credit Cards

Credit cards will by and large prove the cheapest and easiest way to pay for major purchases in Corsica. On the island, as throughout mainland France, Visa (Carte Bleue) and MasterCard (Eurocard) are the cards most widely accepted by hotels, restaurants and stores, while American Express cards are only recognised in the more upmarket establishments. All three cards can be used to pay for air, train and ferry travel. You may also want to check with your credit card company about charges on international transactions before leaving home.

If your credit card is lost or stolen, call **Carte Bleue** (☎ 02 54 42 12 12), **Eurocard** (☎ 01 45 67 53 53) or **American Express** (☎ 01 47 77 70 00).

Moneychangers

You'll find plenty of banks and *bureaux de change* to change money and travellers cheques in the larger places such as Bastia, Calvi and Corte. You should, in fact, stock up on funds in these places as your chances of changing money are greatly reduced in rural and remote areas. Banks and moneychangers often offer a better rate for travellers cheques than for cash. However, a low exchange rate might not be the bargain it appears if you end up paying a hefty commission.

If you are carrying cash and happen to be passing through mainland France before you get to Corsica, you will do well to change your money there. Paris, in particular, but also the provincial cities, are useful places to find places with the kind of low rates and no-commission deals that you're unlikely to encounter on the island.

Travellers Cheques

If you don't want to carry large amounts of cash, and if plastic isn't the right solution for you either, you may want to carry at least some of your money in the form of euro-denominated travellers cheques.

These are widely accepted and as good as cash in many mid-range to top-end places in the major centres.

Bureaux de change, found in larger Corsican towns, often charge inflated commission so, if your object is to get the best possible rate, you will almost always be better off at a bank. Post offices offer a useful alternative with moderate rates. In more rural areas the post office may be the only place where you can actually cash travellers cheques.

PHOTOGRAPHY

Generally print film is both more widely available and cheaper to develop in Corsica, while both buying and developing slide film is a more expensive and time-consuming business – the film is usually sent off to mainland France for processing. B&W and specialist film is also harder to find and tends to be expensive.

Professional snappers arriving armed with a ready supply of film will not be disappointed: Corsica is exceptionally photogenic. However strong light can present a problem in summer and, as such, it's pointless to use very sensitive film. Film with an ISO rating of 100 will be more than sufficient, and a polarising filter may prove a useful purchase.

Lonely Planet's *Travel Photography: A Guide to Taking Better Pictures*, by acclaimed photographer Richard I'Anson, makes for a useful companion on the road.

There are no major restrictions on photography in Corsica, except in museums and art galleries. Of course, taking snapshots of military installations is not appreciated in any country. And, when photographing people, it is basic courtesy to ask their permission first.

POST

Post offices are widespread across the island and, in some rural hamlets, often provide a community focus as they are housed alongside the *mairie* and the local administrative offices. In addition to providing the customary mail services, some will also send and receive faxes, and offer a photocopying or mail-holding service. Some larger branches also cash travellers cheques and perform other modest banking services. Many village post offices survive either by selling postcards or by doubling as tobacconists. Public telephones are either in or near the post office.

Domestic letters weighing up to 20g cost €0.45; postcards and letters up to 20g cost €0.50 within the EU, €0.90 to most of the rest of the world. Aerograms cost €5.84 to all destinations.

Although now dying out with the introduction of email, poste restante is still available at some larger Corsican post offices. Since poste restante mail is held alphabetically by last name, it is vital that you follow the French practice of having your surname or family name written first and in capital letters. To collect poste restante mail, you'll need your passport or a national ID card. Post is generally kept for about two weeks.

SOLO TRAVELLERS

Generally Corsica is a poor destination choice for solo travellers. The mainstay of the tourist season comprises families or couples so single travellers face not only a feeling of isolation but also hefty single supplements on their room charges. Worse still, some restaurateurs are rather hostile to single diners taking a table with two covers.

For single women the macho nature of Corsican society could be an issue, although physical attacks on women are relatively rare. They could, however, be made to feel very uncomfortable – especially if they stray off the tourist beat into some of the more traditional rural communities. Overall, single females would probably feel more at home and less vulnerable in other Mediterranean destinations.

TELEPHONE

The country code for France is 33 and the international access code is 00. All telephone numbers throughout Corsica consist of eight digits and start with the prefix '04'. If calling Corsica from overseas, you would drop the first '0', that is dial '00 33 4', then six digits. All mobile phone numbers start with the prefix '06'. If calling a Corsican mobile number from overseas, you would drop the first '0', that is dial '00 33 6', then six digits. International Direct Dial (IDD) calls to almost anywhere in the world can be made from public telephones, of which there are a reasonable number on the island. But for most you will need a *télécarte* (phonecard; see p230).

Fax

To send or receive a fax the best option is to pop into the nearest post office. Some *tabacs* also offer a fax service. Expect to pay the usual international rates for faxes, plus some nominal fee for the service.

Mobile Phones

Corsica uses the GSM 900/1800 system for mobile phones, which is compatible with the rest of Europe and Australia but not with the North American GSM 1900 system or the totally different system in Japan. If you have a GSM phone, check with your service provider at home about using your mobile phone in Corsica. Beware in particular of calls being routed internationally – this ends up proving a very expensive way of making a supposedly 'local' call. Ask your service provider about international roaming agreements and the charges involved.

Phonecards

Most public telephones in Corsica require a *télécarte* (telephone card), which can be purchased at post offices, *tabacs*, supermarket check-out counters and anywhere you see a blue sticker reading *télécarte en vente ici*. Cards worth 50/120 units cost €7.50/15.

To make a domestic or international phone call with a *télécarte*, follow the instructions on the LCD display. It should first read *décrochez* (if it says *hors service* it's out of order). If the phone has a button displaying two flags linked with an arrow, push it for the explanations in English. If not, when you see the words *introduire carte ou faire numéro libre* (insert the card or dial a toll-free number), insert the card chip-end first with the rectangle of electrical connectors facing upwards. *Patientez SVP* means 'please wait'.

When the top line of the display tells you your credit available, the bottom line of the LCD screen will read *numérotez* (dial). When you key in the number you're calling it will appear on the display.

After you dial, you will hear a rapid beeping followed by long beeps (it's ringing) or short beeps (it's busy). When your call is connected, the screen begins counting down your card's value. To redial, you may have to pull your card out and reinsert it.

If, for any reason, something goes wrong in the dialling process, you'll be asked to *raccrochez SVP* (please hang up). *Crédit épuisé* means that your card has run out of units.

Lonely Planet's eKno global communication service provides low-cost international calls – for local calls you're usually better off buying a local phonecard from a *tabac*. eKno also offers free messaging services, email, travel information and an online travel vault, where you can securely store your important documents. You can join online at www.ekno.lonelyplanet.com, where you will find the local-access numbers for the 24-hour customer-service centre.

Phone Codes

If you want France Telecom's directory inquiries or assistance service (*service des renseignements*), dial ☎ 12. Don't be surprised if the operator does not speak English. This call is free from public phones.

For directory inquiries concerning subscriber numbers outside France, dial ☎ 00 3312 and finally the relevant country code (11 instead of 1 for the USA and Canada). You often get put on hold for quite a while. In public phones, you can access this service without a *télécarte*, but from home phones there is a charge.

Most of the toll-free 1-800 numbers in the USA and Canada can be called from phones in Corsica, but you will be charged at the same international rates as for any other call.

Two-digit emergency numbers and toll-free numbers (those with 10 digits and beginning '08 00') can be dialled from public telephones without inserting any payment.

TIME

Corsica uses the 24-hour clock, with hours separated from minutes by a lower-case 'h'. Thus, 15h30 is 3.30pm, 21h50 is 9.50pm, 00h30 is 12.30am, and so on.

Corsica is on the same time as the rest of France, that is, on Central European Time which is one hour ahead of (later than) GMT/UTC. During daylight-saving time, which runs from the last Sunday in March to the last Sunday in October, France is two hours ahead of GMT/UTC. Without taking daylight-saving time into account, when it's noon in Paris it's 3am in San Francisco

6am in New York, 11am in London, 8pm in Tokyo, 9pm in Sydney and 11pm in Auckland

TOILETS

Public toilets, signposted *toilettes* or WC, are rare on the island so most people tend to stop at a café, have a quick coffee and then use the toilets on the premises. Simply ask, *Est-ce que je peux utiliser les toilettes, s'il vous plaît?* Generally, toilets are fairly clean and the mechanisms intelligible though, in the more remote areas, you may occasionally encounter a squat toilet, with a high-pressure flushing mechanism that will soak your feet if you don't step back in time.

Frustratingly, travellers often find there are no toilet or washing facilities at beaches, and obviously the more remote the beach the greater the likelihood that there will be no toilet facilities at all. Hikers will find a few chemical toilets near PNRC refuges but none, of course, along the hiking trails. Be prepared to go back to nature at times.

You may find that carrying a small supply of paper tissue or medicated wipes in lieu of toilet paper would be a smart move.

TOURIST INFORMATION

There are generally tourist information offices in most main towns across the island. Increasingly there is also some sort of small tourist information kiosk or centre in the more rural areas. Indeed, new branch offices are opening all the time.

However, on the whole, the standard of service and advice from these centres is, at best, patchy. Some are less than useful, with staff who just dish out brochures and seem to have no grasp of the needs of international travellers. Thankfully there are exceptions to this rule – notably in larger centres such as Bastia and Calvi where staff are generally competent, often speak English and/or Italian, and almost always have good local knowledge.

L'Agence du Tourisme de la Corse (ATC; ☎ 04 95 51 00 00; 17 blvd du Roi Jérôme BP 19, 20180 Ajaccio; www.visit-corsica.com), is the overall body responsible for tourism and the place you should report under-performing tourist information offices in the first instance.

For details of French government tourist offices, usually called *Maisons de la France*, in your home country, see p225.

TOURS

With the rise of the budget airlines, Corsica is slowly – very slowly – starting to emerge as a destination for independent travellers seeking more adventurous trips away from the mass-market package deals that have traditionally dominated the packed Corsican summer season. The following are specialist operators who will assist with arranging adventure-based trips for independent travellers.

In Terra Corsa (p200; ☎ 04 95 47 69 48; www.interra corsa.fr; Ponte-Leccia)

Objectif Nature (p82; ☎ 04 95 32 54 34 or ☎ 06 13 86 47 47; objectif-nature@wanadoo.fr; Bastia)

VISAS

By law, everyone in France, including tourists, must carry some sort of ID on them at all times. For foreign visitors, this means a passport (if you don't want to carry your passport for security reasons a photocopy should do, although you may be required to verify your identity later) or, for citizens of those European Union (EU) countries that issue them, a national ID card.

EU nationals have no entry requirements, and citizens of Australia, the USA, Canada, New Zealand and Israel do not need visas to visit France as tourists for up to three months. Others will need a Schengen visa, named after the Schengen Agreement that abolished passport controls between Austria, Belgium, Denmark, Finland, France, Germany, Greece, Italy, Luxembourg, the Netherlands, Portugal, Spain and Sweden. A visa for any of these countries should, in theory, be valid throughout the area, but it always pays to double-check with the embassy or consulate in the country you intend to visit.

When you apply, you will need your passport (valid for a period of three months beyond the date of your anticipated departure from France), a return ticket, proof of sufficient funds to support yourself, two passport-size photos and the visa fee in cash. You may also be asked for proof of pre-arranged accommodation.

If all the forms are in order, your visa will be issued on the spot at the French consulate closest to you in your home country. You can also apply for a French visa after arriving in Europe – the fee is the same, but you may not have to produce a

DIRECTORY

return ticket. If you enter France overland, your passport may not be checked for a visa at the border, but, if you don't have one, major problems can arise later on (for example, at the airport as you leave the country).

Citizens of EU countries and Switzerland wishing to stay in Corsica for longer than 90 days must apply for a residence permit from the nearest town hall or from the *service des étrangers* (foreigners' department) of the Corsican prefecture. Citizens of Australia, Canada and the USA are limited to two stays of 90 days each per year. Those wishing to extend their stay must apply for an extended residence permit from the French embassy or consulate in their own country.

Non-EU nationals wanting to work or study in France or stay for over three months should apply to their nearest French embassy or consulate for the appropriate *long séjour* (long-stay) visa. Unless you live in the EU, it is extremely difficult to get a visa allowing you to work in France.

For more up-to-date visa information, consult the Lonely Planet website and its hot links.

WOMEN

Corsica has traditionally been a male-dominated society with women allocated the status of wives and mothers. Twentieth century economic change, the influence of modern mass media and the explosive growth of the tourism industry in Corsica have improved the status of women. This is particularly true in the cities but much less so in the villages where the traditional ways still prevail.

Women travelling solo, or with one or more other women, should experience no problems in Corsica, and physical attack is rare. As in any country, however, women should remain conscious of their surroundings and of potentially dangerous situations.

France's national **rape-crisis hotline** (☎ 08 00 05 95 95; ☻ 10am-6pm Mon-Fri) can be reached toll-free from any telephone without using a phonecard. Staffed by volunteers, it is run by a women's organisation called *Viols Femmes Informations*.

In an emergency, you can also call the police ☎ 17.

WORK

The tourist season generates thousands of seasonal jobs in hotels and restaurants catering to visitors. But, given the Lilliputian size of most Corsican enterprises, finding a job isn't easy – especially for outsiders.

To work legally in Corsica you must have a residence permit known as a *carte de séjour*. This is relatively straightforward for EU nationals and almost impossible for anyone else except full-time students. Non-EU nationals cannot work legally unless they also obtain a work permit (*autorisation de travail*) before arriving in France, and then a *carte de séjour* on arrival.

The best option for summer work is to arrange your placement through one of the UK-based tour operators such as **Corsican Places** (☎ 0870 160 7503; www.corsicanplaces.com) or **Explore Worldwide** (☎ 01252 760000; www.explore worldwide.com).

Transport

CONTENTS

Corsica does not lie on any international trunk route, and – unless you're hopping across from one of its eyeballing neighbours (mainland France or Italy) – is not an easy place to get to. But it is precisely this that makes the island so exotically charming.

GETTING THERE & AWAY

AIR
Airports & Airlines
Corsica's main hub is the small but serviceable Ajaccio Campo Dell'Oro airport, which is where the bulk of European scheduled and charter flights land. Bad weather often sees charters destined for the even smaller Calvi Ste-Catherine airport, on the island's northwest coast, diverted to Bastia Poretta on the island's spindly northern leg instead. Figari-Sud airport is the strip to land for Porto Vecchio, Bonifacio and Propriano in southern Corsica.

With the exception of flights to/from mainland France operated by the Corsican home-grown CCM Airlines, Air France and Air Littoral, direct international flights are few and far between. In fact, the only other direct options are aboard a couple of seasonal, budget-airline flights (p234).

> **THINGS CHANGE...**
>
> The information in this chapter is particularly vulnerable to change. Check directly with the airline or a travel agent to make sure you understand how a fare (and ticket you may buy) works and be aware of the security requirements for international travel. Shop carefully. The details given in this chapter should be regarded as pointers and are not a substitute for your own careful, up-to-date research.

Many non-French carriers and budget airlines do fly, however, into Nice and Marseille (mainland France), and into Livorno (Italy), from where ferries sail to Corsica.

Airports serving the region include:

Ajaccio Campo Dell'Oro (code AJA; www.ajaccio.aeroport.fr)
Bastia Poretta (code BIA; www.bastia.aeroport.fr)
Calvi Ste-Catherine (code CLY; www.calvi.aeroport.fr)
Figari Sud Corse (code FSC; www.figari.aeroport.fr)
Genoa Cristoforo Colombo (code GOA; www.airport.genova.it)
Nice Côte d'Azur (code NCE; www.nice.aeroport.fr)
Marseille Provence (code MRS; www.mrsairport.com)
Pisa Galileo Galilei (code PSA; www.pisa-airport.com)

Airlines flying into these airports include:
Air France (code AF; ☎ 08 20 82 08 20; www.airfrance.com; hub Paris)
Air Littoral (code FU; ☎ 08 25 83 48 34; www.airlittoral.com; hubs Nice & Montpellier)
BMI Baby (code CWW; ☎ 08 90 71 00 81; www.bmibaby.com; hub East Midlands)
British Airways (code BA; ☎ 08 25 82 54 00; www.britishairways.com; hub London Heathrow)
CCM Airlines (code CCM; ☎ 08 20 82 08 20; www.ccm-airlines.com; hub Ajaccio)
Crossair (code QE; ☎ 08 20 04 05 06; www.crossair.ch; hub Basel-Mulhouse)
EasyJet (code U2; ☎ 08 25 08 25 08; www.easyjet.com; hub London Stansted)
Germania Express (code ST; ☎ 04 95 54 54 13; www.gexx.de; hub Berlin Tegel)
Luxair (code LG; ☎ 08 20 82 08 20; www.luxair.lu; hub Luxembourg airport)
Ryanair (code FR; ☎ 08 99 70 00 07; www.ryanair.com; hub London Stansted)
Virgin Express (code TV; ☎ 08 00 52 85 28; www.virgin-express.com; hub Brussels)

TRANSPORT

Tickets

Air travel has never been better value – assuming you've researched the options carefully to get the best deal. Full-time students and those aged under 26 (under 30 in some countries) occasionally have access to better deals than other travellers.

One increasingly useful resource for checking fares and buying tickets is the Internet: try the web-based budget carriers which only sell direct to travellers (mainly online), airline websites and the ever-increasing number of online agents, such as www.travelocity.com, www.travelocity.co.uk and www.deckchair.com. Be aware however, especially if you're travelling to Corsica from a considerable distance, that online super-fast fare generators are not necessarily a substitute for an old-fashioned travel agent behind a desk, who can take into account your personal requirements.

Paying by credit card offers protection; most card issuers provide refunds if you can prove you didn't get what you paid for. Similar protection can be obtained by buying a ticket from a bonded agent, such as one covered by the Air Travel Organiser's Licence (ATOL) scheme in the UK.

DEPARTURE TAX

Airport taxes in Corsica vary slightly from airport to airport and can add up to around €35. They are almost always included in the price of an air ticket.

From Australia

STA Travel (☎ 1300 733 035; www.statravel.com.au) and **Flight Centre** (☎ 133 133;www.flightcentre.com.au) have offices countrywide. For online bookings, try www.travel.com.au.

Qantas and Air France fly from Australia to Ajaccio, via Paris, from around A$1670/2300 return in low/high season.

From Continental Europe
ITALY
CTS Viaggi (☎ 06 462 0431; www.cts.it) A recommended student- and youth-travel specialist.

SPAIN
Barcelo Viajes (☎ 902 116 226; www.barceloviajes.com)
Nouvelles Frontières (☎ 90 217 09 79; www.nouvelles-frontieres.es)

GERMANY
Expedia (www.expedia.de)
Just Travel (☎ 089 747 3330; www.justtravel.de)
Lastminute (☎ 01805 284 366; www.lastminute.de)
STA Travel (☎ 01805 456 422; www.statravel.de) For travellers under the age of 26.

MAINLAND FRANCE
Anyway (☎ 08 92 89 38 92; www.anyway.fr)
Lastminute (☎ 08 92 70 50 00; www.lastminute.fr)
OTU Voyages (www.otu.fr) Student and youth specialists.
Voyageurs du Monde (☎ 01 40 15 11 15; www.vdm.com) Student- and youth-travel specialist.

Any continental European carrier – **Lufthansa** (www.lufthansa.com); **KLM** (www.klm.nl); **SAS** (www.scandinavian.net); **CSA Czech Airlines** (www.csa.cz); or **Lot Polish Airlines** (www.lot.com) – will sell you a through ticket to any of the Corsican airports but will make you change planes in mainland France to link up with a flight operated by French national carrier Air France, France's regional Air Littoral, or Corsica's CCM Airlines (Compagnie Corse Méditerranée). The latter three operate direct flights from several airports in France, including Lille, Lyon, Montpellier, Nice and Paris.

Charter flights pop up here and there around mainland Europe between April and October and at Christmas. **Corsair** (www.corsair.fr), a public charter airline operated by France's leading budget-minded travel agency, **Nouvelles Frontières** (☎ 08 25 00 07 47; www.nouvelles-frontieres.fr), operates up to 10 Corsica-bound flights a week from Paris and other French regional airports.

No-frills operator Luxair flies seasonally from between Luxembourg and Brussels to Bastia (once weekly May to September). Germania Express links Berlin-Tegel with Bastia once a week year-round (€88 one way, including taxes). At the time of writing, Crossair was uncertain if it would continue its seasonal service (May to August) between Basel-Mulhouse and Ajaccio Campo Dell'Oro airports.

In addition, budget airline easyJet flies to Nice from Amsterdam, Paris and Geneva; and to Marseille from Paris. Ryanair flies to Pisa from Hamburg, Frankfurt and Brussels; and Virgin Express flies from Brussels to Nice.

From the UK

Discount air travel is big business in London. Advertisements for many travel agencies appear in the travel pages of the weekend broadsheet newspapers, in *Time Out*, the *Evening Standard* and in the free magazine *TNT*.

Recommended travel agencies:

Bridge the World (☎ 0870 444 7474; www.b-t-w.co.uk)
Flightbookers (☎ 0870 010 7000; www.ebookers.com)
Flight Centre (☎ 0870 890 8099; www.flightcentre.co.uk)
North-South Travel (☎ 012-4560 8291; www.north southtravel.co.uk) North-South Travel donate part of their profit to projects in the developing world.
Quest Travel (☎ 0870 442 3542; www.questtravel.com)
STA Travel (☎ 0870 160 0599; www.statravel.co.uk) For travellers under the age of 26.
Trailfinders (www.trailfinders.co.uk)
Travel Bag (☎ 0870 890 1456; www.travelbag.co.uk)

There are no direct scheduled flights to Corsica from the UK – but plenty of charters (May to October) are sold via UK-based operators such as **Corsican Places** (☎ 0870 160 5744; www.corsica.co.uk), **VFB Holidays** (☎ 01242-240 340; www.vfbholidays.co.uk) and **Voyages Ilena** (☎ 020-7924 4440; www.voyagesilena.co.uk). Most strive to sell charters as part of a package with accommodation, although **Holiday Options** (☎ 0870 013 1450; www.holidayoptions.co.uk) and **Simply Corsica** (☎ 020-8541 2205; www.simply-travel.com) sell flights only to/from regional airports such as Birmingham, Newcastle, Edinburgh and Manchester; they sell flights only from London as well.

A sensible, cost-effective alternative from the UK is to fly as far as Nice, Marseille, Genoa or Pisa (Livorno) and catch a ferry for the last leg. British Airways flies to all four port cities from London; and there's a rapidly multiplying rash of cheaper airline routes to pick from: non-frilly Ryanair flies to/from London Stansted and Genoa; BMI Baby flies from East Midlands to Nice and Pisa; and easyJet flies to Marseille and Nice from London Gatwick, and to Nice from Liverpool, Luton and London Stansted as well as Gatwick.

From the USA

The North Atlantic is the world's busiest long-haul air corridor and the flight options are bewildering. Flights from the USA to Corsica require a change of aircraft in Paris. Discount travel agencies in the USA are known as consolidators (although you won't see a sign on the door saying 'Consolidator'). San Francisco is the ticket consolidator capital of America, although some good deals can be found in Los Angeles, New York and other big cities. The following agencies are recommended for online bookings:

American Express Travel (www.itn.net)
Cheap Tickets (www.cheaptickets.com)
Expedia (www.expedia.com)
Lowestfare.com (www.lowestfare.com)
Orbitz (www.orbitz.com)
STA Travel (www.sta.com) For travellers under the age of 26.
Travelocity (www.travelocity.com)

SEA

Approaching Corsica by sea is an experience. Whether you do it aboard a nippy NGV (*navire à grande vitesse*; high-speed vessel) or a romantic, slow ferry, afloat a luxury palace or a private yacht, any sea voyage instantly reveals just how remote and isolated from the continent the island really is.

Ferry

By sea, Corsica can be reached from the ports of Nice, Marseille and Toulon in mainland France; and from Genoa, Livorno, Savona and Piombino in Italy. Ferries also link Corsica with the Italian island of Sardinia.

Advance reservations are essential in high season, especially for motorists planning to take a vehicle. Students under 27, seniors aged over 60 and families get reduced rates with most ferry companies; children aged four to 12 years usually pay 50% or two-thirds of an adult fare, and children aged under four sail for free. Taking a bicycle on board costs around €3 one way.

FROM MAINLAND FRANCE

Nice, Marseille and Toulon are linked year-round by ferry to Corsica

In high season, SNCM operates at least one speedy NGV (from Nice) and slower ferry (from Marseille) a day to/from the island ports of Ajaccio, Bastia, Calvi, Île Rousse, Porto Vecchio and Propriano; and a couple of overnight ferries a month in July and August to/from Toulon and Propriano. In winter, services are reduced to just a handful of weekly sailings to/from Nice and Marseille.

Corsica Ferries serves fewer island ports, but sails year-round to/from Nice and Toulon. La Méridionale likewise provides

FERRY 'CROSS THE MED

A plethora of vessels plough the Mediterranean at a variety of speeds between mainland France and Italy, Corsica and Sardinia. Most ferry companies are geared up to accept online reservations and ticket bookings – if you can fathom the often highly convoluted websites they tout. Attempt to secure detailed information from them in any way other than over the Internet and you risk high telephone charges, not to mention acute frustration as you sit on hold for a good 15 minutes or so.

Société Nationale Corse Méditerranéenne
(SNCM; France ☎ 08 91 70 18 01, Italy ☎ 02 66 117 104, UK ☎ 020-749 14 968; www.sncm.fr) This is the largest of the five Corsica-bound carriers. It sails year-round from Marseille and Nice to Ajaccio, Bastia, Calvi, Île Rousse, Porto Vecchio and Propriano and return; and between Toulon and Propriano in July and August.

La Méridionale (CMN; France ☎ 08 10 20 13 20; www.cmn.fr) This SNCM subsidiary has year-round sailings from Marseille to Ajaccio, Bastia and Propriano and return; and seasonal ferries (April to October) from Porto Terres (Sardinia) to Propriano and Ajaccio and return.

Corsica Ferries (France ☎ 08 25 09 50 95, Italy: Livorno ☎ 0586 88 13 80, Savona ☎ 019 215 62 47; www.corsicaferries.com) Year-round ferries from Nice to Ajaccio, Bastia, Calvi and Île Rousse, and from Toulon to Ajaccio and Bastia; and seasonal ferries from Livorno to Bastia (April to early November) and from Savona to Bastia, Calvi and Île Rousse (April to September).

Moby Lines (Corsica ☎ 04 95 34 84 94, Italy: Genoa ☎ 010 254 15 13, Livorno ☎ 0565 93 61; www.mobylines.it) Seasonal ferries (May to September) operate from Genoa and Livorno to Bastia and return. Seasonal boats (April to September) also operate between Santa Teresa di Gallura (Sardinia) and Bonifacio.

Saremar (Corsica ☎ 04 95 73 00 96, Sardinia ☎ 0565 90 89 33; www.traghettiservice.com /saremar) Sardinia's public ferry line has seasonal daily sailings between Bonifacio and Santa Teresa di Gallura, April to September.

a year-round service from its Marseille hub. For routings see the boxed text on the left.

From Nice (the closest French port to Corsica), you can nip across by NGV to Calvi or Île Rousse in three hours. Nice–Bastia and Nice–Ajaccio both take 3½ hours (six to nine hours by ferry); while La Méridionale's three ferry routes (Marseille to Ajaccio/Bastia/Propriano) are 12-hour night crossings.

Single SNCM fares from Nice/Marseille or Toulon to any island port range from €30/35 (low season) to €41/53 (high season), plus upwards of €5/8/28 for a reclining chair/bed/cabin; while transporting a car one way costs €40 to €100 depending on the season. La Méridionale and Corsica Ferries charge equally competitive fares.

Quoted fares do not include port tax – count on an additional €5 per passenger levied by the mainland French port, €3 to €6 per passenger for its Corsican counterpart, plus around €5 to €10 per vehicle.

FROM ITALY

Between April and October, scheduled ferry boats link Corsica with the Italian mainland ports of Genoa, Livorno and Savona, and Porto Terres on neighbouring Sardinia. The season is a tad shorter for smaller boats that yo-yo between Bonifacio and Santa Teresa di Gallura on Sardinia.

Corsica Ferries and Moby Lines are the main operators on these routes; see the boxed text on left for exact routings. From Livorno (near Pisa and Florence) it's a two-hour voyage to Bastia; a Propriano–Porto Terres trip takes 3½ hours; Genoa–Bastia 6½ hours; and Savona to Bastia/Calvi takes six/eight hours.

Fares from mainland Italy are lower than from mainland France. Corsica Ferries charges €40 to €110 to transport a small car one way and upwards of €16/23 per person (up to €33/33 in high season) on a day/night crossing from Savona to Bastia, Calvi or Île Rousse. Passengers sailing with La Méridionale to Ajaccio or Propriano from Porto Terres pay €19, plus €35 for a car.

For port taxes, add about €6 per passenger and €5 per car.

Yacht

Corsica sports some 16 pleasure ports (*ports de plaisance*) and is a yachters' paradise.

BY LAND & SEA FROM THE UK

Corsica is a hop across the Channel, a skip (albeit it a mighty big one) over mainland France and a jump across the Med for Brits with time and a sense of adventure on their hands.

The die-hardy can bus it to Bastia with London-based **Busabout** (☎ 020-7950 1661; www.busabout.com), which does a couple of loops around mainland France before ending up in Nice, from where you can buy a Corsica add-on (UK£45 return) to get across to Bastia. The latter fare is on top of a basic Busabout Pass which is UK£219/359 for two weeks/one month and allows you to get on and off at designated pick-up points. You also need to count an extra UK£40 for the return Channel crossing.

An equally time-consuming (read: 23-hour) alternative is to bus it with **National Express** (☎ 0870 580 8080; www.nationalexpress.com) from London to Nice (via Lyon; UK£105 return) then pick up a Corsica-bound ferry independently.

Travellers able to plan their journey well in advance would do just as well to travel by train: 2nd-class London–Nice or London–Marseille return fares with a change of train (from the cross-Channel **Eurostar** (☎ 0870 518 6186; www.eurostar.com) to a high-speed French TGV (www.tgv.com) in Paris or Lille start at UK£109. Tickets are non-refundable and non-changeable, and can be booked up to 60 days in advance through **Rail Europe** (☎ 0870 584 8848; www.raileurope.com).

Rail enthusiasts with a penchant for experiencing (rather than vaporising) distance can alternatively ride a regular British train to Dover or Folkstone, take a cheap ferry across the Channel to the French mainland ports of Calais or Boulogne respectively, then connect with the French rail network to reach Nice or Marseille ports. Longer channel crossings (with less competitive fares) include Newhaven–Dieppe, Poole–Cherbourg, and Portsmouth–Cherbourg/Le Havre/Ouistreham/St-Malo. Ferries are run by several cross-Channel ferry companies; updated schedules and fares can be found on the web. Motorists can cross the Channel by ferry, or aboard a high-speed **Eurotunnel** (☎ 0870 535 3535; www.eurotunnel.com) train which takes 35 minutes.

Crossing mainland France by train is pure joy (compared to British rail travel). Super-sleek **TGVs** (www.tgv.com) purr along at a whirlwind 310km/h, serving a highly efficient network operated by the state-owned **SNCF** (Société Nationale des Chemins de Fer; ☎ 08 36 35 35 39; www.sncf.com). Ticket reservations can be made in France by telephone, Internet or at any SNCF train station. Marseille is three hours from Paris.

Yachts can be hired with or without a crew at most marinas along the coast; the various tourist offices have lists.

Up-to-date marina and harbour master information is available from the **Fédération Française des Ports de Plaisance** (FFPP; www.ffports-plaisance.com, French only). Follow the 'Ports de Plaisance Corses' link online to get a full listing of Corsican ports.

GETTING AROUND

AIR
Corsica may well sport a handful of civilian airports, but scheduled commercial flights between any two of them remains a pipe dream.

BICYCLE
Corsica, with its dramatic mountain passes and its stunning coast, is superb cycling terrain – for experienced cyclists. For those less accustomed to forging up hills and power-peddling along gravel tracks, the island's mountainous terrain and stifling summer heat can prove too mind- (not to mention muscle-) blowing.

Those fit or foolish enough to brave the island by bike should do so in spring and autumn. Cyclists keen to see Corsica's mountainous interior usually begin by taking the train to Corte or some other starting point high in the mountains. (See p242 for information on travelling by train with your bike.)

By law, bicycles must have two functioning brakes, a bell, a red reflector on the back and yellow reflectors on the pedals. After sunset and when visibility is poor, road cyclists must turn on a white light in front and a red one in the rear. Marked cycling lanes (on roads) or trails (for mountain bikers) are practically nonexistent across the island. Cycling in the Parc Régional Naturel de Corse is not forbidden, but there are no trails suitable for cyclists.

Hire

Mountain-bike (*vélo tout-terrain*; VTT) hire is widespread and costs around €5/15 per hour/day. Most outlets require a deposit (cash, signed travellers cheques or credit card) of anything from €30 to €150 which you forfeit if the bike is damaged or stolen. Rental shops are listed under Getting Around in the Ajaccio, Bastia, Porto, Porticcio, Propriano, Porto Vecchio, Bonifacio, Levie and Golfe de Santa Manza sections of this guide. Several places listed arrange guides, plan itineraries and run biking tours. For an online listing of 40-odd bicycle rental outlets island-wide, follow the Transport/Getting Around link at www.visit-corsica.com.

Bike Organisations

The volunteer-run **Fédération Française de Cyclotourisme** (FFCT; www.ffct.org) liaises between 3100-odd cycling clubs in mainland France and Corsica, and can send you a free information pack in English. It also sells touring itineraries, cycling maps and topo guides for cyclists, and organises bicycle trips, tours and races – including Corsica's legendary **Tour de Corse Cycliste**, a four-day, 400km race in May that has sped around the island since 1920. There's also the family-orientated **Corsica Bik'Up**, which sees mountain bikers (from kids to pensioners) mount up for fun in late March, and the **Six Jours Cyclotouristes de l'Île de Beauté**, a six-day event aimed at uncovering the island's beauty spots by pedal power.

For its members, the UK-based **Cyclists' Touring Club** (CTC; ☎ 0870 873 0060; www.ctc.org.uk) publishes a free information sheet on cycling in France, as well as touring notes and itineraries for several routes in Corsica. The CTC also offers tips on bikes, spares and insurance; it sells maps and topoguides by mail order.

BOAT

There is no scheduled commercial boat service between any two Corsican ports. This said, you could try to persuade one of the tour-boat companies making daily excursions from one Corsican town to another and back to sell you a one-way ticket. You might also be able to persuade them to allow you to go out one day and back another but don't expect bargains. Sailors with their own boats can find information about harbour facilities in Getting There & Away under individual coastal towns.

Tourist boats ply the waters between Calvi and Girolata, Calvi and Ajaccio, Ajaccio and Bonifacio and Bonifacio and Porto Vecchio.

BUS

Travelling by bus requires superhuman time and patience. Corsica's major towns and many of the little ones in between are linked by bus, as are the airports with town centres, but in remoter areas services are scarce, infuriatingly erratic or – quite simply – nonexistent.

Bus services are geared to local inhabitants rather than tourists, meaning services are least frequent during the height of the tourist season when school children are on holiday. In July and August there is often only one departure a day on what appears to be a major trunk route and no departure at all on Sunday and public holidays. Secondary routes often only have service on alternate days or once or twice a week. Many passenger routes year-round are combined with school and/or postal services.

Those with even the slightest desire to get off-the-beaten track can forget travelling by bus. Those that stay on the main tourist trails, and want to travel by bus, should build their itinerary around bus-route maps and schedules; following your own priorities will only court frustration.

Autocars (regional buses) are operated by a muddling host of different bus companies, the odd one of whom might have an office at the bus station (*gare routière*) of the towns they serve. Often one company sells tickets for all the bus companies operating from the same station, although passengers, as a rule, do not need to worry about buying tickets in advance. You can buy your ticket on any particular route, or leg of a route, from the driver – fares average around €13 per 100km. Minibuses serve many bus routes. Tourist-targeted bus passes do not exist.

The island's two main towns, Ajaccio and Bastia, have the largest bus stations. In smaller places, where a bus stop can constitute a 'station', bus schedules are invariably pinned up in the window of the local tourist office. Bus stations do not have left-luggage facilities.

Primary bus routes and companies include:

Autocars Cortenais (☎ 04 95 46 02 12) Bastia–Corte, Porto Vecchio–Bonifacio.

Autocars Ricci (☎ 04 95 76 25 59) Ajaccio–Propriano–Sartène–Levie–Zonza–Bavella; Ajaccio–Tiuccia–Sagone–Cargèse–Piana–Porto–Ota; Ajaccio–Porto Pollo.

Autocars SAIB (☎ 04 95 22 41 99; www.imperialtours-corsica.com) Ajaccio–Porto–Ota; Ajaccio–Cargèse; Bastia–Ponte Leccia–Île Rousse–Algajola–Calvi.

Autocars Santoni (☎ 04 95 22 64 44; www.autocars-santoni.com) Ajaccio–Zicavo.

Eurocorse Voyages (☎ 04 95 71 24 64; www.eurocorse.com) Ajaccio-Propriano-Porto Vecchio-Bonifacio; Ajaccio-Corte-Bastia; Ajaccio-Sartène-Zonza.

Les Beaux Voyages (☎ 04 95 65 15 02/11 35; www.lesbeauxvoyages.com) Bastia–Calvi; Bastia–Aléria–Ghisonaccia–Solenzara–Porto Vecchio; Calvi–Galéria; Calvi–Porto via Col de la Croix.

Les Rapides Bleus (☎ 04 95 31 03 79) Bastia–Porto Vecchio; Bastia–Canari.

See the Getting There & Away sections of the respective regional chapters for detailed schedules, bus frequencies and fares.

CAR & MOTORCYCLE

No other form of transport gives those wanting to dip deep into the island's secret backwaters as much freedom as a set of motorised wheels. Little beats cruising along the island's beautiful and dramatic roads – the D81 linking Calvi and Porto, the D84 between Porto and Francardo (via Évisa, the Forêt d'Aïtone and the Scala di Santa Regina), and the D69 from just below Vivario to Ghisoni, to name but a few memorable drives – in a car, aboard an open-top 4WD or on the back of scooter.

Exhilarating views aside, motoring around Corsica can be hair-raising. Roads are narrow; hairpin bends (lacets) are torturous and blind; and rocky outcrops often prevent you spotting oncoming traffic (or the menagerie of livestock that frequents mountain roads) until it's bang on top of you, or you're on top of it. Use your horn to announce your presence. Drops either side of the road may be sheer and guard rails are usually nonexistent. To top it off, hot-blooded Corsican drivers are not the most courteous of motorists.

Corsica has no motorway (autoroute). The largest roads are routes nationals, such as the N198 which skirts the flat eastern coast from Bastia to Bonifacio, or the rickety old N193 which makes a mockery of the distance and dramatic relief between Bastia, Corte and Ajaccio. Routes départementales, whose names begin with the letter D, are tertiary local roads, invariably pot-holed and far from silky smooth. Routes communales, whose names begin with the letter C (or nothing at all), are rural roads best suited to off-road vehicles and mountain bikes.

Corsican towns are small by any standard and were not designed with cars in mind, making parking an expensive, time-consuming nightmare. Défense de stationer means 'No Parking'.

Michelin's Corsica sheet map No 90 (scale 1:200,000) is indispensable. For suggested driving itineraries, see the full-colour gatefold map at the start of this guide.

Bring Your Own Vehicle

While there is no bridge between the continent and Corsica, the fleet of car ferries operating between French and Italian ports make bringing your own vehicle onto the island a doddle. A right-hand drive vehicle brought to France from the UK or Ireland must have deflectors affixed to the headlights to avoid dazzling oncoming traffic.

By law, motorists (those driving their own car or a rented vehicle) need to carry a national ID card or passport; a valid driving permit or licence (permis de conduire); car ownership papers, known as a carte grise (grey card); and proof of insurance, called a carte verte (green card). If you're stopped by the police and don't have one or more of these documents, you risk a hefty on-the-spot fine. Never leave your car ownership or insurance papers in the vehicle.

By law, a reflective warning triangle, to be used in the event of breakdown, must be carried in your car. Recommended accessories include a first-aid kit, spare bulb kit and fire extinguisher. In the UK, the **RAC** (☎ 0870 010 6382; www.rac.co.uk) or the **AA** (☎ 0870 600 0371; www.theaa.com) can give you more advice.

TRANSPORT

If you're involved in a minor accident with no injuries, the easiest way for drivers to sort things out with their insurance companies is to fill out a *Constat Aimable d'Accident Automobile* (jointly agreed accident report), known in English as a European Accident Statement. Make sure the report includes any details that will help you prove that the accident was not your fault. If problems arise, alert the police.

Petrol *(essence)*, also called *carburant* (fuel), costs around €1.10 per litre (unleaded, 95 or 98 octane). Outside main towns, petrol stations are few and far between, and carrying a spare can of petrol is not a bad idea.

Rental

Cars can be rented upon arrival in Corsica, be it at an airport or in town. Most companies require the driver to be at least 21 years old (23 for some categories of car) and have had a driving licence for at least one year.

Although multinational rental agencies such as Avis, Budget, Hertz and Europcar (Europe's largest) can be expensive for on-the-spot rental, their prepaid promotional rates are usually reasonable. Fly-drive deals offered by Avis and Europcar are also worth looking into. For quick, walk-in rental, domestic firms such as ADA sometimes offer better rates. In Ajaccio, a couple of local firms rent cars and 4WD vehicles at extremely competitive rates; see p154. All major firms have a desk at the airports in Corsica. Most companies charge an airport pick-up or drop-off surcharge of around €20.

Most companies require a credit card, primarily so that you can leave a deposit *(caution)*. Most ask you to leave a signed credit card slip without a sum written on it as a deposit. If you don't like this arrangement, ask them to make out two credit card slips: one for the sum of the rental; the other for the sum of the excess. Make sure to have the latter destroyed when you return the car.

Insurance *(assurance)* for damage or injury you cause to other people is mandatory, but collision damage waivers vary. If you're in an accident where you are at fault, or the car is damaged and the party at fault is unknown (eg, someone dents your car while it's parked), or the car is stolen, the *franchise* (excess/deductible) is the amount you are liable for before the policy kicks in. When signing the rental agreement, you can agree to pay an extra daily fee (anything from to €15 to €50 per day) to reduce the excess (usually €350 to €800 depending on the vehicle size) to either zero or a minimal amount.

The packet of documents you are given when hiring a car includes a 24-hour number to call in case of a breakdown and a European Accident Statement (see the previous section). Check how many 'free' kilometres are in the deal you're offered; *kilométrage illimité* (unlimited mileage) means you can drive to your heart's content.

To rent a scooter or *moto* (motorcycle), you must likewise leave a deposit (of several hundred euro) which you forfeit (up to the value of the damage) if you're in an accident and it's your fault. Since insurance companies won't cover theft, you'll also lose the deposit if the bike is stolen. Expect to pay about €60/350 per day/week for a 125cc motorbike. Rates usually include helmet hire.

A complete list of car- and motorcycle-rental companies is online at www.visit-corsica.com. Local rental outlets are listed under Getting Around in the regional chapters.

Off-roaders can rent a 4WD in Ajaccio (see p154) and there are a couple of companies in Propriano that organise motorcycling tours. Mainstream contacts include:

Ada (Ajaccio-Campo dell'Oro airport ☎ 04 95 23 56 57, Bastia-Poretta airport ☎ 04 95 54 55 44; www.ada-location.com)

Avis (Ajaccio-Campo dell'Oro airport ☎ 04 95 23 56 90, Bastia-Poretta airport ☎ 04 95 54 55 46; www.avis.fr)

Budget (Ajaccio-Campo dell'Oro airport ☎ 04 95 23 57 21, Bastia-Poretta airport ☎ 04 95 30 05 05; www.budget-en-corse.com)

Europcar (Ajaccio-Campo dell'Oro airport ☎ 04 95 23 57 01, Bastia-Poretta airport ☎ 04 95 30 09 50; www.europcar.fr)

Hertz (Ajaccio-Campo dell'Oro airport ☎ 04 95 23 57 04, Bastia-Poretta airport ☎ 04 95 30 05 00; www.hertz.fr)

National-Citer (☎ 04 95 51 21 21; www.corse-auto-rent.fr)

Sixt (Ajaccio-Campo dell'Oro airport ☎ 04 95 23 57 00, Bastia-Poretta airport ☎ 04 95 54 54 70; www.sixt.fr)

Road Rules

In Corsica, as throughout continental Europe, people drive on the right side of the road and overtake on the left. Unless otherwise indicated, you must give way to cars coming from the right. North American drivers should remember that turning right on a red light is illegal.

A speed limit of 50km/h applies in built-up areas; on intercity roads you must slow to 50km/h the moment you pass a white sign with red borders on which a place name is written in black or blue letters. This limit remains in force until you arrive at the other edge of town, where you'll pass an identical sign with a red diagonal bar across the name.

Outside built-up areas, speed limits are 90km/h (80km/h if it's raining) on single carriageway N and D roads and 110km/h (100km/h if it's raining) on dual carriageways. You are nevertheless more likely in Corsica to fall short of the speed limit than to exceed it. Local drivers will consequently close to within a few metres of your rear bumper, flash their lights impatiently and try to rile you – don't let them.

French law is tough on drunk drivers and police conduct random breathalyser tests to weed out drivers whose blood-alcohol concentration (BAC) is over 0.05% (0.50g per litre of blood) – two glasses of wine for a 75kg adult. Licences can be suspended.

Helmets *(casques)* are compulsory for motorcyclists and moped riders. Bikes of more than 125cc must have their headlights on during the day. No special licence is required to ride a scooter with an engine capacity of 50cc or less.

HITCHING

Hitching is never entirely safe in any country in the world, and we don't recommend it. Travellers who decide to hitch should understand that they are taking a small but potentially serious risk. People who do choose to hitch will be safer if they travel in pairs and let someone know where they are planning to go.

The student-inspired **Ecotrajet** (www.ecotrajet .com) puts people looking for rides in touch with drivers going to the same destination: There are no cover charges; you simply split the cost of the trip with the driver and other passengers.

LOCAL TRANSPORT

Most Corsican towns are small enough to get around on foot. Ajaccio and Bastia, the island's two largest towns, both have local bus services. Elsewhere, you may find yourself to some degree dependent on taxis, and if you're on your own, taxis can be expensive. Approximate fares are given in the destination chapters, as are prices for short tours for which you might want to hire a taxi.

Taxis in Corsica have a 'Taxi' sign on the roof; the cars can be any colour. Look for details of taxi companies in Getting Around under individual towns.

TRAIN

Travelling by train in Corsica – a thrilling experience – is way more than a means of getting from A to B. Dubbed *U tringhellu* (literally 'the trembler' by local Corsicans), the 110-seat mountain train trundles along a remarkable railway line constructed in the 1880s and 1890s. With 38 tunnels (the longest is 4km), 34 viaducts and 12 bridges (one designed by Gustave Eiffel no less), it represents one of the great triumphs of man over topography and ranks among the world's great scenic railways.

The network, operated by **Chemins de Fer de la Corse** (CFC; Bastia ☎ 04 95 32 80 61, Corte ☎ 04 95 23 11 03, Ajaccio ☎ 04 95 32 80 57, Calvi ☎ 04 95 65 00 61; www.ter-sncf.com/corse), is limited in the destinations it serves. The principal north–south line runs between Bastia and Ajaccio. From the Ponte Leccia junction between Bastia and Corte, a spur runs to the Balagne towns of Île Rousse and Calvi. In days of old, a third line used to connect Bastia and Porto Vecchio along the flat east coast of the island. But it was badly damaged in German bombing raids in 1943, and for all the talk over the years of restoring it, no one has yet lifted a hammer.

Travelling by train is slower than a bus ride – a factor not helped by the occasional wild goat that wanders on the track, prompting the mountain train to lurch (endearingly so) to a standstill. Trains tout no classes, and advance ticket reservations simply don't exist.

At the train station *(gare),* you can get updated train timetables and information, or alternatively check the website (see above). Left-luggage facilities do not exist at any station.

The train routes are as follows:

Bastia–Ponte Leccia–Corte-Ajaccio – Corsica's primary north–south rail route, with dozens of stops in smaller stations, including Furiani, Biguglia, Casamozza, Ponte Nuovo, Francardo, Vénaco, Vivario, Vizzavona and Bocognano. Trains run year-round in either direction four times daily. It takes four hours to travel the length of the line from Bastia to Ajaccio.

Bastia–Casamozza – Up to 12 trains daily shunt the 30-minute journey from Bastia to Casamoza, stopping approximately every two minutes at every conceivable local station along the way; no Sunday service.

Bastia–Ponte Leccia–Calvi – Corsica's east–west link, this line follows the Bastia–Ajaccio line south to Ponte Leccia then it lurches west towards the coast, stopping en route in Île Rousse. There are two trains daily in summer, otherwise change trains in Ponte Leccia or Île Rousse.

Île Rousse–Calvi (Tramway de la Balagne) – On the same right of way that the CFC uses, these little two-car trains shuttle back and forth all day long, April to October, on the 45-minute stretch of coast between Calvi and Île Rousse. Approximately 20 intermediate stops include Lumio, Sant'Ambrogio, Algajola and Davia. Wherever you happen to be along the line, a train will pass in each direction approximately once an hour.

Costs

Train fares are reasonable, clocking in at around €15 per 100km. Children aged under four travel for free and those aged four to 12 years pay 50% of the adult fare.

In July and August travellers making a return journey of 200km in one or two consecutive days can buy a *billet touristique* for 25% less than the normal fare. Groups of more than 10 people are eligible for a 20% discount on all routes between June and September, and a discount of 30% the rest of the year.

Cyclists can take their bicycles aboard for a €12.50 fee, but be warned – there is only space for four or five bikes on each train, and places cannot be reserved in advance.

GREAT GREEN RAIL ESCAPE

In July and August green-fingered railway buffs can ride the mountain railway as far as Vizzavona (2¾ hours from Bastia, one hour from Ajaccio) then delve deep into the heart of the Forêt de Vizzavona – a fairytale forest of beech and laricio pines – with the help of an experienced guide from the Office National des Forêts (ONF; National Forestry Office).

The two-hour forest discovery walk leads nature lovers to the Cascade des Anglais, impressive winter-time waterfalls which melt into a picture-postcard set of serene pools (to swim in) in summer. The GR20 links the latter with Vizzavona train station.

Tickets covering the return train trip and forest guide cost €45/33 from Bastia/Ajaccio and are available from CFC train stations. The ONF office (☎ 04 95 32 81 90) in Bastia also has details.

Train Passes

Senior travellers holding a one-year **Carte Sénior** issued by the French national rail line, the SNCF, can use it on CFC trains to get a 50% reduction. SNCF's **Carte Famille Nombreuse**, which gives families with three or four children aged under 18 discounts of at least 30%, is likewise valid in Corsica. More information on both annual travel passes is online at www.sncf.com.

In addition, the CFC sells its own rail pass, the **Carte Zoom**, valid for seven consecutive days of unlimited travel throughout the CFC network. It costs €47 and is sold at any CFC station.

None of the major European rail passes – InterRail, Eurail, Eurorail or even the France Railpass – provides for unlimited free travel on the CFC system. The major rail passes do, however, yield a 50% discount on CFC fares between Bastia and Ajaccio (but not on the Tramway de la Balagne between Calvi and Île Rousse).

Health

CONTENTS

Good health during your travels depends on your pre-departure preparations, your daily health care while travelling and how you handle any medical problems that do develop. Corsica is a healthy place to travel. Hygiene standards are high and there are no unusual diseases to worry about.

BEFORE YOU GO

Prevention is the key to staying healthy while abroad. A little planning before departure, particularly for pre-existing illnesses, will save trouble later: see your dentist before a long trip; carry a spare pair of contact lenses and glasses, and take your optical prescription with you. Bring medications in their original, clearly labelled, containers. A signed and dated letter from your physician describing your medical conditions and medications, including generic names, is also a good idea. If carrying syringes or needles, be sure to have a physician's letter documenting their medical necessity.

INSURANCE

If you're an EU citizen, an E111 form, available from health centres or, in the UK, post offices, covers you for most medical care. E111 will not cover you for non-emergencies or emergency repatriation home. Citizens from other countries should find out if there is a reciprocal arrangement for free medical care between their country and the country visited. If you do need health insurance, make sure you get a policy that covers you for the worst possible scenario, such as an accident requiring an emergency flight home. Find out in advance if your insurance plan will make payments directly to providers or reimburse you later for overseas health expenditures. Note that some policies require the holder to carry an E111 form if they are an EU citizen.

RECOMMENDED VACCINATIONS

The World Health Organisation (WHO) recommends that all travellers should be covered for diphtheria, tetanus, measles, mumps, rubella and polio, as well as Hepatitis B, regardless of their destination. Since most vaccines don't produce immunity until at least two weeks after they're given, visit a physician at least six weeks before departure.

ONLINE RESOURCES

The WHO publication *International Travel and Health* is revised annually and is available online at www.who.int/ith/. Other useful websites include www.mdtravelhealth.com (travel health recommendations for every country; updated daily), www.fitfortravel .scot.nhs.uk (general travel advice for the layman), www.ageconcern.org.uk (advice on travel for the elderly) and www.marie stopes.org.uk (information on women's health and contraception).

IN TRANSIT

DEEP VEIN THROMBOSIS (DVT)

Blood clots may form in the legs during plane flights, chiefly because of prolonged immobility. The longer the flight, the greater the risk. The chief symptom of DVT is swelling or pain of the foot, ankle or calf, usually but not always on just one side. When a blood clot travels to the lungs, it may cause chest pain and breathing difficulties. Travellers with any of these symptoms should seek medical attention immediately.

To prevent the development of DVT on long flights you should walk about the cabin, contract the leg muscles while sitting, drink plenty of fluids and avoid alcohol and tobacco.

IN CORSICA

AVAILABILITY & COST OF HEALTH CARE

Good health care is readily available in Corsica, and for minor self-limiting illnesses pharmacists (*pharmaciens*) can give valuable advice and sell over-the-counter medication. They can also advise when more specialised help is required and point you in the right direction. In major towns you are likely to find English-speaking doctors or a translator service available. The standard of dental care is usually good, however it is sensible to have a dental check-up before a long trip.

TRAVELLER'S DIARRHOEA

If you develop diarrhoea, be sure to drink plenty of fluids, preferably an oral rehydration solution eg dioralyte. A few loose stools don't require treatment but, if you start having more than four or five stools a day, you should start taking an antibiotic (usually a quinolone drug) and an anti-diarrhoeal agent (such as loperamide). If diarrhoea is bloody, persists for more than 72 hours or is accompanied by fever, shaking, chills or severe abdominal pain you should seek medical attention.

ENVIRONMENTAL HAZARDS
Bites & Stings

Jellyfish stings are generally just rather painful. Antihistamines and analgesics may reduce the reaction and relieve the pain. Scorpion fish and weevers can also sting if you touch them; although the stings are not serious, you many need to see a doctor. There are no poisonous snakes on Corsica.

Decompression Sickness

Corsica is perfect for two activities that should *not* be tried on the same day: diving and mountain walking. Always avoid climbing at altitude straight after diving; this will allow your body to get rid of the residual nitrogen that it has stored up. Climbing as little as 1500m can prove dangerous if you have been diving only a few hours earlier, and so can air travel. As a rule of thumb, wait at least 12 hours after resurfacing for either.

The **Ajaccio hospital** (☎ 04 95 29 90 90; 27 ave de l'Impératrice Eugénie) has a decompression chamber.

Heatstroke

Heat exhaustion occurs following excessive fluid loss with inadequate replacement of fluids and salt. Symptoms include headache, dizziness and tiredness. Dehydration is already happening by the time you feel thirsty – aim to drink sufficient water to produce pale, diluted urine. To treat heat exhaustion, replace fluids with water and/or fruit juice, and cool the body with cold water and fans. Treat salt loss with salty fluids such as soup or Bovril, or add a little more table salt to foods than usual.

Heatstroke is much more serious, resulting in irrational and hyperactive behaviour and eventually loss of consciousness and death. Rapid cooling by spraying the body with water and fanning is ideal. Emergency fluid and electrolyte replacement by intravenous drip is recommended.

Hypothermia

Proper preparation will reduce the risks of getting hypothermia. Even on a hot day in the centre of Corsica, the weather can change rapidly – carry waterproof garments, warm layers and inform others of your route.

Acute hypothermia follows a sudden drop of temperature over a short period of time. Chronic hypothermia is caused by a gradual loss of temperature over hours.

Hypothermia starts with shivering, loss of judgment and clumsiness. Unless rewarming occurs, the sufferer deteriorates into apathy, confusion and coma. Prevent further heat loss by seeking shelter, warm dry clothing, hot sweet drinks and shared bodily warmth.

Water

Tap water in Corsica is safe to drink. However, the water in most fountains is not drinkable and, like the taps in some public toilets, may have a sign reading *eau non potable* (undrinkable water).

Many people to not hesitate to drink water from streams during their walks. However, given all the free-ranging livestock and other animals, this water is not necessarily safe.

TRAVELLING WITH CHILDREN

All travellers with children should know how to treat minor ailments and when to seek medical treatment. Make sure the children are up to date with routine vaccinations, and discuss possible travel vaccines well before departure as some vaccines are not suitable for children under 12 months old. Lonely Planet's *Travel with Children* includes advice on travel health for younger children.

WOMEN'S HEALTH

Emotional stress, exhaustion and travelling through different time zones can all contribute to an upset in the menstrual pattern. If using oral contraceptives, remember some antibiotics, diarrhoea and vomiting can stop the pill from working and lead to the risk of pregnancy – remember to take condoms with you just in case. Time zones, gastrointestinal upsets and antibiotics do not affect injectable contraception.

Travelling during pregnancy is usually possible but always consult your doctor before planning your trip. The most risky times for travel are during the first 12 weeks of pregnancy and after 30 weeks.

HEALTH

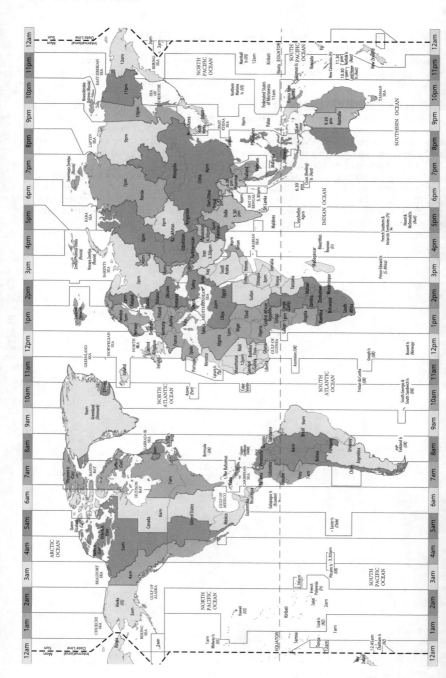

Language

CONTENTS

French is Corsica's official and working language and the language in which Corsicans express themselves most of the time. Corsica is nevertheless impressively bilingual and even trilingual. Many older Corsicans, and even some younger ones, express themselves quite eloquently in Corsican (*Corsu*) and even in Italian – not that the differences between the two are all that vast.

Spontaneous use of Corsican by the native inhabitants has been on the decline, but it has benefited from various forms of life support. It's now even part of the curriculum for the primary and secondary schools on the island. This is a significant turnaround from the days when signs posted in Corsican village schools read: *Il est interdit de cracher par terre et de parler corse* (No spitting on the floor and no talking in Corsican). Young people can, moreover, now study Corsican at the university in Corte. Politicians have seen to it that Corsican enjoys equal status with French on road signs, although the French will often have been edited out with spray paint or bullets!

For more information on Corsican, see the 'Corsican' boxed text on the following page. For a more comprehensive guide to the French language, pick up a copy of Lonely Planet's *French phrasebook*.

FRENCH

PRONUNCIATION

Most letters in French are pronounced more or less the same as their English counterparts. Here are a few that may cause confusion:

j	as the 's' in 'leisure', eg *jour* (day)
c	before **e** and **i**, as the 's' in 'sit'; before **a**, **o** and **u** it's pronounced as English 'k'. When undescored with a 'cedilla' (**ç**) it's always pronounced as the 's' in 'sit'.
r	pronounced from the back of the throat while constricting the muscles to restrict the flow of air
n, m	where a syllable ends in a single **n** or **m**, these letters are not pronounced, but the vowel is given a nasal pronunciation

BE POLITE!

An important distinction is made in French between *tu* and *vous*, which both mean 'you'; *tu* is only used when addressing people you know well, children or animals. If you're addressing an adult who isn't a personal friend, *vous* should be used unless the person invites you to use *tu*. In general, younger people insist less on this distinction between polite and informal, and you will find that in many cases they use *tu* from the beginning of an acquaintance.

GENDER

All nouns in French are either masculine or feminine and adjectives reflect the gender of the noun they modify. The feminine form of many nouns and adjectives is indicated by a silent **e** added to the masculine form, as in *ami* and *amie* (the masculine and feminine for 'friend').

In the following phrases both masculine and feminine forms have been indicated where necessary. The masculine form comes first and is separated from the feminine by a slash. The gender of a noun is often indicated by a preceding article: 'the/a/some', *le/un/du* (m), *la/une/de la* (f); or one of the

CORSICAN

'Good day' in the Corsican language is *bunghjornu*. 'Thank you' is *grazie*. Bread is *pane*. Dog is *cane*. 'Best wishes!' is *pace i salute*! If this all sounds suspiciously like Italian to you, you're not off the mark. The Corsican language – Corsu in Corsican – is descended from, and still related to the Tuscan language that formed the basis of standard Italian. If you think Corsican is Italian or a dialect of Italian, you might nevertheless do well to keep this view to yourself. Though Corsicans are too good-natured to want to punish innocent foreigners for the hasty conclusions they draw on only partial evidence, many Corsicans are committed to the view that Corsican is not a dialect, and still less Italian itself, but a distinct language.

It's not recommended that you make any effort to communicate with Corsicans in Corsican. As Alexandra Jaffe says in her excellent *Ideologies in Action: Language Politics in Corsica*, Corsican is the language of the Corsican heart and hearth. French 'commands the domain of the formal, the authoritative, the instrumental and intellectual'. You may think you are being ingratiating if you attempt a few words of Corsican. More likely, however, you'll be perceived as patronising or condescending, as if the person you are addressing didn't speak French perfectly well. You may be perceived to be baiting the person you are addressing on what is in Corsica a heavily charged political issue. Finally, again Corsican being the language of the Corsican heart and hearth, you may be perceived as intruding on personal and private space – as if, invited into a stranger's living room, you proceeded immediately into their bedroom. Another way to put it is that presuming to address a stranger in Corsican is akin to the liberty you take in addressing a stranger in the familiar pan-Mediterranean 'tu' form rather than in the more respectful 'vous', 'lei' or 'usted' form.

If you speak French or Italian, stick with that. Dedicated Corsophiles can enrol in language courses at the Università di Corsica Pasqual Paoli in Corte or those offered by the association Esse (☎ 04 95 33 12 00) in Bastia.

possessive adjectives, 'my/your/his/her', *mon/ton/son* (m), *ma/ta/sa* (f). With French, unlike English, the possessive adjective agrees in number and gender with the thing in question: 'his/her mother', *sa mère*.

ACCOMMODATION

I'm looking for a ...	Je cherche ...	zher shersh ...
campground	un camping	un kom·peeng
guesthouse	une pension (de famille)	ewn pon·syon (der fa·mee·ler)
hotel	un hôtel	un o·tel
youth hostel	une auberge de jeunesse	ewn o·berzh der zher·nes

Where is a cheap hotel?
Où est-ce qu'on peut trouver un hôtel pas cher?
oo es·kon per troo·vay un o·tel pa shair

What is the address?
Quelle est l'adresse?
kel e la·dres

Could you write it down, please?
Est-ce que vous pourriez l'écrire, s'il vous plaît?
e·sker voo poo·ryay lay·kreer seel voo play

Do you have any rooms available?
Est-ce que vous avez des chambres libres?
e·sker voo·za·vay day shom·brer lee·brer

I'd like (a) ...	Je voudrais ...	zher voo·dray ...
single room	une chambre à un lit	ewn shom·brer a un lee
double-bed room	une chambre avec un grand lit	ewn shom·brer a·vek un gron lee
twin room with two beds	une chambre avec des lits jumeaux	ewn shom·brer a·vek day lee zhew·mo
room with a bathroom	une chambre avec une salle de bains	ewn shom·brer a·vek ewn sal der bun
to share a dorm	coucher dans un dortoir	koo·sher don zun dor·twa

How much is it ...?	Quel est le prix ...?	kel e ler pree ...
per night	par nuit	par nwee
per person	par personne	par per·son

May I see it?
Est-ce que je peux voir la chambre?
es·ker zher per vwa la shom·brer

Where is the bathroom?
Où est la salle de bains? oo e la sal der bun

Where is the toilet?
Où sont les toilettes? oo·son lay twa·let

I'm leaving today.
Je pars aujourd'hui. zher par o·zhoor·dwee

We're leaving today.
Nous partons aujourd'hui. — noo par·ton o·zhoor·dwee

MAKING A RESERVATION

(for phone or written requests)

To ...	*A l'attention de ...*
From ...	*De la part de ...*
Date	*Date*
I'd like to book ...	*Je voudrais réserver ...* (see the list under 'Accommodation' for bed and room options)
in the name of ...	*au nom de ...*
from ... (date) **to ...**	*du ... au ...*
credit card	*carte de crédit*
number	*numéro*
expiry date	*date d'expiration*
Please confirm availability and price.	*Veuillez confirmer la disponibilité et le prix.*

CONVERSATION & ESSENTIALS

Hello.	*Bonjour.*	bon·zhoor
Goodbye.	*Au revoir.*	o·rer·vwa
Yes.	*Oui.*	wee
No.	*Non.*	no
Please.	*S'il vous plaît.*	seel voo play
Thank you.	*Merci.*	mair·see
You're welcome.	*Je vous en prie.*	zher voo·zon pree
	De rien. (inf)	der ree·en
Excuse me.	*Excuse-moi.*	ek·skew·zay·mwa
Sorry. (forgive me)	*Pardon.*	par·don

What's your name?
Comment vous appelez-vous? (pol) — ko·mon voo·za·pay·lay voo
Comment tu t'appelles? (inf) — ko·mon tew ta·pel

My name is ...
Je m'appelle ... — zher ma·pel ...

Where are you from?
De quel pays êtes-vous? — der kel pay·ee et·voo
De quel pays es-tu? (inf) — der kel pay·ee e·tew

I'm from ...
Je viens de ... — zher vyen der ...

I like ...
J'aime ... — zhem ...

I don't like ...
Je n'aime pas ... — zher nem pa ...

Just a minute.
Une minute. — ewn mee·newt

DIRECTIONS

Where is ...?
Où est ...? — oo e ...

Go straight ahead.
Continuez tout droit. — kon·teen·way too drwa

Turn left.
Tournez à gauche. — toor·nay a gosh

Turn right.
Tournez à droite. — toor·nay a drwa

at the corner
au coin — o kwun

at the traffic lights
aux feux — o fer

SIGNS

Entrée	Entrance
Sortie	Exit
Renseignements	Information
Ouvert	Open
Fermé	Closed
Interdit	Prohibited
Chambres Libres	Rooms Available
Complet	Full/No Vacancies
(Commissariat de) Police	Police Station
Toilettes/WC	Toilets
Hommes	Men
Femmes	Women

behind	*derrière*	dair·ryair
in front of	*devant*	der·von
far (from)	*loin (de)*	lwun (der)
near (to)	*près (de)*	pray (der)
opposite	*en face de*	on fas der
beach	*la plage*	la plazh
bridge	*le pont*	ler pon
castle	*le château*	ler sha·to
cathedral	*la cathédrale*	la ka·tay·dral
church	*l'église*	lay·gleez
island	*l'île*	leel
lake	*le lac*	ler lak
main square	*la place centrale*	la plas son·tral
museum	*le musée*	ler mew·zay
old city (town)	*la vieille ville*	la vyay veel
palace	*le palais*	ler pa·lay
quay	*le quai*	ler kay
riverbank	*la rive*	la reev
ruins	*les ruines*	lay rween
sea	*la mer*	la mair
square	*la place*	la plas
tourist office	*l'office de tourisme*	lo·fees der too·rees·mer
tower	*la tour*	la toor

EMERGENCIES

Help!
Au secours! o skoor
There's been an accident!
Il y a eu un accident! eel ya ew un ak·see·don
I'm lost.
Je me suis égaré/e. (m/f) zhe me swee·zay·ga·ray
Leave me alone!
Fichez-moi la paix! fee·shay·mwa la pay

Call ...! *Appelez ...!* a·play ...
  a doctor *un médecin* un mayd·sun
  the police *la police* la po·lees

HEALTH

I'm ill.	*Je suis malade.*	zher swee ma·lad
It hurts here.	*J'ai une douleur ici.*	zhay ewn doo·ler ee·see
I'm ...	*Je suis ...*	zher swee ...
asthmatic	*asthmatique*	(z)as·ma·teek
diabetic	*diabétique*	dee·a·bay·teek
epileptic	*épileptique*	(z)ay·pee·lep·teek
I'm allergic	*Je suis*	zher swee
to ...	*allergique ...*	za·lair·zheek ...
antibiotics	*aux antibiotiques*	o zon·tee·byo·teek
aspirin	*à l'aspirine*	a las·pee·reen
bees	*aux abeilles*	o za·bay·yer
nuts	*aux noix*	o nwa
peanuts	*aux cacahuètes*	o ka·ka·wet
penicillin	*à la pénicilline*	a la pay·nee·see·leen
antiseptic	*l'antiseptique*	lon·tee·sep·teek
aspirin	*l'aspirine*	las·pee·reen
condoms	*des préservatifs*	day pray·zair·va·teef
contraceptive	*le contraceptif*	ler kon·tra·sep·teef
diarrhoea	*la diarrhée*	la dya·ray
medicine	*le médicament*	ler may·dee·ka·mon
nausea	*la nausée*	la no·zay
sunblock cream	*la crème solaire*	la krem so·lair
tampons	*des tampons hygiéniques*	day tom·pon ee·zhen·eek

LANGUAGE DIFFICULTIES

Do you speak English?
Parlez-vous anglais? par·lay·voo ong·lay
Does anyone here speak English?
Y a-t-il quelqu'un qui parle anglais? ya·teel kel·kung kee par long·glay
How do you say ... in French?
Comment est-ce qu'on dit ... en français? ko·mon es·kon dee ... on fron·say

What does ... mean?
Que veut dire ...? ker ver deer ...
I understand.
Je comprends. zher kom·pron
I don't understand.
Je ne comprends pas. zher ner kom·pron pa
Could you write it down, please?
Est-ce que vous pouvez l'écrire? es·ker voo poo·vay lay·kreer
Can you show me (on the map)?
Pouvez-vous m'indiquer (sur la carte)? poo·vay·voo mun·dee·kay (sewr la kart)

NUMBERS

0	*zero*	zay·ro
1	*un*	un
2	*deux*	der
3	*trois*	trwa
4	*quatre*	ka·trer
5	*cinq*	sungk
6	*six*	sees
7	*sept*	set
8	*huit*	weet
9	*neuf*	nerf
10	*dix*	dees
11	*onze*	onz
12	*douze*	dooz
13	*treize*	trez
14	*quatorze*	ka·torz
15	*quinze*	kunz
16	*seize*	sez
17	*dix-sept*	dee·set
18	*dix-huit*	dee·zweet
19	*dix-neuf*	deez·nerf
20	*vingt*	vung
21	*vingt et un*	vung tay un
22	*vingt-deux*	vung·der
30	*trente*	tront
40	*quarante*	ka·ront
50	*cinquante*	sung·kont
60	*soixante*	swa·sont
70	*soixante-dix*	swa·son·dees
80	*quatre-vingts*	ka·trer·vung
90	*quatre-vingt-dix*	ka·trer·vung·dees
100	*cent*	son
1000	*mille*	meel

PAPERWORK

name	*nom*	nom
nationality	*nationalité*	na·syo·na·lee·tay
date/place	*date/place*	dat/plas
of birth	*de naissance*	der nay·sons
sex/gender	*sexe*	seks
passport	*passeport*	pas·por
visa	*visa*	vee·za

QUESTION WORDS

Who?	*Qui?*	kee
What?	*Quoi?*	kwa
What is it?	*Qu'est-ce que c'est?*	kes·ker say
When?	*Quand?*	kon
Where?	*Où?*	oo
Which?	*Quel/Quelle?*	kel
Why?	*Pourquoi?*	poor·kwa
How?	*Comment?*	ko·mon

SHOPPING & SERVICES

I'd like to buy ...
Je voudrais acheter ... zher voo·dray ash·tay ...
How much is it?
C'est combien? say kom·byun
I don't like it.
Cela ne me plaît pas. ser·la ner mer play pa
May I look at it?
Est-ce que je peux le voir? es·ker zher per ler vwar
I'm just looking.
Je regarde. zher rer·gard
It's cheap.
Ce n'est pas cher. ser nay pa shair
It's too expensive.
C'est trop cher. say tro shair
I'll take it.
Je le prends. zher ler pron

Can I pay by ...?	*Est-ce que je peux payer avec ...?*	es·ker zher per pay·yay a·vek ...
credit card	*ma carte de crédit*	ma kart der kray·dee
travellers cheques	*des chèques de voyage*	day shek der vwa·yazh

more	*plus*	plew
less	*moins*	mwa
smaller	*plus petit*	plew per·tee
bigger	*plus grand*	plew gron

I'm looking for ...	*Je cherche ...*	zhe shersh ...
a bank	*une banque*	ewn bonk
the ... embassy	*l'ambassade de ...*	lam·ba·sahd der ...
the hospital	*l'hôpital*	lo·pee·tal
the market	*le marché*	ler mar·shay
the police	*la police*	la po·lees
the post office	*le bureau de poste*	ler bew·ro der post
a public phone	*une cabine téléphonique*	ewn ka·been tay·lay·fo·neek
a public toilet	*les toilettes*	lay twa·let
the telephone centre	*la centrale téléphonique*	la san·tral tay·lay·fo·neek

TIME & DATES

What time is it?	*Quelle heure est-il?*	kel er e til
It's (8) o'clock.	*Il est (huit) heures.*	il e (weet) er
It's half past ...	*Il est (...) heures et demie.*	il e (...) er e day·mee
in the morning	*du matin*	dew ma·tun
in the afternoon	*de l'après-midi*	der la·pray·mee·dee
in the evening	*du soir*	dew swar
today	*aujourd'hui*	o·zhoor·dwee
tomorrow	*demain*	der·mun
yesterday	*hier*	yair

Monday	*lundi*	lun·dee
Tuesday	*mardi*	mar·dee
Wednesday	*mercredi*	mair·krer·dee
Thursday	*jeudi*	zher·dee
Friday	*vendredi*	von·drer·dee
Saturday	*samedi*	sam·dee
Sunday	*dimanche*	dee·monsh

January	*janvier*	zhon·vyay
February	*février*	fayv·ryay
March	*mars*	mars
April	*avril*	a·vreel
May	*mai*	may
June	*juin*	zhwun
July	*juillet*	zhwee·yay
August	*août*	oot
September	*septembre*	sep·tom·brer
October	*octobre*	ok·to·brer
November	*novembre*	no·vom·brer
December	*décembre*	day·som·brer

TRANSPORT
Public Transport

What time does ... leave/arrive?	*À quelle heure part/arrive ...?*	a kel er par/a·reev ...
boat	*le bateau*	ler ba·to
bus	*le bus*	ler bews
plane	*l'avion*	la·vyon
train	*le train*	ler trun

I'd like a ... ticket.	*Je voudrais un billet ...*	zher voo·dray un bee·yay ...
one-way	*simple*	sum·pler
return	*aller et retour*	a·lay ay rer·toor
1st class	*de première classe*	der prem·yair klas
2nd class	*de deuxième classe*	der der·zyem klas

I want to go to ...
Je voudrais aller à ... zher voo·dray a·lay a ...
The train has been delayed.
Le train est en retard. ler trun et on rer·tar
The train has been cancelled.
Le train a été annulé. ler trun a ay·tay a·new·lay

LANGUAGE

the first	*le premier* (m)	ler prer·myay
	la première (f)	la prer·myair
the last	*le dernier* (m)	ler dair·nyay
	la dernière (f)	la dair·nyair
platform number	*le numéro de quai*	ler new·may·ro der kay
ticket office	*le guichet*	ler gee·shay
timetable	*l'horaire*	lo·rair
train station	*la gare*	la gar

Private Transport

I'd like to hire a/an...	*Je voudrais louer ...*	zher voo·dray loo·way ...
car	*une voiture*	ewn vwa·tewr
4WD	*un quatre-quatre*	un kat·kat
motorbike	*une moto*	ewn mo·to
bicycle	*un vélo*	un vay·lo

Is this the road to ...?
C'est la route pour ...? say la root poor ...
Where's a service station?
Où est-ce qu'il y a une station-service? oo es·keel ya ewn sta·syon·ser·vees
Please fill it up.
Le plein, s'il vous plaît. ler plun seel voo play
I'd like ... litres.
Je voudrais ... litres. zher voo·dray ... lee·trer

petrol/gas	*essence*	ay·sons
unleaded	*sans plomb*	son plom
leaded	*au plomb*	o plom
diesel	*diesel*	dyay·zel

(How long) Can I park here?
(Combien de temps) Est-ce que je peux stationner ici? (kom·byun der tom) es·ker zher per sta·syo·nay ee·see?
Where do I pay?
Où est-ce que je paie? oo es·ker zher pay?
I need a mechanic.
J'ai besoin d'un mécanicien. zhay ber·zwun dun may·ka·nee·syun
The car/motorbike has broken down (at ...)
La voiture moto est tombée en panne (à ...) la vwa·tewr/mo·to ay tom·bay on pan (a ...)
The car/motorbike won't start.
La voiture/moto ne veut pas démarrer. la vwa·tewr/mo·to ner ver pa day·ma·ray
I have a flat tyre.
Mon pneu est à plat. mom pner ay ta pla
I've run out of petrol.
Je suis en panne d'essence. zher swee zon pan day·sons
I had an accident.
J'ai eu un accident. zhay ew un ak·see·don

ROAD SIGNS

Cédez la Priorité	Give Way
Danger	Danger
Défense de Stationner	No Parking
Entrée	Entrance
Interdiction de Doubler	No Overtaking
Péage	Toll
Ralentissez	Slow Down
Sens Interdit	No Entry
Sens unique	One-way
Sortie	Exit

TRAVEL WITH CHILDREN

Is there a/an ...? *Y a-t-il ...?* ya teel ...
I need a/an ... *J'ai besoin ...* zhay ber·zwun ...

baby change room	*d'un endroit pour changer le bébé*	dun on·drwa poor shon·zhay ler bay·bay
car baby seat	*d'un siège-enfant*	dun syezh·on·fon
child-minding service	*d'une garderie*	dewn gar·dree
children's menu	*d'un menu pour enfant*	dun mer·new poor on·fon
disposable nappies/diapers	*de couches-culottes*	der koosh·kew·lot
formula	*de lait maternisé*	de lay ma·ter·nee·zay
(English-speaking) babysitter	*d'une baby-sitter (qui parle anglais)*	dewn ba·bee·see·ter (kee parl ong·glay)
highchair	*d'une chaise haute*	dewn shay zot
potty	*d'un pot de bébé*	dun po der bay·bay
stroller	*d'une poussette*	dewn poo·set

Do you mind if I breastfeed here?
Cela vous dérange si j'allaite mon bébé ici? ser·la voo day·ron·zhe see zha·lay·ter mon bay·bay ee·see
Are children allowed?
Les enfants sont permis? lay zon·fon son pair·mee

Also available from Lonely Planet
French phrasebook

Glossary

French (F) Corsican (C)

A

AGENC – Agence pour la Gestion des Espaces Naturels de Corse; Office for the Management of the Natural Areas of Corsica

aiguille (F) – rock mass or mountain peak shaped like a needle

anse (F) – cove

AOC – *Appellation d'Origine Contrôlée*, mark of quality for wines and cheeses

ATM – automated teller machine; cashpoint

auberge (F) – inn

auberge de jeunesse (F) – youth hostel

B

baie (F) – bay

bain (F) – bath

barrage (F) – dam

bastiglia (C) – fortress

bergerie (F) – shepherd's hut, often used as accommodation for walkers

bocca (C) – mountain pass

bouches (F) – straits

brèche (F) – breach, gap

brocciu/bruccio (C) – Corsican goat or ewe's milk cheese

bruschetta – toasted bread rubbed with garlic and topped with any of a number of salads, roasted vegetables or other treats

C

calanques (F)/calanche (C) – rocky inlets

cap (F)/capu/capo (C) – cape

carrefour (F) – crossroads, intersection

cascade (F) – waterfall

casgili (C) – cheese cellar

castagnu (C) – chestnut

castellu, castelli pl **(C)** – castle

chapelle (F) – chapel

charcuterie (F) – cooked pork meats

cignale (C) – wild boar

cirque (F) – a semicircular or crescent-shaped basin with steep sides and a gently sloping floor, formed by the erosive action of ice

clos (F) – vineyard

col (F) – mountain pass

commune (F) – smallest unit of local government in rural areas/districts

Conseil Général (F) – General Council; implements legislation at local level

Conservatoire du Littoral (F) – Conservatoire de l'Espace Littoral et des Rivages Lacustres; Organisation for the Conservation of Coastal Areas and Lakeshores

Corse (F), Corsu (C) – Corsican language

couloir (F) – deep gully on a mountain side

couvent (F) – convent

crête (F) – ridge

D

défilé (F) – gorge, narrow pass

démaquisage (F) – scrub clearance

département (F) – unit of French regional administration

désert (F) – desert

dolmen – megalithic standing stones capped by a horizontal stone, thought to be tombs

domaine (F) – estate, especially one that produces wine

E

écobuage (F) – cultivation on burnt stubble

église (F) – church

étang (F) – lake, pond

F

fiadone (C) – flan made with *brocciu*, lemon and eggs

figatellu (C) – type of liver sausage

FLNC – Front de Libération Nationale de la Corse; Corsican National Liberation Front

fola (C) – folk tale

forêt (F) – forest

G

gîte d'étape (F) – mountain lodge, more comfortable than the basic *refuge*

golfe (F) – bay, gulf

goulet (F) – narrows; bottleneck at entrance to a harbour

H

half-board – bed, breakfast and one main meal

I

île (F) – isle, island

L

lac (F) – lake

laricio – type of pine native to Corsica

lauze (F) – type of stone found only in the area around Bastia

libeccio – southwesterly wind

M
mairie (F) – town hall
maison (F) – office, house
magmatic rock – igneous rock, including granite, formed by magma rising within the earth's crust, which slowly crystallised as it rose
maquis (F) – scrub vegetation
marché (F) – market
menhir – single standing stone, often carved, dating from the megalithic era
mouflon (F) – wild sheep native to Corsica

N
névé (F) – mass of porous ice; also known as a firn

O
ONF – Office National des Forêts; National Office for Forests
optimiste (F) – coracle

P
panini – filled bread rolls
phare (F) – lighthouse
pieve (C) – small region; parish
pinzuti (C) – settlers from the French mainland
place (F) – square
plage (F) – beach
plongée (F) – diving
PNRC – Parc Naturel Régional de Corse; Corsican Nature Reserve
pointe (F)/punta (C) – point; headland
port de plaisance (F) – marina

pozzi (C) – pits
pozzines (C) – interlinked water holes
préfecture (F) – unit of regional administration in France
priorité à droite (F) – give way to the right
prisuttu (C) – Corsican raw ham

R
randonnée (F) – walk
refuge (F) – mountain accommodation, from a basic hut to a simple hostel

S
sanglier (C) – wild boar
Saracen – Moor; Moorish
sec (F) – shallow (diving); dry (climate, wine, etc)
Sécurité Civile (F) – civil defence department
sémaphore (F) – coastal signal station
Shardanes – 'sea people'; ancient nautical race
son et lumière (F) – night-time presentation at a historic site using lighting, sound effects and narration
source (F) – spring

T
tafoni/taffoni (C) – cavities (geology)
torre (C) – circular stone formation or tower; plural *torri*
Torréens – invaders who conquered Corsica around 1100 BC; possibly the Shardanes
tour (F) – tower

V
vallée (F) – valley
vendetta – blood feud

Behind the Scenes

THIS BOOK

This is the 3rd edition of Lonely Planet's *Corsica*. The 1st French-language edition of *Corse* was written by Olivier Cirendini, Jean-Bernard Carillet, Christophe Corbel, Laurence Billiet and Tony Wheeler, and was translated into English as *Corsica* by Atlas Translations in London. The 2nd edition of *Corse* was updated by Olivier and Julien Fouin. The 2nd English-language version was revised and updated by Mark Zussman. This 3rd edition was revised and updated independently of the French-language edition.

The Health chapter is based on text by Dr Caroline Evans. The GR20 chapter was updated by Adrienne Costanzo using material written by Olivier Cirendini and Arno Lebonnois from the 3rd edition of *Corse*.

THANKS FROM THE AUTHORS

Oda O'Carroll Many thanks to Stephanie Coralie at the Cargèse tourist office and the ever-efficient Jean-Phillipe di Grazia at the Ajaccio tourist office, to all the readers who sent in observations and notes from the last edition, to Peter Souter whose love of the island rubbed off, to Jackie Burke and to Corsica-savvied Emma and Francois Lamotte, Celine Cazali, Sevérine Breton and Anna and Laurent Koenig who recommended some top places to visit. Thanks to Etain O'Carroll for the great feedback, my co-authors David and Nicola for the support and to Heather and Sam in the LP London office for all their patience, support and good humour. Thanks to Ashling for keeping the kids at bay and to Eoin, Esa and Mella for all their patience, love and laughs. But final thanks go especially to my sister Lisa, orienteering expert, in-car DJ, confidante and tour manager, who made this so enjoyable.

David Atkinson Thanks: Sharon McManus and Jacques Bellais in Torra, William Keyser in Calvi, Beate Kiehn in Calacuccia, Mat McCann and Fran Hughes of Explore Worldwide, Claire Hall and Nicola Ball of Corsican Places and Sarah Donnelly of VFB.

CREDITS

This title was commissioned and developed in Lonely Planet's London office by Sam Trafford & Heather Dickson. Cartography for this guide was developed by Mark Griffiths. Overseeing production were Ray Thomson (Project Manager) and Kyla Gillzan (Editorial House Style Coordinator). Thanks to the cartographic team, Celia Wood (coordinator), Herman So, Jacqui Saunders, Chris Lee Ack, Chris Tsismetzis, Marion Byass, Karen Fry; to the editors and proof-readers who helped EdInk, including Miriam Cannell, Alexandra Payne, Felicity Shay, Barry Werd and Kate Church; and to Max McMaster for creating the index. Quentin Frayne prepared the language chapter. Maria Vallianous designed the cover. Thanks to P.A.G.E. people, Jenni Quinn and Peter Dyson, who laid the book out and made everything fit on the page.

Thanks also to Yvonne Byron, Julie Sheridan, Vicki Beale, Mark Griffiths, Anthony Phelan, Adriana

THE LONELY PLANET STORY

The story begins with a classic travel adventure: Tony and Maureen Wheeler's 1972 journey across Europe and Asia to Australia. There was no useful information about the overland trail then, so Tony and Maureen published the first Lonely Planet guidebook to meet a growing need.

From a kitchen table, Lonely Planet has grown to become the largest independent travel publisher in the world, with offices in Melbourne (Australia), Oakland (USA), London (UK) and Paris (France).

Today Lonely Planet guidebooks cover the globe. There is an ever-growing list of books and information in a variety of media. Some things haven't changed. The main aim is still to make it possible for adventurous travellers to get out there – to explore and better understand the world.

At Lonely Planet we believe travellers can make a positive contribution to the countries they visit – if they respect their host communities and spend their money wisely.

Mammarella, Jennifer Garrett, Meredith Mail, Bridget Blair, Geoff Stringer, Michelle Glynn, Andrew Tudor, Ben Handicott, David Burnett and Mark Germanchis for their contributions to the title.

Series Publishing Manager Susan Rimerman oversaw the redevelopment of the regional guides series with the help of Virginia Maxwell and Maria Donohoe, and Regional Publishing Manager Katrina Browning steered the development of this title. The series was designed by James Hardy, with mapping development by Paul Piaia. The series development team included Shahara Ahmed, Jenny Blake, Anna Bolger, Erin Corrigan, Nadine Fogale, Dave McClymont, Leonie Mugavin, Rachel Peart, Lynne Preston, Howard Ralley, Valerie Sinzdak and Bart Wright.

Last but not least, thanks to the authors – for all your hard work and patience along the way.

ACKNOWLEDGMENTS

Many thanks to the following for the use of their content:

GR and PR are trademarks of the FFRP (Fédération Française de la Randonée Pédestre).

THANKS FROM LONELY PLANET

Many thanks to the travellers who used the last edition and wrote to us with helpful hints, useful advice and interesting anecdotes:

A Tony Alcock, Beat Amacher, Joseph Antonini **B** Nicole de Baat, Mauro Borneo **C** Paul Cole, Jonathan Cook, Julian Cope **D** Manije Mir Damad, Liz Delleart, Lee Douglas **F** Laetitia Fabri, Jonas Fast, Alastair Ferraro, Fabio Fraulino **H** Eivin Rune Hansen Lea Hartog, Martin Haulrich, Ludo van Hijfte **K** Jessica Kim, Marnix Koets, Esther Koh, Sander de Kroon **L** Duncan Lamberton, Jake Lee **M** Mark Mee, Kevin Molloy **N** Stephen Nelson, J Neordman **O** Mary Anne Okomski, Niall Ó Murchadha, Catherine O'Toole **R** Elizabeth Raymont, Joan Rennie, Dave Ryden **S** Ludek Safarik, Noa and Daniel Sher, Anneke Sips, Ilene Sterns, Nancy Sturm **T** Annie Thorpe, ken Thorpe, Fabian Tourette, Johan Treur **W** Gabriela Weiss, David Whittall, Martin Wood, Laura Wooster

SEND US YOUR FEEDBACK

We love to hear from travellers – your comments keep us on our toes and help make our books better. Our well-travelled team reads every word on what you loved or loathed about this book. Although we cannot reply individually to postal submissions, we always guarantee that your feedback goes straight to the appropriate authors, in time for the next edition. Each person who sends us information is thanked in the next edition – and the most useful submissions are rewarded with a free book.

To send us your updates – and find out about LP events, newsletters and travel news – visit our award-winning website: **www.lonelyplanet.com**.

Note: We may edit, reproduce and incorporate your comments in Lonely Planet products such as guidebooks, websites and digital products, so let us know if you don't want your comments reproduced or your name acknowledged. For a copy of our privacy policy visit www.lonelyplanet.com/privacy.

Index